W9-BNQ-301

CRITICAL PRAISE FOR GARY SOLIS AND *SON THANG*:

"Such an objective dissection of a war crime is rare. This work is valuable to anyone interested in the bringing to justice of violators of international humanitarian law, whether in the former Yugoslavia, Burundi, Rwanda, or any place where such crimes are committed under the colors of armed combat. Gary Solis melds careful research with vivid writing. The result is a deep and useful probing into the dark corners of crimes committed in combat."

—*Major General George S. Prugh, USA (Ret.), Judge Advocate General of the Army, 1971–1975*

"A riveting account of the Marine Corps' worst known war crime in Vietnam and of its legal aftermath. Gary Solis throws valuable light on many little-known aspects of the Vietnam War and on the way the system of military justice operated there. I highly recommend this book."

—*Guenter Lewy, Professor Emeritus, University of Massachusetts, and author of* America in Vietnam

tion contains the complete text of the original hardcover edition.
ONE WORD HAS BEEN OMITTED.

ANG

am Book / published by arrangement with the Naval Institute Press

ISHING HISTORY
Institute Press hardcover edition / 1997
m mass market edition / September 1998

ghts reserved.
right © 1997 by Gary D. Solis
r photos courtesy of U.S. Marine Corps
ry of Congress Catalog Card Number: 97-18512
art of this book may be reproduced or transmitted in any form or by
means, electronic or mechanical, including photocopying, recording,
any information storage and retrieval system, without permission in
ng from the publisher. For information address: Bantam Books.

you purchased this book without a cover you should be aware that
is book is stolen property. It was reported as "unsold and destroyed"
the publisher and neither the author nor the publisher has received
y payment for this "stripped book."

N 0-553-57977-0

ished simultaneously in the United States and Canada

tam Books are published by Bantam Books, a division of Bantam Dou-
ay Dell Publishing Group, Inc. Its trademark, consisting of the words
tam Books" and the portrayal of a rooster, is Registered in U.S. Patent
Trademark Office and in other countries. Marca Registrada. Bantam
ks, 1540 Broadway, New York, New York 10036.

NTED IN THE UNITED STATES OF AMERICA

M   10 9 8 7 6 5 4 3 2 1

SON
THAN

AN AMERICAN WAR C

Gary D. Solis

BANTAM BOOKS
NEW YORK TORONTO LONDON SYDNEY AUCKL

This ed
NOT C

SON TH
A Ban

PUBL
Naval
Banta

All ri
Copy
Cove
Libr
No
any
or b
writ

If
th
to
ar

ISB

Pub

Ban
bled
"Ba
and
Boo

PF

O

For Andrea

Contents

FOREWORD

Five Marines of Company B, 1st Battalion, 7th
Marines, made up the "killer team" that in February 1970 murdered sixteen noncombatant
Vietnamese women and children at Son Thang,
an obscure hamlet southwest of Da Nang. Four
of the five Marines were tried by general
courts-martial. The maximum sentence for premeditated murder is death. This book is the
story of their crime and their fates.

The term "killer team" was local to the war
and to the regiment. There was no agreed definition, just that it meant to kill the enemy. The
killer team had been told to "Shoot first and ask
questions later." The team leader wrote later:
"We'd fired instinctively, just the way we were
trained."

"Body count" was the probable gut cause of
this affair. Statistics were the stuff of life for
Secretary of Defense Robert Strange McNamara. Were we winning or losing in Vietnam?
He wanted numbers. McNamara was gone by
1970, but the iniquitous body count continued.

The motto of the 1st Battalion, 7th Marines,
was "Get Some." In front of the battalion headquarters was a "Kill Board" on which the body
count was kept. (I remember that as the battal-

ion "stood down" to leave Vietnam some months later, "Get Some" was crossed out and changed to read "Got Some.")

Four widely different verdicts resulted from the courts-martial. How could this be so for four participants in the same heinous act? And what of the fifth participant, who was not court-martialed?

The author, Gary Solis, poses larger questions: How do ordinary men become extraordinary murderers? What is the compulsion? How does it happen? And how ordinary were these ordinary Marines?

By one of the coincidences with which wars seem to be fraught, the Army's Calley massacre at My Lai had happened twenty-three months earlier and only twenty-five miles from Son Thang. Some call Son Thang the Marine Corps' My Lai. The author insists that it was not.

Oliver Stone, John Milius, or Francis Ford Coppola would have been accused of worn-out cliches if he had assembled such a cast for a Vietnam war movie: A new and ambitious battalion commander; a tough, overly aggressive company commander; a callow just-arrived platoon leader; a battle-wise platoon sergeant; and a five-man patrol that included an African-American with a criminal record, led by a twenty-year-old who was part Native American.

Shortly before the Son Thang incident, the Uniform Code of Military Justice of 1950 was modified by the Military Justice Act of 1969 and a new *Manual for Courts-Martial* written. The changes brought the military justice system more in line with the federal court system with some differences in form, but few differences in substance. Would such a system work in wartime? (I remember there were great problems, for example, in carrying out such requirements as transcribing verbatim testimony.)

Implementing the code came at a tremendous price. The 1st Marine Division had twenty-six Marine Corps judge advocates, most of them captains, assigned to its staff judge advocate's office in 1970. A full-strength Marine division has twenty-seven rifle companies. The table of organization calls for these companies to be commanded by a captain. In 1970 many of the 1st Marine Division's rifle companies, including Company B, 1st Battalion, 7th Marines, were commanded by first lieutenants. It was that kind of war: more captain judge advocates than captain rifle company commanders.

Under the military justice system, the members of the court, that is, the jury, impose the sentence. In earlier times the president of the court actually presided. Under the Uniform Code he was merely the jury foreman, subordinated to the military judge. Sentencing guidelines were lacking and mandatory sentencing minimums were not stated.

Two of the players in the case, Oliver North and James Webb, would later attain celebrity status. Both were members of the class of 1968 at the Naval Academy. Both took the option of a Marine Corps commission. Both had exemplary combat records in Vietnam. Ollie North returned to Vietnam to be a defense witness for the killer team leader and gave important testimony. Jim Webb, while a law student at Georgetown, became interested in the case, particularly the conviction of the only African-American. He argued that the conviction was flawed by constitutional error. Later, he became a successful novelist (*Fields of Fire*), a Vietnam veterans' advocate, and a controversial Secretary of the Navy whose interest in the case continued.

By 1970, in many ways, the war had descended to a primeval level. The Vietnamese were "gooks," a disparaging term on a par with "nigger." Solis traces its recorded use back to 1912 in Nicaragua. I can add that "gook," which was widely used in the Pacific in World War II and again in Korea, might have been derived from "gugu," a term used by soldiers and Marines for Filipinos during the Philippine Insurrection at the beginning of this century.

Solis tells the story in a straight-forward manner, touched with a bit of hard-edged cynicism. He skillfully leads the reader through the labyrinthine pathways of investigation and trial and the subtleties of law under the military justice system.

Key figures shifted as the case progressed. The division

commander responsible for the investigation phase of the crime was injured when his helicopter was shot down. The new commanding general became the convening authority for the courts-martial that followed the investigation.

The new commanding general and I had served together at Headquarters, Marine Corps, and had become good friends. On our previous tours in Vietnam, as colonels, we had been regimental commanders, he of the 5th Marines and I of the 9th Marines. In the winter of 1970 we learned it would soon be time for us to go to Vietnam once again. He was slated to have command of the 1st Marine Division, and he asked me if I would be his assistant division commander. I readily agreed. He went out early because of the injury of his predecessor. I followed a month or so later, just as the courts-martial were getting under way.

A division commander gives his assistant division commander such duties as he sees fit. My employment was primarily operational, not administrative; rather easy for me because fighting the relatively inactive Viet Cong and North Vietnamese was probably the least of the commanding general's concerns. This was a time of internal deterioration and violence in the 1st Marine Division: soaring venereal disease rates, an unnecessarily high incidence of malaria, too many casualties from accidental discharges and "friendly" fire, racial unrest including a secret "Mau Mau" society, rampant drug use, and "fraggings" (the murder or attempted murder of an officer or NCO, usually by use of a fragmentation grenade).

I was a sidelines witness to the proceedings of the courts-martial. The staff judge advocate reported directly to the commanding general, not through me. I did see the message traffic, incoming and outgoing, on the case. Quite often the commanding general asked me to go over a draft message before it was sent.

The commanding general was a solitary man. He was not well liked. I believe I was his only real confidant. We used to talk almost every night in his quarters, a plywood villa on Hill 327 with a magnificent view of Da Nang. We would watch the pyrotechnic display of outgoing artillery fire, the occasional flaming overhead rush of incoming rockets, and the eerie—almost daylight-bright—illumination of Hai Van Pass and Marble Mountain by so-called "star shells." To our backs, masked from sight by the crest of Hill 327, was the war, such as it was. We could always hear the *crrummpping* of our harassing and interdiction artillery shells, whose efficacy we doubted gravely, and sometimes the crackling of small-arms exchanges that could cause us to wonder if in some hamlet out there another Son Thang was in the making.

The commanding general had been a Phi Beta Kappa at the University of Texas, where he majored in philosophy, many years before. He lost me sometimes in his ruminations over Kant, Kierkegaard, and particularly Schopenhauer. The erratic course the courts-martial were taking greatly disturbed his coldly rational mind. This complex and increasingly bitter man, as convening authority, had immediate powers of review over the courts' proceedings. In this book the reader will learn how he restored a degree of equity to the widely disparate findings and sentences.

The author is pre-eminently qualified to write of the Son Thang tragedy, which did not end with the murders and the trials. Gary Solis, born in Denver in 1941, has lived almost his entire life in a military environment. His parents divorced when he was four and his mother packed him off to a military school on his sixth birthday. For the next twelve years he lived, in a series of such schools, in California. He went on to San Diego State College with the sole intention of qualifying for a Marine Corps commission. He graduated in 1963 and reported to the Marine Corps at Quantico, Virginia, a month later. After The Basic School, the leveling process for all new Marine lieutenants, he was assigned to amphibian tractors, the tracked vehicles that make the run into the beach from the transports and are sometimes used ashore as thinly armored troop carriers. His first duty with troops was on Okinawa as a platoon leader in the 1st Amphibian Tractor Battalion, 3d Marine Division. Immediately after the Tonkin Gulf incident in August 1964, his unit deployed to Da Nang where he spent four months helping defend Monkey Mountain against a nebulous enemy.

He returned to the States in 1965 to be stationed as an instructor at the Tracked Vehicle School at Camp Pendleton, California. He shot rifle and pistol on the Pendleton team.

The Marines landed in force in Vietnam beginning in March 1965 at Da Nang. By telephone and telegram, Solis besieged Headquarters to send him back. The Marine Corps obliged in 1966 and ordered him, a freshly promoted captain, to the 3d Amphibian Tractor Battalion, 1st Marine Division, at Chu Lai. As an amtrack company commander he worked primarily in Mo Duc and Duc Duc districts on both sides of the Que Son Mountains. Amtracks were useful in the rice paddies as personnel carriers and supply vehicles. There were many hamlets; his amtracks may even have trundled through Son Thang.

He resigned from the Marine Corps and went to law school at the University of California at Davis, getting his juris doctorate in 1971. Missing the Marine Corps life, he returned to the Corps as a lawyer. His first assignment was as a prosecutor at Camp Pendleton, about the same time as the 1st Marine Division was coming home from Vietnam.

Promoted to major, he went back out to Okinawa in 1974 to fill the billet of chief trial counsel or lead prosecutor in the 3d Marine Division. Case loads were at an all-time high.

"I wondered what the hell I'd gotten myself into," he remembers. "NCOs selling drugs to their own troops, race riots of the most violent nature, armories being broken into and weapons stolen, UA [unauthorized absence] rates through the roof, literally platoons of returned deserters marching to chow in civilian clothes and long hair, awaiting their uncontested administrative discharges. . . . It was the worst of times, but it put me into the courtroom every day—and often two or even three times a day."

Solis decided that he liked criminal law and liked being a prosecutor. He never defended an accused, then or later. He returned to Camp Pendleton to be the chief trial counsel of the 1st Marine Division. The Marine Corps sent him to George Washington University where he earned a master of laws degree in 1977, specializing in criminal law. His next assignment was in Norfolk, Virginia, where, with a promotion to lieutenant colonel, he was staff judge advocate of Fleet Marine Force, Atlantic.

He moved to Headquarters, Marine Corps, in Washington in 1981. Here he headed the Military Law Branch within the Judge Advocate Division. The billet involved his taking part in a significant revision of the *Manual for Courts-Martial*.

In 1983 he again went to Okinawa, this time to be the chief military judge of the Western Pacific circuit. By then the Corps was accepting only high school graduates and disciplinary infractions were way down. Another tour at Camp Pendleton followed a year later, and again he would be a general court-martial military judge.

"During my legal career I participated in more than 750 courts-martial, either as prosecutor or military judge," he recently told me. "Up to that point, I thought that trial work was what I did, what I was best at. Maybe it was."

His final Marine Corps assignment would be a departure from trial work. He was detailed in 1986 to the Marine Corps Historical Center to write a history of the Marine Corps' military law experience in Vietnam. I was then the director of the center. His product was the landmark *Trial by Fire: Marines and Military Law in Vietnam*. Son Thang could only be treated briefly in *Trial by Fire*. Gary and I frequently discussed the incident, each from his own perspective. We agreed that Son Thang was the nadir of the Marine Corps' Vietnam experience. We both saw a need for a book that would explore Son Thang fully.

Gary Solis retired in 1989 and moved to London, England, to join his wife-to-be Andrea and to pursue a doctorate at the London School of Economics. In two and a half years he had his Ph.D. in the law of war. He stayed on to teach and for three years taught British criminal law and British commercial law. In 1995 he gained a kind of celebrity status by being the nightly commentator on the O. J. Simpson murder trial on Britain's Sky television channel.

In the summer of 1996 he joined the Department of Law at the U.S. Military Academy at West Point. There he is teaching constitutional and military law, a required course. He still looks the part of a combat Marine; he is a cyclist and has run eight marathons. At West Point he hopes to create a new course, Law of War for the Small-Unit Leader. It should be a good one and *Son Thang: An American War Crime* should be required reading.

But this is not a specialist book, just for military lawyers, officers, and cadets. The thoughtful reader must decide: When is killing in war illegitimate? When should orders be obeyed and when do they need to be disobeyed? What constitutes a legal order? When is an order illegal? When can an order be disobeyed? As tested by the Son Thang case, was the system of law prescribed by the Uniform Code of Military Justice adequate? Was justice done? This book gives some answers to these and other questions—tentative answers, not absolute answers.

The reader will most likely be left with a disturbing thought. Americans like to believe that atrocities are committed by others, but we are not immune from such things. We like to think we are, but we are not.

EDWIN H. SIMMONS
Brigadier General, U.S. Marine Corps (Ret.)
Director Emeritus, Marine Corps History and Museums

PREFACE

This account is true. There are no "imagined" or "reconstructed" quotations; every Q and A is from a record of trial, word for word. No names have been changed, no scenes invented.

This rather disturbing story is told not only because it's an engrossing courtroom drama set in an arena with which few are familiar: a court-martial in a combat zone, but also because the outcomes of the trials were unpredicted and tinged with Grecian tragedy. And the account is related because it is both instructive and cautionary.

In a 1961 opinion, *Ball et al. v. U.S.*, the Supreme Court of the United States wrote, "In the Armed Forces, as everywhere else, there are good men and rascals, courageous men and cowards, honest men and cheats." Rascals and worse are found in this story; cowards and cheats as well. But it should be remembered that 448,000 Marines served in Vietnam; only a very small percentage became entangled in the military justice system. Literally millions of patrols encountered Vietnamese civilians without incident.

Since many readers will be unfamiliar with military law and its terminology, I take the liberty of using words more familiar to the lay reader than the usual legal terms, substituting "count" for its military analog, specification; substituting "judge" for military judge, and "prosecutor" for trial counsel. I also use the term "rank" when referring to military position, although grade is technically correct.

A general court-martial ending in conviction is recorded and the transcript is printed verbatim. I use such a verbatim record in detailing the first of the Son Thang-4 trials. It is an exceptional window to the military legal process, and the personalities implementing it.

General court-martial acquittals, on the other hand, result in "summarized" records that merely note the time of trial, who participated, the legal motions raised, and the resulting rulings. Many Vietnam-era court-martial records, verbatim and summarized, have been lost—including two of the Son Thang series of four trials. In reconstructing the two recordless courts-martial I've employed interviews of and letters from participants, plus newspaper and book accounts. Similar materials also augment the available records of trial.

Throughout this account Marine Corps personnel records, command chronologies, official histories, and declassified secret messages are used, in addition to military appellate court opinions. The interviews collected in the Marine Corps Oral History Program were a rich source, as well.

A continuing regret is my inability to detail the lives of the court-martialed Marines after their return to the civilian world. They, and their relatives, decline my efforts to interview them.

I must acknowledge the support of Brig. Gen. Ed Simmons, USMC (Ret.), the long-time director of the Marine Corps History and Museums Division, and dean of Marine historians. He has my respect and thanks. Through his encouragement and example I've learned much about writing, and other things, as well. (Despite his best efforts I still regularly confuse effect and affect.)

Like countless writers before me, I thank Dan Crawford of the Marine Corps Historical Center, and his peerless Reference Section, Bob Aquilina, Ann Ferrante, and Lena Kaljot. At many junctures their assistance and expertise were crucial. I'm fortunate to count them as friends, as well. Steve Hill, also of the Historical Center, produced the Son Thang-4 map.

Maj. Michael J. Benjamin, JAGC, U.S. Army, provided wise and learned comment on the draft text. Laning Thompson, my copyeditor, was a perceptive guide, too. Col. Bob Blum, Lt. Col. Dick Theer, and Lt. Col. Paul St.Amour, all USMC (Ret.), were of invaluable help in piecing together this story, as was Denzil Garrison, who continues to practice law in Oklahoma. I thank Maj. Jon Hoffman, USMCR, among the finest of military writers, for his advice and example. I, of course, remain solely responsible for the opinions and conclusions expressed in this book.

Gary D. Solis
West Point, New York

SON THANG

1 | 1/7, 1st MarDiv

The General Court-Martial

"The court will come to order."[1]

It was 16 June 1970, on Hill 327, a few kilometers southwest of Da Nang in South Vietnam. The makeshift, plywood-lined courtroom was perched on the eastern slope of "Division Ridge," the bustling headquarters cantonment of one of the U.S. Marine Corps's proudest combat units, the 1st Marine Division.

Three lawyers, dressed in camouflage utilities, the Marine Corps field uniform, were seated before the military judge, Lt. Col. Paul St.Amour. The judge wore utilities as well—no black robes for Marines. Two of the lawyers were prosecutors; the third, seated at a separate small table, was a defense counsel. All three were Marine Corps captains and judge advocates, but none wore a sidearm. Weapons are not allowed in Marine courtrooms, even in a combat zone.

As the proceedings opened, the seated lawyers paid little attention to the judge as he intoned the boilerplate preliminaries to the general court-martial. Instead they reviewed notes of witnesses' anticipated testimony, or examined the color photographs of the murder victims.

Crowded together behind a long, waist-high plywood panel, the eight-man Marine Corps jury—a colonel, two lieutenant colonels, and five majors—paid very close attention to the judge. So did the accused Marine, Pvt. Michael Schwarz, who was seated beside his lawyer, Capt. Daniel LeGear; neither the jury nor the accused was familiar with the judge's courtroom litany. Behind the jury a large American flag was thumb-tacked high on the plywood wall.

Inaudible to others in the small room, a Marine court reporter seated beside the judge's bench softly repeated the judge's words into the microphone he clasped over his nose and mouth like an oxygen mask. His closed mike was linked to a Gray Audiograph recorder. Later, the court reporter would type a word-for-word record of the court-martial from the belt recording the Audiograph was making. On the reporter's small table, the open microphone of a battery-powered cassette tape recorder was making a second, back-up, tape—Hill 327's gasoline-powered generators often failed without warning, interrupting the electric-powered primary recorder. Whether based on primary or back-up tapes, every word uttered while the court was in session would be transcribed, typed, and retained.

The general court-martial case of *The United States versus Pvt. Michael A. Schwarz* was called to order at 0912. The heat in the windowless hut was already sweltering, despite the air conditioner laboring on a side wall. Private Schwarz was a member of Company B, 1st Battalion, 7th Marines, 1st Marine Division. He was charged with the premeditated murder of sixteen Vietnamese noncombatant women and children. Under military law, the maximum punishment for premeditated murder is death.

First Lt. Lloyd S. Grant was one of the first prosecution witnesses to be sworn and testify in Schwarz's general court-martial (GCM). Grant had been the intelligence officer of the 1st Battalion, 7th Marines, which was referred to as "one-seven," or "1/7." Four months before, on 20 February 1970, Grant had led a patrol whose mission was to check electronic sensors buried near 1/7's base, Fire Support Base (FSB) Ross.

Grant testified that a Vietnamese woman had approached his patrol and, through an interpreter, had heatedly complained that early the night before, Americans had entered her hamlet and killed many women and children. Although the Army's 23d Infantry (American) Division also operated in that area, Grant believed that only Marine personnel recently had been in the area she described.

After radioing battalion headquarters at FSB Ross for permission to deviate from his pre-planned route, Grant and his men followed the woman to her hamlet, which was no more than eight or nine thatch-roofed huts clustered beside small rice paddies.

Several identically named hamlets grouped within a geographical area are considered to form a village with that name. On 1:100,000-scale military maps, these individual hamlets are numbered for differentiation. It is difficult to make out the small print of village names on such maps, let alone the numbers indicating the component hamlets. Vietnamese who knew of the old woman's hamlet called it "Son 4, Thang Tra Hamlet," although few Vietnamese would have known of her specific village, let alone her hamlet, because both were so small. Some U.S. maps showed the hamlet as "Son Tra." But the Marines of 1/7, in whose tactical area it was located, had been there many times and knew it as "Son Thang-4."

The court-martial's prosecuting judge advocate asked Lieutenant Grant, "Do you recall what time you entered the hamlet?"

"I believe it was just before noon, about 1130," Grant responded.

"Would you describe what you observed when you entered the hamlet?"

The twenty-two-year-old lieutenant, groomed solely for duty in Vietnam, gave the court a horrific description.

"When I first entered the hamlet I arrived at an old decrepit-type hooch. . . . As I was walking into the left of the hooch there was a mass of bodies lying there." He counted six dead Vietnamese, he said. At two other nearby hooches he found another ten Vietnamese bodies. All had been killed by close-range gunshot wounds.

The prosecutor continued his examination: "Could you tell us generally what the ages were?"

Referring to the six bodies he first discovered, Grant replied, "I would say the woman was about fifty . . . and the two boys were about eight or nine, for one, and ten or eleven for the other, and the two girls were . . . I would say about ten to twelve, somewhere in that age group. And then there was a younger child that appeared to me to be about three or four."

Describing the same bodies at an earlier preliminary hearing, Grant had added, "and these people appeared to have multiple wounds, multiple small arms wounds. There were a lot of holes in the bodies . . . mostly on the upper torso and the head. . . . Whatever did it, there had been quite a few rounds that had hit them."[2]

Grant identified a color photograph of the second group of dead Vietnamese he had discovered. Pointing to the body of a child, he testified: "This boy here had a side wound and a head wound. I remember them specifically."

Questioned about another body visible in the photograph, he described it as that of "a young girl, I would say about twelve years old, or so. She had long black hair. She had been wounded, I remember, in the upper torso, the arm, and she was lying on her side, with her head in a northerly type direction."[3]

He recounted finding still more bodies at a third Son Thang-4 site: "There were six. . . . They were all . . . on top of each other. . . . There were two women, each of whom was clutching a young child under her. There was one male and one female." Explaining how he recognized another photo as depicting the third mass of bodies, rather than the first or second, Grant betrayed no emotion in responding that it was "the woman clutching her child. The head wound on the child she's clutching. . . . The large amount of brain matter. I remember it being on the deck there—plus this .45 cartridge."[4] He pointed to the brass cartridge case in the photo. The child had been shot at point-blank range with a large caliber weapon; judging from the cartridge, with a .45 caliber pistol, the standard U.S. military sidearm.

There were no men among the sixteen bodies found by Grant's patrol. Only women and children. Had Marines been involved in this carnage? Could Schwarz, the accused—could any American—have perpetrated this slaughter?

In November of 1969, three months before Lieutenant Grant's grisly discovery, Army 1st Lt. William L. Calley, Jr., had been charged with the murder of "not less than" 109 Vietnamese. Even before the official charges were served on Calley, worldwide publicity made him and My Lai, the scene of his crimes, infamous.

In January 1966, long before the Calley case, a court-martial had sentenced Marine Pfc. John Potter to confinement at hard labor for life for his vicious murder of five Vietnamese noncombatants, one of them an infant, and the rape of another Vietnamese.[5] Army Sgt. Roy Bumgarner was convicted in 1970 of the murder of three Vietnamese noncombatants and, ludicrously, was sentenced to reduction to private and forfeiture of $97 per month for twenty-four months.[6] In 1969, Cpl. Ronald Reese and L.Cpl. Stephen Crider were sentenced to hard labor for life after their convictions by Marine general courts-martial of the murder of four Vietnamese children.[7]

Americans were coming to suspect what every Vietnam combat veteran already knew: U.S. soldiers and Marines could indeed commit heinous crimes like those charged against Schwarz.

If the press was not covering the Schwarz GCM with the same intensity as it did the Calley trial, it was in part because Calley was tried at the more accessible Fort Benning, Georgia. The Marine's court-martial was being covered, however: "Judge Accepts Photos In Viet Murder Trials," a *Los Angeles Times*[8] headline read; "Trial Opens For Marine In 16 Deaths," the *Washington Post*[9] reported, even though the 1st Division headquarters offered few of the amenities usually enjoyed by the civilian press. Hill 327, with its frequent rocket attacks and proximity to the Vietnamese enemy, made it an unlikely site for U.S.-based reporters, and many in-country correspondents considered other stories more interesting. The Marine Corps was fortunate in that regard. The Son Thang murders, although reported in civilian newspapers, would never seize the full attention of the American people or its television pundits. The public, when it thought of war crimes at all, focused on Calley and the My Lai atrocities.

And with good reason. Compared to My Lai, Son Thang involved far fewer victims, far fewer perpetrators, and no attendant sexual crimes. Although often referred to in the press as "the Marine Corps's My Lai," Son Thang didn't equal My Lai. Nor was there any attempt by Marine officers to cover up the crimes charged against Schwarz and other Marines of 1/7. Instead, the offenses, once discovered, were brought to trial as quickly as possible.

Still, among Marine commanders, there was dismay and shame. Could Marines really have committed these acts . . . again? The answer, highlighted in a series of general courts-martial of which Schwarz's was only the first, was complex and rooted in the Marines' long combat involvement in Southeast Asia.

THE WAR IN VIETNAM

In 1946, France was at war in Vietnam with the Communist Vietminh. The United States pursued a French-biased neutrality. In 1950, the Korean War and increasing cold-war tensions in Europe led the United States to extend its European containment policy to East Asia. Fearing a domino effect, the United States finally supplied the

French with direct military and economic aid, and by 1954 it was paying almost 80 percent of France's Vietnam war costs.

The French were defeated at Dien Bien Phu in 1954. Peace agreements reached in Geneva called for the French to withdraw to the south, and the Vietminh to the north, of a newly created ten-kilometer-wide demilitarized zone. Agreed-upon reunification elections were never held, and Vietnam remained divided at the seventeenth parallel.

After the defeat at Dien Bien Phu, the United States formally underwrote what it had long been paying for anyway. An anti-Communist government under Ngo Dinh Diem was installed in South Vietnam and massive aid was instituted to prevent further Communist expansion.

Diem, initially successful in repressing the Communist Vietminh, by 1960 was turning victory into defeat through corruption and ineptitude. His regime was threatened by the newly formed National Liberation Front (NLF), which became a powerful antigovernment insurgency. Through the early 1960s, U.S. military advisers took an increasingly active role in combat operations, but proposals to send American troops were rejected. Meanwhile, Buddhists were threatening government stability in the cities while the NLF was overwhelming South Vietnamese forces in the field.

Alarmed by televised images of monks immolating themselves, the United States finally jettisoned Diem. In 1963 the South Vietnamese army led a coup and Diem was murdered.

The new Vietnamese leaders proved as inept as their predecessors and the NLF consolidated gains and increased its military effectiveness. In August 1964, American air strikes were launched against North Vietnamese naval bases in response to actual and purported attacks against U.S. naval vessels in the Gulf of Tonkin, and in March 1965, the 9th Marine Expeditionary Brigade, the first American combat unit committed to the war, landed

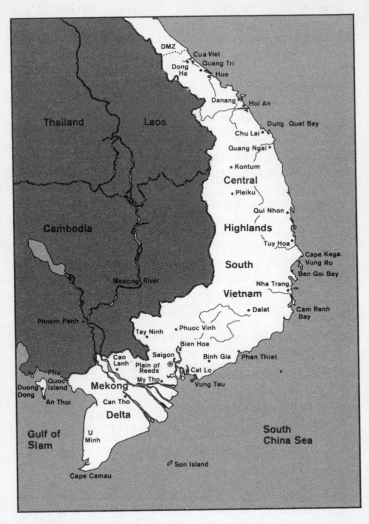

South Vietnam

near Da Nang. By 1966 there were almost 400,000 U.S. ground troops in-country.

Despite the ever-increasing number of American combat personnel in South Vietnam, the North Vietnamese, the Viet Cong, and the NLF retained the combat initiative during the next few years. They usually chose where and when to fight and when to retreat to Laotian and Cambodian sanctuaries or beyond the demilitarized zone (DMZ) to the north.

Eventually, the III Marine Amphibious Force (III MAF), headquartered in Da Nang, was made responsible for the defense of the five northernmost provinces of South Vietnam. Approximately 55,000 Marines and 50,000 Army troops were situated in these provinces, which constituted the I Corps Tactical Zone (ICTZ or, more popularly, "Eye" or I Corps). Although ICTZ was the smallest of the four South Vietnamese military regions in both area and population, its nearness to major enemy and supply routes as well as base areas in Laos, the DMZ, and North Vietnam made it the most strategically located.[10]

Within I Corps, the conflict was not of a piece. Warfare in the southern part was very different from that in the north, which was nearer the DMZ. As Ronald Spector has written, "The conditions and intensity of combat in Vietnam varied enormously; from the World War I–style warfare of Khe Sanh to . . . fierce clashes in the mountains and jungles, to endless patrols in the agricultural lowlands. . . . Even in a single province the pattern of battle and death could vary enormously."[11]

Col. Robert H. Barrow, who commanded the 9th Marines in Vietnam, pointed out that in the north of I Corps, "anything that moved you could shoot at because he was the enemy. You didn't have to separate the armed threat from the civilian population." Barrow, who later became Commandant of the Marine Corps, considered the kind of war that had to be fought down in the Da Nang area to the south, "the most difficult, the most arduous, dirty, psychologically bad situation. . . . Those Marines who went out

day after day, conducting . . . combat patrols, almost knowing that somewhere on their route of movement they were
going to have some sort of surprise visited on them, either
an ambush or explosive device . . . that is the worst kind of
warfare, not being able to see the enemy. You can't shoot
back at him. You are kind of helpless."[12]

By early 1970 the 1st Marine Division was III MAF's
principal infantry command in I Corps. Headquartered
on Hill 327 since it moved north from Chu Lai in 1966,
the 1st Division operated throughout Quang Nam
Province—the southern I Corps of which Colonel Barrow
spoke. By 1968, the division's principal mission was essentially the defense of Da Nang, no small task. Da Nang, with
its giant airfield, its port facilities, and its complex of military headquarters and logistical support facilities, was the
U.S. nerve center of the war in northern South Vietnam.

In 1970, an estimated 78,000 enemy troops opposed
U.S. forces in I Corps. They included about 49,000 North
Vietnamese Army (NVA) regulars, 6,000 main force Viet
Cong (VC), and more than 23,000 VC guerrillas. Although
peace talks were under way in Paris, the war was by no
means winding down. Every week, hundreds of Americans
were dying in combat. Most weeks, more died than in the
entire Persian Gulf War of 1990–91.

Two years after their stinging 1968 Tet military defeat,
however, the NVA and the VC in I Corps were hard-
pressed. Throughout 1969, the U.S., South Vietnamese,
and Korean troops, capitalizing on their greater mobility,
had driven into enemy base areas and inflicted heavy losses
on main force units. An intensified pacification effort had
reduced enemy guerrilla strength. While the NVA and VC
were still able to mount heavy attacks, they increasingly
employed harassing tactics. Large-scale engagements became fewer as the enemy reverted to small unit hit-and-run
attacks, mines, and terrorism. They saw this as the most
economical way to maintain their military position until either the U. S. withdrew or the Paris peace talks achieved
agreement.

I Corps Area, South Vietnam

The 1st Marine Division was a 28,000-man component of I Corps's III MAF. The division consisted of four infantry regiments: the 1st, 5th, 7th, and 26th Marines; an artillery regiment: the 11th Marines; and several support battalions. The infantry regiments were the combat heart of the division.

Each of those 3,950-man infantry regiments was composed of a headquarters battalion and three 1,100- to 1,200-man infantry battalions. The young Marine on trial for the murder of sixteen Vietnamese noncombatants, Private Schwarz, was a member of 1/7—the 1st Battalion of the 7th Marine Regiment. The 7th Marines (in Marine parlance the term "regiment" is omitted when designating regimental-sized units) had been in South Vietnam since early 1966, first at Chu Lai, then in the Da Nang area.

In 1969 and 1970, the ground war was centered in the southern portion of the 1st Division's 1,050-square-mile tactical area of responsibility (TAOR). The division's TAOR ran from the rugged Que Son Mountains in the south, near the boundary between Quang Nam and Quang Tin Provinces, to strategic Hai Van Pass in the north. From the South China Sea, on the east, the TAOR stretched westward into the jungle-covered mountains of the Annamite chain. Almost a million Vietnamese lived in the TAOR, over 400,000 of them in the city of Da Nang.

In the An Hoa Basin, called "Arizona Territory" by Marines who fought there, along Charlie Ridge, and in the area known for all-too-obvious reasons as "Dodge City," the division's four infantry regiments maintained a brutal routine of a thousand patrols every twenty-four hours, day and night.

Patrolling from fixed bases, the Marines of the 1st Division operated primarily along the southern edge of their TAOR. According to the Marine Corps's official history, "This region had experienced much warfare. The ravines, gorges, and caves of the Que Son Mountains hid extensive enemy base camps and headquarters complexes within easy striking range of the coast. The Que Son Valley, with many of its villages and hamlets controlled by the VC, constituted a major enemy food source. Detachments of VC/NVA combat and supply troops infested the area."[13]

In the An Hoa Basin, rifle companies of the 7th Marines sometimes spent up to ninety continuous days in the field, resupplied by helicopters that landed only long enough to unload ammunition cans, water blivets, and food—usually C-rations.

Every two to three months, the 7th Marines rotated its three infantry battalions, 1/7, 2/7, and 3/7, between its three patrol bases, FSB Ryder atop Hill 579, LZ Baldy, and FSB Ross.

LZ Baldy was located on Hill 55, at the intersection of Routes 1 and 535, 30 kilometers south of Da Nang and 16 kilometers east of FSB Ross. The site of the regimental headquarters, Baldy boasted raised plywood offices and living quarters (South East Asia huts: SEAhuts), rudimentary showers, and an actual messhall.

FSB Ross commanded much of the Que Son Valley. Located in the far south of Que Son District of Quang Nam Province, Ross was just south of old colonial Route 535, where Route 536 branches off to cross the Ly Ly river. Ross also lay northeast of Nui Chom, a rugged ridge line defining the northern edge of Hiep Duc Valley ("Death Valley"). No more than two low knolls separated by a saddle, FSB Ross sat close to the road, a small and lonely outpost. Two batteries of six 105mm howitzers, two eight-inch howitzers, a platoon of 81mm mortars, and a light section of two M-48 tanks occupied the easternmost hill, and the infantry battalion's cantonment was on the slightly higher hill to the west. From Ross, the battalion patrolled the dangerous Hiep Duc and Que Son Valleys.

THE BATTALION

In those valleys the infantrymen of 1/7 contended with considerably more than forty-two identified enemy battalions. The Marines' opponents included a Vietnamese civilian population that was not exactly sitting out the war—the civilians often were the enemy. According to Marine historians, it was a war "of snipers, ambushes, and old women who planted booby-traps—and where the Search & Destroy doctrine was most cruelly interpreted by frustrated and inexperienced U.S. forces."[14]

Throughout the summer of 1969, 1/7 was engaged in virtually continuous heavy combat. On 13 August, during a two-day contact with the 90th NVA Regiment in the Arizona, the battalion's commander, Lt. Col. John Dowd, was killed by enemy machine-gun fire while maneuvering his battalion. The engagement in which he died—along with eighteen other Marines and two Navy corpsmen—was one of forty NVA encounters in the first half of August alone.[15] Dowd's posthumous Navy Cross was one of three awarded men of the battalion that summer.[16]

The battalion commander was replaced by Lt. Col. Frank Clark, who arrived from outside the regiment. Methodical and deliberate, he was the antithesis of the brash, swaggering Dowd. Inevitably, Clark proved unpopular with some of the battalion's officers, who preferred Dowd's driving leadership style, which they felt better met the needs of their harsh combat.

First Lt. Ray Hord, a 1/7 platoon commander, was awarded the Silver Star for his part in the battalion's summer combat. He recalls that "1/7 was . . . operationally keen and efficient, a well-oiled war machine."[17] The fighting in Death Valley and the Arizona, often in over-100-degree heat, molded the battalion and imparted a cold and efficient aggressiveness.

The savagery of the summer's action is illustrated by an incident described by Keith Nolan in *Death Valley,* his history of 1/7's summer 1969 combat. Following a firefight with Dowd's 1/7, an NVA soldier who had a light buttock wound was captured by Marines of H&S Company's mortar platoon:

The NVA . . . was stiff, frightened, and in a lot of pain. Two Vietnamese scouts crouched beside him and began firing off questions. The NVA gritted his teeth in a grimace of pain, and shook his head no, no, no. One of the scouts slid his knife up the prisoner's anus, then twisted. The man's eyes almost popped from his head. He talked.

Talked of what, one wonders? High strategy? His unit's tactical plans? Would he have known much beyond the names of those in his immediate unit, and his unit's previous location? Or did it matter what he said?

This brutality—which was to recur in an amplified version at Son Thang-4—was a war crime, plain and simple; a war crime witnessed by American officers. A U.S. serviceman standing by while an ally tortures a prisoner is itself an offense punishable under both the customary law of war and U.S. military law contained in the Uniform Code of Military Justice.[18] But in U.S. infantry units in South Vietnam, such acts were not unusual. Generals will deny it, colonels and majors may doubt it, but any captain or lieutenant and any enlisted infantryman who was there will confirm it. That's just the way it was. Not in every unit, not in the best-led units, but in most.

A hardened 1/7 NCO later said, "We definitely did not go over and just blow civilians away for no reason. . . . We did kill every duck, chicken, and water buffalo that we came across. . . . These people were all supporters of the NVA and VC, and they deserved whatever happened to them. But unless a gook had a weapon we didn't kill him."[19]

As it happened, he was wrong.

Fall of 1969 brought no respite to the Marines of 1/7. Through much of August and September they pursued the 1st and 3d VC Regiments of the 2d NVA Division across the Que Sons. The enemy's summer offensive was over but the war ground on. "All four companies were in the field for the greater part of the month," read 1/7's command chronology for October. "Emphasis was placed on platoon day patrol activities and area saturation by squad ambushes at night."

The entire month of November, too, all four companies of 1/7 were in the field, combing Antenna Valley and the Que Sons for VC rocket launch sites and conducting rice-denial operations. Monsoon rains often prevented normal helicopter resupply, and for several days during that period the battalion was without rations. Fifteen 1/7 Marines were killed that month and eighty-four wounded, but there were no rocket attacks on Da Nang, and the battalion recovered seventeen tons of rice destined for the VC. And they weren't the only ones with combat losses: the battalion claimed 402 NVA KIAs from August through November.

That month 1/7 Pfc. Ralph Dias died earning the Medal of Honor. He was one of four men of the 7th Marines posthumously awarded the medal that year.

On 9 December, after two continuous months of combat, 1/7 was finally pulled back to FSB Ross; Ross's previous occupants, 3/7, in turn replaced Lieutenant Colonel Clark's battalion in the mountains.

Among the 1/7 Marines moving into Ross that day was Randy Herrod, who was new to the battalion and fresh from a court-martial for an unauthorized absence. As a member of the later Son Thang-4 patrol, Herrod, along with Schwarz, would bring more notice to 1/7 than any garnered by its combat exploits.

The new occupants of Ross were worn down but pleased with themselves. They had done good work in recent months and had been recommended for, and eventually received, a Meritorious Unit Commendation. Morale was high.

At FSB Ross the battalion was by no means out of the combat zone. Throughout December, 1/7's patrols around the base encountered sporadic VC and NVA contact. Two Marines died, twenty more were wounded.

That month a new term appeared in 1/7's command chronology—a term not encountered previously in the records of either the battalion or its parent unit, the 7th Marines. Paragraph six of 1/7's Organization and Operations chronology read: "Commencing 9 December 1969 companies started operating independently, using platoon size patrols, squad size ambushes, and Killer teams." The chronology did not describe or define "killer teams."

The battalion saw no relief in the new year, despite the relative comfort of FSB Ross. A semipermanent base camp with a helicopter landing pad, and tanks, mortars, and batteries of howitzers for defensive support, the fire support base was, if not a safe haven, at least a fortified camp offering a modest degree of safety and a respite from the harsher rigors of the field. Beer and soda were usually available and there was a hardback messhall where hot meals were served. Enclosed two-holer latrines, indelicately called "shitters," were an additional luxury. At fire support bases the illusion of security was enhanced by the surrounding concertina, tanglefoot, and razor wire, plus, at Ross, six fifty-foot-tall observation towers and defensive claymore mines. The availability of supporting artillery fire from the 105mm batteries at Ryder and eight-inch howitzers at Baldy added to the sense of safety at Ross. True, some base camps, notably those of the Army's Special Forces, had been attacked and overrun, but those camps were usually even more remote and isolated and were known to be at risk.

Nevertheless, on 6 January 1970 the 409th Local Force VC Battalion attacked Ross.[20] Although not entirely unexpected, the assault was much more intense than anticipated. At 0130, in a monsoon rain that reduced visibility to yards, the VC announced its onslaught with a 200-round mortar barrage. Simultaneously, Ross's 560 defenders took rocket-propelled grenade (RPG) fire from twenty sappers already inside the wire. Satchel charges detonated throughout the base.

Battalion commander Clark was in Hawaii on R&R, which was unusual for the commander of an infantry battalion. In his absence 1/7's operations officer, Maj. Dick Theer, organized the FSB's defense under fire. The battalion executive officer, who would normally have been in command, "was suffering a nervous breakdown in one corner of the [command] bunker,"[21] Theer later explained.

First Lt. Ron Ambort, Company B's young but veteran commander, shifted reaction forces from sector to sector, shoring up weak points, pursuing sappers with small teams, and killing VC as they retreated to the wire. Rain and a low cloud ceiling precluded air support but 105mm fire from Ryder and Baldy, in addition to the mortar and open-sights artillery fire from Ross's own flechette-firing 105s, began to take a toll. Fierce fighting continued until 0330, when the last sappers were finally rooted from hiding places inside the base.

In the morning, the attack's cost was tallied. Thirteen Marines lay dead and sixty-three were wounded, forty seriously enough to be evacuated. Thirty-nine VC bodies and large quantities of weapons were found in and near the compound. Initial confusion among the attackers— sappers killed by their own mortar prep fire—kept Marine casualties from being even higher. Lieutenant Ambort later noted, "we [Company B] were brought in there, actually, because they were expecting to be overrun—and they were. We pulled their ass out of that."[22] But at a heavy toll.

Immediately after the assault there was an investigation to determine how the VC had penetrated Ross's presumably solid defenses. The inquiry was conducted by the 7th Marines' executive officer, Lt. Col. Bain McClintock. Major Theer, the 1/7 operations officer, thought McClintock "was looking for someone to blame for our losses."[23]

Eight days after Ross was overrun, Lieutenant Colonel Clark was relieved of command. Theer bitterly recalls being told not to bother submitting award recommendations he had prepared: the division commander had directed that there would be no medals, other than Purple Hearts, for the defenders of Ross.

Although the assault occurred a month before Private Schwarz joined Company B, its fallout was to have a significant impact on his general court-martial. The battalion got

Richard E. Theer in Vietnam in 1966, as a captain. *Lt. Col. R. E. Theer*

a new commander—1/7's third commanding officer in five months.

Lt. Col. Charles G. Cooper assumed command of the battalion on 16 January 1970. Although the timing suggested that Clark's relief was for cause—for inadequate fortification and defense of his newly inherited base—Cooper says it was not, and indeed, Clark was subsequently promoted to colonel.[24]

THE COMMANDERS

The commander of an infantry battalion has a great influence upon the men of his unit. His personality is reflected in the battalion's performance or non-performance. The CO sets the martial tone, and the level of military competence and achievement. Lieutenant Colonel Cooper possessed a strong personality and he anticipated big things from his new command.

A 1950 Naval Academy graduate, Cooper had been badly wounded as a platoon commander during the Korean War. When the Marines landed in Vietnam years later, he was stationed at the Pentagon as an aide to the Chief of Naval Operations. Following that assignment he remained stateside as a battalion commander, then a division staff officer, and then an Army War College student. Finally reaching Vietnam in mid-1969, he was the III MAF staff secretary—an excellent staff assignment in a series of excellent assignments. But that was not the combat command an ambitious 41-year-old Marine officer needed in order to advance to more senior ranks. In a war where commanders had little time to learn their trade or make their mark, Cooper's opportunity for a combat command was slipping away. General P. X. Kelley, himself a veteran of heavy Vietnam combat, later said of Cooper, "Charlie was very frustrated. . . . He was coming up for general. . . . Even though he was only a lieutenant colonel, his time to shine was probably going by the wayside, unless he got a battalion."[25]

As a staff officer with the MAF commander's ear, Cooper was well-positioned to lobby for a battalion—for his time to shine—after the usual (for Vietnam) six-month staff stint. So now 1/7, with its 1,184 officers and men, the same battalion led in the past by such Marine Corps heroes as Michael P. Ryan, Raymond G. Davis, and Lewis ("Chesty") Puller, was Cooper's.

Cooper later professed, however, that he was unimpressed upon assuming command. "When I looked around

Charles G. Cooper, 1/7 Battalion Commander, in 1973, after promotion to colonel. *U.S. Marine Corps*

Fire Support Base Ross . . . I was appalled. . . . I also was not at all impressed with the XO,"[26] or, he said, the battalion sergeant major, communications officer, or supply officer. Cooper viewed his new battalion as ineffective and beset by disciplinary, morale, and other problems: "Alcohol abuse, drug abuse, and a racial situation. The first day I took over that battalion I became aware of all three of them. The first day!" Nor was that all. "The appearance of the troops and the officers had gotten pretty salty. . . . People were wearing—can you imagine—beads? Peace beads," he recalled. "There was a cadre . . . that I called black militants. . . . There were a lot of drug users, suspected drug users, and a couple or three drug pushers."

Whatever the battalion's problems, real or imagined, Lieutenant Colonel Cooper didn't lack for confidence in his ability to rectify them. Referring to 1/7, which was his first combat command since Korea, Cooper later said, "I kind of feel like the good Lord put me on the face of the earth to take over an outfit that was down, that was disillusioned and discouraged, and to bring them back to life. . . . They saw me everywhere. Wherever troops were the most miserable, I would show up."

Cooper's dissatisfaction with the battalion was not universally shared. Major Theer, 1/7's operations officer, conceded that the infiltration of Ross had briefly discouraged the men, but disagreed that the outfit was in poor shape. "The battalion was charged up, it was proud. . . . Cooper's remarks . . . simply reflect his lack of understanding of what the war at the company level was really like."[27]

On the other hand, author Keith Nolan cites a 1/7 company commander who groused that "his company was a body of teenagers. The grunts were mostly new graduates or dropouts from high school, and most of his NCOs had been promoted early due to the manpower drain of Vietnam. He had sergeants who weren't old enough to drink beer legally. His platoon leaders were all rushed through a shortened version of Basic School for only one use."[28]

But such complaints, often heard in any Vietnam-era unit, did not add up to the troubled, even cowardly unit that Cooper recalled: "I felt that, just my sensing of things . . . a lot of times they were dogging it. They'd put out a couple of patrols and the company would go off and hide somewhere and crap out. I began to sense this."

By that point in the war, "ghost patrols" were, in fact, common. But company-size ghost operations? Considering the number of killed and wounded that 1/7 suffered month after month, Cooper's suggestion that entire infantry companies, and their officers, had avoided combat until their exposure to his leadership is, at the least, surprising.

Cooper had a higher opinion of Company B and its CO, however. Company B, he said, was "certainly the brightest and most aggressive company in 1/7. It was commanded by 1st Lt. Ron Ambort. . . . He had by far the preponderance of successes and kills of the enemy. He had developed a technique he called 'killer teams.'"

1st Lt. Louis R. Ambort in August 1968. *U.S. Marine Corps*

Louis Ronald Ambort of Little Rock, Arkansas, was commissioned in the Marine Corps Reserve in June 1968. He was a graduate of a six-week Vietnamese language course when he arrived in Vietnam in March 1969. Assigned to 1/7, he would have plenty of opportunity to employ that training.

Ambort commanded a rifle platoon for five months. After a brief transfer to the battalion's civil affairs billet, he became executive officer (second in command) of B Company. In October, seven months after arriving in-country, he was promoted to first lieutenant and given command of the company. Twenty-three years old and eight months out of Basic School, he was leading 207 Marines in combat—swift advancement even in Vietnam, where one-year tours of duty forced young officers to mature quickly.

Ray Hord, Ambort's fellow first lieutenant and company commander, years later recalled Ambort as "a very aggressive young man, capable in the profession. He knew what he was about, tactically. . . . A man, I would say, that had a very hard time taking his pack off. . . . Extremely intense."[29]

During Ambort's pretrial investigation, Major Theer agreed, saying: "I've always felt that Lieutenant Ambort was perhaps our most aggressive company commander, and I had a great deal of respect for his ability, tactical sense, for one so young. . . . I feel that Lieutenant Ambort is a fine officer."[30] Eventually Theer would have second thoughts.

As Lieutenant Colonel Cooper recalled, Ambort was "my best company commander. . . . His only flaw . . . was his youth and inexperience. . . . But his company carried well above its share of the load in the battalion. It had taken more than its share of suffering, too."

Yet another view of Ambort was disclosed by 1/7's S-2 (intelligence) clerk: "He would usually come over and take a look at our charts. . . . He noticed the Kill Board. . . . Charlie Company was ahead at that point for the month, and I overheard a comment . . . that the situation would be changed. . . . He was the only one who went in the COC [combat operations center], would check that, and would seem to know exactly how many [kills] his company had at a particular point."

Few battalions maintained a "kill board." One-seven kept one prominently displayed.

Ambort was not the originator of killer teams; Lt. Col. Cooper was mistaken. They figure in the battalion's command chronologies prior to Ambort's takeover of Bravo Company. The same source indicates that Ambort's company wasn't that much more effective than the other three companies in the battalion, either. Company B was more aggressive, perhaps, and that was significant enough. In a battalion that erected a large sign reading "Get Some" outside its patrol base, and whose intelligence section displayed a kill board comparing the companies' body counts, aggressiveness counted for much. The problem was in knowing how to control and when to rein in that aggressiveness.

The Briefing

In February 1970, B Company was in the bush. Again. Ambort, who had led the company for four months, was tired. The Category II company patrols, primarily rice-denial missions, had been virtually continuous. Catching "rice humpers," who gathered rice in the valley and carried it to VC mountain camps, was more demanding a mission, and more dangerous, than it sounded.

B Company's operating area was covered by rice paddies that gave way to jungle-like tree lines and low hill masses. Many of the paddies were untended and overgrown, as most of the area's Vietnamese had fled or been forcibly relocated. Lieutenant Colonel Cooper described Company B's operating area as "pretty much ruined villages, thinly populated now. This area is honeycombed with bunkers, trench lines, spider holes, a million and one places a unit could be ambushed, or that the enemy could hide himself."

Since taking over the company in October, Ambort had seen eighty-five of his men wounded and fourteen killed. Nine KIAs had been suffered just during the previous week, from the 12th to the 19th of February. Ambort described "a lot of harassing fire at night, mortars and M-79s. . . . The enemy activity just picked up to a frantic rate by around the first of February." Major Theer concurred: "Almost every day after the 12th, they [Ambort's company] had contact of one sort or another. Either a booby-trap, snipers, or incoming small-arms fire. . . . They were harassed almost continuously, day and night."

Any combat death affects the entire company to some degree. The loss of SSgt. Jerry E. Lineberry was particularly disheartening. Lineberry, an eight-year Marine and the platoon sergeant of B Company's second platoon, was competent and well-liked, a spark plug around whom younger Marines rallied. Although in-country a relatively short time, he had formed strong bonds within the unit. On 12 February, Lineberry's platoon was ambushed by a unit of the 31st NVA Regiment. Lineberry, in an exposed position, was wounded in the initial fusillade. Under constant sniper fire, he directed a counterattack and called in supporting artillery fire. Two hours later, still pinned down and having been shot several times more, Lineberry bled to death. His widow and two sons received his posthumous Navy Cross.

A week later, 19 February, Ambort's company was in a defensive perimeter on the high ground of Hill 50 for the night. By day the company was making its way toward FSB Ross; it was due there in two days. They had taken intermittent sniper fire throughout the day—single shots that hit no one, but required repeated halts, dispersals, and squad sweeps with no result.

Hill 50 was familiar to both Company B and the VC. Bravo Company and other U.S. units had overnighted on its shallow slopes many times before. From Hill 50's top one could see Ross, only two-and-a-half kilometers distant. That closeness ensured fire support from Ross's 81mm mortars, but, as the Marines knew, no place in the Arizona was safe. Ambort later commented, "It was just standard that anytime I return to a position that I had once occupied, that I can expect to find at least one booby-trap. To combat this, I left 'stay-behind' ambushes on these positions. More often than not I was called by the ambush, saying that 'we got people spotted on the position,' and that they were women and children, and they can't open up on them—and they don't. And, just by magic, a booby-trap springs when we go back. . . . This is just a general way of this area."[31]

The harsh truth of Ambort's statement was demonstrated on Hill 50 that afternoon, near the base of the hill. In the impersonal, telegraph-like argot of 1/7's operations journal, "MP(00832) WHILE CHECKING OUT CAVE TRIPPED 01 BOOBY TRAP 60MM OR 81MM HE RD [HIGH EXPLOSIVE ROUND] PRESENT PRESSURE RELEASE DETONATED RESULT 01 KIA AND 01 WIA USMC MEDEVAC."[32] When the booby-trapped high-explosive mortar round detonated, it wounded one grunt and killed Pfc. Richard Whitmore. He'd been a Marine for less than a year.

After the medevac helicopter departed with the wounded Marine and Whitmore's torn body, Ambort didn't have the luxury of contemplation. He had to consider his tactical options for the coming night: "I had a pretty good-sized perimeter to occupy, so I wanted to conserve the majority of my people there. . . . I decided to just send out one killer team."

By radio, Ambort confirmed his plan with Major Theer, who, as usual, was manning the operations bunker at Ross. Then Ambort radioed Lt. Bob Carney, his second platoon commander, whose men were only now approaching Hill 50. He told Carney to select the men for that night's killer team. Then Ambort began to work out its route.

Second Lieutenant Carney, twenty-two, son of a general and grandson of a former Chief of Naval Operations, had been commissioned for eight months. Six of those months had been spent in Quantico's Basic School, every Marine officer's initial training course. Having joined B Company only twelve days earlier, Carney had not yet learned his trade, nor earned the confidence of his platoon. As Major Theer said, "most everyone knew the platoon was really led by his platoon sergeant."[33] That is a not an uncommon circumstance where very junior officers are concerned.

As Carney recalled, "I had run two killer teams prior to this," so he knew what to do. Between 1600 and 1630, after his platoon was settled on a finger of Hill 50, he said, "I asked the person I usually had on these killer teams if he'd run a killer team. He said 'no,' he was tired. So I asked my platoon sergeant if he'd see what he could do about rounding up four volunteers, which he did."[34]

Sgt. Harvey E. Meyers, the platoon sergeant, was on a voluntary extension of duty in Vietnam. Meyers approached his first squad leader, LCpl. Larry Creel, who canvassed his men. Three Marines, LCpl. Michael Krichten and Pfcs. Thomas Boyd and Sam Green, volunteered for the team. Creel also approached Pvt. Randy Herrod, a machine-gun team leader from the second platoon's weapons squad. Herrod also volunteered.

Pvt. Michael Schwarz, a new man in the headquarters

section and a company sniper, approached Meyers, asking to join the killer team. "I said it wasn't up to me—to see the team leader [Herrod], he picked the men . . . and he [Schwarz] went over and talked to my people," Meyers recounted. It was the first time any of the other four had met Schwarz. Okayed by Herrod, Schwarz offered to walk point and became the fifth and final member of the team.

In later testimony, Sergeant Meyers said, "I told Private Herrod to get his team over to Lieutenant Carney and that he would brief them." The examining judge advocate, focusing on the unusual circumstance of a private leading a team of Marines who were all senior to him, asked Meyers:

Q. Why is it you refer to it as "Private Herrod's" team?
A. Because he was the one put in charge.
Q. And who had put him in charge?
A. I believe it was myself and Lieutenant Carney. . . . Herrod had been on previous killer teams. He did a good job and he knows what was going on, so we thought he'd be the best man for the job.

Lieutenant Carney concurred. Herrod "was cool under fire. He was aggressive . . . and I thought he would probably be the one who would be able to get them around the best of the group. . . . He seemed like a natural leader with the men. And I just—my personal judgment."

Actually, Carney's subsequent testimony suggests that Meyers made the decision that Herrod lead the team. Carney, not unreasonably, considered his own twelve days in Vietnam against his platoon sergeant's sixteen months, and offered no objection to Meyers's decision.

The Marine Corps, perhaps more than other services, respects and adheres to the priority of rank. When the leader falls, the next senior Marine takes over: higher rank assumes command. Within the same rank, date of rank controls.[35] Wherever there are two Marines, one of them is in charge.

But in the fifth year of the war in Vietnam, as in Korea

in 1952, there was an acute shortage of experienced non-commissioned officers. An unaccustomed and uneasy flexibility pervaded the usual system of seniority. Often, "authority appeared to be derived exclusively from the position occupied rather than supported by the rank of the occupant."[36] In some units "bush rank" became as real as official rank. Lieutenant Colonel Cooper noted that "at this time in Vietnam, this type of small unit jury-rigging was unfortunately not unusual. . . . In my opinion, the problem started here. It was a judgmental error of considerable magnitude."[37]

Academics agree with Cooper. Behavioral norms break down more easily when group identification is lacking, and Herrod's small team was a prototype of disunity. Schwarz, from another platoon, was unknown to the rest of the team until an hour before the patrol departed Hill 50. Green had been in Vietnam for less than three weeks and met the team leader only that afternoon. Herrod, with the company for only a month and a half, was from another squad. Only Boyd and Krichten had served together before the team's formation. All that united the team was the eagle, globe, and anchor stenciled on the left breast pocket of their utilities. That's a significant bond, to be sure, but no substitute for an established relationship tested under fire, nor a basis for immediately smooth teamwork.

A significant factor in Herrod's selection to lead the killer team—the first patrol he ever led—was that he had been recommended for the Silver Star Medal while in another unit. The medal, very seldom awarded to enlisted Marines, had not yet been delivered, but Herrod's recommendation was common knowledge within the company. Schwarz said, "I believed he had to be an NCO . . . because all the teams I had been out with, corporals and sergeants had been in charge, and a man with a Silver Star should be an NCO."

Lieutenant Carney, having been briefed by Ambort, in turn briefed Herrod as the rest of the killer team looked on and listened. They were to proceed by a prescribed route to the northwest of Hill 270 where, three weeks before, there had been VC contact. Ambort later explained, "I wanted to get them back in that area to see if we couldn't make some more money." Carney gave Herrod the map coordinates the team was to follow, their five checkpoints, and their radio call sign: "Big Lions 4," a conscious if tenuous reference, Carney said, to the recently killed Staff Sergeant Lineberry. The team's roughly circular route would eventually bring them back to Hill 50, their final checkpoint. Carney told Herrod to be particularly careful near checkpoints two and three, since a recent team had there encountered and killed nine NVA.

Herrod, making little allowance for Carney's newness to combat, considered him hesitant and confused; he later remembered thinking, "that stupid son of a bitch is going to get us killed."[38] But he thought of Ambort as an easy-going officer who let his men alone, as long as they did their job.

After Carney briefed Herrod and his team, Lieutenant Ambort called them to the company command post (CP), a little before 1830. Herrod led the team to Ambort's position.

With the five Marines assembled around him, the company commander gave Herrod "more or less a pep talk," Ambort recalled.

"I told him . . . I didn't want any casualties. . . . Since they were out there alone, there wouldn't be much I could do. And I emphasized the fact to him not to take any chances, to shoot first and ask questions later. I reminded him of the nine people that we had killed on the 12th of February and I reminded him of Whitmore, who had died that day. I said, 'Don't let them get us any more. I want you to pay these little bastards back.'"

Krichten's recollection of the pep talk: "He told us to go out and kill as many enemy as we could find." Boyd recalled: "Kill anything moving around." Schwarz heard: "Kill any gooks in the area."

"I told him [Ambort] that I understood perfectly," Herrod later wrote. "We were all ready to get our pound of flesh."[39] Krichten, a veteran of four killer teams, said that he found nothing unusual in the briefing. When Ambort concluded, the men of the team looked briefly at one another. They were going to be in VC country, on their own, and they knew it.

Soon thereafter, Herrod approached Meyers to ask if the team's departure time could be delayed from 1830, when it would still be light, to a later time. Ambort okayed a postponement to 1900 or 1915, and Meyers passed this on to Herrod.

Meyers later testified that he also "heard this rumor that the killer team was supposed to kill anything that moved. So I asked Herrod about it. . . . And he said that the skipper told him to kill anything that moves. And I told him not to do it. I said, 'Don't do anything stupid. Just go out and do your job and get some.'" And what, Meyers was asked, does "get some" mean? "It means going and getting as many kills as possible," Meyers replied.

After making up (applying their camouflage) the team saddled up. When they moved out Schwarz, as promised, took the lead. He carried a rarely seen M-16 rifle with a permanently attached silencer, as well as a Marine Corps-issue Ka-Bar fighting knife and a holstered .45-caliber pistol. Herrod followed with an M-79 grenade launcher and a .45. Behind him, Boyd humped the AN/PRC-25 radio on his back, along with his M-16 and a .45. Krichten followed, and Green brought up the rear. Both carried M-16s.

Between 1900 and 1930, as the last light faded, the killer team left Hill 50. Moving north, they passed through the third platoon's lines, walking down a clearly defined tank trail that lead to the flatland and its rice paddies. The team's first checkpoint, less than 500 meters away, was a small hamlet the company had passed earlier that day: Son Thang-4.

2 | SON THANG-4

KILLER TEAMS

"Killer teams" do not appear in the training syllabus of any Marine Corps instructional program or school. They are unmentioned in any official account of the Vietnam War, except in relation to the Son Thang incident, and they are rarely encountered in appellate records or other archives of the war.[1] Unrecorded even in the parent 7th Marines' command chronology, killer teams appear to have been essentially unique to 1/7, their genesis unknown.

Asked to define the term, Lieutenant Ambort described a killer team as a four- or five-man night patrol, intended, he said, "to search out, locate, and destroy the enemy. Its purpose is to provide an effective reconnaissance-type force. You might say to effectively control my area. . . . An ambush only covers one point and your chances of catching the gooks moving in that one point are a lot slimmer than they are if you've got people roving around."[2]

Harvey Meyers, platoon sergeant of the second platoon, gave a different definition of killer teams: "They go out in small teams of four to five men and search out hamlets for weapons, rice, different types of caches, and to make contact with the enemy, and kill as many as possible."

Cpl. Larry Creel, a second platoon squad leader and a bit lower on the chain of command, was questioned about killer teams during the course of his testimony in the court-martial of Schwarz. He responded, "A killer team is to go out and rove around and try to catch the enemy off guard, trying to hit quick and fast, and try to get out of the area as quickly as possible without getting any casualties."

The defense lawyer who was questioning Creel knew his witness had been a member of several killer teams. He asked Creel a further question without knowing how the witness would respond:

Q. Would you please describe for the court some of these missions that you've been on, so they can understand what a killer team does.
A. Yes, sir. Like, let's see. . . . There was five of us and we went into a ville area. There was movement and talking in this one hooch, so—it was after dark—so we went in . . . and found three mama-sans in there, and they started hollering real loud. Then we heard movement and this man—we'd been through that area that same day; there wasn't any men. . . . and this man from another bunker starts hollering. . . . He starts clamoring with a lot of racket and stuff. He's got a rifle or something. So I went over and fragged him. Then, when I did that, all of the women started to run for the hooch—went around back. So my men opened up on the three mama-sans. And the next morning we came back, we found one man and one mama-san dead.

More than a bit surprised by Creel's casual recitation of having committed at least one apparent murder, the defense lawyer stared dumbly at the corporal. The prosecutor immediately stood and addressed the judge. "Colonel, the government requests that this witness be warned of his rights [to silence and against self-incrimination]. . . ."

Caustically, the judge replied, "It's a bit late in the day, isn't it, captain?"

Lieutenant Colonel Cooper, asked about the rules within his battalion for nighttime killer teams, replied, "The expression the troops use, and quite accurately so, 'anything that moves at night is fair game.' Now, this doesn't mean within the villes. My troops had authority . . . to search villes at night just because we knew there were numerous [VC] meetings conducted at night."

Was a killer team's mission, then, one of "hit and run," or reconnaissance? Was it to search, or just to kill whoever was encountered after nightfall?[3] The killer team's mission was unclear to those who undertook it. Neither listening post nor observation post, neither an ambush nor an intelligence foray, a killer team was a nighttime roving band whose vague and elastic mission was interpreted differently by different individuals. The only common understanding was that they were to kill the enemy. The problem was in defining who was "the enemy."

Herrod's state of mind while leading the team is indicated by an exchange he and his men had with Lance Corporal Creel shortly before the team left Hill 50. Asked about that exchange in a pre-trial hearing, Creel instinctively appreciated its potential significance and was clearly reluctant to reveal the conversation. But the prosecutor would not be put off:

Q. Would you describe what happened just before they went out?
A. I can't remember anything just before they went out.
Q. Do you recall having any conversation with them, with any members of this killer team just before they went out that night?
A. I remember talking to them. I can't think right now what I said. I can't remember, right now.
Q. Do you recall telling me about a conversation you had with these individuals in which they said they were going to go out and kill more than you got on your killer team?

A. We were just joking around. I had gotten four, one night before that. We were all kidding around. We were all saying we were going out and get some stuff, and they said, maybe we can get more than you got that night, that other night. We were all joking around about it.

Q. Do you remember who said that?

A. Herrod, I think, said it. . . . Just like, when you go out on a patrol or something, they say, "Go out and get some," you know, just joking around. Saying, like, you know, you're against the gooks, and all that stuff, so they say you're going to go out and get some. Stuff like that.

Q. Did he put that in words, in terms of, he was going to beat your record?

A. He said, "I'd like to get more than you got, maybe I'll beat your record," or something. He was just joking around.

So, on 19 February 1970, five young and very junior Marines made their way toward Son Thang-4 ("Son Tra" on many U.S. maps). Upon reaching the base of Hill 50 they angled to their left, slightly westward toward Hill 270, whose steep slope began almost where Hill 50's ended.

Team leader Pvt. Randy Herrod, walking cautiously behind the point man, Schwarz, was no combat novice. For that matter, neither was he a private.

FIVE YOUNG MEN

Randell Dean Herrod, part Creek Indian from Calvin, Oklahoma, was twenty years old when he led the Son Thang killer team. He stood six-foot-four and weighed a lean 170 pounds.

He had enlisted in October 1968, sixteen months earlier. After boot camp at San Diego and infantry training at Camp Pendleton, newly promoted Private First Class Herrod was transferred to Vietnam. In 1969, as the Commandant then said, there were only three kinds of Marines:

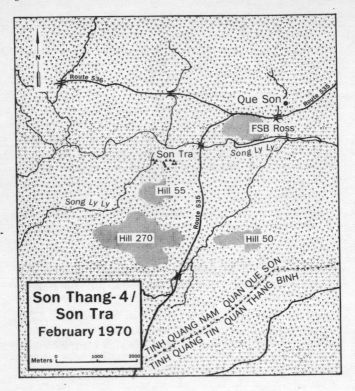

Son Thang-4 /
Son Tra
February 1970

those who were in Vietnam, those who were just back from Vietnam, and those who were about to go to Vietnam.

Once in-country, Herrod was assigned to the 3d Marine Division's 3d Battalion, 3d Marines (3/3), based in Quang Tri's Leatherneck Square—the far north of I Corps. As Marine Corps historians described that area: "In the north . . . the enemy tended to concentrate regular units in the uninhabited, jungle-covered mountain area, close to border sanctuaries. The war in the north, then, was one fought between allied regular units and North Vietnamese Army regiments and divisions . . . not little guys in black pajamas."[4]

SON THANG-4 / 37

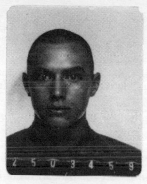

October 1968 boot-camp photo of Pvt. Randy Herrod, leader of the Son Thang-4 killer team. "I want these people killed," he reportedly yelled. *U.S. Marine Corps*

Vietnamese noncombatants were not an issue for 3d Division Marines—there were no noncombatants. If you saw a Vietnamese you shot him. Or shot her. That was the war Herrod came to in June of 1969.

In Company K, 3/3, Herrod was an assistant machine gunner. His platoon leader was 2d Lt. Oliver L. North, the same Ollie North who, as a White House aide seventeen years later, would create a name for himself in other pursuits. In the seventy-four days before Lieutenant North was transferred to another battalion, Herrod formed a lasting and heroic image of him, an image cemented by North's combat leadership. In *Blue's Bastards*, Herrod's account of his Vietnam service, he writes of meeting North: "There's a quality about some men . . . and North had it, even that first day. It was in his eyes: They burned with a bright light. . . . I felt like I had a chance with this man leading me."[5] Herrod thought of North "as an older brother. . . . We looked up to him, went to him for advice, and listened when he talked."

On 28 July, Herrod's company was in a night defensive position supported by tanks, near Cam Lo, when a large

NVA force attacked. In the initial fighting Herrod was wounded by shrapnel in the right leg, but he continued firing his M-60 machine gun at the approaching NVA. When North was wounded, Herrod clambered from his foxhole and pulled the unconscious lieutenant into his defensive position. North recounts in his own autobiography, *Under Fire,* that "Herrod threw me into his hole and stood over me, firing his machine gun as the NVA swept up the side of the hill behind a barrage of mortar fire and a hail of RPGs." North regained consciousness and crawled from Herrod's foxhole, only to be wounded again. "For the second time in half an hour, Herrod left the protection of his fighting position . . . and again dragged me to safety. . . . During the attack, he had saved our entire position."

The citation that accompanied Herrod's subsequent Silver Star Medal read that he "delivered such accurate fire . . . that the enemy soldiers were forced to abandon their mission. . . . Disregarding his own painful wound [Herrod] resolutely maintained his exposed position and continued to fire . . . until reinforcements arrived."

Herrod received a Purple Heart for his leg wound, which was treated in the field. He was initially recommended for a Bronze Star Medal (a fact unknown to Herrod and not later mentioned by North), but reviewing authorities upgraded it to a Silver Star.[6]

The Silver Star is high recognition and honor for any serviceman or woman. For an enlisted Marine it is a particularly significant and unusual recognition of combat valor. "I didn't think I was the world's greatest hero," Herrod wrote, "but I thought I was okay." His fortunes quickly changed.

In late 1969, U.S. troop drawdowns were accelerating along with the Vietnamization of the war. The 3d Marine Division, including Herrod's battalion, 3/3, was one of the first units designated to leave the combat zone; 3/3 was to redeploy to Okinawa in early November. Those Marines who had been in Vietnam for less than six months, however, were to be transferred to other Marine units remaining in-country. Herrod had arrived five months before the scheduled departure date.

It is frequently noted that in World War II, soldiers trained together, went overseas together, fought together, went on liberty together, and returned home together. In 1970, soldiers and Marines arrived in Vietnam alone, had to integrate themselves into already-formed, highly stressed units, went on R&R alone, and often rotated back to "the world" alone. Personnel were rotated into and out of Vietnam like so many shift workers.

While still with 3/3, Herrod was promoted to lance corporal. A week later, on 26 September, he was transferred south to Da Nang and assigned to the 1st Marine Division and Lieutenant Ambort's B-1/7. The move was not to the lance corporal's liking. "I liked the thought of it less than when I'd first landed in Saigon," he wrote, confusing Saigon with Da Nang. "Now it was going to be worse, though how much worse I didn't know." After nine days with 1/7, Herrod resolved his uneasiness with his new command by taking unauthorized absence—"going AWOL," as it is commonly called.

While the rest of his new unit was on patrol and facing enemy fire, Herrod made his solitary way to the coastal city of Da Nang and its rear-area pleasures. He spent the next two months there, hanging out at Freedom Hill's P.X., drinking at enlisted clubs, watching free movies. Sunning on the white sands of the China Beach in-country R&R facility, he could even ogle the occasional nurse or Red Cross woman. He slept and ate at various temporary billeting facilities that dotted the area. After fifty-eight days, out of money and tired of his nomadic existence, Herrod finally turned himself in. He was promptly returned to 1/7, his new command, to await inevitable disciplinary action.

In other times a two-month unauthorized absence (UA)—particularly in a combat area—would have been a serious matter. But in 1970 Vietnam, where hard drugs were common currency and fraggings were unremarkable even in Marine ranks, it was difficult for military legal authorities to be too concerned over a UA of any length.

On 16 January, Herrod was trucked from 1/7 to 1st Marine Division headquarters on Hill 327 for a special court-martial. He later wrote: "The punishment a summary court-martial could hand out was limited, and no one raised an eyebrow when they saw it on your record. Plenty of guys had gotten a summary." Sadly, Herrod was correct—even though his was a special, not a summary court-martial. Disciplinary problems beset all the armed services in Vietnam at that time. Still, there was the possibility of receiving a special court's not inconsiderable maximum punishment: six months confinement at hard labor, a bust to private, loss of all pay, and a bad conduct discharge.

At the trial, Herrod was defended by Capt. Robert C. Williams, a Marine judge advocate with whom he later would have much closer contact. But that day Herrod's case was merely one of several petty courts-martial to be disposed of as expeditiously as possible by 1st Division lawyers. Through Captain Williams, Herrod opted to be tried by a military judge, sitting without a jury. He pleaded guilty to the charge of UA and received a sentence that, most likely, defense counsel Williams, the prosecutor, and the judge, Maj. Robert J. Blum, had agreed upon informally beforehand, as was common in that period. Herrod's rank was reduced from lance corporal to private, and for three months he was to forfeit seventy dollars of his monthly pay and be confined at hard labor. As a matter of clemency, the judge recommended that the confinement be suspended for six months. At the time, it was felt that short-term confinement like Herrod's was better served in the malefactor's unit in the field, rather than "skating" in the crowded but safe III MAF brig in Da Nang. From start to finish, Herrod's special court took less than half an hour.

Under the Uniform Code of Military Justice (UCMJ), the military criminal code that applies to all members of every U.S. armed service, confinement begins to run immediately upon its imposition by the court. Military judges do not have the power to suspend any portion of their sentences, however; only the officer ordering the convening of the court-martial—in Herrod's case, Lieutenant Colonel Cooper, the battalion commander of 1/7—could suspend punishment. Herrod's confinement was promptly suspended in accordance with the code, and he was returned to Bravo Company without ever having seen the inside of a brig.

Another provision of the 1970 UCMJ is that reductions in rank do not take effect until the court-martial record has been typed, reviewed, and approved by the convening authority. Herrod, unaware of this provision, removed the black metal lance-corporal insignia from the collar of his utilities upon returning to B Company from his court-martial. He had just been busted, hadn't he? Besides, few infantrymen wore rank insignia in the field. In relating the results of his court-martial, Herrod thought of himself, referred to himself, and was viewed by fellow Marines as a private; they were all unmindful of the niceties of appellate review. Actually, Herrod was not yet busted. He would remain a lance corporal until his court-martial was approved, on 22 February.[7]

As he led the killer team from Hill 50 toward Son Thang-4, "Private" Randy Herrod was a lance corporal and would remain a lance corporal for three more days.

Although the sun had gone down, the moon was full. At FSB Ross, as battalion operations officer Theer recalls, it was "so bright I could read a report outside the COC."[8] Pfc. Boyd, marching northwest with the team, noted that "the weather was clear and we could see good."

Still, the team moved carefully and without haste. Their flak jackets were unzipped because shell fragments could jam the zipper, making it difficult to reach and treat a wound. Bamboo dipped and swayed with the breeze. The open rice paddies were broken by frequent hedgerows and tree lines, each a potential ambush site. Impenetrable shadows created by the bright moonlight increased the men's caution. Although Herrod later complained of constantly "moving back and forth over the same territory," in fact he had been in that area only since returning to Ross from his court-martial a month before.

The point man, Schwarz, walked about fifteen meters ahead of Herrod, but was no help in navigating or recognizing landmarks. He had joined Company B only six days before, and without Herrod's whispered directions he would have been completely lost.

Pvt. Michael A. Schwarz, from rural Pennsylvania, was at twenty-one the oldest member of the patrol. He had been in Vietnam for exactly four months and, like Herrod, initially had been assigned to the 3d Marine Division, in northern I Corps. As a member of Company E, 1st Reconnaissance Battalion, he had participated in several reconnaissance patrols behind enemy lines, far from friendly forces. When transferred southward to B-1/7, Schwarz's combat experience lent him considerable cachet among the young Marines of his new unit. They sometimes referred to him as "Recon," in recognition of his former command. The infantrymen of grunt battalions often viewed reconnaissance duty as adventurously romantic—Recon guys got to wear picturesque gear that war correspondents liked to photograph. Also much admired was the silencer-equipped M-16 that Schwarz brought with him to 1/7.

As it happened, Recon Battalion had been pleased to rid itself of Schwarz. Only two months after his arrival in-country he had "office hours" punishment for being drunk in the Recon Battalion camp. A month after that, he was formally counseled, and considered for an administrative discharge from the Marine Corps "because of unfitness."[9] In normal times Schwarz probably would not have been accepted for enlistment; if he had been accepted, he already would have been sent packing with an O.T.H.—other than honorable discharge—based upon his frequent involvement with military authorities. But not in 1970, not in Vietnam.

Schwarz had stolen the silenced M-16 he carried. The specialized rifle was 1st Recon Battalion property, and he was obliged to turn it in to the armory when he was trans-

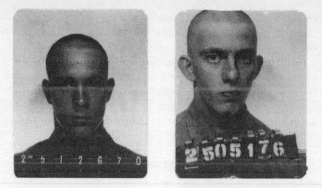

Left, January 1969 boot-camp photo of Pfc. Thomas R. Boyd, the courtroom's reluctant warrior. *Right,* February 1969 boot-camp photo of L.Cpl. Michael Krichten, who testified against the other killer team members in exchange for immunity from prosecution. *U.S. Marine Corps*

ferred from the unit. But in the confusion of the battalion's departure from Vietnam, Schwarz had managed to hold on to the weapon. "I liked it and no one asked for it," he freely admitted. He was not held accountable for the wrongful appropriation of government property, and that crime was never recorded in his service record book. A number of other military offenses were, however. Schwarz had enlisted in the Marines after one year of high school. Now in the fourth year of his four-year enlistment, he had accumulated a formidable record of disciplinary problems stretching from boot camp to Ben Hoa.

Following in trace of Schwarz and Herrod, Pfcs. Thomas R. Boyd, Jr., and Michael S. Krichten were, comparatively speaking, model Marines (Boyd's "office hours" for a one-month unauthorized absence notwithstanding). Both Boyd and Krichten had two years of high school. They had joined B-1/7 within four days of each other in August 1969, and they had served in the same fire team of the same squad of the same platoon since then. Together, the two nineteen-year-olds had been through the heavy combat of the previous summer.

Several months before the Son Thang killer team was assembled, Boyd had received a minor shrapnel wound to his left hand. A week before that, Krichten (known within the platoon as "Cricket") had been lightly wounded in the right shoulder. The two were close as only those who have shared combat can be close.

Bringing up the rear of the killer team, Pfc. Samuel G. Green, Jr., stopped when the others stopped, scanned the tree lines when the others did, and marched on when the others moved. He had arrived in Vietnam only twenty-nine days before, and was still considered an FNG—fucking new guy—by many in the second platoon. This was his first patrol. The short, stocky eighteen-year-old had been a Marine for less than five months and many things he now encountered were firsts.

Like Herrod and Schwarz, Green had weathered problems with authority; in his case, civilian authority. After a series of difficulties with the Cleveland, Ohio, police, beginning when he was fifteen years old, Green had been convicted of incorrigibility, truancy, and running away. The juvenile court also noted his history of drug abuse.[10] When he failed to adjust to the probation imposed by the court, Green had been committed by his parents to the permanent care of Ohio state authorities and had served twenty-three months' confinement in a juvenile facility.

Despite Green's pre-enlistment problems, his brief military record was excellent. His proficiency and conduct marks were consistently high, and even though Marine Corps discipline was difficult for a street-hardened black teenager, Green had avoided any disciplinary note. Platoon Sergeant Meyers said of him, "He was a good man. He followed orders."

A WAR CRIME

Although Son Thang-4 was only a few hundred meters from Hill 50, it took the killer team almost half an hour to reach the village. Each man knew that if they were ambushed, they would have to rely upon themselves until a reaction force from Hill 50 could reach them. They moved slowly, cautiously, prepared to fire on anyone they encountered.

It was understood, at least by the Marines, that a dusk-to-dawn curfew applied to all Vietnamese civilians. "If we spot someone at night, we kill 'em," their platoon leader, Lieutenant Carney, said. "The villagers know better than to walk around. Most of them won't even go to the bathroom at night, out of the hooches." That was the killer team's understanding of the rules of engagement. Besides, Son Thang was on the boundary of a free fire zone, so they felt they could fire at will. "On the boundary" was close enough.

Free-fire zones were geographic areas designated by the South Vietnamese government as pre-approved for the employment of military fire and maneuver because they were ostensibly free of Vietnamese civilians. Since the VC lived among the rural civilian population, the theory was that if that population were removed, whoever remained must be VC. Areas often were cleared by forcibly removing civilians, allowing them to take only what they could carry to refugee camps. In *After Tet,* historian Ron Spector notes that "live stock, furniture, rice paddy, and farm implements, which often represented most of a family's real wealth, had to be left behind."[11] In the resulting free-fire zones the enemy could be taken under fire as soon as detected. Otherwise, permission to fire was first required from a military coordinator and the Vietnamese province chief, via time-consuming radio relays.

But the rural Vietnamese, some of whom had never been more than a few miles from the villages where they were born and their forebears entombed, disliked the refugee camps. Many crept off to return to their former homes, more concerned with what the VC could do *to* them in the

Aerial view of Son Thang-4. Small numbers mark the three hooches where Vietnamese were murdered. The killer team approached via the trail at the lower right.
U.S. Marine Corps

refugee camps than what the Americans could do *for* them. Sometimes the villagers managed to evade resettlement or drifted back into cleared areas out of sympathy or familial loyalty to the VC. One way or another, noncombatants were often in harm's way during combat operations. Gen. William Westmoreland wrote that the only way to establish control over some VC-dominated parts of the countryside was "to remove the people and destroy the village. That done, operations could be conducted without fear of civilian casualties."[12] That assumption, however, usually did not correspond to reality. As Bilton and Sim note in *Four Hours in My Lai,* "The belief that the people had been given a chance to get out and had made their choice made the [free-fire] strategy morally workable. In a free-fire zone, the pursuit of a high body count could proceed unencumbered by the need to discriminate between combatants and civilians at all."[13]

The South Vietnamese government had, in fact, urged Son Thang-4 residents to move to "secure" areas, warning them that their huts were on a free-fire zone boundary line. Company B's 1st Platoon leader, 2d Lt. Peter Kimmerer, had himself escorted numerous civilians from the Son Thang area. "They have no choice but to cooperate," he said, "at least, if they want to go on living they have to cooperate."[14] Villagers who remained were considered with some basis to be, at the least, VC sympathizers.

As Herrod's killer team edged its way down a narrow dirt track that led to Son Thang-4's assemblage of huts, they were locked and loaded. Herrod had a round chambered in his M-79. The shoulder-fired, single-shot grenade launcher was an excellent weapon. Usually loaded with 40mm high explosive/fragmentation rounds, its effective range was 340 meters. It also could be loaded with an M-576 canister round, a particularly effective antipersonnel load with twenty-seven double-aught buckshot pellets that could nearly rip a body in half. Herrod was using canister rounds.

Crossing rice paddies and passing burial mounds, the team approached Son Thang-4. Boyd and Krichten had patrolled that area often enough to know that the ville could not be considered sympathetic to Marine interests. As Lieutenant Colonel Cooper noted, "This was a very unfriendly hamlet. . . . We had much contact around there." A "hooch," a rough, thatch-roofed hut, came into view close beside a waist-high hedgerow. Banana trees grew in front and beside the darkened dwelling. The killer team had reached checkpoint one.

They stopped close to the hooch. At Herrod's whispered direction, Schwarz edged inside the hut's entry, using a flashlight given him by Lieutenant Ambort when the team

A Marine fires an M-79 grenade launcher similar to the one used in Son Thang-4 by the killer team leader, Randy Herrod. *U.S. Marine Corps*

left Hill 50. A moment later Schwarz emerged, saying the hooch was empty.[15]

One might wonder why the team was searching a hooch in a civilian-occupied ville known to be unfriendly. This was, in fact, outside Herrod's briefing, and beyond anyone's understanding of a killer team's mission. It foretold an ominous intent.

The team turned toward another hut about twenty-five

meters distant, from which voices now came. Krichten thought he heard two men: "In my mind I thought there were VC in the area." In front of the hooch was a small cleared space, a patch of hard-packed dirt referred to in subsequent trial testimony as a "patio." Boyd quietly moved to the rear of this second hooch to cut off any escaping Vietnamese. Schwarz stood in front while the other Marines spread out around the edge of the patio. Herrod told Schwarz to call out the hooch's occupants.

"*La dia*," Schwarz barked. "*La dia!*" After a few moments four Vietnamese slowly emerged to stand nervously on the patio. There were no males—only an old woman, a younger woman, and two girls. The younger female, who was led outside by the youngest child, had long, dark hair and unnaturally white, unblinking eyes. Herrod noted to the others that she was blind.

The killer team assembled ten or fifteen feet in front of the Vietnamese. At Schwarz's later court-martial, Krichten described what happened next: "Schwarz handed me his M-16 and he went inside with a flashlight and a .45 and searched out the hooch."

"I went in and proceeded to shake down the hooch," Schwarz later testified. "There was a couple hammocks and a rack like the Vietnamese use for a bed. I went down on the floor, looking under this and, all of a sudden Herrod started yelling, 'Shoot them! Shoot them all! Kill them!' . . . I jumped up and ran out."

Krichten continued his testimony: "I seen him [Schwarz] coming back out," and at the same time, "one of the mamasans ran towards the tree line, and Private Herrod shot her with an M-79. . . . Then he told Schwarz to go over and finish her off." Those in the courtroom were left to fill in the details implied by Krichten's broad-stroke testimony.

As Herrod ejected a casing from his M-79 and loaded another buckshot round, the woman he had shot lay writhing on the ground, screaming in pain. Krichten watched Schwarz move toward where she lay and point his .45 at her. Schwarz fired twice.

In direct examination, Krichten was asked what happened next. His testimony of the cacophonous violence and carnage pales in the retelling, as measured courtroom recitations of violent events usually do. It is even more difficult for a witness to convey the body-quivering tension of anticipated gunfire; the sweaty, heightened sensory awareness and super-slow-motion perception of a firefight, with its adrenaline rush and deafening, yet unheard, sounds. But Krichten's stark testimony was effective enough:

A. Herrod gave the order to kill the rest of the people, and I told him not to do it. . . . Then he says, "Well, I have orders to do this by the company commander, and I want it done." And he said it again, "I want these people killed!" And I turned to Pfc. Boyd, and I said to Boyd, "Is he crazy, or what?" And Boyd said, "I don't know; he must be."

Q. And then what happened?

A. And then everybody started opening up on the people. And by that time it was all over, all the people were on the ground.

Q. Now, did everyone, in fact, shoot?

A. Everyone except for myself.

For a moment the team stared at the results of their point-blank firing. The four bodies, all female, were later identified as Nguyen-Thi-Anh, fifty years old; Le-Thi-Nguyen, a blind twenty-year-old; Nguyen-Thi-Ngoc, sixteen years old; and Nguyen-Thi-Tria, five years old. All of them lay in the dirt, dead or dying. As the team stood transfixed on the patio, the woman shot first by Herrod, then by Schwarz, briefly continued to moan.

This was the first time Green had seen anyone killed by gunfire, let alone women and small children. He was shaken. Television and movies don't prepare one for the sight of actual death by high-velocity military munitions. The human form, when hit by concentrated rifle and pistol fire delivered at point-blank range, does not simply crumple and fall to the ground as though suddenly sleeping. Instead, bodies recoil and jerk with the impact of each round. Bits of flesh, torn from the body by the force of a bullet's impact, tumble crimson in the air. Then the bodies do not fall, but drop heavily to the ground, to lie with limbs splayed in unnatural, seemingly impossible postures, twisted and broken. Often, the acrid odor of urine and excrement fills the air. Flesh is ripped. Unrecognizable organs, glistening and multi-hued, protrude from torn body cavities. Blood pools on the ground, not red, but dark, almost black, soaking into the dusty earth, leaving a sweetish, repulsive smell of its own.

Gunshot victims don't die upon being shot, either. Not right away. Not always. Often they lie in their grotesquely twisted positions, emitting wordless moans and gurglings, animal-like sounds that may continue for minutes. Finally, open eyes grow dull, staring, sightless. No, cowboy movies didn't portray death as it was in Son Thang-4.

Looking down on the bodies, no one spoke. Language and that experience were irreconcilable. Finally, Herrod said, "Let's get out of here." No team member checked the victims for signs of life. There was no need. Moving through a tree line back toward the hooch Schwarz had first entered, the killer team now heard excited voices from inside. Again approaching the first hut's patio, Herrod told the team to spread out.

According to Krichten's sworn testimony, Schwarz once again edged his way inside the hooch's entry. Now he found six Vietnamese. Presumably they had emerged from the small underground "bunker" that many Vietnamese hooches concealed. The family bunker provided refuge from nearby bombing, shelling, or small-arms fire. Once again, the hooch occupants, six this time, were ordered out and assembled on the patio. Once again there were no men among the Vietnamese.

Suddenly Green shouted that one of the women was reaching for something in the waistband of her black *ao abab* trousers, and a single shot was fired by one of the team—by Green, most thought. No one was hit, but the six Vietnamese froze. Two of the younger children began to cry. "Then Private Herrod called us all in and told us to get on line," Krichten said, recalling the event in stilted, self-conscious courtroom language. "Schwarz was just coming out of the hooch and Boyd and myself were just coming up on line, when Private Herrod gave the order to kill them all, and everybody hesitated. Then again he hollered at us, and said, 'I want these people killed immediately!' And then everybody started firing. . . . I fired about three rounds over the people's heads."

The children screamed at first, clinging to the women until they fell. Green recalled firing on the group until his M-16's twenty-round magazine was empty. "The only thing that caused the shooting to stop," Krichten said, "was when all of them were on the ground." There was no need for him to add *why* the Vietnamese were "on the ground."

Later, at Schwarz's trial, Krichten was asked about the propriety of Herrod's orders, a central legal issue in the case. "If you had a question," Krichten's defense counsel asked, "weren't you taught to obey first and ask questions later?" Krichten replied, "That's what we were told by our company commander; to do it and ask questions later."

Again, the team stood over their victims, not speaking. Le-Thi-Lam, a forty-three-year-old woman, lay beside Duong Dong, a twelve-year-old boy. Two ten-year-old girls, Ngo Cam and Nguyen-Thi-Liem, lay sprawled on the patio along with two little boys, Ngo Mien, five, and Ngo Cu, three. Ngo Mien wore a bright checkered shirt. All were dead.

Herrod again reloaded his M-79 and directed the team to move out. As they turned away, Schwarz, working the charging handle of his M-16, said that his rifle wouldn't fire. (Boyd noted that he had used his .45 on the Vietnamese instead.) "Don't worry about it," Herrod told Schwarz. "We'll get it cleared at the next rest stop—at the next checkpoint." Schwarz draped the M-16 over his shoulder by its sling and, as he walked, slapped a fresh magazine into his .45.

The team retraced its steps, passing close by their original victims. Krichten noticed that the woman shot by Herrod and Schwarz still had not died—but he knew she soon would. The men continued on, paralleling another stand of trees to approach another dwelling about sixty meters away.

The third hooch stood where the team emerged from the tree line. A light glowed inside. Again the team took up positions around the hooch and again Herrod had Schwarz call out the occupants. Schwarz later testified that he recalled six people already standing on the patio when the team approached. In either case, once again six Vietnamese, no men among them, now stood on the patio before the killer team, assembled from positions around the hooch. The women and children had heard the heavy firing moments before. One can only imagine their terror.

"I don't know who shot first," Krichten told the court-martial. "But I think it was a -79 that went off first. And then Herrod said to kill them all. And everybody hesitated again, and he hollered at us again, 'I told you that I want these people killed, and I mean it!' By that time, everybody started opening up on the people."

Schwarz, describing the same scene, said Herrod "fired his -79, then he reloaded. And all this time he was reloading he was yelling, 'Shoot them! Kill them all! Kill all of them bitches!'"

Even Herrod, although contending he fired only after having been fired upon, recalled the event in similar terms. "'Shoot. Kill them all,' I shouted, and fired the M-79, as the others blasted away. . . . 'Jesus!' I heard someone whisper."

Responding to a prosecutor's questioning, Krichten resumed his description of the third encounter:

Q. Now, would you explain how Private Herrod was using both a -79 and a .45?
A. Well, first of all he shot his -79 into the people, and then after that, he started using his .45.
Q. And how many rounds did you fire into these people?
A. I put my rifle on automatic and fired into the position as

I did at the first hooch. I just pulled the trigger and just shot the rounds left in my magazine.

Q. What direction did you fire them in?

A. Over the people's heads and into the trees.... They were just all lying on the ground, screaming and crying.... They were all lying on the ground, and there were a few babies crying, and ...

Krichten paused, shaken by his own testimony, but the prosecutor didn't lose his momentum: "Now, what happened after all of the shooting stopped?"

"I heard Private Herrod, I heard Private Herrod tell Private Schwarz to go shoot the baby that was crying. But I don't know if he did it. I don't know if he did. All I heard was a .45 go off."

Boyd similarly reported, "after the firing was over we heard a baby crying and Mike Schwarz got down next to it and fired his .45, and the crying stopped."

Lieutenant Grant, who found the bodies the next day, confirmed the child's death. A dead woman at the third hut, he testified, was clutching a dead child, "about five or six years old, at the most.... its head had just been blown apart, and its grey matter was laying on the ground." The child, Vo-Thi-Minh, was five.

The dead woman holding him was fifty-year-old Vo-Thi-The. When asked to estimate her age, a Navy corpsman with the patrol that found the bodies replied, "I couldn't, because her face was completely blown off ... just completely gone." Ending his description, the corpsman noted, "I could see her intestines hanging out in the back, on the side.... There were ants all over the bodies."

Three other females were killed at the third hooch: Nguyen-Thi-Van, forty; Huynh-Thi-Nhan, twelve; and Vo Hai, six years old. Vo Khuong, a ten-year-old boy, was killed as well. When discovered by Lieutenant Grant, the dead ten-year-old still remained in a kneeling position, face down, his head on his hands.

Krichten's testimony continues: "Then we got a [radio]

call to come in, and we left there and went in to our pos [position], which is Hill 50."

Q. What was the condition of the Vietnamese at hooch number three, after all the firing had settled down?
A. There was still a little moaning, like, stuff, after we left.
Q. Now, to the best of your knowledge what, if any, enemy contact did the team have, while it was in the hamlet?
A. Well, up until the time that Herrod gave the order to fire, as far as I know, there was none.
Q. And how about after that time?
A. I'd say the same thing: there was none.
Q. Now, what, if any, weapons were—did the Vietnamese have in their possession, the Vietnamese living in that hamlet?
A. None.

THE SPOTREP

The killer team, having been recalled, took less than fifteen minutes to retrace their route to the company CP, arriving around 2015. From departure to return, they had been gone slightly less than an hour. In court, Sergeant Meyers related that there had been concern for the team on Hill 50 before they finally returned. The men on the hill had heard a loud burst of gunfire about twenty minutes after the team left, Meyers estimated. "It was a real heavy volume of fire. It was M-16, anywhere from 120 to 160 rounds. . . . There was more than one being fired. . . . We immediately tried to raise the killer team on the radio, and we called them about seven times, but we couldn't get any connection with them."

A minute or two after hearing the first burst of fire, still not knowing what the team might have encountered, they heard a second burst, Meyers said. "It was a much smaller volume of fire. About forty to sixty rounds and it lasted about twenty to thirty seconds. It was all M-16 rifles. I couldn't say exactly how many rifles were firing, but I know there was more than one."

The sounds of small-arms fire are distinctive and usually identifiable to the experienced ear. An M-16, whether firing semiautomatic or automatic, sounds different from, say, a Soviet SKS carbine, or an AK-47. And all of those, even when fully automatic, sound quite different from a crew-served machine gun. Which weapons were heard became a crucial courtroom matter, and the recollections of the veteran Marines did not all agree.

Lance Corporal Creel, on Hill 50 with Meyers and the rest of B Company, heard the gunfire, too. "AK fire, a lot of automatic fire, and I thought they'd been hit. So I got my squad and saddled up for a reac [reaction force]." But the killer team finally responded by radio, saying they were okay, they were coming in, and, Creel added, "said they had some confirms [confirmed enemy KIAs]."

The word quickly spread through the company: the killer team had some kills—six KIAs. "I was pretty excited about them getting six confirms," platoon leader Carney said. "The skipper [Ambort] and myself were real excited, we were pretty happy!"

The team arrived back at Hill 50, still on an adrenaline high. As they were dropping their weapons, body armor, and web gear, Herrod and the team (except Green, who was drawing ammunition) were debriefed by Lieutenant Ambort. Recounting the debrief, Ambort was asked:

Q. And as near as you can remember, what, what happened during that debriefing?
A. Well, I told them all, "Real good shooting, real good job." Then I had to get the spot [report] worked up for battalion, and so I got the information on what had happened. . . .
Q. And what, what were you told, what had happened?
A. They spotted eighteen-to-twenty, fifteen-to-twenty, eighteen-to-twenty, something like that, gooks moving

... towards Hill 270. They moved up to their rear, set up a hasty ambush, opened fire, resulting in six confirms, eight probables, I mean two probables.

Q. Did they indicate the location? . . .

A. Right around checkpoint one.

Herrod wrote of his part in that initial debriefing, "It was a lie, or at best a half truth; and I would live to regret it. . . . we probably hadn't killed any Cong, though we might have blown away some women and children." He knew. He knew from the beginning.

Some team members thought Ambort was suspicious from the moment of their return. Schwarz claimed to recall Ambort saying that "as soon as he heard the shooting, he knew Herrod had gone to wipe out a ville." But throughout the aftermath of the incident, Ambort was firm in saying he had no reason to doubt Herrod. Not yet.

Continuing the debrief, Ambort asked Herrod and the team if they had captured any weapons. No, he was told. "No sweat," the lieutenant responded. "We have one."[16] Then Ambort radioed battalion to give them the first outline of the killer team's contact.

Before working up the spot report, Ambort, aided by Herrod, called an artillery fire mission on the area of the killer team's reported ambush, a post-contact procedure to catch the enemy retrieving bodies, treating wounded, or making an escape. For the next few minutes 160 HE rounds of 105mm artillery plowed the fields and paddies just east of Son Thang-4, where Herrod reported his contact occurred. The spring rice crop had been transplanted the month before.

An infantry battalion's operations officer, its S-3, is vitally important to the unit. The "three" advises the commanding officer on matters relating to combat operations and training of the battalion and, the CO aside, is often the most competent and able senior officer in the command. Usually, the "three" formulates the battalion's tactical plans, which are ratified by the CO, then passed to the company commanders for execution.

Lieutenant Colonel Cooper and 1/7 were fortunate in that their "three" was particularly competent. Maj. Dick Theer, a career Marine, was on his third Vietnam tour. As an adviser to the South Vietnamese and a company commander in past years, Theer had fought over the same ground now being traversed by 1/7's Marines.

The night Ambort submitted his killer team's spot report, Theer was where he spent most of his waking hours (and many of his sleeping ones) since becoming S-3 four months before: in 1/7's COC—the combat operations center bunker—at FSB Ross, where, among other activities, all of 1/7's spot reports were received. From his field desk in the center of the COC, Theer monitored battalion and company tactical radio nets, as well as air and artillery nets. All were on speakers, and when the battalion was engaged the din and confusion were considerable. On the night of Ambort's spotrep it was relatively quiet in the COC.

Theer's radio operator and his operations clerk wrote down the time and general content of Ambort's initial report of the team's success—Ambort had repeated the sketchy information the team had radioed to him before they got back to Hill 50.

Theer had questions. Hoping to sharpen the focus of the spot report the lieutenant would soon submit, Theer asked Ambort the number of VC Herrod's team had encountered, their direction of march, what they were carrying. "I also asked him if they had any weapons; if the men had retrieved any weapons."

About half an hour later, at 2030, Ambort's completed spotrep was received in the COC and entered in condensed form in the battalion's operations journal: SPOTTED 15-20 VC SOME CARRYING ARMS WITH NEG PACKS MOVING SOUTH WEST ALONG TRAIL SET UP HASTY AMBUSH KILLED 06 NVA AND ONE FEMALE PATROL WITHDREW TO CO CP. AND 01 SKS.[17] (The journal is in error. Ambort actually indicated two male and four female KIAs, rather than five male, one female.)

Maj. Dick Theer, 1/7's S-3 (Operations Officer), during an earlier Vietnam tour. Theer was the driving force in uncovering and documenting the Son Thang incident. *Lt. Col. Richard E. Theer*

The final phrase of the report, "and 01 SKS," betrays Ambort's report as false, and suggests his slowly dawning suspicion of what really might have occurred in Son Thang-4. Herrod had not recovered an SKS—a 7.62mm semiautomatic carbine manufactured by the Soviets and Chinese. But Ambort was experienced enough to know that a report of a successful ambush with several enemy KIAs would be viewed with skepticism if there were no captured weapon to corroborate the claim. Although Ambort, too, might have wondered why there were no weapons to show for the engagement, he still wanted his team to receive the credit and recognition that a successful contact merited. And he had been in Vietnam long enough to know how to skirt the problem of no weapon.

Misinterpreting Ambort's motive for adding the SKS to the spotrep, Herrod concluded that Ambort "wanted to protect us, I guess, hoping the detail of the rifle would stave off an investigation. So he told a small lie, too—understandable, maybe, but in the long run one more mistake to contend with."

Reporting the recovery of a VC weapon required more than simply writing it in a spotrep. Following his initial radio transmission with Theer, Ambort walked to the second platoon's position. He could have raised them by radio, but they were close by and he didn't want his conversation monitored by battalion. At Lieutenant Carney's position, Ambort called for an SKS carbine that one Pfc. Clark had found after an ambush a week or so earlier. (After being registered and turned in to an armory for temporary safekeeping, SKS rifles, unlike AK-47s, could sometimes be kept as war souvenirs and taken home when the "owner" left Vietnam.) "It was one of the best-looking SKSs we had found," Sergeant Meyers said. "When my man hit the enemy it splattered blood all over the stock, and it had blood stains on it."[18] Now Pfc. Clark's loss was to be the spotrep's gain, and its validation.

After the report was radioed to battalion, Schwarz brought his own rifle to Ambort's attention. His M-16's nylon stock appeared to have been hit by two rounds, one strike on the receiver above the selector switch, and another in the butt of the rifle, exposing the buffer spring. Ambort questioned Schwarz as he examined the weapon, and Schwarz appeared surprised at the damage. "He said his weapon wasn't firing right, or wasn't firing at all, wouldn't fire, and he just thought it was a malfunction," Ambort said. The M-16 did appear to have been hit.

Schwarz finessed the obvious question of how his weapon could have been struck—twice, without his having noticed—by implausibly suggesting it was hit after he left it lying on the ground when he entered one of the Son Thang-4 hooches. Ambort didn't examine the issue too closely. The damaged rifle was simply further confirmation of the killer team's ambush and resulting exchange of fire with the enemy.

SUSPICIONS

Meanwhile, Major Theer radioed Ambort regarding the spotrep. Instead of the "well done" Ambort expected, Theer said he wanted still more detail. What was the composition of the VC group that had been ambushed? Was Ambort sure about the number of women? Did children appear to be among those fired upon? Were no other weapons recovered?

Ambort may or may not have had suspicions before, but Theer's questions raised red flags. The company commander's concern was further heightened later that night, when the battalion commander, Lieutenant Colonel Cooper, radioed to ask the serial number of the SKS. Did Cooper think the enemy carbine might be imaginary?

Actually, Theer and Cooper were merely anxious that the killer team's engagement not be yet another contact in which, despite multiple kills, no weapons were seized. They wanted to be sure the SKS was genuine, at least. Asked about his suspicions regarding the spotrep, Theer later replied that he had none: "I had no reason to feel that there might be something wrong with it."[19] But if they had to forward a weaponless contact report to regiment and division, Theer and Cooper would have their own credibility concerns. Hence their caution.

But the battalion's three inquiries following what Ambort initially viewed as a fairly ordinary combat engagement led him to believe that "battalion showed an unusual interest in this. I wanted to clear up in my own mind that nothing had happened down there that was out of place, and so I did ask—ask them." Ambort called for the killer team to return to his CP. He wanted to talk to them about their contact again.

He was asked about his motive for the further questioning:

Q. Did you at that time suspect, actively suspect, that they had committed a crime? . . .

A. I suspected that they could have. . . . I was afraid to ask the questions for fear of the answers.

Krichten later wrote that Ambort "called us all back up and said that he wanted to know the truth that really what did happen. So Herrod and I told the lieutenant that we killed about twelve women and children." Although the team still held to having been fired upon by the victims, this was an entirely new scenario for the lieutenant to consider. But dead women and children did not necessarily mean the worst.

Ambort related that he asked the team, "'Are you sure the people were outside of the hooches?' and they said yes. Positive. Again, 'There's no way they were inside the hooch?' He [Herrod] said, 'No, they weren't, they were right outside.' I said, 'Right, okay.'"

Ambort was asked about his response to hearing this. "Well, it sounded strange. . . . The three main things, as far as I was concerned: number one, were these people [Vietnamese women and children] outside, on the trail? Yes, they were. Two, did the killer team take fire? Yes, they did. Number three, we had all heard firing. And number four, the two holes in Schwarz's weapon. . . . I thought it was unusual that, that they didn't tell me this right off, but as soon as I got it cleared up in my mind . . . I didn't bother to call battalion."

In explaining his wishful thinking, Ambort continued, "If some of the group, speaking of the children in the group, had been in fact killed, which was unknown, he [Herrod] said he wasn't sure if they were in fact killed, there was no sweat." Child combatants, after all, were common in Vietnam.

Ambort went on, "I mean, you don't normally go out and shoot kids unless it's an accident, or unless you find one carrying a rifle. . . . And, naturally, whenever a child does get shot or killed, it's of great concern to me and everyone else in the company. And so I told them, 'No sweat, don't worry about it.'"

So Ambort concluded on thin evidence that, because Vietnamese who were violating curfew had fired on the team, the consequential killing was justified, even if they were women and children. He was satisfied.

Ever the commander, Ambort concluded his evening by directing Herrod and his team to saddle up again and finish their assigned patrol, this time reversing their route; from Hill 50 (checkpoint five), to checkpoint four, and so forth, by-passing checkpoint one to return to Hill 50. At a little after 2200, with considerable grousing at having to leave Hill 50 for a second time that night, the team again departed. They returned at daylight.

The next morning, 20 February, B Company received a call from FSB Ross. Battalion warned Ambort that the S-2 (the intelligence officer, Lieutenant Grant) and his patrol would be inspecting the battalion's antipersonnel sensors to the north of Bravo's position. Ambort passed that word to his men so they would not fire on the friendlies.

Shortly after that, Theer called Ambort to ask how long it would take to get the company assembled and moved back to Ross. That struck Ambort as odd, since they were not due for their "rehab" period for one more day, but he responded that they could start for Ross within minutes. He was directed to do so.

As the company prepared to move out, Ambort received one more radio call: "Lieutenant Grant called and said he wanted a working party down there. He didn't give me the coordinates. . . . I said, 'What working party?' . . . He said, 'The one with the E-tools [entrenching tools; small folding shovels].' I said, 'E-tools? What for?' He said, 'For burying some dead people.' And I said, 'Well, what's going on?' He said, 'Well, I can't tell you. You'd better call battalion.'"

3

DISCOVERY AND
INVESTIGATION

MY LAI'S LEGACY

My Lai was in the back of Lieutenant Ambort's
mind even as he debriefed Herrod's killer team
on the rocky slope of Hill 50.[1] My Lai was less
than twenty-five miles from Son Thang-4. Was
Son Thang, like My Lai, a war crime? For that
matter, was My Lai a war crime?

Technically, the March 1968 murder of hundreds of South Vietnamese noncombatants by
Army troops under the command of 1st Lt.
William L. Calley was not a war crime; a crime,
certainly, but not a war crime. As Maj. Gen.
George S. Prugh, the Army's judge advocate
general, noted, "the victims were citizens of an
allied nation, not enemies protected under the
Geneva Conventions, but citizens protected by
the law of Vietnam. . . . Within the scope of the
Uniform Code of Military Justice, the My Lai
murders were not legally distinguishable from
other homicides."[2]

Telford Taylor, former chief prosecutor for
the Subsequent Nuremberg proceedings, dis-
agrees, pointing out that My Lai was regarded
as VC-controlled and armed, and enemy resistance was expected: "It would be highly artifi-

cial to say that this was not 'hostile' territory within the meaning of the Hague Convention, or to question the applicability of the laws of war."[3] The same could be said of Son Thang-4. Indeed, under customary law of war, or the Nuremberg Principles, or the U.S. Army's own definition,[4] My Lai and Son Thang were not only crimes by any domestic definition, but also war crimes—grave breaches of the law of war.

Calley, finally convicted by general court-martial of the premeditated murder of twenty-two Vietnamese and one assault with intent to commit murder, was sentenced to dismissal from the Army and confinement at hard labor for life. To the dismay of many who served in Vietnam, Calley was lionized by large segments of the American public who were unfamiliar with military law and the law of war, and ignorant of the horrific circumstances of My Lai. An Army lawyer wrote of Calley, "Some who seemingly bathe in unawareness have even suggested that to prosecute a person who violates the law of war is to make the accused a scapegoat. Certainly this is a confusion of terms in that 'scapegoat' implies a sacrifice of an innocent thing."[5] Calley was no innocent.

But My Lai did change the way U.S. armed forces were trained. Regulations had long required minimal training in the law of war during initial indoctrination of enlisted personnel, and periodic updating of instruction. Refresher training was required for troops in Vietnam also. But that training, if given, was perfunctory at best.

Brig. Gen. Mike Rich, who directed the Marine Corps' Judge Advocate Division in the late 1980s, was an infantry captain in Vietnam for thirteen months. He received none of the required law of war training ("Zero," as he put it), nor did his Marines (again: "Zero").[6] Former Commandant of the Marine Corps Gen. P. X. Kelley, who spent two years in Vietnam combat, echoed that neither he nor his men received the training. ("None.")[7] "The law of war," wrote Marine Corps lawyer Hays Parks, "is often viewed as . . . an unnecessary, unrealistic restraining device inhibiting the combat commander."[8] Maj. Gen. William K. Suter, a post-Vietnam acting judge advocate general of the Army, now clerk of the Supreme Court of the United States, admits, "it's no secret that we had gotten lax in the military about teaching . . . the law of war. . . . After the [My Lai investigation] all hell broke loose and we started teaching law of war day and night."[9] Still, as 1/7 CO Lieutenant Colonel Cooper derisively noted, "You could have spent three weeks talking to troops about . . . the rules of land warfare and it wouldn't have helped."[10]

In his autobiography, Gen. William Westmoreland writes, "Since murder is so obviously a major crime, surely it was unnecessary to put out a specific order . . . not to murder unarmed civilians."[11] Major General Prugh adds, "Much law of war material . . . sprouts from basic morality and common sense. It is very late to try to teach an eighteen- or nineteen-year-old rifleman . . . that he should carefully distinguish combatants from noncombatants and that he should not kill helpless people."[12] Prugh's observation echoes that of Brig. Gen. S. L. A. Marshall: "[An infantryman] is what his home, his religion, his schooling, and the moral code and ideals of his society have made him. The Army cannot unmake him."[13]

Perhaps the most significant outcome of My Lai was that the law of war and its prohibitions against killing noncombatants became a constant consideration in the minds of commanders. Few were likely to disregard breaches of that law and ignore the moral and legal responsibilities they now understood themselves to carry. And, cynics might add, neither would they disregard the career-ending damage a cover-up, once discovered, would wreak.

That awareness of legal breaches and sense of responsibility did not reach as far as the Son Thang killer team, but it did reach far enough to ensure discovery of their crimes.

MAJ. DICK THEER

The morning after Ambort's spotrep was logged in at Fire
Support Base Ross, Col. Gildo S. Codispoti, the 7th
Marines' fiery regimental commander, helicoptered to B
Company's position on Hill 50 for a command visit. Ac-
companying him was Ambort's battalion commander, Lieutenant Colonel Cooper, who recalled that he and Codispoti
"both were anxious to get out and see how they were doing"[14]—and to see for themselves Schwarz's damaged rifle
and the SKS reputedly recovered in the previous night's action. After their brief visit, Codispoti and Cooper were satisfied that the weapons substantiated the previous night's
contact.

Shortly after Cooper returned to FSB Ross, however,
Major Theer apprised him of Lieutenant Grant's recently
reported discovery of sixteen bodies—all women and children—in Son Thang-4. Moreover, Theer reported, Grant
had returned to Ross with a sandbag full of M-16 shell casings, two M-79 casings, numerous .45 casings, and a variety of spent lead slugs, all found near the bodies. Theer
didn't like the way this was shaping up.

He recommended that Company B immediately return
to Ross so the incident could be looked into. They were
scheduled to return in a day or two, in any event. "I based
[the early return] primarily on the fact that we had a patrol
operating in there the night before," Theer reasoned. "They
had made a contact . . . I believed that perhaps these individuals, the bodies they had found, they may have been the
result of that contact."[15]

Cooper agreed. Theer radioed Ambort to return to Ross
immediately. Even though Ambort's company might have
had nothing to do with the Vietnamese deaths, the directives of Military Assistance Command, Vietnam (MACV), I
Corps, and the division required investigation of all potential war crimes. Bringing Bravo back to Ross early would fa-
cilitate that investigation. Besides, Company B had been
through a lot over the last two weeks. "Almost every day,"

Theer said, "they had contact of one sort or another. Either a booby trap, snipers, or incoming small-arms fire. . . . From one sector to another, they were harassed almost continuously, day and night. . . . Bravo Company lost nine Marines."[16]

B Company arrived at Ross that afternoon, 20 February. As a precautionary measure, Theer had Ambort split up the killer team and post each man to a different perimeter tower. The team immediately realized that all was not well. But Ambort reassured each Marine as he posted him that everything was okay, things were in hand.

The six fifty-foot observation towers, each manned by three or four Marines, looked out over the inhospitable terrain surrounding FSB Ross. Each tower had receivers for the electronic personnel sensors that were planted beyond the perimeter wire; an AN/PVS-2 Starlight night scope mounted on a sniper rifle, and a reassuring .50 caliber machine gun. Team leader Randy Herrod nevertheless viewed each tower as merely "one small jail where each of us could sweat it out."[17]

At early chow that evening Theer discussed with Cooper Lieutenant Grant's report and its possible consequences. The CO had already briefly spoken to Ambort upon his return to Ross. Concerned, Cooper orally appointed Theer to investigate the incident. He told Theer to be thorough and absolutely certain the patrol members' rights were protected. "The colonel had no information . . . just the same as myself," Theer said. "That's why he ordered the investigation." Then Cooper phoned Colonel Codispoti to apprise him of the situation. Dick Theer would determine what had happened at Son Thang-4.

Cooper and Theer had met at Quantico's Basic School eleven years earlier, when Cooper was a company commander and Theer, then a second lieutenant, was a student. Theer was a former All Big Ten guard at Iowa, where he played on the 1957 Rose Bowl team. Now thirty-four, he was a six-foot-three 205-pounder with an exemplary Vietnam record.

Theer first saw combat in 1964 as an adviser to the 3d Battalion, Vietnamese Brigade. In May 1965 he went ashore again at Chu Lai, as a company commander, and remained in-country, and in combat, for a year. He earned the Silver Star for valor under fire in Operation Harvest Moon.[18] Theer returned to South Vietnam again as a major in April 1969, nine months before the Son Thang incident. During this third Vietnam tour he already had earned one Bronze Star for bravery in a Que Son NVA engagement, and he would earn a second, again under fire.

As 1/7's operations officer, Theer commonly spent up to twenty hours a day in the combat ops center, often sleeping in the bunker. No one had a better feel for the battalion's operational activities, and few were better leaders of men.

Theer's abilities in the legal arena, for which he had never been trained, would demonstrate the wisdom of Cooper's appointment. Theer was to be the driving force in uncovering and documenting the Marine Corps' worst known war crime during America's long war in Vietnam.[19]

THE INITIAL INVESTIGATION

"This is an initial report of possible serious incident involving elements of B-1/7 and Vietnamese civilians," the secret message began. "Civilians allege U.S. Marine unit entered hamlet on 19 Feb 1970 and killed women and children. Patrol sent to check allegation found the bodies of approximately sixteen women and children recently slain by small arms fire. . . . Earlier a patrol from B-1/7 had reported a contact . . . in the same area with an estimated 25 VC resulting in 6 enemy kills. There are some indications that this report is inaccurate. Full scale inquiry commencing immediately."[20] That message, from the commanding general (CG) of the 1st Marine Division to the commander of III MAF in Da Nang, was preceded by the words, "Eyes only for Lt. Gen. Nickerson." It was sent at 1800 local time on 20 February. The Marine Corps, having learned from My Lai, had wasted no time in investigating its own.

The next day's sun was hardly up when Dick Theer, by chance, ran into Lieutenant Ambort outside the FSB Ross COC. Theer told Ambort that he was assigned to investigate what had happened in Son Thang-4, and would have to talk to him.

Article 31 of the UCMJ mandates that warnings must be given any service person suspected of a crime before a statement, written or oral, may be taken. The warnings are akin to, but broader than the Miranda warnings long employed by civilian law enforcement agencies across America. But when Theer mentioned Article 31, Ambort interrupted him. Theer recalled, "He said he clearly understood, but he wanted to tell the truth, the whole story, and would be glad to provide me with statements."

Before Ambort wrote his statement, Theer asked him to pass the word to the patrol members that he would speak to each of them shortly. Soon after 0830, the entire team, Herrod, Schwarz, Green, Boyd, and Krichten, met Theer outside the battalion briefing hut. After explaining his purpose and intent, Theer released everyone but Herrod. He would start his inquiry with the killer team leader. This was to be the first of their several encounters.

Inside the briefing hut, Theer informed the young man seated beside his desk that he was investigating the recent killing of sixteen Vietnamese in Son Thang. Reading from a printed wallet-size card he customarily carried, Theer advised Herrod of his Article 31 rights to remain silent, to have a lawyer, to end the interview at any point, and so forth.[21] Herrod, after confirming that he understood his rights, for the next hour related a version of what had happened two nights before. He asserted that his team had been fired upon while questioning Vietnamese villagers, and that some of the villagers they confronted could have been parties to the firing. The villagers may have been hit in the team's return fire, Herrod stated. Moreover, this sequence of events occurred not once that evening, but three times.

Theer, although surprised to hear this new account, did not find the repetitive nature of the team's encounters unbelievable. It was an old story in Vietnam, and Theer knew that such events were all too possible. As Theer later testified, "These [Vietnamese] people might have been killed by a cross fire, or exchange of gunfire between the enemy and the Marines, which sometimes occurs in any war. I had no reason to suspect otherwise."

Asked if he would reduce his statement to writing, Herrod readily agreed. At Theer's invitation Herrod moved to Theer's own nearby quarters—a smaller hut—and was left to write his account.

The three-and-a-half-page document related the killer team's briefing and departure from Hill 50. Once in Son Thang-4, Herrod wrote, they heard voices, a male among them, coming from a hooch. Upon bringing the occupants onto the patio to investigate, the team confronted only women and children. "Then," Herrod wrote, "a shot zinged over our heads, one female started to run toward a tree line so we cut them [Illegible]." Seeking the source of the shot, he continued, the team ran toward another hooch. They forced its occupants outside and began to search them when "two shots rang out and a female hit the deck. We . . . assumed that she just ducked and that we were being set up, so we opened fire on the area again, and on them." Once more seeking the source of fire, Herrod wrote, the team then ran to yet another hooch. Its occupants "were brought out and shot because we thought they had been another part of the set up, or the snipers." Recalled to Company B's position, the team retraced its route to Hill 50. "Upon returning to the pos I gave the CO a false spot report. For fear of what we had done. Later I told him the truth to the best of my knowledge. He then said that I had really messed up."

While Herrod was writing his statement, Theer returned to the briefing hut and began his interview of Pfc. Thomas Boyd. The major offered him a cigarette and urged him to relax. After repeating the same Article 31 rights he had given Herrod, he began the same interview process. Boyd started by saying that he wanted to tell the whole story. He caught Theer's attention when he went on to say that he, along with two other team members, met with Lieutenant Ambort after returning to Ross the day before, and the lieutenant said he was going to tell the truth about the incident, and urged them to do the same. They all had agreed to speak truthfully.

After Boyd described the patrol, Theer asked him if he, too, would write his account. Boyd agreed and was shown to Theer's now-empty quarters and left to pen his statement. "He was in there by himself," Theer recalled, "and I returned to the briefing room [and] invited the next member of the patrol in to repeat the sequence."

While Pfc. Sam Green talked with the major, Boyd wrote a page-and-a-half account that closely paralleled Herrod's: As the team was confronting several Vietnamese at the first hooch, one round was fired at them and "we opened up on them"; the Marines did the same thing with the second group, when fired upon at the next hooch. At the third location, "one of us opened up and then all of us did"; Boyd mentioned no enemy fire.

About that time Theer received Ambort's written statement, which interrupted his interview of Green. Reading the statement in light of what he had learned from Herrod and Boyd, Theer now understood that the lieutenant's spotrep was false in regard to the captured SKS, at least. A sickening suspicion began to grow: perhaps there was more to all this than he had realized.

After examining Ambort's statement, Theer asked him about the meeting on the previous day that Boyd had mentioned. Ambort readily confirmed it, explaining that he met with Herrod, Boyd, and Krichten after talking with Colonel Cooper. The platoon leader, Lieutenant Carney, also was present, but Ambort could not immediately locate Schwarz and Green. The company commander had warned the three that events were taking a serious turn; that it would be best to tell the truth, and that he intended to do so himself, starting by revealing that he'd made a false contact report. Ambort had already told Cooper that his spotrep was not true and that the "recovered" enemy weapon was actually from an earlier firefight.

While Colonel Cooper felt Ambort made a serious judgmental error in falsifying the report, he generously believed that "his motivations were based on a rather difficult situation. He reacted in protection of his men."[22]

As it happened, Ambort didn't learn how many Son Thang victims there actually were, or that the team had fired on them at least once without first receiving fire, until Theer told him. Ambort's earlier vague suspicions were then realized: His men had lied to him and involved him in much more than a false weapon report.

Theer, for his part, was now concerned that the statements he was taking from the team might be subtly influenced by Ambort's well-meaning admonition to his three men that they should tell all—that, in effect, they should make self-incriminating admissions.

"I felt that perhaps each of these men might have been under some duress. . . . Having been a company commander myself . . . you have a family relationship. . . . There are very tight bonds. If the commanding officer said something, I'm sure the men would . . . take it as authoritative. Like your father speaking to you."

Theer recognized what psychiatrists and academics have long known to be true: "Combat calls forth a passion of care among men who fight beside each other that is comparable to the earliest and most deeply felt family relationships."[23] Even with the Article 31 warnings, were the men's statements truly voluntary in light of Ambort's admonitions?

Returning to his inquiry, Theer picked up with Private Green, repeating the Article 31 warnings despite his new concern about their adequacy. Theer listened to the now-familiar recitation volunteered by Green. Although willing to reduce his story to writing, Green said he wasn't much of a writer; he accepted Theer's offer to write the statement as he dictated it, a not-uncommon practice for such investigations.

When the statement was completed, Theer handed it to Green, reminded him that he did not have to sign it, and had him read it. Green's account was virtually identical to Herrod's and Boyd's, except Green offered that at the third Son Thang hooch, he had been the first to fire on the Vietnamese when one of the women "suddenly reached into the waistband of her pants."

By now it was noon, but at FSB Ross there was no such thing as a lunch break. Theer carried on, knowing what to expect from the remaining two team members. Krichten talked to him next, mentioning the meeting with Ambort on the previous day. Krichten, too, agreed to write his statement, and soon gave it to Theer, who had already begun his interview of Schwarz, the last team member.

Half an hour later, while Theer was still talking to Schwarz, Krichten re-entered the briefing hut and asked for the return of his written statement, explaining that he had left out several details. Theer handed it back, only to watch Krichten wad it up, then ask to write another. Puzzled, Theer told him to return after he had completed his talk with Schwarz.

Like the others, Schwarz agreed to write his statement. When he later gave it to Theer, however, it was illegible and differed significantly from his oral recitation. Asked if he would mind clarifying the writing, Schwarz agreed, and took up Theer's offer to write the statement per Schwarz's dictation. But when Schwarz was asked to sign the completed new version, he said, no, he would rather rewrite it in his own handwriting. "A matter of pride on his own part," Theer presumed.

As anticipated, Schwarz's statement approximated the others, with the notable addition that at the first and third hooches the team had been "ordered" to fire—by whom, Schwarz did not say.

By 1730, Theer also had Krichten's new written statement, this time dictated to Theer. Predictably similar to the other accounts, Krichten recited that at the first hooch, they "shot the women and children because we thought they were part of a trap," as they did at the second hooch. At the third, Green fired, Krichten said, then Herrod ordered all of them to fire.

Putting the best possible light on the events at Son Thang, Dick Theer still told himself there was no firm basis for suspecting the worst. "I had no reason to suspect these men of murder. . . . I was simply investigating the . . . deaths of these sixteen civilians."

Despite his lack of training in the law, Theer knew something was wrong, however. Schwarz had altered his initial statement, and his account of his rifle having been hit by enemy fire rang false to Theer. All five team members related firing on the civilians at the third hooch without first having been fired upon. You didn't have to be a Supreme Court justice to recognize the wrongfulness of such an act. Had the team's meeting with Ambort, almost accidentally mentioned, influenced their stories? To Theer, the five statements as a whole were suspect. "They were too pat," he recounted, as if "every man had gotten together, made up a story . . . like it was rehearsed." He wanted to see Son Thang 4 for himself.

He needed help, and he knew it.

Late that afternoon, Theer approached Lieutenant Colonel Cooper, who, once he heard the story, concurred with Theer's assessment. Things were looking even worse than the previous evening's message to III MAF had implied.

Cooper contacted division headquarters in Da Nang to request Criminal Investigation Division (CID) assistance. He also asked that Col. Robert Lucy come to Ross. Recognizing the potential seriousness of the matter, division promptly agreed to both requests. Two CID NCOs would arrive at Ross the next morning and Bob Lucy, the division staff judge advocate (SJA), would arrive later that very day.

Col. Robert M. Lucy, who had graduated from the Naval Academy three years ahead of Cooper and was his close friend, had been an infantry officer in the Korean War, earning a Bronze Star at Inchon as a weapons company commander. At Da Nang he had been the division's SJA—its senior lawyer—for six months, directing roughly a score of lawyers through a series of particularly difficult cases, several of which had involved circumstances like those shaping up at 1/7. Always responsive to the commanders his office served, Lucy helicoptered to Ross just before nightfall.

Upon landing, Lucy met with Cooper and his ops officer in the CO's quarters. For two hours the three of them discussed the now-suspected homicide of sixteen Vietnamese noncombatants. Theer related the warnings he had given each man, and the possibility that the team had been influenced by their conference with Ambort the day before. As Theer later testified, "I wanted his advice to ensure that each man, his rights were not violated. And I told him that I intended to question them again . . . that I was afraid that each of the men had somehow or another incriminated themselves by virtue of this conference."

Colonel Lucy agreed that Theer, when re-interviewing the team, should again warn them in writing of their Article 31 rights. Theer also suggested that this time he include additional written advice that they could freely withdraw any prior statement, whether oral or in writing, and that a statement so withdrawn could not be used against them in any way.

Then Lucy, having become involved in a potential court-martial case he might later review for legal sufficiency, went to chow. Afterward, he bedded down in Cooper's quarters; it was too dark for a chopper flight back to division. Around 2000 Cooper and Theer left Colonel Lucy for the COC, where they spent the night monitoring the battalion's on-going field operations. They still had a battalion to run. Theer firmed up preparations for his own patrol to Son Thang the following day.

REVELATION

Early the next morning two CID agents, Staff Sergeant Slagle and Staff Sergeant Dye, arrived at Ross by helicopter. At their suggestion, the killer team's weapons were collected and placed in a wooden crate, and new weapons were issued. The crate was nailed shut and placed in the COC. Theer later learned from Boyd and Krichten that Herrod had substituted a weapon he had not carried, but, although the weapons were taken to the Army's criminal investigation laboratory at Long Binh for ballistics tests, neither the test results nor Herrod's deception became an issue.

The hump from Ross to Son Thang-4 was about two miles, and it was hot. Several of the Marines wore soft covers and T-shirts under their fourteen-and-a-half-pound flak jackets. Lieutenant Grant led the patrol; Major Theer and a radio operator were near the front, followed by the CID sergeants and two scout dogs with their handlers. A *chieu hoi* interpreter and a photographer were in trace, along with other infantrymen for security. Theer intended to go, he said, where "the men had described that they had taken fire. . . . Put myself where I would have believed a sniper would have been hidden."

The patrol approached Son Thang from the northeast, reaching it without incident. The fresh graves, pointed out by the villagers in nearby manioc and potato fields, were evident. The Vietnamese told Theer where each victim was buried. Grant showed him the patios where he had initially found the bodies. "I scooped the dirt away with my hands and felt the soil," Theer said. "It was still wet, tacky, and there was some human matter there."

He looked in each hooch, every thicket, each tree line. "I examined the outside of the houses very carefully, looking for marks that a rifle shot might have made . . . I walked around and looked at all the trees." He found spent .45 slugs and an M-16 cartridge. There were gouges apparently made by bullets on structures near where the bodies had

Members of Maj. Dick Theer's patrol examine the area around the third hooch. On the left, Marines extract bullets from a tree trunk. *U.S. Marine Corps*

fallen. "I was looking specifically for spent cartridges . . . bent or broken brush where someone [VC] might have been. . . . They would have to force an opening in the hedgerow . . . in order to shoot." Again Theer went to the three locations where the bodies had been found. Placing himself where the team members said they had stood, he turned, looking for fields of fire, for distant positions from which the team might have been fired upon. "I wanted to make sure that I looked in every possible place where a sniper could have been standing, to have seen them on the patio. And I couldn't find any place." He examined any potential cover, close or distant. "I was looking for footprints, or any sign that there was, or had been, a soldier there, or a guerrilla, or what have you. I found nothing."

After inspecting the ville for four-and-a-half hours, Theer was satisfied. He was no longer looking into how sixteen Vietnamese had died. He was investigating sixteen murders.

• • •

Theer's patrol returned to Ross at about 1800. There was a flap when electronic sensors detected movement outside the perimeter and a 100 percent alert was effected. When no one was found the base stood down and Theer began the process of requestioning the killer team. It was 2130.

Again, he started with the team leader. Randy Herrod arrived at the major's quarters to find the two CID staff sergeants there as well. Theer again advised Herrod of Article 31, but now, in addition to the usual rights, the neatly typed warnings included the statement, "I have been informed . . . that I am suspected of unlawfully killing one or more of . . . sixteen civilians." The new warnings went on to say that his statement of two days before would not be considered, or used against him if he wished to withdraw it. An additional warning read: "I should not be influenced into making a statement merely because my commanding officer, 1st Lt. Ambort, told me to tell the truth and to tell the whole story."

Herrod read the paper, confirmed that he understood it and had no questions. He initialled the spaces indicating he did not desire a lawyer, and did not wish to withdraw his prior statement. He signed it. Herrod did offer to make a new oral statement, however.

Briefly interrupted when Theer had to monitor a patrol's enemy contact, Herrod again related his account, making no essential change to his written statement of two days before. Herrod later recalled, "I assured him over and over again that we'd been attacked, that the civilians had made the moves, that we'd fired instinctively, just the way we were trained." Briefly questioned by Theer, then by the two CID agents, Herrod finally returned to Yankee tower. He was a cool one, Theer thought. This second encounter with Herrod was a draw.

Herrod writes of that second interview, "I was more than a little worried about what the others might do. Not Green and probably not Schwartz [sic]—I'd fought beside them and I knew what they were made of. But I didn't know much about either Boyd or Krichten. I just hoped they weren't easily intimidated."

Theer's other duties kept him occupied in the COC for the rest of the night. He catnapped while monitoring the various battalion nets, Son Thang always in the back of his mind.

At about 0600 the next morning, 23 February, Pfc. Tom Boyd again reported to the major. In Theer's quarters, with Staff Sergeants Slagle and Dye again present, Theer advised Boyd of his now-augmented rights. Boyd said he wanted to be truthful, and again began to recite his story.

When he mentioned sniper fire, Theer interrupted: "I said that I had been out there in the hamlet . . . I could find no evidence that an enemy sniper had been in the area." Theer told Boyd of his detailed inspection of hooches, bushes, trees, and terrain. "After I had described this, I asked him point-blank, I said, 'There weren't any snipers there, were there?' And at that point he said, 'No, there weren't.'"

Theer sighed. His fears were confirmed.

The major accompanied Boyd, Slagle, and Dye to the officers and staff mess tent. It was too early for chow, but Theer had the cooks prepare something for the four of them. They ate in silence, then returned to Theer's quarters for a discussion of what had really happened in Son Thang-4. After brief conversation, Boyd offered to write a new statement. He wrote for the next hour in the rear of the hut while Theer and the CID men read magazines or wrote letters.

Boyd's simply written, almost childlike account made chilling reading: At the first Son Thang hooch, he wrote, "R.H. [Randy Herrod] called the pepple out side and got them all togather and opened up on them with the M79. We heasateated and R.D. [sic] said to kill them and we opened up on them to." At the second hooch, "the same thing happened," and at the third the killer team "did the same thing . . . I think it was R.H. or M.S. [Michael Schwarz] idea to tell the CO that we had snipr fire. . . . If I had it to do over, I don't think I wood, Becaus I don't think that we did right and Im truley sorry I had a hand in it. We did not recive sniper fire as far as I know. and R.H. told me to say that we did. We had no contacked on the partrol. . . . At the 3rd hooch after the friing was over we heard a babby crying and Mike Schwarz got down next to it and fired his 45 and the crying stoped."

Theer had Boyd swear to the new statement's truth in grimly formal fashion: "I told him to raise his right hand and repeat after me, 'I do solemnly swear that the information contained in this statement is true to the best of my knowledge, so help me God.'" Boyd swore and signed, and then the nineteen-year-old returned to his perimeter tower in the morning cold.

After attending to other battalion matters, Theer asked L.Cpl. Mike Krichten into his quarters. As he had with Boyd, the major advised Krichten of his augmented rights, pointing to each one on the typed page as he read it aloud, including the admonition that Krichten was now suspected of "unlawfully killing" Vietnamese civilians. After Krichten indicated his understanding by signing the page, he was offered a cigarette. Cricket agreed to discuss the incident once again.

Midway through his recitation, Krichten mentioned sniper fire. The major interrupted as he had with Boyd, saying that he did not believe there had been a sniper. After Theer recited his observations in Son Thang-4, he told Krichten that he had the true story from Boyd already. "I asked him, I said, 'Now, was there a sniper, and were there any enemy?' And he said, 'No, there weren't.'"

Krichten moved to a small desk in the office portion of Theer's quarters, and for the next hour wrote his new statement, a sad repetition of Boyd's recent admissions. "Herrod said to open up on all of these people. . . . I didn't think it was right at all."

At 1330, a weary Theer summoned Pfc. Sam Green to his quarters. Green eyed Slagle and Dye suspiciously as he was advised of his augmented rights. After brief consideration, Green elected not to write another statement. But like the others, he was willing to discuss the incident again. In doing so, like Boyd and Krichten, he mentioned sniper fire. Theer said, "Now, wait a minute, Sam. You know and I know that there wasn't any sniper fire." At that point, Theer said, Green "became very hostile . . . and turned towards me with fire in his eyes and said, 'What do I care about some gook woman or child! It's them or me. If they get in my way, that's too bad!'"

Continuing, Green mentioned a particular Son Thang-4 hooch. Theer interrupted him again. "'I've been out there. The area that you are describing was impossible for anyone to see where you were, if you were standing on the patio.' And with that he said that he wasn't going to answer any more questions, that . . . he had been in jail for some twenty-three months prior to coming in the Marine Corps, and he wasn't going back."

The conversation ended. The major excused him. Although Green had seen the rough streets of Cleveland, he was not prepared for Son Thang-4.

Theer was still primarily concerned with current enemy contacts, and throughout the day the ops officer's presence was frequently required in the COC. Fire Support Base Ross was still in a contested zone and operations in the field never shut down, regardless of time or weather. Like all the men at Ross, Theer took catnaps and continued his duties, as well as his investigation, through the night.

Shortly after 0100, the major again sent for Private Schwarz. "When Schwarz came into my quarters . . . he had a very bold approach. Very confident air about him, and I asked him to sit down." Theer introduced him to the two CID men. Cigarettes were lighted. After the now-usual preliminaries, the discussion began. Schwarz soon began to grow less confident, more nervous; he said he preferred to let his original statement stand, but he was willing to answer questions about the patrol.

As Schwarz talked, the major noted that "he seemed to take a great deal of pride . . . that he was the searcher of the houses. . . . This is rather a risky chore." Theer asked about sniper fire at the first hooch, then at the second, and then about Schwarz's illogical account of his rifle having been struck by enemy fire. As the questioning continued and Theer's disbelief became ever more apparent, Schwarz's self-confidence dwindled.

Theer finally asked Schwarz, "Now, the statement that you submitted to me earlier is not really what happened?" Schwarz said, "That's true," that it wasn't what really happened. Theer asked if he was willing to make another written statement. This time, Schwarz said yes.

For the next hour and a half, alone at a desk in the rear of the major's quarters, Schwarz labored over his hand-printed, six-page statement. Theer recalled, "I could hear him sobbing in there, crying in the office, and I gave him a Pepsi, or coffee, or something; offered him more cigarettes."

His comments completed, Schwarz handed the pages to Theer. Reading it, the major realized that Son Thang was even worse than he had feared.

At the first hooch, only women and children were found, Schwarz wrote. He was checking the hooch and, "when I was nearly done the team was orderd to kill them and when they opened fire I joind in. When the fireing quieted all the people were dead." At the second hut, more women and children were herded outside. "I was returning to the team when the team leader orderd to kill them all. I started to fire along with everyone else as order." Finally, at the third hooch, "the team was again orderd to shot every one. The team hesetated and were again orderd to fire, so we did." Back on Hill 50, "The team leader told we had recieved sniper fire of witch we all wen along with for fire of what would had if it was disuverd what had really happen. . . . We were given the odrers by Pvt Harred each time we were told to fire and what to do."

Near the end of his statement, the twenty-one-year-old father of a three-year-old son wrote, "When I relised what was happpening I got scard and sick but was ordred to shot the people and knew if I did not obay the order I could get court marialt. From the time we started shotting I regretted ever going with this team."

On 22 February, 1st Lt. Ron Ambort was relieved of command of Company B. After conferring with Colonel Codispoti, Lieutenant Colonel Cooper decided that the killer team members should be transported to the III MAF brig near Da Nang for pre-trial confinement.

Taking an odd view of these events, Herrod wrote, "The My Lai cover-up had just come to light. The Army was catching hell for it. Lieutenant Calley was headline news. And now the Marines had an opportunity to wash their dirty linen in public, and in so doing, 'one-up' the Army."

But Marine Corps commanders, whether motivated by one-upmanship or the pursuit of justice, could not be accused of a cover-up.

THE PRE-TRIAL INQUIRY

The Continental Congress in 1775 adopted the first American code governing land armies, based upon the British Articles of War. The Rules for the Regulation of the Navy adopted the following year also followed the British model. Over the next 175 years American military law, of both land armies and the sea, underwent evolutionary change. By the middle of the twentieth century military law, stained by World War II injustices, had fallen into public and political disfavor.

The Uniform Code of Military Justice, a largely civilian-written reform and consolidation of the eighteenth-century codes, became law in 1950. The UCMJ, and the *Manual for Courts-Martial* for its implementation, applies to all U.S. armed forces. The 1950 Code was a landmark improvement in military justice, but over the years inevitable flaws and gaps in that initial effort became apparent. Congress mandated a new Military Justice Act, which took effect in

1969. It significantly revised the 1950 UCMJ and introduced an entirely new *Manual for Courts-Martial*. They were the military criminal law in effect during the Son Thang trials.

The 1969 UCMJ brought military trial procedure generally into line with civilian federal court practice. For the first time, military judges—senior military lawyers with lengthy trial experience—were mandated in virtually all courts-martial; their powers were roughly equivalent to those of civilian federal judges. Another significant change was the requirement that, free of charge, every military accused, with rare exceptions, be represented by a judge advocate from initial confinement or charging, through trial and appeal. Those two revisions alone dramatically altered military law practice. From 1969 onward, there were "relatively few important procedural differences between civilian and military trials, and some of the obvious ones are indicative of form rather than substance."[24]

General courts-martial, as opposed to summary and special courts-martial, are reserved for serious criminality such as rape, murder, desertion, and war crimes. GCMs require a verbatim record of trial, lawyer representation of the accused, and a GCM-certified military judge. The trial may be before the judge alone, or before a panel of "members" (essentially jurors in uniform), at the option of the accused. Military rules of evidence, akin to federal rules of evidence, are applicable throughout trial.

All rulings of the Supreme Court of the United States are binding on military courts. Likewise, GCM convictions and special court convictions are federal convictions, with the attendant disabilities and stigma. A body of military case law applies to military trials, as case law does in civilian jurisdictions. The GCM's maximum punishment, if authorized for the charged offense, is death.

GCMs such as those faced by the five Marines of 1/7 must be preceded by a formal pretrial hearing. That hearing is called an "Article 32" investigation because of its placement among the 140 articles of the 1969 UCMJ. The Article 32 is often described as the military analogue to a civilian grand jury proceeding, but an Article 32 is actually more discriminating and demanding of legal evidence. The civilian grand jury, the creature of the prosecution, would indict a ham sandwich, if the prosecutor vigorously proposed it.

The purpose of an Article 32 is to have the allegations examined by a disinterested officer, in Marine practice usually a senior judge advocate, to determine if there is, or is not, probable cause to bring charges against the accused at a GCM. The hearing invariably consists of the prosecution offering evidence through its witnesses. At its conclusion, the investigating officer (IO) submits a written report to the senior officer with the authority to convene a GCM for that case—usually the division's commanding general. The IO may either recommend proceeding with a GCM, or taking lesser legal action or none at all.

The Son Thang Article 32 was unusual in that its verbatim record would also be used as the war crime investigation[25] required by MACV orders.[26]

Two days after the Son Thang five were placed in confinement, Maj. Robert J. Blum of the division staff judge advocate's office was appointed to conduct their Article 32.

Herrod had a bleak view of the military justice system from his cell in the Da Nang brig: "I knew how the Uniform Code of Military Justice worked: you were guilty until proven innocent. . . . So I figured I was already on that old railroad, chugging down the track, with a firing squad waiting at the end of the line."

Within hours of the crimes' discovery, a military defense counsel had been assigned to each accused and to Lieutenant Ambort. Each defense counsel immediately wrote to his client's family to advise them of his assignment and prospective efforts on behalf of their son. The accused Marines also were offered free calls to their families via the MARS (Military Affiliated Radio Stations) network, but their defense lawyers objected because privacy could not be ensured. The MARS calls were cancelled, and free telegrams were offered instead. Telegrams were sent by all except Herrod.

A series of secret Son Thang messages was initiated on 27 February. Labeled "specat" (special category) and "Marine Corps eyes only," the messages were from the CG of the 1st Marine Division to, by name, the commander of III MAF in Da Nang, the commander of Fleet Marine Forces, Pacific, in Hawaii, and the Commandant of the Marine Corps, in Washington, D.C.

The first specat message advised that disciplinary action regarding Ambort would await completion of his men's Article 32. It also read, "Vietnamese district and province officials are not disturbed over incident since all families involved considered to be VC. . . . U.S. newsmen expressing very active interest."[27]

Indeed, on 28 February, three NBC, three CBS, and two Associated Press reporters, as well as United Press International, *Stars and Stripes*, and *New Yorker* writers, were flown by helicopter to FSB Ross, where they were briefed and escorted around the perimeter by Lieutenant Colonel Cooper. "I was on the evening news the next day, all over the country," he recalled. "We got tremendous coverage. It's not the kind of thing you want to get so much coverage on, but it was almost favorable."[28] A *Newsweek* stringer had made his own, unauthorized, way to Ross earlier that day. He had been turned back without a story. Such visits by newsmen and women, authorized and unauthorized, were to become frequent disruptions at Ross.

A *Los Angeles Times* story on 27 February, under the headline "Marine Officer Tells Pressures on 5 Charged in 'New My Lai,'" quoted Colonel Cooper as saying: "Just because they are charged doesn't at all mean they are guilty." The three-column story repeated Cooper's description of the area as "real Indian country."

On 4 March, Tony Sargent of CBS News reported that the sixteen Vietnamese victims had been decapitated and dismembered with knives. The 1st Division CG was quick to assure the Commandant by message that Sargent's report was incorrect: "Some mutilation and dismemberment of bodies did result from gunfire because of short range," the general wrote, but no knives or bayonets were used. The story arose, the CG opined, when "local residents told gory story of deaths even though none were witness to actual incident."[29] The erroneous story was not repeated.

The defense lawyers spent several days at Ross interviewing potential witnesses in preparation for the Article 32 hearing. They were experienced advocates, most of them having been involved in murder trials in the past.

Twenty-six Marine Corps judge advocates were assigned to the SJA's office. That number rose and fell through the year as lawyers ended their one-year tours of duty in Vietnam and were replaced by others.

Among them were four or five senior lawyers who were career Marines. They had served in a variety of legal billets and possessed broad experience in military law. The Marine Corps, unlike the Army and Navy, and despite the career lawyers among its own ranks, has no separate judge advocate corps. All Marines, including lawyers, are considered potential riflemen. Indeed, a number of Marine Corps judge advocates acted as infantry platoon and company commanders in Vietnam combat. One, 1st Lt. Michael Neil, was awarded the Navy Cross, Purple Heart, and six Air Medals. Many other lawyers were recognized to varying lesser degrees.

Ironically, 1st Lt. James Schermerhorn, a law school graduate, was a platoon leader in B-1/7 during the heavy combat of the summer of 1969. He was awarded the Silver Star Medal for his combat heroism shortly before his transfer to the 1st Division's SJA office.

The SJA's twenty or so junior judge advocates were, to a man, reservists—volunteer officers serving their first and, in all but two cases, last tours of uniformed service. Upon initial arrival at division headquarters they were assigned to defend or to prosecute, according to office needs and va-

Nine days before the Son Thang-4 incident, Staff Judge Advocate Col. Bob Lucy (left) poses with 1st Marine Division judge advocates newly certified to act as special courts-martial judges. Next to Lucy: Maj. Jim King, Ambort's Article 32 investigating officer; Capt. Mark Haiman; Capt. Dan LeGear, Schwarz's defender; Capt. Bob Williams, Herrod's assigned defense counsel; Capt. Adrian King, Krichten's lawyer; Capt. Gary Bushell, assistant prosecutor in the Green, Boyd, and Herrod trials; and Maj. Gen. Edwin B. Wheeler, Division CG. *U.S. Marine Corps*

cancies. Most of them switched roles in mid-tour. After serving their time in Vietnam, they would return to the United States for another year of duty to complete their three-year military obligation, then return to civilian life. They were the young lawyers who tried whatever cases went to trial—and the caseload was higher than ever before in Marine Corps history. During the preceding year in Vietnam alone, 123 general and 1,023 special courts-martial had been tried, even though in-country troop strength had dropped by 32 percent compared to the previous year.

The Son Thang Article 32 investigation was called to order on Thursday, 12 March. Usually there is a single accused at a 32, but this was a joint investigation. The small courtroom was crowded with the five accused Marines, their five lawyers, the IO, two prosecuting lawyers, and a court reporter with his recorders and closed-mike reporting system.

Maj. Bob Blum, the Article 32 investigating officer, had been one of the first Marine judge advocates to serve in Vietnam, having been in-country during an earlier tour in 1963. He also had previously met Randy Herrod.

Within minutes of the hearing's start, Herrod's defense counsel, Capt. Robert Williams, asked Blum about Herrod's special court-martial for UA:

Q. Are you the same Major Blum who sat as military judge . . . in a case involving Private Herrod on 16 January last?
A. I am.
Q. Is there any way possible for this to have . . . influence on your decisions here, today?
A. I don't think so, no. . . . That was an entirely different matter. I might also indicate that . . . I was favorably impressed with Lance Corporal Herrod, and I believe I signed and submitted a recommendation for clemency.

Captain Williams resumed his seat, not entirely content.

The prosecutors, Capts. Franz P. Jevne and Charles E. Brown, Jr., called Lieutenant Grant as their first witness. Grant testified to having found the bodies when summoned to Son Thang-4 by a Vietnamese woman, and described the wounds of the dead he and his men assisted in burying. His cross-examination by the five defense lawyers did not conclude until the following day.

Maj. Dick Theer, the battalion operations officer, was the next government witness. He testified to the radio contacts with Company B on the night of the homicides, and to details of his own examination of Son Thang-4. He related the tangled sequence of events once Bravo returned to FSB Ross and his own inquiry began. It was Saturday evening before he left the stand.

Theer was followed by a 1/7 corpsman who had been with Grant's initial patrol to Son Thang-4. He confirmed the lieutenant's observations, detailing each victim's wounds and their lethality. Over the next few days, the corpsman testified that they had all been killed by small-arms fire, and he described the many spent M-16 and .45 casings he and others had found, most of them adjacent to where the bodies lay fallen.

Subsequent government witnesses included the battalion armorer, who identified the casings retrieved by Grant's patrol as fresh brass from U.S. weapons. Other men from Grant's patrol described the state in which the bodies were found, and how their sex and approximate ages were determined before the patrol assisted in their burial. Spider holes, favored by VC snipers, were described in the vicinity of the hamlet, but the absence of enemy brass was also noted.

Lieutenant Carney, B Company's second platoon leader, told of the formation of the killer team. Introducing a theme to be repeated to later effect, Carney also described hearing gunfire from Son Thang: "I heard a long burst of heavy automatic weapons fire. . . . I thought it was M-60 machine gun. . . . It sounded like it was 20, 15, 30 rounds, somewhere in that area." Upon the killer team's return to Hill 50, Carney testified, he heard Herrod admit to Ambort that actually twelve to sixteen Vietnamese had been killed.

He also related Ambort's conversation with the team after they returned to FSB Ross. Ambort told Herrod, Schwarz, and Boyd that sixteen bodies had been discovered; that he had submitted a false report concerning the SKS, and he was going to make a clean breast of it; Ambort said he thought being honest about the incident was the best course, and he urged his men to be truthful. The three agreed, Carney said, and, with Herrod as their spokesman, again insisted to Ambort that they had taken enemy fire before they fired.

Carney's platoon sergeant, Sergeant Meyers, also heard Ambort urge the three team members to be truthful, and echoed Carney's account. As to the team's activity on the night of the incident, he said that he had warned Herrod he should not "do anything stupid . . . go out there killing women and kids." After the team's departure from Hill 50, Meyers, too, heard bursts of automatic fire from Son Thang, but reckoned it to be M-60 machine gun and M-16 fire.

Over the course of several days, the Article 32 made fitful progress, interrupted by electrical power losses and, more often, problems with keeping so many lawyers under control. Tempers were short and multiple objections frequent. At one point, Capt. Adrian King, Krichten's lawyer, stood and heatedly addressed Blum: "I'd like to register an objection to the investigating officer and request that he disqualify himself. . . . It is apparent to this counsel, judging from the questions that the investigating officer is asking, and his tone of voice, that . . . he has prejudged these individuals, and for this reason he cannot make a fair recommendation as to what to do in this case."

Blum, the third most senior lawyer in the SJA's office, responded, "Let the record indicate that all counsel have joined—is this a request? . . . I have not prejudged these people. I consider myself to be fair and impartial at this point," and he recessed the proceedings for an hour and a half so passions, including his own, might cool.

The next witness, a squad leader from Carney's platoon who was experienced in leading patrols, related the killer team's return from Son Thang to Hill 50, and his conversation with Herrod, Krichten, and Boyd shortly afterward.

A. They said they ran into some gooks. . . . They weren't supposed to be out, so they just blew them away.
Q. Did anyone explain to you at that time what gooks they were referring to?
A. Gooks are gooks. That's all there is to it. If you see them . . .

He left his pregnant implication unfinished. Continuing, he recalled that Green, hearing the others joking about Son Thang, had shouted that "they were cold-blooded killers," and was clearly upset by the killings. "Yeah, then they all laughed, started laughing about it," he said.

Over the objection of Herrod's lawyer, the squad leader testified that Herrod had indicated what the team had done. "They just more or less, he said, you know, count to three and open up."

Lieutenant Ambort, the next witness, repeated much of what had been heard in preceding testimony. He added that upon B Company's return to Ross, he had been called to the battalion commander's hut. Lieutenant Colonel Cooper, he said, "told me that something very serious had happened, that he didn't know who was involved, that they found sixteen dead women and children . . . and that it looked bad and did I have the details for him? So I told him that I'd talk to my men and get back with him." Minutes later, standing outside the company office, Ambort had urged three of the team to tell the truth. Later that day, he told the other two team members, Krichten and Green, the same thing. The five had lied to him back on Hill 50, he surmised, "because it does, it looks bad."

Ambort adamantly recalled hearing what he thought was automatic fire—M-14s, an M-60, or an enemy .30 caliber—from the area of Son Thang 4 while the killer team was there. "Did any of these accused here ever tell you that they received heavy weapons fire?" the IO asked. That was crucial, of course. "No, I don't believe they did, because I didn't ask," Ambort replied.

Questioned about Vietnamese noncombatants in his company's operating area, Ambort expressed the opinion shared by many bush Marines. "It's the same old story in every ville. . . . You take fire from a ville, you walk in there, you find mama-sans, baby-sans. Papa-san was blown up in an air strike. . . . Papa-san has gone to Que Son, or he's been killed. You know, and they've got these little babies—I don't know where they are getting them from, there's no papa-sans around. . . . Papa-san . . . is out with the VC and mama-san is feeding him every night, and takes care of his house for him, plows the rice paddy while he goes out and kills Marines. That's my opinion of the people in this area."

Outside the hearing room, the 1st Marine Division's CG advised the Commandant and other senior commanders by secret message that Herrod's Silver Star Medal was approved and awaiting presentation at the time of the Son Thang incident. But, in keeping with long-standing federal law,[30] the CG would "postpone delivery . . . until after disposition current charges."[31]

The general also reported that a civilian lawyer from Oklahoma, Herrod's home state, would appear on Herrod's behalf. The lawyer, Gene Stipe, conferred via MARS radio with Herrod's military lawyer, Captain Williams. Stipe said he would skip the Article 32 and arrive in-country later.

A separate "Secret—Marine Corps eyes only" message to the Commandant noted that two members of the patrol that initially discovered the Vietnamese bodies had taken black-and-white and color photographs of the dead. The film was confiscated, the CG said, and was hand-carried to Camp Smith, Hawaii, for developing in a Marine Corps photo lab, since there were no facilities in-country. The photos, returned to Da Nang by special courier, could become evidence in subsequent courts-martial.

Newsmen were beginning to gather daily outside the hearing room to photograph and attempt to interview participants as they came and went. Others also took an interest in the case. A public affairs officer (PAO) in the Da Nang press center answered a call from Saigon. The PAO reported: "Individual on phone identified himself as Melvin Belli, indicating he had just finished Green Beret court-martial. . . . Wondered if accused Marines would like to talk to him. He offered to fly up if they needed him."[32] When referred to the SJA's office, the San Francisco defense attorney said he didn't care to talk to any judge advocate. Belli's offer was never passed on to the accused because, as Colonel Lucy said, obtaining civilian defense counsel was the personal choice—and responsibility—of every accused. With a staggering case load that reflected ever-increasing hard-drug use, fatal racial incidents, fraggings, and a frightening in-country desertion rate, Lucy had enough problems. Offers of outside legal help would not be routed by his office.

Nor were things particularly smooth inside the hearing room. The IO often had to fend off the probes of one or another defense counsel wanting to know with whom he had discussed the case, and what had been said. "My statement [to Colonel Lucy]," Blum replied at one point, "was something to the effect that I felt that the defense counsel were not—the defense counsel did not understand the function of an Article 32 investigation. . . . I made some statements that I thought that Captain Williams [Herrod's counsel] was attempting to provoke me into anger, which I believe to be the case."

Williams, one of only three black Marine Corps lawyers ever to reach Vietnam, not only irritated Blum, but repeatedly submitted a motion to add another black Marine lawyer to the defense team. The IO repeatedly denied the motion.

Blum also was disturbed to note that Herrod and Green continually read magazines as the hearing was in progress. "I do not consider it appropriate," Blum caustically told the defense lawyers, "for an accused presently being investigated for murder to read a magazine during the proceedings." Blum later added that he thought that Herrod did so "just to send me, and the Marine Corps, a message that he didn't give a damn about Son Thang-4 or my investigation. . . . And Williams certainly would not have corrected his courtroom conduct."[33]

As the Article 32 continued, Le-Thi-Thiem of Son Thang-4 was called by the government. Testifying through a Vietnamese army interpreter of dubious ability, she related that her daughter and sister had been killed on the night of 19 February. Although not asked to identify any of the accused, she recalled seeing several Marines enter her hamlet that night, and described the firing she heard. Yes, she said, one hamlet resident was currently detained as a VC and, yes, other VC do sometimes spend the night in Son Thang-4, but there were none present on 19 February, and there was no fire from any VC that night. She also related that the families of the dead had each received 4,000 piasters (about $33.40) in solatium payments—monetary compensation from the American government for the loss of a noncombatant family member due to U.S. military action.

On 19 March, the government's case concluded. The defense enterprisingly located and called an Army lieutenant assigned to MACV Intelligence Team 15, based in Hoi An. Among his duties was the coordination of Project Phoenix operations in Quang Nam province. Asked about Phoenix activities to eradicate VC infrastructure in the province, the lieutenant fastidiously corrected, "We like to use the word 'neutralize' because anything else connotes distaste." He went on tastefully to detail enemy units known to be operating in the Son Thang-4 area: elements of the 105 Main Force Battalion, the 1st and 31st Regiments, and the 270 Transportation Battalion. He further informed the investigating officer that an M-16 rifle, capable of automatic fire, had recently been captured near Son Thang-4.

Another Army lieutenant testified for the defense that Son Thang was classified by the Hamlet Evaluation System as a "D" hamlet: contested. No news there.

The brief defense case having concluded, the prosecution reopened to offer three final Vietnamese witnesses, among them the district chief, who identified the Son Thang victims by name, age, and sex.

After nine hearing days, the Article 32 pretrial investigation concluded on 23 March and Major Blum began his review of the case. Did he consider the evidence to present probable cause to believe that a crime had been committed, and that the five accused had committed it? Proof beyond

Maj. Bob Blum conducted the difficult pre–general court-martial Article 32 investigation. He already had met Randy Herrod in another courtroom. *Col. Robert J. Blum*

a reasonable doubt was the required standard at trial, but Blum only needed to find probable cause in order to recommend further legal action.

It wasn't even close. He had death certificates, the testimony of surviving relatives and Vietnamese officials, and the testimony of members of Grant's patrol to establish the commission of the alleged crime.

The testimony of Major Theer indicated the absence of signs of the enemy in Son Thang-4. Fresh American brass and the absence of enemy brass at the scene bolstered Theer's assessment, as did the testimony of Son Thang-4 residents. But Blum found even more significant the sworn written statements of Boyd, Krichten, and Schwarz detailing what they said happened, including their assurances that there had been no enemy fire, no enemy contact.

Finding probable cause, Blum then had to recommend what further action should be taken. That too was clear. A charge of murder of sixteen individuals could only be tried by the highest level court-martial.

Four weeks after concluding the 32, and after the verbatim record and its multiple carbon copies were completed, Blum submitted five similar reports to the CG of the 1st Marine Division, Maj. Gen. Edwin B. Wheeler, the officer empowered to convene general courts-martial. In his reports concerning Boyd, Krichten, and Schwarz, Blum specifically noted that the three asserted in their written statements that Herrod had ordered them to fire on the victims. He recommended that all five killer team members be tried by GCM, each charged with the premeditated murder of sixteen noncombatant victims.

4 | PRE-TRIAL

CIVILIAN LAWYERS ASSEMBLE

Krichten cut a deal with the prosecution. In return for immunity from prosecution he agreed to testify truthfully in the courts-martial of the other four team members. "I didn't blame Krichten at this point," Herrod writes. "He was smart to save his own ass."[1]

Actually, Krichten's lawyer, Capt. Adrian King, was smart to save his client's ass. King appreciated that the prosecutors might be willing to grant immunity to one of the five in order to ensure (to the degree that anything may be ensured in a criminal trial) stronger cases against the other four.

Herrod and Schwarz were not likely candidates for immunity, King knew. Their involvement was too deep. He saw Green, Boyd, and his own client as the only possibilities—but Boyd and Krichten especially, as they had admitted all in their written statements. In an environment where the lawyers for both sides slept, worked, and ate together, testing the waters for immunity had not been difficult.

Had Herrod actually been a private, as everyone in Son Thang believed him to be, L.Cpl. Michael S. Krichten, nineteen, of Hanover, Pennsylvania, would have been the senior man in the killer team. As it was, he had made no objection when "Private" Herrod was appointed the killer team honcho, over him. The youngest of six children, Krichten had left school after the tenth grade and immediately enlisted in the Marines. He was the only member of the team who had neither civilian nor military court convictions. He arrived in Vietnam in early August 1969 and reported to B-1/7 the day after landing.

In a pre-immunity letter to President Nixon requesting his assistance, Krichten wrote, "The people that were supposed to be civilians were founed out to be V.C. and I sure can't see the goverment hang five of us Marines for them."[2] A second letter to the president ended, "I think that the Marine Corp is trying to screw us."[3] Now, with immunity, he was home free.

Krichten's agreement was to "testify truthfully," not to testify *against* the others. In practice there would be no distinction, but it is far easier to sell a young man on immunity if his lawyer can argue that he won't have to rat on his comrades, but merely tell the truth. The prospect of immediate release from pretrial confinement was a further sweetener. Upon his release Krichten was transferred from 1/7 to 1/11, the 1st Division's artillery battalion. Ostensibly assigned to the artillery observers' section, for the next four months he would spend so much time at "legal" that the Son Thang cases effectively became his assignment.

Considering the government's evidence, it would not appear necessary to have granted immunity to any participant in order to gain convictions of the others. On the other hand, since it was impossible to know whether some prosecution witnesses might be wounded or killed before trial (it happened all the time), or rotated back to the States to be discharged before a legal hold could be slapped on them, or how the case might develop between charging and trial, it no doubt seemed a reasonable trade-off. Krichten appeared the least culpable of the five, and his testimony would be a powerful weapon in the government's trial arsenal—perhaps enough to nudge one of the other four into a guilty plea with a pretrial agreement. As it turned out, it would require more than Krichten's testimony.

The one-page grant of transactional immunity was signed on 26 April by the division CG, Major General Wheeler, who was the only officer authorized to grant immunity in a court-martial tried within his command. The charges against Krichten were not dismissed, but would not be prosecuted as long as he kept the agreement. Krichten was released from the brig the same day.

Lieutenant Ambort, in separate proceedings, had been charged with three offenses. The first charge alleged a failure to obey lawful orders, specifically, a division order to report an incident thought to be a war crime; the second, dereliction of duty, for failing to take effective measures to minimize noncombatant casualties and making no efforts to ensure his men were aware of the rules of engagement. The final charge alleged that he made a false official statement with intent to deceive: that the killer team had captured an enemy SKS rifle.

The final accusation appeared well-grounded, and the first was reasonably supported by the evidence. The second was not the solid charge usually found at a GCM. But the prosecution could always agree to drop the second charge in return for a guilty plea to one of the others, a common trial tactic.

The SJA, in a change of mind, decided to proceed against Ambort immediately, instead of awaiting the outcomes of his subordinates' trials. Ambort's pre-GCM Article 32 was scheduled for 30 March.

Thanks in part to media attention, civilian lawyers in the U.S. were showing interest in representing the five killer team members—four, now that Krichten would not be tried.

The UCMJ specifically provides for civilian representation of an accused at trial, and a surprising number of civilians made appearances in Vietnam courts-martial. Although the financial arrangements always were between the civilian defense lawyer and the uniformed client, fees and expenses usually were paid by the accused's family, who often mistrusted the quality of military legal representation. Few enlisted men could afford a civilian lawyer on their own. Civilian attorneys often appeared *pro bono*—without fee, even paying their own expenses. In Vietnam they ate in unit messhalls, used officers' and enlisted men's clubs, and were billeted in officers' quarters.

Civilian representation at court-martial is a two-edged sword. The civilian usually brings a degree of trial experience outweighing that of the opposing military prosecutor. On the other hand, civilians are often unable to develop the rapport with uniformed juries that is important to courtroom persuasion. They seldom know how to deal effectively with a convening authority in negotiating for the withdrawal or downgrading of charges, or when bargaining for a pretrial agreement. Civilian lawyers did not know how to locate military witnesses in the field, or secure their presence.

An accused's military defense counsel normally continued in that capacity even when a civilian lawyer was retained. The civilian would enlist his military counterpart to carry out trial functions relating to the soldierly aspects of the case, such as dealing with the convening authority, securing witnesses, and marshalling evidence of a military nature. But at trial the civilian was always lead counsel.

There was widespread feeling among military defense lawyers that they did the onerous scut-work in preparation for trial while the civilian was viewed, and paid, as if he alone had conducted the case (the military defense lawyer was, of course, assigned free of charge to the accused). But often, a mutual respect eventually arose between civilian and military lawyers in Vietnam.

All of the charged Son Thang Marines were looking for civilian help. Schwarz was so far unsuccessful. Boyd was in touch with an Evansville lawyer. Green was said already to be represented by a Cleveland attorney.

Even before the opening of the joint Article 32, Randy Herrod was represented by Oklahoma State Senator Gene Stipe, who had chosen to forego attending the 32. Stipe arrived at Da Nang on 15 April, along with Herrod's grandfather, Alvin Self, who had played a major role in Herrod's upbringing. Over the next few days Stipe, a stocky, brown-haired man who was an experienced and able trial lawyer, began to prepare his case. He visited Herrod, who now spent most days in his military lawyer's office rather than the brig. Stipe conferred with the other military defense lawyers and the other accused Marines, interviewed potential witnesses, and also visited LZ Baldy, where 1/7 was then positioned.

In a shrewd move, Stipe advised the 1st Division's SJA that he required a delay of Herrod's trial until July, three months hence, due to the extensive preparation required for such a major case. The SJA reluctantly accommodated him. Stipe was well aware that such a delay would result in his man's case being tried last, a significant advantage.

Herrod writes, "Gene and my grandfather told me that I had all sorts of support back in my home state, that everybody was pulling for me. The city of Calvin [Herrod's home town] had even raised the money for my grandfather to come over and see me."[4] Stipe's recollection was that while he paid their way from Oklahoma to California, "every dime that they raised, I spent on taking his grandfather with me on [that] first trip. . . . Voluntary financial support for attorney fees is never a very satisfactory way to get paid."[5]

It was Marine Corps policy to provide transportation on civilian-contract airliners complete with stewardesses and in-flight meals of dubious quality. The flights originated at Travis Air Force Base near San Francisco, the principal transit point for Vietnam-bound Marine personnel, and terminated at Da Nang. Reimbursement was customarily waived for civilian defense lawyers, the interminable ride on the crowded, often hot flight probably considered price enough. Relatives like Herrod's grandfather were expected to reimburse the government for their transportation to and from Vietnam, however. It was rare for a relative to visit an accused in Vietnam; that usually occurred only in cases involving multiple homicides.

Lawyer Stipe had been kept apprised of the case's progress. As soon as a civilian lawyer made known his representation of a killer team member, the lawyer was mailed a mimeographed copy of the entire 791-page verbatim record of the joint Article 32 investigation and its eighty-seven exhibits. Photocopy machines were unknown in Vietnam field commands.

EVADING TRIAL

There would be no civilian lawyer for B Company's commander, 1st Lt. Ron Ambort. He would take his chances within the military legal system.

Lt. Col. James P. King, the 1st Division's deputy SJA, was appointed to conduct Ambort's Article 32. King (no relation to Krichten's defense lawyer, Capt. Adrian King) was a former infantry officer with broad experience in military law. His previous assignment was the sought-after billet of senior Marine instructor at the Navy's Justice School in Newport, Rhode Island. Even-tempered and calm, King was highly respected.

Ambort's father, Louis Ambort of Little Rock, Arkansas, requested, and the Marine Corps agreed to provide, a combat-experienced non-lawyer to assist in his son's defense, presumably so someone could tell the judge and jury what things were really like in the field, away from the relative luxury of a division headquarters. The younger Ambort and his military lawyer, Capt. Frank G. Roux, Jr., declined the offer, however. By secret message, the division CG warned the Commandant, "[Ambort's] Father seemed very insistent and indicated he would go to congressman, if necessary, on this issue. He may not agree with decision made by son."[6]

With reporters in attendance and congressional inquiries anticipated, Ambort's Article 32 convened in a tin-roofed plywood hut at LZ Baldy at 1425 on 9 April.

In an unusual move, one of the two prosecutors was the initial witness for the prosecution. Capt. Charles E. Brown, Jr., had twice interviewed Ambort while preparing for the 32, and on the stand he described Ambort as "completely candid. Completely honest . . . no hesitation . . . no reluctance at all to go into any area which I wanted to pursue."[7] Ambort's defense counsel had been present during both interviews. Since Ambort surely would not testify in a proceeding seeking probable cause to try him, Brown instead related Ambort's statements to him—statements given only after Ambort had been formally warned that his words could be used against himself. Ambort's earlier sworn testimony, given in his men's joint Article 32, also would be considered by the investigating officer.

Prosecutor Brown, after relating what Ambort told him of the killer team's formation, repeated what the company commander forthrightly admitted saying to the team just before they departed Hill 50.

"He said that he told them to go out and get some, to pay the motherfuckers back, to pay them back good. To shoot everything that moved. To shoot first and ask questions later and to give them no slack. . . . If the killer team . . . saw anyone moving along a trail, that if they saw anyone cutting across a rice paddy, that they were to shoot these people."

Those were extremely strong words for any leader to utter to men of his command. Ambort's exhortation, which he had described as a "pep talk," raised the volatile issue of superior orders: Were those who obeyed the orders free of legal responsibility? But this was Ambort's pretrial hearing, not that of his men. What is the law regarding an officer who, although not at the scene of the offense, issues possibly illegal orders which are executed by his troops? A commander is responsible for the crimes, including the war crimes, committed by his troops if he orders the offenses, or has actual knowledge of them, or *should have knowledge* of them.

During the Spanish-American War (1898), Army Brig. Gen. Jacob H. Smith, in writing, ordered a patrol leader: "I want no prisoners. I wish you to burn and kill; the more you burn and kill, the better it will please me," and he ordered that anyone capable of bearing arms, down to ten years of age, be killed.

President Theodore Roosevelt, when he approved Smith's conviction for inciting and ordering subordinates to commit atrocities, could have been writing about Vietnam: "That warfare is of such character as to afford infinite provocation for the commission of acts of cruelty by junior officers and the enlisted men, must make the officers in high and responsible position peculiarly careful . . . to keep a moral check over any acts of an improper character by their subordinates."[8]

Thus, in February 1946, Japanese Gen. Tomoyuki Yamashita was hanged for failure to control his troops after their capture of Manila, his appeal denied by the U.S. Supreme Court.[9] In Vietnam, Capt. Ernest L. Medina, Calley's immediate superior at My Lai, briefed his soldiers in a manner not unlike Ambort's and was tried by GCM for failure to control his subordinates. He was acquitted after an error in a crucial jury instruction.[10]

Seventy years after General Smith's conviction, there remained a "long-standing Marine assumption that discipline, as exemplified by immediate obedience to orders, is the overriding factor in combat success."[11] According to Brig. Gen. Edwin H. Simmons, the 1st Marine Division's assistant commanding general shortly after Son Thang, "There is a predisposition . . . stronger in the Marine Corps than it might be in other services, to accept orders without question. . . . In many cases, the better the Marine, the less apt he would be to challenge an illegal order."[12]

So the investigating officer, after hearing the rest of the evidence against Ambort, would have the additional legal task of deciding whether the company commander's briefing made him as responsible for what happened in Son Thang-4 as the Marines who actually committed the charged offenses. If so, Ambort would be charged with the crimes alleged against his men—sixteen counts of premeditated murder—in addition to the charges the IO was already investigating.

In any event, the question of obedience to orders was a major issue, and one that would not be concluded with Ambort's case.

Captain Brown's testimony ended, he rose from his chair—there was no witness box at Baldy. Brown was followed by Maj. Dick Theer, who within a few days would complete his Vietnam tour and return to "the world." Theer repeated for the IO, Lieutenant Colonel King, what he had told the first IO, Major Blum, adding that Son Thang was on the edge of a free-fire zone, and was a particularly dangerous area.

"You say you wouldn't go out there with less than a company, is that right?" King asked him.

"Yes, sir. . . . It's an area in which you wouldn't want to go out to take a stroll. It's an area where you would go prepared for anything, and particularly at night. It would be considered extremely hostile. . . . The people that live in the hamlet are the VC cadre . . . and they support actively the enemy forces."

Asked during defense cross-examination about pre-patrol "pep talks," Theer recalled such "frequent" talks by Lt. Col. Frank Clark, the 1/7 battalion commander preceding Cooper: "I heard Colonel Clark tell the commanders, 'Let's get some, tonight,' 'Let's pay them back for what they've done to us,'" words similar to those Ambort had uttered, if somewhat less inciting.

Nor was it unusual to have enemy KIAs without attendant weapons, Theer said. Many kills were laborers or bearers who would have no weapons. That could explain the killer team's failure to retrieve weapons, had their contact been with the enemy, rather than unarmed women and children.

Asked if a curfew was in effect for the Vietnamese civilians, Theer said, "There is a curfew throughout Vietnam during the hours of darkness."

Ambort was charged with not making his men aware of the rules of engagement (ROEs), the directives delineating circumstances and limitations under which U.S. forces may initiate or continue combat engagement with opposing forces. The effectiveness of Vietnam ROEs has often been questioned, both by historians and by those who had to implement them.[13] When Ambort was asked about ROEs during the earlier joint Article 32, he replied, "I remember some officer gave me some publication about a thousand pages long, so I didn't get through it."[14]

James Webb, author of *Fields of Fire* and Reagan-era Secretary of the Navy, earlier had arrived in Vietnam as a new Marine infantry lieutenant, like Ambort. Webb "was told to read and sign a copy of the rules of engagement. The document ran seven pages. Some of it made sense, but a lot of it seemed an exercise in politics, micromanagement, and preemptive ass covering, a script for fighting a war without pissing anybody off."[15]

Theer, asked about ROEs in cross-examination, responded, "I am aware of the fact the order states that troops must be reminded or reorientated every three months on the rules of engagement. We have not done that in this battalion." He gave an unconvincing explanation: ROEs were essentially repeated in the battalion's every operational order, providing a kind of rolling periodic re-indoctrination.

Such testimony from a highly regarded and decorated operations officer was not likely to support the charges against Ambort. The prosecuting lawyers' hands were tied, of course. They could hardly keep their own witness from truthfully responding to defense cross-examination. The defense counsel continued:

Q. What type of Marine is [Ambort]? What type of individual, a person is he?
A. He's always been very professional, and I believe his

company's record proves that. I've always felt that Lieutenant Ambort was perhaps our most aggressive company commander, and I had a great deal of respect for his ability and operational, tactical sense.

If Theer was the prosecution's best witness against Ambort, the case for probable cause was not going well. And subsequent prosecution witnesses weren't noticeably more effective. Another B-1/7 company commander was questioned about ROEs by Ambort's defense counsel:

Q. Did you discuss between yourselves the rules of engagement?
A. Most affirm.
Q. Did you pass this word on to your own troops?
A. Most affirm.
Q. And what did the ROEs say, for example, about Vietnamese children out at night?
A. If it was at night, if it moved, that's tough.

After being read Ambort's "pep talk," his fellow company commander considered it little different from what he himself often told his men. "You have to get the men aggressive so they can get a kill." And where did the nighttime shoot-to-kill rule come from? "Self-survival in the bush," he replied. Rather than approach an apparently wounded villager at night, the lieutenant went on, "blow them away before you approach them, because I've had too many killed from wounded NVA and VC [but] if you kill anybody, I don't want any ninety-five-year-old mama-sans, or I don't want any two- or three-year-old baby-sans."

Lieutenant Grant, the next prosecution witness, once again described his discovery of the victims' bodies at Son Thang-4. Under cross-examination he agreed with prior witnesses, saying that, at night, "if I saw something moving, I'd shoot at it. . . . It would be crazy not to fire."

The CO of 1/7, Lieutenant Colonel Cooper, next testified that Ambort was "my best company commander . . .

imaginative . . . energetic . . . dedicated. His only flaw, at the time, was his youth and inexperience. . . . Ambort's company carried well above its share of the load. . . . It had taken more than its share of suffering, too." Prompted by the IO, Cooper quoted a letter he had written to his senior, the 7th Marines CO, describing Ambort in glowing terms and saying that the lieutenant had, in his false SKS report, "let me down," although his motivation was based "on a rather difficult situation," presumably referring to the inconvenient fact of sixteen dead noncombatants.

Cooper concluded by telling the investigating officer, "What he did in addressing his men was a charge to them to carry out their mission. I do not feel in any way that he gave them an illegal order or implied that they should harm civilians. . . . I feel he gave them a good pep talk. . . . I feel quite strongly that the charges forwarded are not valid, in my opinion."

Despite the prosecution's best efforts, it seemed that a celebration of Ambort was taking place rather than a prosecution. That tack continued with the next witness, Sergeant Meyers. After an account of the formation of the killer team, Meyers was asked, this time by the prosecution, "What kind of company commander is Lieutenant Ambort?"

"I think he is a real good company commander," the veteran infantryman replied. "The best I ever worked for." And the men in Meyers's platoon? "They felt the same way I do, sir. That they couldn't have a better leader."

Six days after initially convening, the Article 32 heard its final witness, 1st Lt. R. Peter Kimmerer, Ambort's 1st Platoon commander. By then the location had changed; Kimmerer testified at Hill 327, the division headquarters cantonment.

In recounting the night the killer team went to Son Thang-4, Kimmerer related hearing fire, as did others. He heard only American 5.56mm M-16s firing on automatic, however, and he thought something was not right: "Because I didn't hear an [enemy] SK, and I didn't hear an [enemy]

AK, and I have never been shot at by the gooks by a 7.62 [M-14] machine gun, yet."

On cross-examination Kimmerer, like others before him, had no doubt about the ROEs under which Company B operated. "Night combat, in the area where we were operating in, anything that moved after dark . . . he was the enemy and you killed it." He thought Ambort "the best company commander I have seen in the battalion. . . . He is a good tactician and he cares for his men. We all trusted him, had complete faith in him, and I think he's a real fine Marine."

After Kimmerer was excused, the prosecution had no further witnesses; it had shown what it viewed as probable cause to send Ambort to a GCM, charged with sixteen counts of murder. King turned to the defense counsel, Captain Roux, who was seated next to a silent Ambort. Roux had heard the government's evidence and now knew what he would have to defend against at trial. The defense had no duty to present evidence, as the hearing was only to determine probable cause. He stood and said, "The defense will call no witnesses." King adjourned the Article 32 investigation at 1745 on 15 April.

Jim King was a highly competent and ethical officer and lawyer, clearly destined for greater responsibility. Indeed, eight years later, he was promoted to the grade of brigadier general, there being only one judge advocate general officer in the Marine Corps. As Ambort's IO, he had to decide what action to recommend. Clearly the prosecution had been burdened with a difficult task, as well: finding probable cause to try a popular and respected combat leader for failing to report the Son Thang incident as a war crime, which was not the most grievous of sins in the eyes of most infantry officers and NCOs. Moreover, contrary to the first charge against Ambort, the evidence showed that 1/7 was informed of the incident almost immediately, albeit untruthfully in some respects.

The prosecution also had a difficult task in demonstrating that Ambort had not minimized civilian casualties and

At LZ Baldy, Lt. Col. Jim King conducted the pre–general court-martial investigation of 1st Lt. Ron Ambort. Was the commander responsible for his subordinate's war crimes? *Brig. Gen. James P. King*

had not kept his men apprised of the ROEs. It was apparent to King that Ambort did as much as anyone in the battalion in those regards, as even Dick Theer's testimony had confirmed. On the other hand, Ambort had freely admitted he made a false statement that the Herrod patrol had captured an enemy SKS, and that would merit official punishment.

But King's more challenging decision was not in regard to the accusations on the charge sheet. It was whether Ambort's "pep talk," telling the patrol "to pay the motherfuckers back, to shoot everything that moved, to shoot first and ask questions later," made him, in the eyes of the law, a principal to the crimes of his men.

In terms of the 1969 *Manual for Courts-Martial*, did Ambort intend to aid or encourage the persons who committed the crime? Did Ambort share the criminal intent or purpose of the perpetrators? For Ambort to be chargeable as a principal, military law required that he share, along with the patrol members, the specific intent to murder.

If King found probable cause to believe that high threshold had been reached by the "pep talk," he was obliged to add a charge of sixteen murders to Ambort's offenses. Then, if the CG agreed with King's assessment (and CGs invariably do agree with IOs), Ambort would stand before a GCM that could, upon proof beyond a reasonable doubt, find him guilty of the Son Thang murders, just as if he had personally pulled the trigger at all three hooches.

"I agonized over the recommendation," King said. "I believed it to be close—very close! But given the testimony I had heard . . . and the analysis of criminal intent . . . Ambort's conduct amounted, under the circumstances, to a high (very high) degree of negligence but did not amount to an order to kill women with children in their arms. His words came perilously close."

As he evaluated the evidence against Ambort, King considered Herrod's assertion that the team received enemy fire. King found the falsity of that report a key to Ambort's conduct because, he said, it suggested that "Herrod *knew* that Ambort had not authorized the kind of killing that went on." King later noted that "it was Ambort's own low-key admission of the words [through prosecutor Brown's testimony], but denial of the intent, that was more influential on me." Finally, King believed that no court-martial convened in Vietnam would have convicted Ambort.[16]

In a contemporaneous report to the 7th Marines CO, King eloquently wrote:

In this shadowy war where friend, enemy and neutral are virtually indistinguishable, and where women and children have often set booby-traps . . . "minimizing noncombatant casualties" is translated in the field, rightly or wrongly . . .

to shoot anything that moves at night. If the instructions given by Lieutenant Ambort were inconsistent with standard Battalion operating rules it would be a different matter. The fact is, they were not. To the Marine in the field the word "gook" means enemy . . . [Ambort] failed to comprehend that his words . . . might, on this occasion, provide the "spark" that sent the team on its rampage. But these are judgment and experience factors not, in my opinion, properly measurable under the Uniform Code of Military Justice. If his words did indeed act as a catalyst then he must answer to his own conscience and to a higher authority than the members of any court-martial.[17]

King recommended that Ambort receive only a letter of reprimand at non-judicial punishment (NJP) for making a false official statement. No court would have the opportunity to measure and judge the impact of Ambort's words to the patrol.

NJP is an administrative-type hearing for relatively minor offenses. It is not a court-martial and it does not enjoy that forum's procedural safeguards, such as lawyer counsel or observance of rules of evidence. Often referred to in the Marine Corps as "office hours," or in the Navy as "captain's mast," NJP is a brief, one-officer procedure with punishments severely limited by *Manual for Courts-Martial* provisions. Officers subjected to NJP, a very infrequent occurrence, are heard by the commanding general of their division, wing, or base. Although a finding of "not guilty" is theoretically possible, in officers' cases guilt is almost always a foregone conclusion, as the offender would otherwise be before a court-martial.

If the individual recommended for NJP wishes, he or she, officer or enlisted, may refuse NJP in favor of a court-martial. A court ensures the accused's right to a judicial procedure, but also greatly increases the possible punishments if the individual is convicted. Except when charges are clearly ill-conceived, the wise accused always accepts an offer of NJP. Its bite is brief and not so deep.

In retrospect, King's recommendation of NJP for Ambort appears lenient, but perhaps the wiser course.

The Mere Gook Rule

"Gooks are gooks," a pretrial witness unabashedly declared. Early in the war, U.S. troops were better trained and disciplined, but over time, increased manpower needs, lowered recruiting standards, and the war's political unpopularity were reflected in the soldiers' and Marines' attitudes toward the Vietnamese. Servicemen grew distrustful of all Vietnamese: "You begin to think they're all your enemies. And that all of them are something not quite human. . . . You give them names to depersonalize them, to categorize them. . . . They become dinks and slopes and slants and gooks."[18] "The rule in Viet-Nam was the M.G.R.—the 'mere gook rule': that it was no crime to kill or torture or rob or maim a Vietnamese because he was a mere gook."[19] Telford Taylor confirms this in *Nuremberg and Vietnam*: "The trouble is no one sees the Vietnamese as people. They're not people. Therefore it doesn't matter what you do to them."[20]

A Marine Corps judge advocate recalls a Vietnam rape prosecution he conducted. The evidence was overwhelming against the accused, who raised the victim's consent as a defense. The jurors found him not guilty. The judge advocate later spoke to the senior member, a colonel, who said, "There's not much doubt what happened there, but we're not going to ruin the lives of these young Marines for some Vietnamese." But "Vietnamese" wasn't the word the juror used, the lawyer noted.[21] It was the "Mere Gook Rule" in action in the courtroom, and it was not unusual.

The word "gook" originally referred not to Vietnamese, but to Nicaraguans, its first use noted during the 1912 U.S. intervention in Nicaragua. The term was ubiquitous in Vietnam. "Ordinary soldiers under the strains and stresses of modern warfare can hardly be expected to bear [law of war] injunctions in mind," writes a prominent international legal scholar, "when the enemy has been denigrated by their high command, their political leaders and the media to the level of uncivilized sub-humans."[22]

But passing the buck of prejudice against Vietnamese to the media and senior commanders is too easy, too facile. Few wars have seen the national leadership raise so little propaganda against the enemy. Significant segments of the U.S. population even viewed the Viet Cong with respect and admiration. The mind-set illustrated by the Mere Gook Rule, however, was common in conversation among U.S. forces of all ranks in Vietnam and reflected casual, un-thinking racism and cultural arrogance. True, combatants have always used appellations of varying crudeness to de-scribe their enemies—redcoats, rebs, or krauts, for exam-ple. And the military doesn't hold a copyright on the use of such terms. But "wherever such antipathies exist, the prospects for limitation, restraint, and humanity in warfare have always been . . . poor indeed."[23]

Lt. Gen. William Peers, senior member of the panel that investigated the My Lai incident and its cover-up, reported, "The most disturbing factor we encountered was the low re-gard in which some of the men held the Vietnamese . . . considering them subhuman, on the level of dogs. . . . Some of the men never referred to Vietnamese as anything but 'gooks.' . . . We thought that perhaps the [My Lai] units had included an unusual number of men of inferior qual-ity. . . . The result [of a personnel analysis] concluded that the men . . . were about average as compared with other units in the Army."[24]

Sociologists and psychologists are too familiar with the result of such dehumanization. "Distance in war is not merely physical," writes Lt. Col. Dave Grossman in his study *On Killing*. "There is also an emotional distance process that plays a vital part in overcoming the resistance to killing . . . permitting the killer to deny that he is killing a human being."[25] Others point out, "When victims are de-humanized . . . the moral restraints against killing or harm-ing them become less effective. Groups of people who are systematically demonized, assigned to inferior or dangerous categories, and identified by derogatory labels are readily excluded from the bonds of human empathy and the protection of moral and legal precepts."[26]

The part played by the Mere Gook Rule in Son Thang cannot be documented. But the attitudes held by the killer team toward Vietnamese, no different than those held by most American servicemen in South Vietnam, were significant.

As anticipated, Son Thang attracted congressional inquiries like flies to honey. On 8 May, Pfc. Green spoke by MARS radio-phone to his congressman in Washington, D.C. (three days before, the Commandant had directed the division CG to ensure the call went through). Green and his military lawyer, Capt. John Hargrove, informed the congressman of their assessments of the case and its progress. The congressman asked for a copy of Green's Article 32, which was sent to him in Washington via Marine Corps headquarters.[27]

On 13 May, Private Boyd was temporarily released from the brig and, along with his lawyer, Capt. Michael Merrill, travelled by jeep to Chu Lai, forty-six miles south of Da Nang. There they met with Boyd's congressman, who was on a fact-finding trip to South Vietnam as a member of a subcommittee of the House Armed Services Committee.[28] Neither congressional contact produced any noticeable result.

Whether instigated by a constituent's letter or by personal interest, congressional interrogatories directed to the Marine Corps always receive swift response. They are informally called "congrints," short for "congressional interest." In fact, both congresspersons and the Marines understand that in most cases the legislative inquiry is pro forma, just as the Marine Corps's initial response to the legislator is usually a standard form letter. The exchange of official missives allows legislators to assure constituents of their concern and personal involvement, and the Marine Corps to show its attention to the legislator's need to respond to constituent voters.

That having been said, congrints often work their way down the chain of command to field commanders. As unit commanders receive few such inquiries, they return a prompt and detailed response. That response makes its way to the office in the Judge Advocate Division of Marine Corps headquarters where congrints are routinely endorsed and re-routed.

Although congrints receive the attention of field commanders, they are usually little more than bureaucratic minuets. There were to be many congrints during the Son Thang trials, but few that evidenced special or extraordinary concern on the part of a legislator. So the congrints were given corresponding attention by the Marine Corps: not much.

On 5 May, twenty days after his Article 32 adjourned, 1st Lt. Ron Ambort was called to the office of the staff judge advocate. Colonel Lucy's cramped work space was located just inside the doorway of a long, low, arched building constructed of curved corrugated tin sheets. Blistering hot in summer, damp and refrigerator-like in monsoons, it was uncomfortable all of the time, although as Ambort might have pointed out, any roof was superior to the rough comforts of the field. Known as Butler huts after their pre-World War II designer, or Quonset huts, many of these unattractive but functional buildings stood on Hill 327's slopes and served as the division's headquarters.

Lucy advised Ambort that he remained suspected of making a false official statement—the charge to be disposed of at non-judicial punishment, if Ambort agreed. Ambort quickly consented and, in writing, attested that he had discussed his case and his options with his defense counsel, Captain Roux.

Ten days later, on 15 May, Ambort stood at attention before the desk of Maj. Gen. Charles Widdecke, Commanding General, 1st Marine Division. Widdecke had assumed command from Major General Wheeler only a few days before, when Wheeler had seriously injured his back in a helicopter crash. Also present was the general's lawyer,

Colonel Lucy. There is no record of what was said at the brief meeting.

As Ambort left the office, General Widdecke handed him a two-page document headed "Letter of Reprimand." After mentioning the Son Thang patrol, the reprimand detailed Ambort's false report. Paragraph four continued, "Conduct such as this cannot be condoned on the part of any Marine. It is particularly reprehensible for an officer."[29]

Ambort's punishment was that letter of reprimand, plus his forfeiture of two hundred and fifty dollars pay for two months, a total of five hundred dollars. It was the maximum punishment permitted at office hours. A letter of reprimand effectively ends a military career, although that was largely insignificant to Ambort, a Reserve officer who had no apparent career aspirations. Any reprimand, however, deeply wounds a conscientious and capable combat commander. Ambort was a young leader who had made a serious mistake and paid what was, to him, a serious price. The officers' joke, that a letter of reprimand is better than no mail at all, is wrong. But he knew it could have been a hell of a lot worse.

Lieutenant Colonel Cooper, in writing Ambort's final combat zone fitness report, the semiannual critique of officer performance, stood by his company commander ("With the exception of one incident of poor judgment")[30] despite the letter of reprimand. As required, Cooper attached a copy of the letter to the fitness report. But he also attached a recommendation that Ambort be awarded the Bronze Star Medal ("superb leadership, steadfast devotion to duty and personal courage").[31] Predictably, the award recommendation was not approved. The letter of reprimand was not appealed. Although his thirteen-month tour of Vietnam duty was completed, Ambort remained in-country on "legal hold" as an essential witness to the upcoming courts-martial of his men.

Cooper, in a written recommendation to the division CG, urged that the killer team's charges be reduced to lesser offenses. That surprisingly unrealistic and naive recommendation was ignored.

CHARGING WAR CRIMES

In the staff judge advocate's office, lawyers from both the defense and prosecution sections were preparing for the first of the Son Thang courts-martial. Colonel Lucy, constantly in the eye of civilian television and print reporters, oversaw the efforts of both teams. He later said, "I don't remember any pressure from anybody [higher in the chain of command] to do anything other than to bring them to trial. . . . We were not going to put it under the table. We were going to bring everything out in the open and get it done."[32]

There was brief consideration of a joint trial, a single court-martial of all four remaining accused. But in view of Major Blum's unpleasant and difficult experience in controlling five defense lawyers in one hearing, that course was, wisely, not taken. The difficult legal problems involved in admitting the prior written statement of one accused without its improper use against another accused would have raised thorny appellate issues.

It was also easily decided that the charge against the killer team would be alleged as a violation of UCMJ Article 118—murder—rather than the war crime of murder under the law of war. Indeed, those involved in the case probably did not even consider charging war crimes. Battlefield war crimes committed by one's own forces are almost never charged as such. Instead, they are simply alleged as the UCMJ offenses of murder, rape, or aggravated assault, whichever the case might be. They are denominated war crimes only if committed by enemy nationals.[33]

When U.S. military personnel are accused of crimes amounting to violations of the law of war, UCMJ Article 18 incorporates such war crimes into military law, and within the jurisdiction of GCMs.[34] "The military court, by punishing the acts, executes international law even if it applies . . . its own military law. The legal basis of the trial is international law, which establishes the individual responsibility of the person committing the act of illegitimate warfare."[35] The fact that the Son Thang courts-martial would, in international law, be trying war crimes, went unnoticed by those involved.

The murder of noncombatants, whether enemy nationals or co-belligerents, is a war crime under a variety of international agreements, as well as under international case law, including Nuremberg's post–World War II International Military Tribunal.[36] U.S. military case law earlier reached that same conclusion.[37]

The Son Thang prosecutors, "trial counsels" in military parlance, were assigned by the SJA. They would be the same two judge advocates, Capts. Franz P. Jevne and Charles E. Brown, Jr., who had presented the prosecution's evidence in the joint Article 32. Jevne and Brown decided to try what appeared to be their strongest case first—that of Private Schwarz, who was represented by Capt. Dan Le-Gear.

Some advocates might have been overwhelmed by a contested multiple-murder trial. As Colonel Lucy said, "they were getting experience in a hurry."[38] But there were no tyros on the trial team, and this was by no means their first murder case.

The military judge was not a member of the SJA's office, or even a member of the 1st Marine Division. General court-martial judges were assigned their cases by the senior military judge in the Navy-Marine Corps Judicial Activity at III MAF headquarters in Da Nang. The Judicial Activity's principal office was in Yokosuka, Japan; there were usually only two GCM judges in Vietnam.

Once assigned, the military judge has final authority over case progress, including continuances, witness requests, and other pre-trial matters. During the trial, the judge is the sole arbiter and legal authority. The UCMJ removes judges from all local command authority, such as

Lt. Col. Paul St.Amour, the irascible but practical general court-martial judge in the Schwarz, Green, and Boyd trials. *Lt. Col. Paul A. A. St.Amour*

watch and duty rosters and performance ratings, making them answerable only to their senior military judge. It would be virtually impossible to bring pressure to bear on a judge—if a senior officer would be so foolish as to try.

Lt. Col. Paul A. A. St.Amour was the military judge assigned to hear Schwarz's case. An experienced judge, St.Amour had first served in South Vietnam in 1967 as SJA of the 1st Marine Aircraft Wing. He had a reputation as a difficult and argumentative man, but he was also considered an independent thinker, willing to make difficult decisions that ran contrary to the expected, even at the expense of his relations with other senior lawyers and commanders. In fact, one Vietnam SJA had made official complaints about St.Amour's judging and judicial temperament. Such assertions were debatable, and it is not uncommon for strong-minded SJAs to grumble, usually to no effect, about equally strong-minded judges and their handling of courts.

PREPARING FOR TRIAL

As the parties prepared for trial, Capt. Bob Williams, Herrod's defense counsel, made headlines in both America and Vietnam. "Murder Trial Called Political," read the *Stars and Stripes* headline.[39] The UPI story continued, "The lawyer for one of four U.S. Marines accused of killing 16 Vietnamese civilians said Tuesday that high-ranking commanders ordered a court martial for political reasons to avoid any charges of a cover-up. The attorney, Capt. Robert Williams . . . said the case was 'political' in nature and controlled by headquarters to make sure that 'the Marine Corps is not going to get caught up like the Army did, covering up at My Lai. . . . They don't even care if these kids are convicted or not, but the political decision was that they had to be tried.'" The story concluded by quoting Williams's assertion that, "evidence presented against the men at a pretrial hearing was not sufficient to warrant a court-martial, but that one was ordered by 'authorities higher than the 1st Marine Division.'" The defense lawyer's allegations were widely aired on Armed Forces Vietnam radio, as well.

Contrary to Williams's assertion, there was no direction from higher authority as to handling the cases. It was true that Marine Corps headquarters required all replies to press questions to be cleared through Washington. That presented considerable difficulties for the division CG on Hill 327, who was constantly faced by reporters asking legitimate questions about the cases. Instead of providing a prompt response, the CG had to send proposed answers via secret message to Headquarters Marine Corps in Washington to be staffed through the Public Affairs Division and the Commandant's office. Days later, their decision was re-

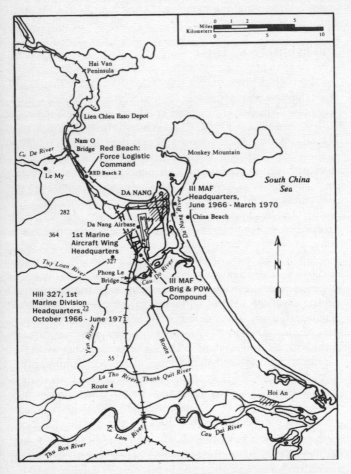

Legal Office Locations in the Da Nang Area

layed back to Da Nang for dissemination, or not, to the civilian press corps.

Eventually, Major General Widdecke sent a plaintive request to the Commandant: "Please advise if it is still desired that all queries be cleared through Headquarters Marine Corps."[40] The requirement for approval of press statements was dropped.

Colonel Lucy later recalled, "The only instructions that I had was the commanding general's . . . in regard to concluding the investigation and proceeding. I don't remember any pressure from anybody to do anything other than to bring them to trial."[41] Lieutenant Colonel Cooper, who dealt with significant media interest while directing the initial investigation of the incident, said, "No one, absolutely no one, ever put any pressure on me as an individual, or tried to influence my actions."[42]

Bob Williams was an abrasive but effective defense counsel. He was often requested by black defendants who might have heard of the Malcolm X and other black power posters hanging prominently in his quarters. Lieutenant Colonel King diplomatically recalled that "Williams had quite a few rough edges. . . . He was not the easiest to get along with."[43] Among the other 1st Division attorneys he was referred to as "X," or "Brother X," an appellation intended and accepted in good humor. Williams's goal in making accusatory statements to the press was not apparent, however. Hard evidence for the statements was nonexistent.

Five days after Williams's comments were reported, Colonel Lucy delivered a letter to the captain which read, in part, "[American Bar Association] Disciplinary Rule 7-107 . . . cautions all lawyers in a criminal matter against expressing publicly opinions 'as to the guilt or innocence of the accused, the evidence or the merits of the case.' I do not intend to take any further action in relation to the statement attributed to you . . . however . . . any further public communications of this type will be closely examined and may require trial counsel to request official consideration of them prior to trial, by the . . . military judge."[44]

Not long afterward, Herrod's civilian lawyers took over the direction of his defense, and Williams remained on the defense team in a lesser capacity.

Schwarz was unsuccessful in locating a civilian defender, so he would go to trial with his assigned counsel, Capt. Daniel H. LeGear, Jr., of Kirkwood, Missouri. LeGear, like the other judge advocates trying the Son Thang cases, was only three years out of law school, the University of Missouri. He had spent the last two years constantly in military trials. This would be his fifth premeditated murder defense since arriving in Vietnam nine months before. He knew it would not be an easy case.

After consulting with his client, as required by the *Manual for Courts-Martial*, LeGear informed the prosecutors that Schwarz desired his case to be heard by members.

After the 1969 revisions to the UCMJ, and consistent with civilian practice, courts-martial could be heard by either a judge alone or by members—a jury. Military juries are frequently the target of critics, having never fully shed their World War II image as the commander's lackeys.

In Marine Corps practice, members are usually selected from rosters of officers at the division level, where GCMs are convened. No member may be from the accused's unit. An administrative officer, often the adjutant, makes a random selection, guided by availability and common sense. Operations officers are seldom selected because they must be constantly available to carry out their critical duties. Military police officers and provost marshals go unpicked because of the possibility of their disqualifying familiarity with pending cases.

There is no standard number of GCM members, but the minimum is five. A seven- or eight-member panel is common and allows for challenges. The commanding general signs the order appointing members to a specific case, as he is the only officer with authority to convene GCMs. In a sense, then, military jurors are selected by the commander. In fact, selection is an administrative matter accomplished by mid-level officers of the commander's staff who have no idea (or interest in) what case may come before that panel. Instances of commanders deleting or adding officers to a members list to achieve bias are rare, and the mere "appearance of impurity"[45] is sufficient to overturn a conviction rendered by a panel discovered to be so tainted.

Critics argue that commanders need not make changes to member assignments; the mere fact that members come from the officer ranks is sufficient bias in and of itself to ensure convictions. Ignoring what such a broad charge implies about officer integrity and intelligence, it must be admitted that courts-martial have a very high conviction rate. In 1970, the year of the Son Thang incident, 94.6 percent of the Army's 2,647 GCMs resulted in findings of guilt. Marine Corps figures are unavailable but no doubt comparable.[46]

A significant factor elevating the military's conviction rate is its unique offenses—unauthorized absence, culpable loss of government property, breaking restriction—common charges, the courtroom proof of which is administratively simple. Another factor is the common military practice of, before trial, disposing of cases that lack reasonably strong proof via administrative action.

So, although Captain LeGear knew Schwarz would not be an easy case, he was experienced enough to know that neither was any case impossible.

In the U.S., press reports of the charges provoked letters of protest from citizens to Marine Corps headquarters. Most writers objected to what they perceived as the prosecution of young men for doing the killing they had been trained for. Many writers stressed the emotional toll of counter-guerrilla operations as a mitigating factor. In replying to such letters on the Commandant's behalf, the Judge Advocate Division avoided comment on the pending cases but commonly noted in its standard reply, "there is no denying that the ordeal of combat puts extreme pressures on the Marines fighting in Vietnam. However, the Marine Corps is fighting in Vietnam in the name of a nation which requires certain standards of civilized conduct to be maintained even under the trying circumstances of combat. Those standards do not permit the intentional killing of persons, such as civilians or prisoners of war, who are not actually participating in combat. When there is an allegation that such an event has occurred appropriate action must be taken in accordance with the law."[47]

5

U.S. v. Pvt. M. A. Schwarz

PROJECT 100,000

Pvt. Michael Schwarz had a checkered past. By his own account, he was suspended twelve times from his Pennsylvania grade school and finally quit after his second expulsion, having completed ninth grade. He had already left home, at fourteen. Supporting himself by working in garages as a mechanic, he rode with local motorcycle gangs—the War Lords, Vigilantes, and Hell's Messengers—and at fifteen had a civilian conviction for fighting. His infrequent drug involvement was, for those times, unremarkable.

In February 1966, when seventeen, he married. Six months later he enlisted for a four-year hitch in the Marine Corps, and shortly thereafter was the father of a son. His wife remained in Bulger, Pennsylvania, living in a house trailer while her husband completed boot camp, infantry training, and an initial Camp Lejeune assignment.

Schwarz arrived in Vietnam in October, 1969, just after his twenty-first birthday, relatively old for an infantryman in that teenager's war. He was initially ordered north, assigned to the 1st Reconnaissance Battalion, 1st Marine Division, near the DMZ. He participated in four long-range patrols. His conduct was poor when he wasn't in combat, and even in Vietnam he was the frequent subject of disciplinary action. Transferred to B-1/7 on 13 February 1970 after four months in-country, he walked point for Herrod's killer team just six days later.

It is Marine Corps policy to inform the families of those accused of serious crimes personally, to spare them learning of their children's difficulties through the media. The lieutenant colonel sent to advise Schwarz's parents of their son's criminal charges recalled that they received the news calmly; they may have found solace in the fact that he would not face execution if convicted of the charges against him. The colonel reported that Schwarz's wife, however, "was bitter and very emotional. . . . Neighbors . . . managed to cool her down."[1]

Under the UCMJ, the maximum punishment for premeditated murder was (and remains) death. For that punishment to be applicable upon conviction, however, it must be specifically authorized before trial by the officer convening the court-martial. General Widdecke did not do so. Unlike civilian law enforcement authorities who must weigh similar sentencing options, the general did not have to consider the political aspects of his potential life-or-death decision. Widdecke had no constituency to impress, appease, or woo, but made the decision based upon his own assessment of the facts, and his own sense of fairness and justice.

Instead of execution, Schwarz faced a maximum punishment of confinement at hard labor for life—although he might receive any lesser term imposed by the court, if convicted.

Besides the wounding testimony anticipated from Krichten, and his own sworn, hand-written statement, Schwarz had one other notable problem as he faced his trial. He had a general classification test (GCT) score of seventy-four. GCT scores are rough equivalents of IQ scores, a GCT of 100 being average. A score of 120 is required of officer candidates. A GCT of 74 was very low, even by the relaxed standards of the day: Schwarz was a Mental Category Four enlistee. Such individuals were sometimes referred to as "Project 100,000" Marines.

Few outside the ranks of Vietnam-era military officers realize the harm done the armed services and the conduct of the war in Vietnam by Project 100,000—most Americans would not even recognize the term. But military lawyers, having dealt with the criminality that Project 100,000 engendered, were particularly aware of its disservice.

Project 100,000, called "an ill-conceived program,"[2] and an "unmitigated disaster,"[3] was implemented after a 1964 federal task force found that each year the armed services rejected about 600,000 men who failed to meet intelligence standards. The task force suggested that some of these men were suitable for military duty. With the war's need for increased manpower, the military was required to accept many of those previously rejected.

Armed forces enlistment examinations, standard for all services, classify prospective entrants into five intelligence categories. Those scoring in categories one, two, and three are automatically acceptable for service; those in category five are automatically rejected. A small number of category fours, like Schwarz, had always been enlisted, but now the Department of Defense was requiring all the services to accept many more.[4] In October 1966, the DOD required that 40,000 category fours ("cat fours") be enlisted for service the following year, and 100,000 each year thereafter. Hence the program's name, Project 100,000. Schwarz enlisted two months before the mandatory cat four enlistments were instituted so, although a cat four in terms of enlistment test scores, he was not a *mandatory* cat four.

Under Project 100,000 it became necessary to turn away better-qualified volunteers to meet the new cat four quotas.[5] In his authoritative book, *America in Vietnam*, Guenter Lewy writes, "Through 'Project 100,000' they had to accept men of lower intelligence ratings who were ill-suited for the exacting demands of a counterinsurgency war like Vietnam. The results could have been expected."[6]

The influx of cat fours, mandatory and otherwise, had an immediate negative effect on discipline. Gen. William Westmoreland bluntly said, "Category four is a dummy. . . . That [program] introduced a weak-minded, criminal, untrained element. . . . When those people came to Vietnam . . . that's when disciplinary problems began on the battlefield."[7] Cat fours initially had both desertions and court-martial convictions at about double the rate of other servicemen, and significantly lower promotion rates. A later Pentagon study revealed that their "attrition-by-death" rate, too, was nearly double that of other Vietnam veterans.[8] Their court-martial rates did eventually decrease to levels only slightly higher than those of other mental categories.

Gen. Robert E. Cushman, CG of III MAF in 1967 and '68, said, "We just had a hell of a time with quality. . . . I was always massaging the number and trying to get the mental group fours down to the lowest possible level."[9] Maj. Gen. Rathvon McC. Tompkins, a Vietnam 3d Marine Division CG, added, "That was a very grave problem. . . . [Category] four was a guy who could see lightning and hear thunder, maybe. . . . Great waste of effort, great waste of time, and a very dangerous thing."[10] The Commandant of the Marine Corps, Gen. Leonard F. Chapman, declared, "We're going to fight to the highest levels of government, projects like Project 100,000. . . . They've got a lot of merit in the social sense, but they don't contribute a single thing to the readiness of the Marine Corps, to the combat capability of the Marine Corps."[11] But the cat four requirement continued until June 1971, the enlistments extending until after the war's end.

Gen. Colin Powell could have had Michael Schwarz in mind when he wrote, "I can never forgive a [political] leadership that said, in effect: These young men—poor, less educated, less privileged—are expendable . . . but the rest are too good to risk. . . . Of the many tragedies of Vietnam, this raw class discrimination strikes me as the most damaging to the ideal that all Americans are created equal."[12]

By the time of Schwarz's GCM, 7 percent of Marine Corps enlisted strength was cat four, their relatively small number illustrating the military adage that commanders spend 90 percent of their time dealing with 10 percent of their men. To a large extent untrainable, and needing close supervision, many cat fours became disciplinary problems requiring the attention not only of commanders, but military police, investigators, judge advocates, and warders. Ultimately, the manpower dividend gained by enlisting cat fours resulted in a manpower deficit. Although a number of Marine Corps ills have been wrongly attributed to Project 100,000, there is little question that a cat four would have difficulty in assisting in his own defense at a GCM.

Clemenceau reportedly remarked that military justice is to justice as military music is to music. When he said that, in the early twentieth century, the statement was apropos even if many individuals were partial to martial tunes. But by 1970, American military justice had greatly matured. The case of *United States v. Private Michael A. Schwarz* was a gauge of the military criminal justice system's maturity and fairness.

The first of the Son Thang general courts-martial began a little less than four months after the alleged offenses. "Trial Opens For Marine In 16 Deaths,"[13] a *Washington Post* headline said.

The "courtroom" was one of two such rooms that sat close beside the Quonset hut housing the division legal office; it was the same cramped space where the joint Article 32 investigation was held. The military judge, Lieutenant Colonel St.Amour, was seated on a metal folding chair at the right end of the raised "bench" that ran along the wall opposite the entrance. A stack of legal manuals lay on the table before him. Like everyone else in the small room, St.Amour wore rumpled camouflage utilities and scuffed, dusty jungle boots.

The court reporter sat next to the bench, tending his belt recorder and back-up cassette recorder. There was a witness box containing another folding metal chair to the left, across the room from the judge. The lawyers and the accused sat with the judge's bench to the front right and their backs to the courtroom door. Schwarz and his lawyer, Captain LeGear, were at one small table, prosecutors Franz Jevne and Charley Brown squeezed behind another. They all deposited their shapeless utility covers on the deck beside their chairs. Directly across from the lawyers, facing the door, was the jury "box," essentially a desktop that ran the width of the room. Behind it were several folding chairs for the members. A five-by-four-foot American flag was tacked on the wall behind the members box. Two doors on that same back wall, one at either end of the box, led to an even smaller members' deliberation room littered with out-of-date magazines and rancid ash trays.

The plywood walls featured Navy Seabee decor: each panel was laboriously hand-blowtorched to bring out the grain of the wood. The price for such inter-service materials and labor was usually several pairs of new jungle boots or, if the sailor was lucky, a captured SKS or even an AK-47. Four triple-tube fluorescent light fixtures lit the room—except when the generators died, as they occasionally did on Hill 327. Then the windowless courtroom became dark and claustrophobic and all hands filed out into the humid heat of the Vietnamese summer.

CRITICAL PRE-TRIAL MOTIONS

Capt. Franz P. Jevne, twenty-eight, was chief trial counsel—senior prosecutor—of the 1st Marine Division. A 1964 Harvard and 1967 University of Minnesota law graduate, he was approaching the end of his Vietnam tour. Jevne had already tried "a bunch"[14] of Vietnam murders and was well-regarded by seniors and peers, although also considered humorless. Meticulous, Jevne wrote out in advance each question he planned for every witness, seeking to make his prosecutions as objection-free as possible. Judge St.Amour considered Jevne "the more active, aggressive, and intense"[15] of the three defense and prosecution lawyers, but neither Jevne nor defense counsel LeGear struck St.Amour "as being professionally distinctive."[16] St.Amour was a hard man to impress.

Jevne had decided to try Schwarz first because the facts in his case made him a likely candidate for conviction. In Jevne's view, Schwarz was no more than "a thug."

Assisting Jevne was Capt. Charles E. Brown, ten days short of twenty-eight and a 1967 graduate of Cleveland's Western Reserve Law School. Brown, who had conducted Ambort's 32, would be taking over the Son Thang prosecutions after Jevne's imminent return to the States, and was intimately involved in all the preparations for trial.

The court was called to order at 0904 on Monday, 15 June 1970. The jury was not yet present. To the judge's inquiry, Schwarz replied that he would be represented by his assigned military defense counsel, Capt. Dan LeGear.

LeGear, twenty-eight, was a graduate of the University of Missouri law school. Like Jevne and Brown, he was unusually experienced in the trial of major cases: military law is like that, particularly from the mid-1960s to mid-1970s when case loads were staggeringly high. Like Jevne and Brown, LeGear had been on active duty for less than three years.

In sixteen separate counts, the charge sheet alleged that Schwarz "did, at Hamlet 4 Son Thang . . . on or about 19 February 1970, with premeditation, murder [each count naming a different victim], a Vietnamese civilian, by means of shooting [her or him] with an M-16 rifle, a .45 caliber pistol, and an M-79 grenade launcher." (After the prosecution's proof was submitted, the court would routinely grant a prosecution motion to amend each count to strike out the weapon not applicable as the means of death.)

As in any civilian or military trial of major consequence, motions, some more substantive than others, were submitted at the outset.

Capt. Franz Jevne *(left)*, Schwarz's prosecutor, outside the Officers Club on Hill 327, with Capt. Ted Padden and Jevne's hoochmate, Capt. Dan LeGear. *Col. Robert J. Blum*

LeGear initially moved to alter the format of the charge sheet. Instead of sixteen separate counts he argued for three, each count naming the victims at each of the three hooches. LeGear figured that if he could not gain a complete acquittal—and he knew how slim a chance that was—he might at least convince the jury that his man had played no part in the killings at one or another of the hooches.

After lengthy argument, St.Amour denied the defense motion. He felt the jury should consider each alleged killing individually. Otherwise, they might tend to apply a defense concerning one victim to all the victims at that particular site.

LeGear then asked for a list of all radio-telephone calls from division headquarters to the Commandant of the Marine Corps since the case came to light, and for copies of all classified messages between those parties for the same period. He already had copies of the unclassified message traffic.

For what purpose? St.Amour asked the defense lawyer. "To determine," LeGear replied, "if there has been any undue influence or pressure put upon this command to send this case to trial, or the appeasement of the Vietnamese government . . . on the theory that it's probable there has been some [improper] command influence."[17] It was a long shot that such material existed, an even longer shot that if it did he would get it. But no harm in asking; it might be a decent appellate issue if Schwarz were convicted.

But St.Amour bristled at LeGear's assertion of improper command influence. "Do you mean to suggest that a commanding general . . . if some officious ass comes along and tries to interpose his opinion . . . that he is disqualified from referring the case to trial?"

Uh-oh. Unable to offer any specific evidence, however flimsy, that General Widdecke might have been pressed to act one way or another regarding the case, LeGear heard his motion summarily denied.

LeGear next moved that the Son Thang victims be disinterred and autopsies conducted to determine causes of death. Now he was on more solid legal ground. After all, a conviction required the prosecution to prove the victims were in fact dead, and that they had died at the hands of the accused by the means charged—rifle, pistol, or M-79. LeGear knew there had been no autopsies. In fact, no doctor had ever seen the bodies. He also knew the bodies had been buried four months previously.

Displaying his rough judicial temperament early on, St.Amour demanded of LeGear, "And who has control, as it were, over these bodies?"

"I have no idea. . . ."

"You're not suggesting I go out and disinter the bodies," St.Amour said, sarcastically. "Are you suggesting Captain Jevne go out and disinter the bodies?"

No, but some governmental agency should do it, LeGear responded. He added that he merely wanted the prosecution to prove the victims hadn't been killed by, say, VC fire, or by artillery.

LeGear was unsurprised when that issue, his final pretrial motion, was denied as quickly as his prior motion.

No matter what the jurisdiction, judges receive great deference in their courtrooms. That innate institutional respect is further enhanced in military courtrooms by the judge's superior rank; not only was St.Amour one of only fifteen GCM judges in the Marine Corps, he was a lieutenant colonel, commissioned for twenty years, dealing with uniformed lawyers who were captains only by virtue of their law degrees, and who had less than three years in Marine green. The judge's combination of rank and office made most disagreements with the bench very brief.

The government counsel stood next. Jevne made the first of two motions that may well have determined the outcome of the GCM before the members even entered the room. The prosecution asked for a determination of the admissibility of nine color photographs of the victims' bodies, photos taken by Lieutenant Grant's patrol the day after the killings.

Before the motion was decided, Grant was called to the stand to satisfy St.Amour that the photos were authentic and accurate. Having already recounted his patrol and its actions numerous times, Grant concisely repeated his account for the judge, saying that a Navy corpsman, HM1 Jones, took the pictures with his personal camera.

On his feet to object to admission of the pictures, LeGear said, "The sole purpose of the prosecution attempting to introduce [the photos] is to inflame the minds of the jury, and he may claim that, well, these members are Marines and they're used to seeing bodies like this, but I say, hardly are they used to this!"

Inflame the jury? Probably. But to let them see the method and the savagery of the killings, as well. Besides, as Marine Corps judges are taught in their training courses, the members should not be disallowed from seeing the handiwork of the accused. St.Amour was not about to.

Objection overruled, motion to admit granted. The members would see the photos.

Then, in a final and crucial motion, the government sought to admit Schwarz's statement of 23 February, the last of the three statements he had given Major Theer at FSB Ross shortly after the homicides had been discovered. Here was the prosecution's "smoking gun," Schwarz's confession to the charges to which he would shortly plead not guilty, written in his own hand and sworn to before witnesses. If that statement were admitted, LeGear knew he would have a hell of a job explaining it away to the jury.

But significant legal issues militated against its admission. And Dick Theer was again the critical cog.

The stumbling blocks to be overcome by prosecutors Jevne and Brown were a result of Theer's inexperience in legal matters. Because the initial investigation at 1/7 had been undertaken without the detailed guidance and participation of an experienced judge advocate—despite the Division SJA's awareness of the seriousness of the case—the most significant documentary evidence relating to the homicides might be ruled inadmissible.

The legal issue was two-fold: the voluntariness of Schwarz's statement, and the correctness of Theer's Article 31 warnings to Schwarz—not for the third and final 23 February statement, but for his first statement on the 21st.

Voluntariness was at issue because Schwarz had come to Theer shortly after having spoken to Lieutenant Ambort, who had questioned him and urged him to "tell the truth." This exhortation from Schwarz's CO, an officer who had promised the battalion commander he would find out more about Son Thang, had been unaccompanied by legal warnings of any sort. Ambort's innocent, even laudable, motive in talking to Schwarz and the others was irrelevant in the eyes of the law: his encouragement, and lack of legal warning, could render Schwarz's statement involuntary, in the sense that the statement was the product of government pressure. If the court considered Schwarz's subsequent statement to the unknowing Theer to be a result of Ambort's influence, not even the Article 31 warnings given by Theer would negate the legal taint of Ambort's prior exhortations. The initial statement to Theer would be inadmissible as the product of governmental coercion. Worse for the prosecution's case, that taint would pass through to the second and on to the vital third statements, as well.

The related issue threatening to keep the statement out of evidence was the completeness of Theer's initial rights warning to Schwarz. The defense contended that, independent of the voluntariness issue, Theer's initial Article 31 warnings were deficient because he had failed to inform Schwarz of the offense of which he was suspected, as required by Article 31. If Theer countered that he did not, on 21 February, suspect Schwarz of an offense, LeGear would argue that he *should* have suspected him. After all, the defense would point out, Theer had already talked to Lieutenant Grant and to Colonel Lucy, the division SJA. And as with the issue of voluntariness, if the warnings given for the first statement were legally incomplete, that deficiency could carry through to Schwarz's second and third statements, they being the products of the first, tainted, statement. The repeated and enhanced warnings later received by Schwarz would be to no avail if the first statement required warnings that were not given.

These were to be very close matters. Years later, St.Amour would say of the two warnings issues, "in retrospect, that was probably the diciest legal question" of the entire trial.[18]

To determine the third and final statement's admissibility, Theer, who by now had completed his third tour of combat duty and been transferred to Virginia, was returned to Vietnam to give evidence again. He was called to the stand by the prosecution solely to testify as to the admissibility of the third statement, the "smoking gun" statement he had taken from Schwarz.

After relating the circumstances of all the statements,

Theer was cross-examined by LeGear. The defense counsel went directly to the issue of the completeness of Theer's warnings to Schwarz before the first statement. Had he advised Schwarz of what crime he was suspected, as required by Article 31?

Theer replied, "It was my duty, of course, to talk to him about it, to see if the Marines were involved in any way. As far as I was concerned, when I began my investigation I didn't feel, I didn't suspect there was any criminal intent on the part of the Marines whatsoever." So Theer had no suspicion of wrongdoing, therefore no crime of which to warn. Fair enough.

But was that reasonable? Theer really suspected no wrongdoing? With raised eyebrows, LeGear asked, "In spite of the fact that you had access to a spot report? You knew where the patrol had been in that area. . . . You also knew Lieutenant Grant's report the next day. . . . You suspected a possible false report about an SKS . . . and you still didn't suspect nothing wrong?"

"No, I did not."

Variations of the same disbelieving theme continued for several minutes, Theer continuing to maintain his lack of suspicion while LeGear's questions made plain his skepticism.

"Were you aware," LeGear asked Theer, "that a person who is neither a suspect nor an accused need not be advised of his rights?" If Theer did not suspect Schwarz of a crime, then why did he give him any warning at all?

Theer dodged. "I told them that I was looking into the circumstances surrounding the deaths of these people, and as far as suspecting, I did not suspect them."

"Was there anything in your mind, deep down, that caused you to think that possibly . . . some criminal act could have been performed down there [in Son Thang-4], in relation to this incident?"

"No, none whatsoever." Theer knew where LeGear was trying to drive him, and was having none of it.

"Now, on the 23d [the date of the controversial third

statement] you said you talked to him again, he filled out a rights statement. At that time did you suspect that a criminal offense may have been committed?"

"I did." The warnings given Schwarz on the 23d, two days after his first statement, were legally impeccable and reflected Theer's then-awakened suspicions.

But was Schwarz cognizant of what he was signing, on the 23d? That, too, went to the voluntariness of the statement. LeGear pointed out that Schwarz was questioned by Theer at 0100, having been in a perimeter tower all day before. Theer responded, "There was nothing to do in the tower during the daytime except rest, clean your weapons for the coming night, which, of course, was a dangerous time."

Unable to shake Theer, LeGear concluded his cross and muttered, "I have no further questions of this witness."

Judge St.Amour promptly took up the matter of whether Schwarz could have been coerced by Ambort into making an incriminating statement, either to Ambort himself, or later to Theer.

Q. Do you know . . . whether Lieutenant Ambort had more than one confrontation or interview with Schwarz?
A. After talking to the men, yes, sir. He had two meetings with the men.
Q. I didn't ask you "with the men." I asked you, "with Schwarz."
A. He had one meeting with Schwarz. . . .
Q. To your knowledge, Major, did Schwarz in fact make a statement to Lieutenant Ambort, oral or written, as a result? . . .
A. I have no way of knowing, sir. . . .
Q. You are not aware of any statements that Schwarz might have made to Lieutenant Ambort as a result of this confrontation?
A. No, sir. He didn't reveal anything to me.

After pursuing the same line for several more minutes, St.Amour concluded by asking Theer, "Search your memory now, and tell the court whether you consciously suspected Schwarz at that time of any wrongdoing whatever, moral or legal, in the broadest context possible of the word." If Theer had suspected Schwarz of *anything*, he would have been required to tell Schwarz of what he was suspected.

But Theer didn't waver in the face of the judge's questioning. "I did not, because, as I've said previously, we've had incidents before where civilians have been killed in exchanges. . . ."

St.Amour, through his own questioning of Theer, had now established both a lack of suspicion on Theer's part, and a reasonable legal basis for admission of the "smoking gun" statement that would probably satisfy an appellate court, if he ruled to admit it.

In a final effort to keep the damning third statement from the jury, LeGear called Schwarz to the stand for the limited purpose of testifying to the circumstances of his *first* statement. If LeGear could not show the warnings to be legally deficient, perhaps he could convince the judge that, despite Theer's testimony, the first statement was involuntary, only given because it was coerced by the government through its agent, Ambort. All following statements would then be inadmissible against their maker, Schwarz. It was a more convoluted chain than any defense lawyer would like, but it was all LeGear had to work with.

Schwarz took the stand, raised his right hand, and was sworn. Prodded by LeGear's questions, he related details of his conversation with Lieutenant Ambort, and the lack of Article 31 warning from him. Schwarz described being urged—by an officer he considered "outstanding"—to "tell the truth, cooperate to our fullest," and finally, Schwarz related his resultant initial statement to Theer. Having seemingly established the requisite links for a chain that could exclude the third statement from evidence, LeGear passed the witness to the prosecution.

But cross-examination of Schwarz quickly revealed that, despite pre-trial preparation by his counsel, Schwarz did not appreciate or recognize the thrust of prosecutor Jevne's questions. After several minutes of innocuous probing, Jevne asked:

Q. At any time did you feel, when you had this conversation with Lieutenant Ambort about what had taken place on the patrol, that he was trying in any way to get you to incriminate yourself?
A. No, sir.
Q. That he was in any way trying to elicit information which could get you in trouble?
A. No, sir.
Q. It wasn't that type of conversation at all, was it?
A. No, sir. . . . He talked to us just like he was my older brother, trying to explain something to us.
Q. You didn't get the feeling that he was talking in any official capacity?
A. No, sir.

Schwarz's opinion would not determine the official or nonofficial character of the exchange. But in reply to the prosecutor's questions, he continued to paint a picture of a group of buddies, just us and the lieutenant, talking over recent events. No questioning, no need for a warning.

LeGear could only look on, knowing too well what his client was walking into, but powerless to stop him. Even if he objected in an effort to alert Schwarz to the danger, it seemed clear that his man would not see the red flag. The prosecution barreled on:

Q. He wasn't directing you to do anything? He was just, more or less, talking to you in a brotherly manner?
A. He was giving us advice, suggestions.

Question by question, Jevne did his best to negate Ambort's official capacity—his status as an officer and an agent of Marine Corps authority—as far as his conversation with Schwarz and the other team members was concerned. If Ambort were acting in a purely personal manner, he had no duty to advise the team of their Article 31 rights.

"Now, would it be a fair statement," Jevne continued, "to say that Lieutenant Ambort's relationship with you on the 20th was, more or less, a close group of friends, all of whom had certain information, [and] you were discussing with this close group of friends what was to be done about this information? Is that a fair description?"

Clueless, Schwarz agreed: "Yes, sir."

And what about Schwarz's later statements to Major Theer? Jevne went on to ask him about his understanding of his rights upon giving his first statement to Theer, and then his third statement to him:

Q. Did you understand . . . that you were suspected of killing one or more of the sixteen Vietnamese civilians they were investigating?
A. Yes, sir . . . I definitely believed it. . . .
Q. Did you understand, that night when he [Theer] read your rights to you, that you did not have to make any statement at all? . . .
A. Yes, sir, I did.
Q. And did you feel at that time that you were free of any influence by Lieutenant Ambort?
A. Yes, sir.

Jevne went through each individual right contained in Article 31. Schwarz confirmed that, yes, when he gave his third statement to Theer he did understand each of those rights. And, yes, he also understood that he was free to withdraw his prior two statements, and if he chose to do that, no use could be made of them.

Nailing it down, Jevne closed his cross-examination:

Q. And did you write that statement all completely in your own handwriting?
A. Yes, sir.

Q. And these are completely your words?
A. Yes, sir.

On redirect, LeGear could do little to rehabilitate his client. He merely added a defense shading to the decidedly unhelpful responses already elicited by the prosecution.

Schwarz was about to step from the stand when the judge stopped him. St.Amour held up the third written statement for Schwarz to see, and asked him, "Did you make this statement on 23 February because of the statement that you had made [earlier] to Lieutenant Ambort?"

It was a key question that cut to the heart of the issue: did Schwarz make his statement to Theer as a result of previously talking with a Marine officer representing the command, the entity now prosecuting him for murder?

"No sir."

Ron Ambort, having received his letter of reprimand exactly a month before, was the second and final defense witness on the issue of the admissibility of Schwarz's third statement.

LeGear, after preliminary questioning, asked Ambort about his conversation with Lieutenant Colonel Cooper, during which Cooper related the extent of the killings in Son Thang-4. LeGear could overcome his own client's testimony by showing that whether or not Schwarz thought so, when Ambort talked to the team at Ross, he had indeed been an agent of the command.

Q. Did the colonel ask you to go get some more facts for him?
A. Right. He wanted me to tell him everything that I knew about it and I said, "Well, I don't know much . . . but I'll go talk to the team and find out. . . ."
Q. Did you elicit any information from the team?
A. Yes, sir, I did.
Q. Prior to eliciting this information, did you suspect that anything was wrong?

A. Yes, sir. I couldn't help but suspect, after I had talked with the colonel and he told me directly what they found.
Q. Prior to talking to [the team], did you warn them in any way?
A. No, sir, I didn't.

Finally, a break for the defense. Ambort confirmed he was on a mission for the command when he talked to the killer team, and had suspected them of serious crimes when he did so. It was a seemingly clear combination of circumstances that required he warn the team of their legal rights under Article 31, including what they were suspected of, or any resulting statements were not admissible against them. But it remained for the defense to show that Schwarz's subsequent statement to Theer was a result of Ambort's talk, a chore that, so far, was beyond LeGear's reach.

Jevne's deft cross of Ambort quickly pushed that linkage still further from the defense's grasp. Jevne first asked Ambort if, when the team returned from Son Thang to Hill 50 and reported killing women and children, he had suspected them of wrongdoing.

No, Ambort replied. Such things happened. He had been concerned, worried even, but not suspicious of a crime. Come to think of it, when Colonel Cooper had talked to him after the company returned to Ross, he *still* did not actually suspect any criminal act.

Jevne continued: "Lieutenant Ambort, [at FSB Ross] when you went to see the members of your killer team, to talk with them, were you doing that in an official capacity, or personal capacity?"

"Official capacity," in this instance, was a status for the court, not the witness, to determine. But LeGear did not object to the question and St.Amour did not interject.

Ambort answered: "I wasn't—it wasn't put like you indicate, as far as the colonel ordering me, or I was his runner, or his messenger, or his information gatherer. It wasn't like that. He asked what I knew about the incident and I said, 'Nothing besides what I've already told you last night.' He said, 'Well, we're going to have to have a little bit more than that.' . . . So I wanted to go down and debrief the team again, so I could come back to him and brief him. . . ."

"Would you say this conversation you had with these people was a personal or official conversation?"

"Well, I considered it to be personal. . . . I wanted to go down there and give them as much advice as I could, try to help them out. . . . No official report." Although it remained highly arguable, Ambort's official mantle, and the warnings required by that status, were receding further into the legal distance with his every answer. The lieutenant continued: "I didn't consider myself to be investigating. All I considered myself doing was getting myself some information."

It was a fine distinction that continued to tip the balance the prosecution's way.

Q. And the reason that you did not warn them of Article 31 at that time, was that you definitely felt that you were not acting in an official capacity?

A. Yes, sir. . . .

Q. And would you say . . . they understood that, from the manner in which you presented it to them, that this was nothing more than a brotherly advice type of conversation?

A. Yes, sir. . . .

Q. Did you in any way intend to rob them of their own personal free choice to follow whatever course of action they felt appropriate, despite your advice?

A. No, sir.

With Jevne's cross concluded, the judge, as before, clarified through his own further questioning that nothing Schwarz had said to Ambort had, in Ambort's estimation, been incriminating.

After impassioned argument from both co-prosecutor Brown and from LeGear on the prosecution's motion to ad-

Pvt. Michael Schwarz and his lawyer, Capt. Dan Le-Gear, walk to court on the second day of Schwarz's general court-martial, 16 June 1970. The door to the jury deliberation room is on the right. *UPI/Corbis-Bettmann*

mit the "smoking gun" statement, the judge sat silent for a long moment. The parties squirmed on the uncomfortable metal chairs. There clearly was sufficient testimonial evidence to allow St.Amour to deny the motion. Whether or not Ambort viewed his acts as official, he was an officer and a member of the killer team's command structure, seeking information to relay to the battalion commander.

On the other hand, there was contradictory testimony that, if not nearly so clear-cut, would support the statement's admission. Schwarz's own belief was that Ambort had been acting not as an officer, but as a . . . a what? A buddy? Adviser? Brother? Whatever, Schwarz's opinion carried some weight, although it was not legally determinative.

St.Amour knew that if he admitted the statement the case would be infinitely easier for the prosecution, although that had no bearing on his legal decision. If there were a conviction, would his admission of the statement pass appellate scrutiny by the Court of Review in Washington?

Paul St.Amour was not one to make rulings based upon what an appellate court might later think. The statement was simply too significant not to allow the jury to consider it.

"Prosecution exhibit 10 [Schwarz's first written statement] and prosecution exhibit 11 [his third written statement] are received in evidence."

For all practical purposes, the trial was decided.

THE PROSECUTION CASE

The general court-martial resumed at 0912 the next morning, Tuesday, 16 June. All hands stood as the eight-officer panel filed into the crowded room for the first time. The members, not realizing that all were standing in respect for them, also stood behind their metal chairs, looking around in mild confusion until the judge motioned them to sit. Each had in front of him a new lined tablet and a sharpened pencil, laid out by the court reporter.

It was an impressive panel, as most GCM juries are. The senior member—the foreman, in civilian terms—was a colonel, first commissioned during World War II, twenty-seven years before. He had commanded an infantry company in Korea and had a son at the Naval Academy.

The next-senior member, a lieutenant colonel with eighteen years service, had been an infantry platoon commander in Korea and a company commander at Camp Lejeune. The next senior, another lieutenant colonel, had seventeen years commissioned service and five years enlisted time. He had lengthy infantry service, as well, including prior command of 1/9.

Five majors rounded out the panel. Two were mustangs—former enlisted Marines—and three of the five had infantry backgrounds. Another, in past assignments, had been a CID officer for seven years.

Although the members were drawn from the division headquarters staff, their extensive infantry experience was a plus for the defense. They had been through the rigors of ground combat and were aware of the moral ambiguities often encountered in Vietnam.

The members were sworn, their oath administered by the prosecutor. They were given their initial orienting instructions by the judge. As they scanned their respective charge sheets, they were told the general nature of the charges, and then were questioned by both sides as to their qualifications and their possible knowledge of the case. Most of them had read something about Son Thang in *Stars and Stripes,* the service-published newspaper available in the "rear" area. Some had heard the case mentioned on Armed Forces Radio, as well. All assured the court that they were unaware of specifics of the case, and that any reports they had read or heard would not influence them in determining a verdict.

The defense and the prosecution, in turn, announced they had neither challenges for cause nor peremptory challenges.

Captain Jevne's opening statement for the government was less than five minutes long, a sketch of the proof he intended to present. Captain LeGear reserved his opening: he would make the defense's opening statement after the prosecution concluded its case-in-chief.

The first prosecution witness was Sgt. Harvey Meyers who, like several other witnesses the jury would hear, had testified in both the initial joint Article 32 investigation and in Ambort's 32.

Meyers again recounted that, in the field, Marines often did not wear rank insignia. (Herrod, the jury would learn, wore none.) Meyers described the killer team's departure from Hill 50, as well as his warning Herrod not to just "kill anything that moved." He noted having heard automatic fire from the direction of Son Thang, and related the subsequent false report of the recovery of an SKS.

Lieutenant Grant, the next witness, repeated his story

yet again, detailing the bodies he found upon entering Son Thang-4. This time, however, Jevne displayed a color photograph of several bodies and asked, "How are you able to recognize that picture?"

"I recognize it from—she's lying on the dirt ground, on the trail next to the tree line," Grant replied. "The pool of blood next to her head. She had the dark clothing on, and the age of her, and the wound she has is bleeding by the right ear that you can see in the photograph, and from the mouth. . . . I specifically remember that two women were each clutching a younger child under them."

Grant remembered each body, and Jevne would make sure the jurors kept the victims, and their horrific deaths, in mind.

LeGear's renewed objection to showing the photo was again overruled, as were his objections to eight further pictures identified by Grant. As a photo was admitted into evidence Jevne handed it to the senior member. From colonel to major, each member of the panel grimly examined each eight-by-ten photo before passing it on. They had all seen their share of dead bodies, but these were kids and old women, with no weapons or signs of military involvement in sight. Every one of the jurors had school-age children.

Grant was followed on the witness stand by a corporal who testified to finding spent rifle and M-79 casings in Son Thang. He also testified to the number of spider-holes, favored VC sniper positions, around the ville.

Next, a corpsman with Grant's patrol testified to picking up brass around the bodies. He was not asked his opinion regarding the condition of the bodies, whether they were in fact dead, and, if so, from what cause.

Dick Theer, his crucial role continuing, then returned to the stand. He took the oath and sat down. As many times as he had detailed his story, this was his first appearance before members. They listened closely as he told of taking Schwarz's first and second statements and, finally, his third.

Throughout Theer's testimony LeGear often objected, fighting a delaying action whose fruitlessness was preordained by St.Amour's ruling to admit the "smoking gun" statement, prosecution exhibit eleven.

Jevne, closing his direct exam, turned to the judge. "At this time, I would offer prosecution exhibit eleven into evidence. . . ."

"Do you have an objection, or a motion, Captain Le-Gear?" the judge asked.

Addressed by the court, LeGear stood and replied, "No, sir." He remained standing, searching for some means, any means, to keep the statement from the members.

"Well, then, please be seated," St.Amour gently admonished. "Would you present prosecution exhibit eleven to the members, Captain Jevne?"

Each member slowly read what was essentially Schwarz's confession, while Schwarz watched. As one finished reading he would pass the exhibit to the next man, then turn his eyes to the accused.

LeGear's brief cross of Theer did nothing to repair the damage to the defense case.

At 1452, Jevne informed the court that his next witnesses, two Vietnamese women, had not yet arrived at Hill 327. Nontactical helicopter scheduling was notoriously unreliable, so the court recessed until the next morning.

The next day at 0900, an Army major, the senior Que Son District U.S. adviser, took the stand to explain the government's difficulty in finding the two female prosecution witnesses. Despite his responsibility to locate them and put them aboard a court-bound chopper, he could not find them and, in fact, had no real authority over them even if he did locate them.

Securing the presence of witnesses for combat zone trials was a constant problem, the *bête noire* of prosecutors who, under the UCMJ, were required to produce both government and defense witnesses. Vietnamese witnesses were particularly difficult to entice to court; a Vietnamese farmer could never understand why he had to tell his story repeatedly to different legal forums. And Americans searching for a Vietnamese witness could hardly look up the number in the phone book. Villages had confusingly similar names, or the same village sometimes had different names, depending who was asked. Some Vietnamese, never having travelled more than a day's walk from the ville where they were born, were unaware that it even had a name. Witness fees, payable when the Vietnamese arrived at the U.S. compound (so they could make purchases while near the shops that surrounded rear-area bases) were an enticement to appear, but no guarantee of attendance.

One of the missing women, the major told the court, was about seventy. "The reason I remember the older woman is because she got sick every time we put her on the helicopter."

Jevne rose and addressed the judge. The two women were important witnesses, he urged, and if they could not be located the government moved that, as a substitute, their testimony from the earlier Article 32 investigation be read to the jury.

"Would you address yourself to the significance of the anticipated testimony of the witnesses?" St.Amour asked.

Jevne explained that the women lived in Son Thang-4 and would testify that on the night of the murders, they saw the killer team arrive and heard the shootings; they could also identify the dead.

St.Amour, unmoved, considered the prosecution's efforts to locate the women inadequate, and would not allow their Article 32 testimony to be read to the members, who were absent throughout the exchange. It was not a great setback for the prosecution, but one more issue Jevne would have to figure a way around.

Then, after a short trial day, court was recessed for two days.

At 0900 on Friday, 19 June, LeGear addressed the court before the members of the jury entered the courtroom. "Certain information has been made aware to the defense," he said, "that one of the members has been talking to one of the witnesses. . . . I would request that the military judge inquire into the matter."

Asked how this information came to his attention, Le-Gear replied, "Lieutenant Grant, sir." He explained that, contrary to the court's instructions to the members and the oath they had taken, a major on the panel had discussed the case with Grant, and indicated he had been reading about the trial in *Stars and Stripes*.

The major was summoned to the courtroom from the adjoining deliberation room. He took his assigned seat in the jury box, alone.

St.Amour asked, "Have you, since the start of this trial, had a conversation with Lieutenant Grant?"

"No, sir. I have not. . . ."

"Did you, in reading the *Stars and Stripes*, have an occasion to notice any item pertaining to this trial?"

"I read none of them about this trial."

As quickly as that, the major was excused and left the room. Lieutenant Grant then entered and was seated in the witness box. At least he would have a new story to tell.

Again placed under oath, Grant responded to St.Amour's opening question that, yes, in the Headquarters Battalion officers' club, the major had spoken to him the night before. "I heard someone say, 'Lieutenant Grant,' and I turned around and [the major] was sitting there. And he said, 'Come over, a minute. . . .' He said, 'I see you made the headlines. . . . Your name was in the paper, today. It said . . . that you patrolled the ville, and you identified some photographs. . . .' I said, 'Yes, sir.'

"Then he said, 'Lieutenant, that must have been real hard on you, having to take the photographs, and the condition of the bodies. . . . I don't know, if I had been in your spot, if I could have done a good job. . . .' I said, 'Yes, sir.'

"Then he said, 'Well, I shouldn't be discussing the case with you, should I?' I said, 'No, sir, I don't think so.' Then he said, 'Well, to change the subject, we just had another case, and the man was a real shitbird, and up for premeditated murder. And the man was lucky he got off with manslaughter. And then we had someone who we were not really after, and he ended up getting life.' At this time,"

Grant continued, "I stated I would rather not talk about it because I had been instructed not to talk outside the courtroom."

To ensure the identity of the intemperate major, St.Amour had all five majors called into the courtroom. They took their seats.

"Lieutenant, do you see the gentleman you spoke to last evening?"

The young officer, commissioned for some eighteen months, looked the offending major in the eye and answered, "Yes, sir," and named him. It was the same officer who, minutes before, had denied speaking to Lieutenant Grant.

St.Amour directed the other four majors back into the deliberation room. He then excused Grant, and turned to the prosecutor.

"Captain Jevne, would you please put [the major] under oath?" The new oath differed from the member's oath the major had taken when the case began. Lowering his right hand, he looked expectantly at Jevne. But it was the crusty St.Amour, who at age seventeen had enlisted to fight in World War II, who asked the questions.

Q. Major . . . were you in the Headquarters Battalion officers' club yesterday evening at about 1900 hours?

A. Yes, sir.

Q. Did you have occasion to talk to Lieutenant Grant?

A. Yes, I talked to him . . . I really don't remember exactly what I said. . . . That he must be getting a little rest. I think I mentioned something about the patrol.

Q. What patrol?

A. The patrol that entered the village.

Q. His testimony in court?

A. No, sir. I said that it must have been a pretty bad scene. . . . I really didn't discuss it. . . .

Q. You discussed the patrol with Lieutenant Grant, in Hamlet 4, is that correct?

A. No, I didn't discuss the patrol.

The major's omission of the word "sir" in addressing Lieutenant Colonel St.Amour was not missed.

Q. What *did* you discuss?
A. I just said that it was a pretty bad scene. . . .
Q. Did you mention to Lieutenant Grant that you read an article concerning this trial in the *Stars and Stripes*?
A. I stated that I saw an article. . . .
Q. Did you discuss with Lieutenant Grant your having sat on prior cases where murder was alleged?
A. Yes, I did. I think I did. . . .
Q. Did you characterize prior accused . . . as "shitbirds"?
A. I don't know. Maybe.
Q. Were you in a condition, yesterday evening, that you cannot recall because of the condition you were in, yesterday evening?
A. I didn't have a drink at the club, if that's what you're getting at. . . .
Q. Major . . . do you recall at the commencement of this trial, when I addressed the members, that you not discuss the matters pertaining to this trial with anyone?
A. Yes, sir.
Q. Do you recall . . . I instructed the members not to have recourse to any outside source, concerning this trial?
A. Yes, sir.

As a puzzled Schwarz looked from the judge to his lawyer, St.Amour turned the questioning over to the government and defense lawyers. They asked the major if he had already formed an opinion as to the facts in this case. No. Had he formed an opinion as to the guilt or innocence of Schwarz? He had not.

But the major was not to escape his irresponsible actions. "Does either side have a challenge against [the major]?" St.Amour finally asked.

"The defense does."

With a derisive glance at the juror, St.Amour immediately responded, "The challenge is sustained," and he directed the major from the courtroom. The officer had violated the instructions of the judge, violated his sworn duty as a member, and now, had lied to the court while under oath.

Over the years, military law struggled mightily to escape the burden of civilian derision and distrust that past injustices had earned. Betrayals of the system such as the major's were taken seriously, and he had not heard the last of the matter. A letter of reprimand was in his future.

When the remaining seven members were called in and seated, St.Amour turned to them. "You may notice that [the major] has been dismissed from further participation in the trial. I caution you from speculating as to the reason," he said, repeating his direction to not discuss the case or read or listen to outside sources of information. After questioning each member as to possible conversations about the case, or their reading about it, all parties were satisfied that the remaining panelists were following the court's instructions.

The trial resumed with the appearance of LCpl. Mike Krichten, Schwarz's fellow killer-team member. As Krichten took the oath, his lawyer, Capt. Adrian King, took a seat in the minuscule spectators gallery just inside the door. King would ensure that no problem arose concerning his man's immunized testimony.

Schwarz shifted in his seat. Although he and Krichten had been in Son Thang together, and were from the same company, Schwarz really had no idea who Krichten was. He only knew that he was going to be bad news.

Krichten briefly described being a member of four prior killer teams, then related Ambort's briefing of the Herrod team. In response to a question from Jevne, he said there wasn't anything unusual about this particular briefing.

Then Jevne, through his direct examination, led Krichten to Son Thang-4, eventually asking about Schwarz's involvement in the shootings.

Krichten sketched in details of the first hooch and the

initial moments of the team's encounter with their Vietnamese victims. He related that Herrod had shot and wounded an escaping mama-san with his M-79, then directed Schwarz to "go over and finish her off . . . but," Krichten punctiliously noted, "I didn't see him shoot the mama-san. All I heard was the .45 go off."

Continuing hesitantly, Krichten explained that Herrod then ordered the team to kill the remaining Vietnamese, "and then everybody started opening up on the people, and by the time it was all over, all the people were on the ground."

The most savage violence tends to seem antiseptic and almost orderly in legal accounts. In the hushed quiet of the tiny, stuffy courtroom it all sounded so mundane. Jevne continued:

Q. Now, did everyone in fact shoot?
A. Everyone shot, except for myself.
Q. How can you be sure that everyone but yourself shot?
A. Because Pfc. Boyd and Private Schwarz was on my left, and I could see them shooting. And Private Herrod and Pfc. Green was on my right, and I could also see them. And I was standing behind them, sort of behind Private Herrod and Pfc. Boyd. And if I had shot, I would have shot them; shot them right in the back.

When he came to the second hooch, Krichten essentially repeated the same story, but with a significant difference concerning Schwarz: he could not swear that Schwarz had actually fired on the assembled Vietnamese.

Krichten testified that Herrod, after herding the Vietnamese from their hut and onto the patio, again ordered the team to fire on the women and children. Obeying Herrod, they opened fire.

Q. Again, how did you know that everyone was firing?
A. Pfc. Green was standing right beside me, and he was firing a -16, and Boyd was on the other side of me,

shooting, and Private Herrod was firing the -79 and, Private Schwarz, I'm not sure if he was firing or not. . . . I fired about three rounds over the people's heads.

Oddly, neither prosecution nor defense followed up Krichten's casual statement that he was unsure of Schwarz's participation at hooch two.

Questioned about events at the third hooch, the witness said that once the victims were forced onto the patio by Schwarz, the team again formed a line: "Then Herrod said to kill them all and . . . everybody started opening up on the people. I could see Private Schwarz right beside me. He was using his .45. I was using my -16, Pfc. Boyd was using his -16, Private Herrod was using a .45, and a -79 also, and Pfc. Green was using his -16."

Q. And how many rounds did you fire into these people?
A. I put my rifle on automatic and fired . . . over the people's heads and into the trees. . . .
Q. Now, what happened after all of the shooting stopped?
A. I heard Private Herrod tell Private Schwarz to go shoot the baby that was crying, but I don't know if he did. I don't know if he did. All I heard was the .45 go off.

Krichten had again identified Herrod as the slaughter's moving force and Schwarz as the executioner, delicately failing to observe the *coups de grâce* personally, while clarifying that he had himself never fired at the Vietnamese.

Q. What, if any, enemy contact did the team have, while it was in the hamlet?
A. Well, up until the time that Herrod gave the order to fire, as far as I know, there was none.
Q. And how about *after* that time?
A. I'd say the same thing. There was none.
Q. What, if any, weapons were—did the Vietnamese have in their possession? The Vietnamese living in that hamlet.
A. None.

Captain LeGear's cross-examination would have to be a matter of damage control. But things went poorly from the first question.

"Lance Corporal Krichten," he began, "I want you to set your mind, now——" At this point the judge broke in: "Question the witness, don't make a speech."

As the jury looked on, LeGear recovered what poise he could and continued, referring to the point when the team had finished firing at the third hooch. "What were your thoughts at this time? Can you remember?"

Jevne quickly stood. "I really have to object to this. I do not see that the witness's state of mind is relevant."

Judge: "What are you trying to establish, Captain Le-Gear?"

"The defense theory is——"

"I'm not asking for your theory, I'm asking what you're trying to establish."

"I'm trying to establish that what was in this individual's mind was nothing out of the ordinary. There was no intent on anyone's part to blow these people away."

Reasonable enough. Premeditated murder, with which Schwarz was charged, does require proof of a specific intent to kill.

"You can establish it via the surrounding circumstances," St.Amour replied. "You can rephrase your question. . . . The objection is sustained." Defense lawyers face uphill battles in courtrooms all over the world. It was no different in Vietnam.

LeGear asked Krichten, "Up to this point, you weren't aware of everything that was going on around you, were you?"

"Not really. . . ."

"Had you been taught to obey orders?"

"Yes, we had."

"If you had a question, weren't you taught to obey first and ask questions later?"

"That's what we were told by our company commander, to do it and ask questions later."

Through Krichten, the prosecution witness, LeGear was laying a foundation for the classic military defense: I was only following orders. Civilians, understandably, might think that defense had been finally discredited at Nuremberg in 1946. LeGear and the other judge advocates in the room knew better.

The cross-examination moved on. Krichten, a fire team leader, agreed that he had not met Schwarz until the killer team was formed. But Green, he said, was in his fire team; he'd known him for almost a month. Boyd was his assistant fire team leader and longtime friend.

Krichten confirmed that in the Son Thang area Vietnamese women and children frequently acted as combatants.

"There has been a lot of women and children that have been leading Marines into ambushes. . . . On the 12th of February . . . we saw this woman and this child out in the rice paddy, and they started to run, and we follow them, and we walked into a regimental group's CP. We had nine men killed that day. . . . Nine men out of our platoon, and three wounded, also."

"So you have learned that women and children can be as dangerous as men, in this war?"

"Yes, I have."

Indeed they were. "Women recruited as fighters fought like their male counterparts," VC main-force officers have confirmed.[19] Douglas Pike, an authority on the Vietnamese army, notes, "the Vietnamese communists erased entirely the line between military and civilian by ruling out the notion of noncombatant. . . . Not even children were excluded—particularly not children, one might say. All people became weapons of war."[20] Children aged ten and eleven were Vietminh members; those as young as seven were employed as lookouts.[21] A Viet Cong member confirmed, "Children were trained to throw grenades, not only for the terror factor, but so the government or American soldiers would have to shoot them. Then the Americans feel very ashamed. And they blame themselves and call their soldiers war criminals."[22] The tactic worked.

After countless instances of children killing U.S. soldiers and Marines from ambush, and women victimizing them through booby traps and deadly ruses, servicemen grew wary and suspicious of all Vietnamese, regardless of age or sex. The operations journal of Schwarz's command, 1/7, reflects that two days before the Son Thang patrol "a child" lured a squad into an ambush that resulted in two dead and three wounded.[23] Two days before that, a female enemy soldier was killed by men of 1/7.[24] The day before that, a VC estimated to have been eleven years old was taken under fire, captured, and detained.[25] Everyone in the courtroom knew of similar instances.

Finally, Krichten left the stand. As anticipated, he had badly damaged the defense. He swore that he saw Schwarz participate in the killing of Vietnamese at the first and third hooches, and had essentially said he witnessed Schwarz personally execute a wounded woman and a small child at point-blank range.

The final prosecution witness was Le-Thi-Thuong, the seventy-year-old Son Thang-4 resident who had finally been located and brought to court. She was there to identify the killer team's victims for the jury, which she briefly did, testifying through a Vietnamese army interpreter. Seeing a cross-examination opportunity, LeGear seized upon the woman as a means of showing the court the political sympathies of the hamlet: "Isn't it true that VC come into your hamlet, often?"

Jevne jumped to his feet. "Colonel, I'm going to object to the question on the grounds of relevancy. . . ."

"Don't tell me what you're *going* to do, counsel," St.Amour testily shot back. "Either do it—"

"I object!"

"Objection overruled."

In short order, the witness acknowledged that her thirty-five-year-old son had been a VC, killed by Marines. Another villager, she said, was a VC held by South Vietnamese authorities. One of the female victims had been a member of the Communist Association of Sisters and Mothers, and the father of another was a VC. But, the woman said, there had been no VC in Son Thang-4 on the night of the killings.

LeGear quit while ahead. It wasn't much, but it was more than he had gained from most of the prosecution witnesses. Son Thang-4 was riddled with VC sympathizers and members, but how far would that go with the jury in negating the actions of the killer team?

Once again, Jevne rose to his feet. "The prosecution rests."

THE ACCUSED TAKES THE STAND

Now Dan LeGear stood. As permitted in military practice and some civilian jurisdictions, he had opted to delay his opening statement to the members until just before the defense case-in-chief. Now it was time, and he was brief.

"Gentlemen, you've heard the prosecution's case. . . . You know the defense Private Schwarz is basing his innocence on, and that is that he acted in accordance with the lawful orders of his patrol leader." He went on to say that the judge would later instruct them on the legal essentials of such a defense while he, as defense counsel, would show the circumstances under which the killings had occurred.

Nothing flashy. Nothing novel. It was about the best one could do, given the facts. Obedience to orders was a defense resorted to numerous times in Vietnam in similar general courts-martial with similar circumstances. And it was rarely successful.

B Company's commander, Ambort, again took the stand for the defense, this time before the panel. LeGear would use Ambort's testimony to show the members the dangerous nature of Son Thang-4, and the character of the people the men of 1/7 were fighting. He opened by asking Ambort: "In what areas have you worked?"

"Charlie Ridge area, Son Duc Valley area, Arizona, Gonoi Island area, Dodge City, Que Son Valley, Que Son mountains, and Antenna Valley. That's about it," Ambort replied. It was a roll call of the most deadly areas in the III MAF combat zone, as the members well knew.

Ambort described his company's operating area, and the dramatic increase in VC contacts just before the Son Thang incident: "Just a lot. The enemy activity just picked up to a frantic rate by around the first of February. . . . Since the first part of November, we had ninety-nine casualties; eighty-five wounded and fourteen killed." Booby traps had similarly increased, he said. Particularly troublesome were enemy contacts involving children.

"On the 7th of February, I was out checking my lines during the day. I spotted a one-legged Vietnamese child, about twelve years old. He'd been hanging around the perimeter all day long. . . . I noticed him carrying some stuff in a bundle. . . . I went out there to check him out. He was dismantling one of my trip flares, and he had a Marine claymore mine. . . . He was proceeding to make his bird with all our equipment.

"On the 11th of February, I had another 'stay behind' ambush . . . the same general area where I was ambushed on the 12th. My people saw three Vietnamese boys, ranging in age from nine to twelve years old, wearing green utilities, carrying two AK-47s and one SKS rifle, coming up on our position. We killed one of them. The other two got away.

"On the 12th of February, my men were on a patrol . . . [and] they had two mama-sans running to the east . . . and they were in pursuit. Shortly thereafter they walked into a reinforced NVA platoon. . . . It killed nine Marines and wounded nineteen."

Ambort went on to describe three more contacts involving female and child VCs, painting a picture of an area awash in enemy, the enemy often being women and children. Women and children, perhaps, like those killed by Schwarz and the killer team?

Ambort recounted the formation of the Herrod team.

LeGear unwisely allowed him to include his graphic "pep talk" to the five Marines, surely no help to the defense cause.

"And I emphasized the fact to him [Herrod] not to take any chances. To shoot first and ask questions later. . . . 'I want you to pay these little bastards back.'"

He detailed what happened in Son Thang on the night of 19 February from his perspective, including his recollection of hearing small-arms fire, "what sounded like SKS fire to me."

Although Ambort might have deflected a degree of responsibility from Schwarz, even going so far as to assume some of that responsibility himself, he had not materially hurt the prosecution. Jevne's cross-examination was brief:

Q. Would it be a fair statement that it troubles you to see any people in your company get in any amount of trouble?
A. Of course. Yes, sir.
Q. And you wouldn't like to see that happen, would you?
A. Not if there was something I could do to prevent it.
Q. That's what I wanted to know, Lieutenant Ambort.

Jevne moved on to the problem of noncombatants in 1/7's tactical area, his initial question eliciting a response that a law professor would approve:

Q. What is your definition of a noncombatant?
A. A noncombatant is a momentary thing. It's somebody who's sitting there right now, not doing anything.
Q. What is your policy, your company policy, in regard to handling . . . noncombatants?
A. Treat them with the utmost of suspicion, but make sure, you know, protect them as well as you can. . . .
Q. And, do you know whether or not this policy was disseminated down to Private Schwarz?
A. Not for positive, no, sir.

Q. Do you know whether it was disseminated down to Private Herrod?

A. No, sir, I'm not positive.

Concluding, the prosecutor sought to lift from Ambort the share of the responsibility he had assumed during LeGear's direct exam. Jevne asked about the "pep talk":

Q. Did you at that time give any orders to shoot noncombatants?

A. No, sir.

Q. Did you at any time order that killer team to enter hooches, bring people outside, and shoot them?

A. No, sir.

Q. Did you ever make any suggestion as to that type of order, or intimate that type of order, in any way?

A. Not that I know of.

Had Ambort's testimony mitigated, or negated, Schwarz's role in the murders? A scan of the members' faces revealed nothing.

Two subsequent defense witnesses, a civil affairs lieutenant and a junior battalion operations clerk, were called to further emphasize the dangerous nature of operations in the Son Thang area. But upon Jevne's objection, the Hamlet Evaluation Survey[26] (HES, the system for evaluating pacification and enemy activity) was ruled by St.Amour to be irrelevant, and the civil affairs officer's testimony was cut off before it began.

The operations clerk authenticated a pile of spot reports generated by enemy contacts around Son Thang during January and February.

Looking at the bundle of spotreps, LeGear said to the judge, "I request that the reporter mark these exhibits, [and] I have further documents to be marked. It might be proper to take a recess at this point while we mark the documents."

"You can't conduct the court's business during a recess,

Captain LeGear." The judge paused, examining the stack of spotreps. "Captain LeGear, how are these so-called 'spot reports' any more relevant than the so-called 'H.E.S. reports'?"

LeGear replied, "these are the . . . contacts which took place in that area at the time leading up to the incident in question."

St.Amour remained dubious. "I'm lost and puzzled as to how this could have any bearing upon what Schwarz did or did not do on the date of 19 February."

Clearly, LeGear hoped to persuade the members that Son Thang was so consistently a killing ground that the Herrod patrol reasonably viewed its inhabitants, women and children included, as probable VC and threats to their lives. This could arguably account for the team's deadly rampage when confronted by the slightest provocation.

Granted, that would require the members to accept, or at least sympathize with, the team's asserted viewpoint and to find a provocation where there seemingly was none. But for a defense hobbled by bad facts, as well as a hostile witness/participant, and a written admission by the accused, it was a legitimate effort to raise reasonable doubt.

The judge, with equal legitimacy, saw it differently. St.Amour wished to confine the defense to the facts of the incident and inferences reasonably raised from those facts, and to the testimony of the witnesses. Other judges might have allowed LeGear's tack. But, as in any courtroom, it's a matter of judicial discretion—the judge's call.

"It's your position," St.Amour said skeptically, "that these so-called 'spot reports' might have a tendency to show that some of the alleged victims . . . were, in fact, militants of one type or another?"

Again, LeGear was not dissuaded by judicial sarcasm. The spot reports, he retorted, "show that the area . . . was definitely an enemy area with a lot of enemy activity going around, and the victims aren't here, so we don't know. . . . [The reports] will not show . . . that they were for sure combatants or noncombatants."

It was a weak argument for admission of the spotreps. Whether soldiers or civilians, combatants or otherwise, un-armed prisoners may not be shot to death at point-blank range, even if documents proved Son Thang-4 an enemy CP. St.Amour paused, considering the spotreps sitting before the defense counsel.

Aloud, he postulated, "It might remotely have some bearing on the intent of the participants in this incident; their apprehension." In response, Jevne argued that a bundle of reports could hardly prove the character of a hamlet.

But St.Amour had decided. He admitted all 123 spotreps.

Schwarz's squad leader, Cpl. Larry E. Creel, next took the stand. And almost immediately incriminated himself.

Asked to describe a killer team mission he had participated in, he unhesitatingly told about the patrol in which he had dropped a fragmentation grenade into a Vietnamese family's bunker to silence an old man who was yelling to another Vietnamese: "He starts clamoring, with a lot of racket and stuff. He's got a rifle or something, so I went over and fragged him." This unblushing recitation was followed by another describing how his team had "opened up" on several Vietnamese women unwise enough to have then run from him.

Jevne promptly asked that Creel be warned of his Article 31 rights, including that to remain silent.

"Captain LeGear," the judge dryly inquired, "what is your expectation with regard to further testimony from this witness? Is it going to be in the nature of his personal experiences in the field in Vietnam, here?"

"Yes, sir."

The judge turned to the witness. "Corporal Creel, has anyone suggested to you that you might talk to an attorney . . . before testifying in this court, today?"

"No, sir." A stranger in a strange land.

"Captain LeGear, I'll allow you to continue examining this witness, however, Corporal Creel, please do not answer any questions . . . unless I specifically indicate that you are to answer the question. Do you understand?"

"Yes, sir."

The judge personally was going to ensure that the witness would not unwittingly further incriminate himself by his responses ("unwittingly" seemed the operative word with this witness). "Proceed, Captain LeGear."

"I want you to continue and describe generally—"

St.Amour angrily broke in, "I want you to *question* this man, I don't want you to tell him to continue."

No narrative was to be allowed from the witness; no "tell us a story." It was to be question and answer, by the book, not only because that is the correct method of trial examination, but also to avoid Creel's further self-incrimination.

The corporal, in response to LeGear's direct questions, told of incidents near Son Thang-4 where he had been fired upon by women and children. Some had already been heard by the jury, some were new.

One such event occurred on the very morning of the Son Thang incident, Creel said. And a week before that, he and his squad had fired on ten- or twelve-year-old children who carried SKSs. Two days before that, an unarmed female VC sentry had been killed when she raised an alarm. Only three weeks before Schwarz's trial, a Creel-led patrol had killed another woman, this time armed with an AK-47. It must have seemed to the jury that there were no adult male combatants around Son Thang.

Concluding his direct examination, Creel testified that B Company killer teams had been particularly effective in locating and killing VC. On cross, Jevne immediately went to that assertion: "Was that one of the killer teams that you were describing earlier, when you . . . fragged the bunker and shot down the three women—"

Now St.Amour interrupted the prosecutor: "Don't answer that question! Captain Jevne, a moment ago you were rather solicitous about this witness's welfare, and now I find you making an effort to attack. Please remember, you represent the government."

"Yes, sir. I understand that."
"Conduct yourself accordingly."
Jevne tried another question:

Q. Have you ever known a killer team to hit one hooch in
   one ville, and then move along to the next hooch and hit
   another one, and move along to yet a third hooch and
   hit that hooch?
A. It depends on the situation.
Q. Have you ever known it to happen, Corporal Creel? . . .
A. No, sir. . . .
Q. Has it ever been a part of your procedure to bring people outside a hooch, who were not moving around outside to begin with, and to simply shoot them down? . . .
A. No, sir.

There being no further questions, St.Amour said, "Corporal Creel, you're excused." Creel rose, starting for the
door, but the judge spoke again: "One moment, please,
Corporal Creel!" Creel froze in mid-stride. "Before you talk
to any of the reporters it might be good if you talk to a
lawyer yourself." There were quite a few reporters just outside the courtroom door.

Next up was 2d Lt. Bob Carney, still the commander of
B Company's 2d Platoon and still less than six months in-
country. He related how Herrod had been selected to lead
the team, but he was asked little else.

The GCM had convened on the preceding Monday
morning. After Carney's brief defense testimony, the court
recessed at 1616 on Friday afternoon. It was to reconvene
the next morning.

Schwarz stood, as did everyone else in the room except
the judge, as the jury filed out of the room. Then Schwarz
and his counsel walked out of the makeshift courtroom,
wordlessly pushing through the gathered television and
print journalists waiting just outside the door. Courts-martial, like civilian trials, are open to the public, even in Vietnam where there was no public to speak of. Reporters

could observe the trial from inside the courtroom, and one or two did, but most loitered outside, where they could smoke and joke with fellow journalists. They knew that a criminal trial, civilian or military, is for the most part boredom of a high order.

LeGear and Schwarz discussed the next day's events in LeGear's cubicle-cum-office in the defense counsel's hut, several yards up the hill from the courtroom. They also considered whether Schwarz should testify. Putting him on the stand would be risky, but LeGear was coming to believe it was necessary, to give them a chance of convincing the members that Schwarz had only been Herrod's tool.

Finally, LeGear nodded to Schwarz's chaser, the armed Marine escort who shadowed the accused whenever he was not in the courtroom. Chaser and prisoner climbed into the waiting Jeep-like Mighty Mite and drove off toward the III MAF brig, several miles away. There, Schwarz and several hundred other prisoners would get chow and spend the night in their cinder-block huts.

At 0905 on Saturday morning, the first witness for the defense was Lt. Col. Cooper, 1/7's commander.

In an earlier, curiously defense-oriented interview for a *Los Angeles Times* article ("Marine Officer Tells Pressures on 5 Charged in 'New My Lai'"),[27] Cooper was quoted as saying, "You've got to realize the tremendous mental pressure these men are under," and he described the Que Son Valley as "real Indian country . . . everything that moves out there after dark is the enemy, it's that vicious." All Vietnamese, even children, he added, were potential enemies.

Not often does a battalion commander testify on behalf of a Marine accused of multiple murder. Drawing a fine distinction in this regard, Cooper later wrote, "I did not ask to be a defense witness but offered to testify for any or all of the defendants on the complexities and obfuscations of the battlefield. . . . They needed to be judged by people who had an in-depth understanding of the frustration, constant danger, and fog of war these young troopers lived under in Que Son Valley."[28]

Army psychologist Dave Grossman writes, "The sheer horror of atrocity serves . . . to generate disbelief in distant observers. . . . It is difficult to believe and accept that anyone *we* like and identify with is capable of these acts against our fellow human beings."[29] Maj. Bob Blum, who conducted the initial joint Article 32 investigation, commented that Lieutenant Colonel Cooper "could never quite accept as true that *his* Marines could commit murder. . . . Cooper would have rationalized the facts away if he could have."[30]

This was not the first time Cooper had been a GCM defense witness. Seven years before, he had testified on Okinawa for a Marine charged with black-market sales of U.S. ordnance. The accused was a Korean War veteran. Cooper, who was a platoon commander in that conflict, had been very seriously wounded by machine gun fire during the battle for the Punchbowl. One of the men who pulled him from the line of fire was the NCO later charged with black-marketeering. Cooper remembered, and did what he could for that Marine.[31] Perhaps he viewed Schwarz, too, as worthy of his assistance.

After describing 1/7's operating zone, Cooper testified that the area around Son Thang "is honeycombed with bunkers, trench lines, spider holes, a million and one places a unit could be ambushed, or that the enemy could hide himself very effectively. . . . There was constant contact, day and night . . . the area was loaded."

Asked about the role of women and children in enemy operations, he replied, "Unfortunately, a good percentage of the kills in my battalion . . . had been women VC. Armed women usually, nurses, and there is no way to distinguish them at night when they are moving with other units, but they're fighters." He related contacts in which his men had killed teenagers and even younger children. A small child, he said, had motioned a patrol over, leading them into a booby trap that killed one Marine. "Then, when the rest of the squad moved forward, this individual picked up an AK and killed one of the men and wounded two others. . . . We've had relatively small children, not babies, but very young people involved."

The colonel described instances of VC employing U.S. M-16s against Marines. "You could tell by its distinctive sound," he noted.

Although he had not been in Son Thang when the alleged crimes were committed, and could say nothing about the actual events for which Schwarz was on trial, the battalion CO was a definite asset for the defense, essentially a witness in extenuation and mitigation in the midst of the defense case-in-chief—a witness who also anticipated and responded to several prosecution thrusts.

His testimony suggested to the members that the Son Thang victims were not necessarily innocents, and that the firing heard from Son Thang by Marines on Hill 50 could have been enemy fire, even if it sounded like American M-16s. There were even instances, Cooper pointed out, of VC personnel wearing portions of U.S. uniforms. One thought remained unspoken: Was Cooper suggesting that perhaps the victims had not been killed by Marines, after all? Le-Gear did not pursue that line of questioning, the implication being sufficient.

"The one characteristic of the enemy," Cooper testified, "was that he almost religiously policed up . . . places where we had an extended fire fight. Frequently, we would go in there and there would be little evidence that he had been there. . . ." LeGear looked at the members. There was no need to tell them that could explain why Theer's patrol found no enemy shell casings in Son Thang.

Then, in a bit of hearsay to which there was no objection, the colonel noted that the Vietnamese district chief had told him the area "was strictly a VC haven, and it was mostly VC families, and even though there were quite a few people out there that were not interested in helping the VC, they were being forced to do so." Another score for the defense.

LeGear then probed the sensitive issue first raised in his examination of Krichten: obedience to orders.

He asked the colonel, "In your battalion, and throughout your Marine Corps career, have you ever given any instruction regarding when the individual Marine has a duty to disobey an order?"

Cooper responded, "I'd have to say, frankly, in my twenty years commissioned service, I know of no time, or period of instruction, where an individual Marine was told he could disobey an order. . . . During the instruction to the men on the rules of engagement the subject of war crimes was briefly mentioned. But as far as I know, no instruction given to my knowledge—I've never heard of any—would indicate to a man on any certain occasion that he could disobey an order."

"Who," LeGear continued on another tack, "is ultimately responsible for determining who the enemy is, and when to fire on them, when to engage them?"

Cooper's thoughtful answer nicely fit the thrust of the killer team's defense. "This question, particularly in the crux of this war, who is the enemy—I could talk for a long time on this. But, basically, the leader in charge of the sub-unit is the one that has to make this decision. Whether it be at company level, platoon, squad, fire team or small patrol. . . . So, basically, at one time or another every Marine in-country has to make a decision as to whether it's the enemy or not. And . . . if he doesn't fire, it may endanger him. This is really the never-ending difficulty of this war, and something that we have to stay on top of all the time when we're having close contact in amongst civilians, really in many instances."

LeGear thanked his witness and sat down. Jevne stood.

Cooper was not an easy witness to cross-examine. In courts-martial it is unusual for a hostile witness to be senior in rank to the examining lawyer. Not only must the judge advocate conduct a legally probative questioning, he or she must also keep in mind the witness's seniority and the military deference it demands. That need to maintain military respect for a senior officer was particularly important with a panel of majors and colonels watching the exchange. The fact that Cooper commanded a heavily engaged infantry battalion did nothing to lessen Captain Jevne's task.

In fact, he made no effort to shake or dissuade Cooper from his testimony. Instead, he sought to reinforce testimonial chinks with a few brief questions.

Q. This particular hamlet that is involved in this case, Colonel. Are you familiar with the location of that hamlet?
A. Yes, I am.
Q. That's actually reasonably close to Fire Support Base Ross?
A. Yes. I forget the exact distance. It's 1,500 meters, approximately, from Ross.
Q. So, this is not one of those hamlets which was way down in the uncontrolled, in the free-fire zone, at that time?
A. This was a very unfriendly hamlet, I might say. We had much contact around there. . . .

Now the members appreciated, if they had not already, that the killer team had not been isolated, alone in a sea of enemy women and children. They were less than a mile from their own patrol base, by Cooper's reckoning, well within range of supporting artillery, even mortar fire, and a strong reaction force at Ross, minutes away by helicopter.

Q. Colonel, you indicated that you knew or had heard about these VC or NVA using women as fighters. Have you ever seen or heard about the VC or NVA using blind women as fighters?
A. Using blind women?
Q. Blind women.
A. No.
Q. What about three- and four-year-old children? Have you

ever heard about the VC and NVA using them as fighters, as actual combatants?

A. I—No. I know of no instance. . . .

Jevne asked about the rules of engagement discussed on direct examination: What were the rules when Marines were in a village at night?

A. The intent of the rules of engagement are that the ville itself was a sanctuary and a privileged place for the VC—I mean, for the Vietnamese civilians. . . .

Q. Under what circumstances could [Marines] shoot at those Vietnamese outside the hooch?

A. I'd say, if the enemy, or if an individual threatened them in any way . . . or if they received fire. . . . That's my judgment.

Q. Yes, sir. And would you say that generally would be the philosophy that's passed on down to your troops? . . .

A. I don't believe in our formal instruction at battalion level we got this specific. We couldn't. That's my interpretation of what was passed on at company and platoon and squad level. It's an understanding of what could be done. . . .

Q. Yes, sir. Now, Colonel . . . do you know whether or not all the new people that came into your battalion went through this instruction?

A. I know that all the new people were programmed to go through it. I have no doubt that possibly under the pressure of various missions that we had, some people missed it. I know one officer in particular in Bravo Company was immediately put into a job and didn't get this . . . briefing. It was Lieutenant Carney. . . .

Although Schwarz's platoon commander had not received the instruction mandated by Marine Corps and MACV orders, Schwarz had. On the day he arrived in-country in October of the previous year, he received "individual responsibility instruction as required by DivO

1610.5," according to an entry in his service record, signed by his Recon Battalion company commander.

There was no redirect examination, and the colonel was excused.

The final witness for the defense was the accused. Private Schwarz and his lawyer decided that they had little choice, risky as it might be.

The person charged in a military trial has the same right to silence as his civilian counterpart. No military accused may be forced to testify, and the members are instructed by the judge that they may draw no negative conclusion from the accused's decision not to testify. But every criminal trial lawyer knows that a jury wants the accused to look them in the eye and swear he didn't do it—the court's instructions be damned.

In this GCM, particularly, Schwarz *had* to try to explain his own written statement, already admitted in evidence and read by each member.

All eyes were on the young Marine as he walked the few steps from his position beside his lawyer to the stand. He was sworn, then sat on the metal chair.

"Private Schwarz, I want you to start—" LeGear stopped short before the judge could admonish him to just ask a question. He began instead, "How old are you?"

"I'm twenty-one years old, sir."

"Where were you born?"

"I was born in New Brighton, Pennsylvania."

"How far did you go in school?"

"I went through the ninth grade, sir."

Schwarz related that he had two brothers, a sister, four stepbrothers, and a stepsister. All of his male siblings had been in military service, several having served in Vietnam. Photographs of his wife and three-year-old son were offered, but not allowed in evidence, having no bearing on guilt or innocence.

"What is your GCT?"

"Seventy-four, sir."

"Excuse me?"

"Seventy-four, sir."

That shockingly low mental aptitude score, repeated for impact, registered with those in the courtroom. Were we *that* desperate for manpower?

LeGear reviewed Schwarz's initial Marine training, then moved to the heart of his defense.

Q. Did you receive any instruction . . . with regard to obeying orders? . . .

A. About the same as boot camp. That if I'm given an order, to obey it. All of us in formal classes were given this.

Q. What if you had a question about an order?

A. Then to go up the chain of command and question it through the proper steps.

Q. Have you ever had occasion to discuss when it would be wrong, or when it would be right, to obey an order? . . .

A. Once at ITR [Infantry Training Regiment] I asked the sergeant or corporal about this; if there was any occasion, instance, when you were permitted to disobey an order, and he said there was.

Q. What was that?

A. He used the example, if I'm told to scrub out a toilet with my hands, that I didn't have to do that, that I should refuse to do it. There wouldn't be any trouble. But if I was going to refuse, to make sure that I was right.

Q. Did you run into any other occasions?

A. Yes, sir. When I was in Recon, after I got to Vietnam. It wasn't a formal class, but . . . I asked a man who was with me about it. If it comes down, you're supposed to do it. If you're ordered to do it, you have to do it. The only time that you disobey is only when it's completely ridiculous; that there's no way that you should or could do it.

Although Lieutenant Colonel Cooper, in twenty years of service, knew of no instruction permitting a Marine to disobey an order, Schwarz recalled receiving that information several times—but never in relation to refusing an order in combat.

Upon reporting to 1/7 in February, Schwarz continued, he received a briefing by Lieutenant Ambort that touched on obedience to orders. Because he had already been in-country for four months, he had received no briefing at battalion. And no instruction, he testified, had mentioned women or children as the enemy. But he was aware of the danger they represented.

"In the rear, I really didn't worry about them. In the bush, I use extreme caution, because they could do you in just as good as anybody else."

Schwarz recounted volunteering for Herrod's killer team after having joined Company B less than a week before.

"Why did you want to go out with this team?"

"To make a good impression, sir. To show that I was trying."

"Okay. Did you know any of the men on the team?"

"No, sir, I didn't."

"What did you know about Private Herrod?"

"He's a team leader for second platoon, on gun teams, and he rates the Silver Star . . . I believed he had to be an NCO or better, sir. . . . All the teams I had been out with, corporals and sergeants had been in charge, and a man with a Silver Star should be an NCO."

LeGear took Schwarz through the brief march from Hill 50 to Son Thang-4, and the stop at the apparently empty first hut, an account with which the jury was by now familiar.

Then, Schwarz testified, "We heard men's voices over in [another] hooch."

Q. What was your thought at that time? What was in your mind?

A. I figured we snuck up on some VC, and we got some. . . . We got right next to them. . . . I called him [Herrod] up to me, and we were listening. I still heard men's voices. . . . We jumped over the hedge, and over there was a porch, and in front of the porch was a bunch of people. . . . The people looked at us, started yelling and screaming. Just shouting real loud.

Q. What was in your mind at that minute?

A. I thought they were signalling the VC. . . . I went on in and proceeded to shake down the hooch. . . . I was inside, and there was a couple of hammocks, and a rack like the Vietnamese use for a bed. I went down on the floor looking under this and all of a sudden Herrod started yelling, "Shoot them. Shoot them all! Kill them!"

Q. What was in your mind at that time?

A. To get some. . . . I jumped up and ran out. . . . I grabbed my rifle, started firing, got with them in the direction they were firing and fired the same way.

Q. And what was in your mind at this minute?

A. That we had some gooks in the bushes, firing at us.

Q. What about the people?

A. I didn't even see the people. I didn't even remember. I had forgotten completely about the people. I didn't know where they were at.

Q. And how did the firing stop?

A. Someone yelled "cease fire." . . . Then it dawned on me that these people, a bunch of people were lying there in front of me, and I switched on my light. . . . Herrod yelled, "Shut the damn light off!" So, I shut it out. Then he said, "Shut that woman up! Shoot her!"

"And, who was he referring to?" LeGear and Schwarz knew they would have to account for Krichten's recitation of the two point-blank shootings in Son Thang.

"There was a moaning coming from over there. . . . So I went over there and there was a body lying there. I didn't know if it was a woman or a man, and it was covered with blood all on the back. So, I took my .45. I fired two rounds next to her head."

"Why did you fire *next* to her head?"

"She wasn't bothering me. She wasn't going anywhere. I just couldn't see shooting her."

After not shooting the wounded woman, he returned to the others. Schwarz could offer no explanation or rationale, other than Herrod's shouted words, for the team's outburst of violence and killing.

Shortly thereafter, Schwarz said, the team again heard talking, this time from the hooch they had passed by earlier. "I stopped, drawed it to Herrod's attention. He just said, 'Lead the way.'" The men moved toward the voices.

As the team approached that dwelling, Vietnamese civilians began to file from the hooch, Schwarz testified, offering no explanation for why they should have done so. Herrod, he said, was going to throw a grenade into the hut but Schwarz dissuaded him, fearing a booby-trap's secondary explosion. Instead, as at the first hooch, Schwarz entered to inspect the interior.

"I finished checking out the hooch when . . . all of a sudden Herrod yelled, 'Open up! Shoot them! Kill them all!'"

"What was in your mind at that time?"

"The gooks had come back. We had more gooks. . . . I grabbed my rifle. I started firing . . . I was firing, and it dawned on me the women and people were right there in front of me. Before I could even figure it out in my mind, my rifle quit firing. . . . I started to clear it. That was my main concern, my rifle. I reached down, I pulled it [the charging handle] back once, and she wouldn't go home. As I was walking forward I was watching it to see if it chambered a round. I was firing my .45 at the same time."

As before, Schwarz recounted someone yelling to cease fire. Then, without a pause, the team moved off, Schwarz in the lead. Again, no rationale was proposed for the fusillade that left six women and children dead on the ground.

"And, what was on your mind at this time?"

"Well, what I was thinking of was the people, back there. How I could've avoided it, if it ever came up again. I was trying to figure out, was there any way I could have avoided that?"

"What do you mean, 'avoid it'?"

"Because all the people lying back there—I just couldn't see that."

The team passed down a trail, turning left upon reaching a tree line, Schwarz continued. Another hooch came into view.

"When we got to it, all these people were standing out on the patio. It just didn't look right."

Nevertheless, Schwarz entered the third hooch. He found "an old woman," whom he escorted out onto the patio.

"Just as I started back in, a shot went off. I came running out."

LeGear asked his now-standard question, "What was in your mind when you heard that shot?"

"It was somebody out there shooting at us. . . . I turned around and just hauled out there . . . and I saw this one woman falling over. . . . I just thought, she got shot by someone. So, I got there and Herrod said, 'Open up, kill them all, kill all of them!' Then it dawned on everyone that he meant the people. Me, I made up my mind I wasn't going to shoot them unless I seen someone to shoot at. He fired his -79, then he reloaded. And, all this time he was reloading he was yelling, 'Shoot them, kill them all, kill all of them bitches!' Then, before he, just as he fired the -79, all the rounds started going off simultaneously."

"Did you ever fire your .45?"

"Yes, sir, I did. . . . There was these two people standing there in this space about this wide . . . all of a sudden, I started catching these flashes in that little opening. So I started firing through there, right on the other side of there. There were four, maybe five flashes in the bushes. I thought they were muzzle flashes, so I started hoping to hit something over there."

"What about these people? Did you shoot at these people?"

"I shot towards the people, but I didn't shoot at the people."

"You shot between them?"

"Yes, sir. I was trying to put my rounds between

them. . . . I thought I had me a couple of snipers in the bushes who were shooting at us, so I just hoped that, a wild chance, I might hit one."

Once more, "cease fire" was yelled. What happened then, LeGear asked?

"I was standing there. I heard a baby cry and Herrod said, 'Recon! Go shoot the baby and shut it up!' . . . I went over there. When I found the one that was crying, it was on my left—it would be on the right side of the group. I got down. I couldn't see no baby, but I could hear him crying, and something snapped in my mind. If you clapped your hands in front of a baby, he's going to shut up, and that's all my concern was, to keep the baby quiet. So, I put my .45 down and fired two rounds over the right shoulder—the left shoulder—the right shoulder."

"You didn't hit anybody?"

"No, sir. I know definitely, I didn't hit anyone. . . ."

"Why didn't you obey that order that Herrod gave you?"

"I just couldn't see shooting a baby."

Yet again without comment, as Schwarz told it, the team moved out, only to immediately be ordered by radio to return to Hill 50.

In his testimony, Schwarz had alleged enemy fire only at the last hooch. Even there, he irreconcilably asserted that it was Herrod's direction to fire on the assembled and defenseless Vietnamese, rather than to return fire on the enemy. It was a confused and inconsistent description.

His direct examination concluded, LeGear resumed his seat. He knew that direct exam was the easy part. He bunked with Franz Jevne and knew the kind of prosecutor he was. Jevne was personally incensed by this crime and he would give Schwarz no slack on cross. Schwarz wouldn't easily be allowed to shift responsibility to Herrod.

Sure enough, Jevne attacked from his first question.

Q. When your brothers were telling you about the women and children in Vietnam, did they ever tell you it was lawful to bring women and children out of a hooch and shoot them down, unarmed women and children?

A. No, sir. . . .

Q. Private Schwarz, you did know that there were some orders that you could refuse to obey, did you not?

A. Yes, sir.

Q. In fact, on that particular night, you claim you *did* disobey some of those orders?

A. Yes, sir. But not for the fact that I thought they were illegal orders. I just thought, morally, I couldn't do it.

Q. You didn't think it was an illegal order? It was just your own moral compunction?

A. Right, sir.

Q. You said that if you were going to disobey, you better make sure that you were right?

A. Yes, sir

Q. Were you sure that you were right when you disobeyed one of the orders, by not shooting the child, for example?

A. To me, it was right, sir. . . . Because that's what I'd been ordered. As far as I knew, these were the enemy.

Jevne left the members to ponder the juxtaposition of Schwarz viewing the Son Thang victims as the enemy, and his prior assertions that he had been shooting at an enemy firing at him from beyond the victims. Were the dead to be considered enemy or victims?

"Were you actually ever in danger on the night of the 19th?"

"Yes, sir."

"When was that?"

"On the killer team, sir. Any killer team that goes out is in danger."

"When were you specifically in danger, other than just being in Vietnam and on a combat operation? When were you in danger that night?"

"Sir, could you explain that more?"

"The question seems clear to me."

St.Amour broke in. "Let's not have any argument with the witness, please. Rephrase your question, Captain Jevne."

Q. Did you ever receive any enemy fire, that night?
A. I don't know, sir. . . . It's very possible we did—that we were fired at.
Q. Private Schwarz . . . do you recall saying in the signed confession that you made for Major Theer, "In my opinion, the patrol received no sniper fire." Do you remember saying that?
A. Yes, I do.
Q. You swore to the truth of that statement, so help you God, didn't you?
A. Yes, sir.
Q. And you did that in this courtroom, just a little while ago, didn't you?
A. Yes, sir.
Q. Which one of those statements is true, Private Schwarz?
A. Both of them, sir.

All eyes were riveted on Schwarz. Here was his explanation of his earlier written confession. But, caught in the prosecutor's double-bind, he was attempting to have it both ways.

After a long moment Jevne asked, incredulously, "*Both of them are true?*"

"Yes, sir. The statement says, 'in my opinion.' My opinion is we could have, yet we could not have taken sniper fire." Schwarz continued, "See, that night, they'd been sitting, talking to me most of the night . . . and they told me that they talked to everyone else, they knew what had happened. It just made sense to them, having believed that we didn't take no fire, and at the time, I didn't believe we took fire. In my opinion, we couldn't have taken fire."

That logic was followed by Jevne confirming that at all three hooches the alleged enemy fire came from directly behind the Vietnamese gathered before the team. Correct, Schwarz verified, at all three locations—although the panel had just heard him testify that he saw muzzle flashes only at the third hooch and, at the other hooches, had seen no indication of an enemy presence.

And, Schwarz further confirmed, at all three hooches, when he and the team returned fire, the Vietnamese were directly in the cross-fire.

Jevne asked him about the first group of victims:

Q. How many feet away from you would you say they were?
A. Ten, fifteen feet, sir.
Q. And yet you didn't notice them until the end of the firing?
A. No, sir. I didn't.
Q. Then, after this VC contact, you then turned on your flashlight?
A. Right, sir. . . .
Q. It's your testimony that you heard Private Herrod shout, "Kill them," so you came out and started firing, thinking that there were gooks in the bushes. Is that correct?
A. I figured there had to be some reason that the team leader yelled "Open up." He just wouldn't yell "Open up" for no reason. . . .
Q. Did it begin to seem to you to be a little strange that with all this enemy contact your patrol was still standing right out in the open, in the middle of the patio?
A. Yes, sir.

The testimonial fencing continued, Jevne emphasizing incongruities and inconsistencies in Schwarz's account, while Schwarz accented as best he could his lack of criminal intent and his obedience to the orders of Herrod. The more significant points had been made, but the prosecution still had additional, lesser issues to attack.

"So," Captain Jevne continued, "at the time you made this statement to Major Theer, you thought that, at that time, you had definitely seen muzzle flashes on that patrol?"

"I didn't remember seeing them, sir. I forgot about those when I first got there [FSB Ross], because no one else mentioned them." The questioning wore on, and as it did, Schwarz grew less sure of himself, beginning to falter. "Private Schwarz, as far as you were concerned . . . was all the shooting that had been done so far that night lawful?"

"I thought it was, because guys just don't open up on a bunch of people for no reason. . . . I thought, well, the second hooch—the first hooch we hit, number two hooch, well, I didn't know what to think. Then the second hooch, number one hooch, I thought there had to be some reason they were firing and people were getting killed. I just figured it was just one of those things that happens."

"But you really didn't know what was going on, then?"

"No, sir, I didn't . . . I didn't know if we were taking fire or what, and I just knew that the team leader had ordered to shoot, because I wasn't there. I was going along. I thought he knew what he was doing, because he ordered it. . . ."

"Then why, when the patrol went back in, did you not tell the company commander what happened?"

"Well, sir, Herrod started telling the story. . . . I figured that he knew some stuff that I didn't know. . . ."

"Did you go along with that story?"

"I did, sir."

Judge St.Amour suddenly spoke up. "One moment, Captain Jevne. The court will disregard the last question . . . and the answer given by the witness. What are you trying to establish here, Captain Jevne?"

"I'm trying to show that by the accused's conduct after this incident—"

St.Amour cut him off. "That, I believe, is beyond the scope of direct examination. You'll cease that line of questioning."

"Colonel—"

"You'll cease that line of questioning!"

Long pause. "I have no further questions." Jevne sat down.

As Schwarz strode back to his place at the defense table, Captain LeGear stood. "The defense rests its case." Had Schwarz negated the volume of evidence arrayed against him? It was the prosecution's burden to prove the case beyond a reasonable doubt. The accused need prove nothing. But given the daunting evidence against Schwarz, he needed to show something convincingly exculpatory with which to counter the prosecution. Only the members could say if he had.

Long after the trial was concluded, St.Amour depicted Schwarz's story as an "absurd defense," but sympathized, "What was LeGear to do? He played out the game as best he could."[32] But what appears "absurd" to the experienced jurist is not always so to a jury.

Final Arguments

The trial was not over yet. Prosecutors Jevne and Brown had evidence to refute the defense case. Jevne was on his feet again.

"The government would request a recess until 1300, to prepare its case in rebuttal."

It was 1100. St.Amour gave them until 1230.

When the rebuttal case got under way, the prosecution offered three witnesses. All were brief. First, the company first sergeant from Schwarz's previous assignment, the 1st Reconnaissance Battalion, told the court that, although he had known Schwarz for only six weeks before he was transferred to 1/7, he had seen him on a daily basis. Did he have an opinion as to Schwarz's character for truth and veracity? He did. Would he believe Schwarz if he were testifying under oath? He would not.

On cross, LeGear emphasized the short time the first sergeant had known the accused, but did not shake his low opinion of him.

A corporal from Schwarz's Recon Battalion platoon testified to the same effect: He would not believe Schwarz under oath. Another corporal from that platoon noted Schwarz's vocal hatred of Vietnamese—Schwarz said they had killed his brother. (In fact, no brother had been killed.)

"The government has nothing further, sir."

Before the case was turned over to the members, the judge had to instruct them as to the law in the case. That law is contained in the *Manual for Courts-Martial,* the instructions in Department of the Army Pamphlet 27-9, *Military Judge's Bench Book.* The members decide the facts of the case, and apply the law to those facts, in that manner reaching their verdict.

Without the members present, the judge and counsel for both sides discuss the instructions to be given them. Both sides may propose instructions they think applicable, the judge deciding disagreements between the sides. It is an important phase of the trial, for instructions can reinforce a counsel's theory of the case, or neutralize all his previous efforts.

The members were excused for the day but the court was still in session and on the record. The discussion moved quickly for such a lengthy and complex case. St.Amour later said, "My whole purpose in instructing the court was always to make the thing as short and simple as could conceivably be done and still meet the minimal requirements of the law."[33]

St.Amour told the lawyers, and Schwarz, who was present whenever the court was in session, that he would instruct the members that if they did not convict Schwarz of premeditated murder they could still find him guilty of the lesser offense of *un*premeditated murder. LeGear's protestation that the defense did not want the jury instructed concerning lesser offenses—an "all or nothing" gamble—was correctly brushed aside.

Other instructions were briefly discussed. St.Amour

asked if either side desired him to instruct as to the accused's character in regard to truth and veracity.

LeGear, not being foolish, replied, "I do not desire that instruction."

"Captain Jevne, what's your position?"

"The government doesn't feel that's necessary."

"Do you want it or don't you want it?" St.Amour was overbearing, but no appellate court would suggest he left the legal positions of the parties unclear.

"No, sir, we don't desire it."

"Does anybody want to talk about duress and compulsion?"

"The government doesn't see that raised," Jevne replied.

St.Amour was not so sure. "How about the compelling effect of the orders . . . in regard to what Herrod had to say?"

"I didn't think you were talking about that. . . . I think the order business *is* raised," LeGear said. He desired that instruction as well, since it went to his defense, obedience of orders. Also, he said, "The defense would like an instruction regarding self-defense and mistake of fact, in that, mistake of fact that they were under enemy attack. The accused testified he was definitely in fear of his well-being." Schwarz, sitting through it all, may finally have understood something of the legal argument swirling around him.

"Let's take these one at a time," St.Amour replied. The first topic was self-defense. "Captain LeGear, are you suggesting that one of the victims here was attacking Schwarz?"

"What I'm suggesting is that this instruction is relevant to the evidence in the case. He heard the order [Herrod's, to open fire], came running out, and they were shooting, and he was definitely in fear for his own well-being."

"Yes, but this fear has to be grounded in some source that he takes action against! Just because Chicken Little thinks the sky is going to fall on your head doesn't give you cause for shooting up the world. Do you really suggest that the evidence here indicates that one or more of the sixteen victims were actually assaulting, attacking, Schwarz? I'm willing to go whole hog with you, Captain LeGear, but I think you're getting to a point, to coin a phrase, off the wall."

LeGear would not forfeit this defense-oriented instruction without a fight. "In a combat situation, say a soldier starts shooting at you, and you have a weapon to defend yourself, and you shoot back in self-defense, and this mama-san is shot. That is self-defense, in a combat situation."

"Isn't that more akin to an accident?"

"Well, he indicated that he definitely felt they were coming under fire. He felt that the Viet Cong were out there! This is 'comprehension of fear,' and 'bodily harm' to himself [as called for in the self-defense instruction]. That's why he opened fire."

"At the victims, or at the supposed source of attack?" (By this time, Jevne must have been secretly pleased to hear the judge essentially arguing the prosecution's position.) St.Amour continued, "Do you think, as a legal proposition, one has the right of supposedly shooting an innocent person, if one feared he was . . . being attacked by another third party?"

"In a war zone, this is one of the things we can't apply: standard rules of law and evidence . . ." LeGear started to reply.

But that was precisely what was being applied in the Son Thang case. One can commit murder in combat just as in any other situation. Advocates LeGear, Jevne, and Brown and Judge St.Amour had the difficult task of sorting out the conflicting legal priorities while implementing the Uniform Code of Military Justice. For the first time in American history, criminality in combat was, as a matter of course, being tried in the very combat zone where it occurred. It was an inherently difficult task in the best of circumstances and calmest of venues. That it was attempted at all in South Vietnam was a testament to the commanders and judge advocates who, day after day, year after year, made the effort. If that effort may have sometimes fallen short, it far more often validated one's faith in military law, and the beleaguered judge advocates who labored to make the system apply wherever American armed forces were found.

At LeGear's appeal, Jevne interjected: "I can't conceivably see self-defense raised. I think what we're talking about is a mistake of fact. . . . The accused testified that he mistakenly believed . . . they were under attack . . . the people standing in the patio were performing hostile acts."

"Further," LeGear persisted, "as the evidence pointed out, a woman reached into her trousers for—whatever."

"She was probably scratching lice," St. Amour dryly responded.

LeGear gave up on self-defense.

Finally, at 1517, they agreed upon the instructions to be given the members. Judge St. Amour called a recess; the court was to reconvene at 1130 the next day, Sunday.

All hands were seated in the courtroom. "Are both sides ready to proceed with argument?" St. Amour asked. Because the prosecution had the heavy burden of proving the case beyond a reasonable doubt, it would argue first, followed by the defense. The government would then have a final argument, limited to responding to points raised in the defense's closing. The lawyers' arguments would be followed by the judge delivering the agreed-upon instructions. Then the members would take the case.

"Proceed, Captain Jevne."

The chief trial counsel of the 1st Marine Division rose. In Marine practice, counsel stand when addressing the court, and remain more or less behind their tables. No pacing about as in the movies, no jangling of change, no leaning into the jury box—just stand up and argue, let's see how good you are.

"Gentlemen, the government has presented a wealth of evidence," Jevne began, and for the next fifty minutes he recalled that evidence—witnesses' testimony, participants' statements, maps, shell casings, reports, photographs, and documents. Hooch by hooch, he took the panel through the events at Son Thang-4 the way the government contended they occurred.

"The government showed," Jevne argued, "that at each house the victims were removed from inside the house by the patrol. The government showed that at each house the only persons present were women and children. The government showed that none of these people was armed. . . . The government showed that they were shot down in an organized manner, the same procedure being followed at every single hooch."

He reminded the members of the child, his skull shattered by close-range fire, his brain exposed and spilled. A shell casing from a .45, a weapon Schwarz carried, was beside the child's body. Such evidence reminded them that this case was not an exercise in legalities, a test of opposing forensic skills. In Son Thang a crime of monstrous proportion, evil and debased, was committed against defenseless women and children.

Jevne reminded them of Schwarz's written statement with its unambiguous admissions, and asked the members to compare it to his assertions on the stand. And to recall Major Theer's inability to find the slightest evidence of an enemy presence in Son Thang.

He questioned the defense testimony, the recitations by Colonel Cooper and other witnesses of the dangers of the Que Son Valley: "That evidence conclusively proves what I suspect all of you might have suspicioned . . . namely, there is a war going on in this country. . . . It's no dark secret that women and children down to a reasonable age participate in this war. . . . Gentlemen, the government contends that this was not war, on the evening of the 19th of February. This was murder."

In that argument Jevne unknowingly echoed the closing argument of Brig. Gen. Telford Taylor, chief prosecutor at Nuremberg, twenty-four years earlier. In the Allied prosecution of Nazi Gen. Erich von Manstein, Taylor thundered:

"This was not war; it was crime. This was not soldiering; it was savagery."[34]

In Son Thang, even if the victims had been uniformed male NVA, Jevne said, they still would have been unarmed and defenseless. "Should they just be herded together and exterminated? No! No more than a group of unarmed American Marines or civilians should be."

He continued, "The defense has gone all the way back to . . . boot camp to show you that Marines are trained to obey orders. Of course, Marines are trained to obey orders. All of us are! . . . At the same time, gentlemen, there are some orders that a Marine cannot, must not, obey. And those orders are ones that are palpably illegal on their face.

"For example, a Marine is ordered by his company commander to rob the Freedom Hill P.X. Should the Marine obey that order? And if he does obey that order, should he be excused because he only did it after being ordered to? . . . If the order appears on its face to be lawful and the Marine obeys it, and it later turns out to have been *unlawful*, then the law gives that Marine the benefit of the doubt. We don't expect our Marines to make technical judgments about the lawfulness of orders they're given. . . .

"An order to rob a bank is inherently illegal on its face, and the government contends that an order to shoot down a group of unarmed women and children is inherently unlawful on its face! . . .

"The question you must decide is whether or not you believe it's possible that Schwarz *honestly* believed the order he was given, when he first shot . . . was a lawful order. And then you must decide that it was *reasonable* he thought the order . . . was a lawful order. . . . Could any man believe that this is a lawful order that he should follow? Or that he would be punished [if he didn't]? To shoot down three groups of unarmed women and children? Commit the offense of murder? If you think so, if you think it's reasonable to believe that's a lawful order, then you should acquit Private Schwarz."

What of Schwarz's assertion that he mistakenly fired on,

and accidentally killed the victims because he thought he was himself under fire? Read his written statement of 23 February, four days after the event, Jevne urged, and note the absence of any such declaration in that sworn document. Then Jevne held up Schwarz's statement and read from it. "The statement *does* say, and I quote, 'I don't remember whose idea it was, but it was decided back at the CP that we would say we received sniper fire.'"

For a hit-and-run killer team, the patrol was oddly unconcerned with tactical considerations, repeatedly gathering in the open, in bright moonlight. There was no testimony from any party that the team ever took cover while in Son Thang, despite enemy fire. And then, at the third dwelling, the Vietnamese filed from their hooch after hearing nearby firing. "This was certainly cooperative," Jevne noted.

What about the muzzle flashes, he rhetorically asked? Consider that Schwarz remembered them only as his trial approached. And, if he honestly thought Herrod's shouts to "Kill them all!" related to an unseen enemy, would Schwarz have leaped from cover, the hooch, into an open illuminated clearing? Twice? And then move on to another hooch without trying to evade the supposed enemy, or use the team's radio to call for support? And firing towards people standing ten feet away without noticing them, even though, three times—"coincidences and coincidences," as the prosecutor scathingly put it—the enemy targets happened to be directly behind the gathered women and children?

What of Krichten's account of Schwarz's actions? Krichten is immune from prosecution, Jevne pointed out, and there is no suggestion of animosity between the two. Is it Krichten or Schwarz who has a motive to lie? Jevne concluded, "So, there are the two defenses, gentlemen. . . . The first defense is that Schwarz did knowingly participate in those shootings, knowing what he was doing, but believing that it was okay because he was doing it pursuant to a lawful order. Or defense number two . . . Schwarz *didn't* knowingly participate in each of these shootings; rather, on each of the three occasions he was firing at the attacking enemy and it was just a mistake that the sixteen women and children, at the three different locations, just happened to be in the line of fire."

The prosecutor sat down. It was a masterful closing that clearly defined the legal issues and cogently outlined the government's case. It also revealed the defense as illogical and inconsistent.

Capt. Dan LeGear stood and faced the seven members. Schwarz, seated beside him, looked up at him expectantly. A trial lawyer's old joke goes: When the facts are against you, pound on the law; when the law is against you, pound on the facts; when both the facts and the law are against you, pound on the table.

In a military court LeGear was not allowed the luxury of pounding on the table, even though both the facts and the law were surely against him.

"Gentlemen, I want you to remember one thing: the prosecution's argument took longer than the whole patrol took on the 19th of February. Leaving the hill, the action in the ville, and returning to the hill. His argument took longer than that whole patrol."

LeGear went on to stress the lack of a ballistics report, or even an autopsy. The prosecution had failed in as basic a matter as proving how the victims had died.

Remember, he said, it is Schwarz alone who is on trial, not the killer team as a whole. Accepting, for the sake of argument, that the patrol may have acted unlawfully, that was not a sufficient basis for convicting Schwarz of their acts. What, LeGear asked, had been proven as to *this* accused, individually?

He stressed the law, reminding the jurors of the prosecution's requirement to prove Schwarz guilty beyond a reasonable doubt; the defense need not prove his innocence.

He stressed detail: shell casings were found at the hooches in places where testimony showed Schwarz had not been. When the firing had commenced, each time Schwarz had been removed from the others, inside a hooch.

He stressed alternatives: without proof that the team's weapons were the cause of death, could the jury preclude the possibility that the victims did not die at the hands of the team? LeGear reminded the jury, "Colonel Cooper said he suspected that possibly these people were trying to use us, use the Marine Corps; blame them. . . . Colonel Cooper told you who they might have been."

Could the jury say that the VC were not, as Schwarz said, firing at the team? "Colonel Cooper testified that there were many spider holes all over the place, good places to hide and to shoot from."

Krichten testified only after making a deal with the prosecution, LeGear pointed out. Krichten wasn't going to make a deal with the defense, because the defense had nothing to offer Krichten. Of course he would nail Schwarz—while declaiming his own lack of involvement!

"To get to the crux of the defense . . . Schwarz was taught to obey. . . . In combat, if you want to live, if you want to get home, you do what you're told, and *then* ask questions. Let's not substitute our hindsight, sitting back here in this courtroom today, where we can view everything after the fact . . . after we've had a long time to think about it and decide what should have been done."

Yes, the defense agreed that patently illegal orders were to be disobeyed. But the Marine Corps certainly did not stress *dis*obedience! "You never tell a Marine that! It's just impractical." Was it reasonable to expect a rifleman to assess the legalities of an order, at night, in enemy territory, in a fast-developing combat situation? "There's a wide middle ground where the ultimate legality and propriety of orders depends . . . upon circumstances and conditions of which it cannot be expected that the inferior [rank] is informed or advised." In such cases, LeGear argued, the authority of the superior should insulate the subordinate.

"The prosecution is trying to separate the defense in two. It is one defense. . . . The order was to open up, to fire, to shoot. That's what he did. . . . He's just following orders.

"Be realistic! We are over here in time of war! We are not

back in the world! These [Vietnamese] *children* are not innocent, as the prosecution would have you believe. They are as much the enemy as the gun-carrying VC or NVA in uniform. You just don't know."

The prosecution says Schwarz shot a small child at Herrod's order, LeGear continued. "But he has a child of his own—a three-year-old son. And he said, 'I couldn't do it. But I knew if I didn't shoot I would get court-martialed.'" So he feigned shooting the child. And the government could offer nothing other than Krichten's tainted testimony to support their assertion—and even at that, Krichten testified only that he heard a weapon fire, expressly noting he had not seen the actual act. Was that sufficient proof for a conviction of murder? Hardly!

What of Schwarz's written statement, LeGear asked. "Whose statement is that? His? Or Major Theer's and the CID agents'?" They talked him into those words, he did not volunteer them. How much credence should be given such a document? Little, if any, LeGear argued.

"About those pictures. . . . The prosecution is trying to have you convict Private Schwarz because those pictures are gruesome. I can't bring any pictures of *Marines* that have been shot.

"Who is the leader? Private Herrod. Private? Not according to Private Schwarz. He thought he was a corporal, or sergeant. He had a Silver Star. . . . Now, put yourself in that position." Not in daylight, not in Da Nang, LeGear emphasized. But in darkness. In an enemy ville where fellow Marines had very recently been killed—by women and children. And "you have a GCT of seventy-four, with a ninth grade education. That is you, as Private Michael Schwarz. Can *you* determine what to do?"

Finishing his own hour of argument, LeGear sat, his cammy shirt now sweat-stained and clinging. Jevne, who had been furiously writing notes for his own final argument as LeGear spoke, again rose. He was brief, pointing out for the members what he saw as the legal fallacies and logical weaknesses of the defense argument. As Jevne spoke, Le-

Gear could only sit silent, registering no visible emotion for the panel to interpret. He had done all he could; now it was out of his hands.

After final argument, the members looked to the judge. Instructions, they knew from their prior courts-martial, were lengthy, tedious, and *very* boring. Instructions are read directly from the bench book, or from written notes, adding to their eye-glazing dullness. But judges know that the bulk of reversals on appeal are due to instructional error, so they take no chances by extemporizing. Better judges use vocal inflection, eye contact, and pacing to hold the attention of the members. Like much of a lawyer's in-court work, delivering instructions is in large part theater.

General court-martial members are predominantly college-educated officers and well-trained senior NCOs, personnel used to obeying orders and paying attention to detail. Those ingrained habits make them ideal jurors, conditioned to dispassionately execute the tasks mandated by the judge's instructions, even if in disagreement with some aspect of their direction. The military member's intelligence and conscientiousness are usually safeguards against the inexplicable results occasionally seen in civilian jury decisions.

Lieutenant Colonel St.Amour covered the standard "how to" details: the presumption of innocence; reasonable doubt; the prosecution's heavy burden of proof; elements of the crimes the prosecution must prove; that rank may play no part in reaching a verdict; and the mechanics of voting on guilt or innocence.

Having tailored the instructions to fit Schwarz's case, he also detailed the law of principals, and aiders and abettors. If the members found that Schwarz had not himself killed any victim, but they believed he knowingly assisted the others in doing so, he was, in the eyes of the law, as guilty as they.

Mistake of fact, they were told, could result in a finding of not guilty. If they found that Schwarz mistakenly, but reasonably, believed that he was returning enemy fire, and shot the victims only by accident, they must acquit.

Moreover, they must agree that Schwarz's written statement was voluntarily given, not a product of any coercion by Theer, Ambort, or anyone else representing the government—that is, the Marine Corps. Otherwise, they must disregard it.

Krichten's testimony for the prosecution, they were warned, should be viewed with "great caution," as he was an accomplice, and his testimony was offered only after a deal for immunity. Similarly, they should consider Schwarz's reputation for truth, when assessing the credibility of his testimony.

Of particular importance was the so-called *Keenan* instruction. Contained in neither the *Manual for Courts-Martial* nor judge's bench book, it had become all too familiar in both Marine and Army courts in Vietnam. Obedience to orders had been raised as a defense in Vietnam long before the Son Thang incident. Military appellate courts had dealt with it numerous times, approving the instruction given in the 1969 case of *United States v. Keenan*, which involved a feckless Marine convicted of murdering two elderly Vietnamese noncombatants.

"There has been evidence in the case," St. Amour intoned, "regarding orders to the effect of, 'shoot those people,' given the accused by Herrod, the accused's team leader. The general rule is that the acts of a subordinate done in good faith and in compliance with a supposed duty, or orders, are legally justifiable. . . . This justification does not exist, however, when the act done is manifestly beyond the scope of [the senior's] authority, or the order was of such a nature that a man of ordinary sense and understanding would know it to be illegal. . . .

"If you find beyond a reasonable doubt that the accused, under the circumstances of his age and military experience, could not have honestly believed the order issued by his team leader to be legal under the laws and usages of war, then the killing . . . was without justification."

Glancing at the jury for emphasis, St.Amour concluded, "A Marine is a reasoning agent, who is under a duty to exercise judgment in obeying orders. . . . Where such orders are manifestly beyond the scope of the authority of the one issuing the order, or are palpably illegal upon their face, then the act of obedience to such orders will not justify acts pursuant to such illegal orders."

Were there any questions concerning the instructions, the judge asked the members? There were none. He told them they were to retire to reach their verdict.

Everyone in the room stood. Among the onlookers was Howard Trockman, a casually dressed civilian who had been seated in the spectators section for a couple of days. St.Amour assumed him to be a member of the press. He was, in fact, a civilian lawyer from Evansville, Indiana.

Schwarz watched the seven-officer panel file into their deliberation room. No one knew when the most junior of the seven would eventually lean out of the doorway to tell the waiting court reporter that they had reached a verdict. But military panels are usually swift in their decision-making, and so it would be in this case.

6

U.S. v. Pfc. T. R. Boyd, Jr., and U.S. v. Pfc. S. G. Green, Jr.

A War Crime Sentence

"Unaware of Massacre, Marine Defendant Says."[1] The *Los Angeles Times* summarized Schwarz's testimony in a few lines: "He put the blame for the slaughter on the patrol leader, Pvt. Randell D. Herrod."

In Oklahoma City, Herrod's two civilian lawyers, Gene Stipe and Denzil Garrison, were aware of Schwarz's finger-pointing. Weeks before, they had arranged government transportation to Vietnam, timing it to arrive two days prior to Schwarz's GCM. After sitting in on the trial along with Herrod's military defense lawyer, Captain Williams, the two civilians returned to "the world." They required no newspaper account to know of Schwarz's testimony in regard to their man, or enemy fire in Son Thang. Herrod's defense strategy began to evolve in Oklahoma even before Schwarz was convicted in Vietnam.

At the 1st Marine Division's headquarters, Howard Trockman walked the short distance from the courtroom up Hill 327 to the defense counsels' hooch to meet with Capt. Michael P. Merrill. Although it was Sunday, Trockman's client, Pfc. Tom Boyd, was in Merrill's cubicle, temporarily released from the brig to confer with his lawyers.

Earlier, the commanding general had denied Trockman's request for government transportation to Vietnam for two Evansville ex-Marines Trockman wanted as witnesses in defending Boyd. Based on their prior service near Son Thang, the two would have testified to local terrain, the Vietnamese in the area, and to ROEs. Major General Widdecke wrote in his denial (actually drafted by his staff judge advocate), "Neither one has any personal knowledge of the subject incident, and numerous other witnesses in this area [Vietnam] could testify to same defense points."[2] The general instead generously invited Trockman to bring the two potential witnesses to Vietnam at his own expense. (Eventually, one of the two *was* brought to Vietnam by the Marine Corps, and did participate in Boyd's trial.)

In the GCM deliberation room, the members discussed Schwarz's case. No reporter or observer is allowed in deliberations. Unless the panel is later interviewed, one may only surmise what went on in that small room. But, because the procedural instructions are explicit, the sequence of events in any military panel's deliberations is known.

After discussing the case for an hour or so, the senior member, the colonel, asked the others if they favored taking a vote on Schwarz's guilt or innocence. They did. As instructed by the judge, they began with the charge listed sixteen times on the charge sheet, premeditated murder.

The junior member, one of the majors, passed out slips of paper previously cut into small squares and left in the room by the court reporter. Each member secretly marked his "ballot" guilty or not guilty, folded it in half, and returned it to the major. The senior member acts as "foreman," but he or she may not employ rank to influence the others in their votes. The senior's ballot carries no special weight. Military law requires the agreement of at least two-thirds of the members for a finding of guilt. With seven members, five would have to vote guilty to convict Schwarz. If fewer than five voted guilty, Schwarz would thus be found not guilty of premeditated murder; the members would next discuss, then vote upon, the lesser included offense of *un*premeditated murder.

In conformance with their instructions, the junior major carefully unfolded each ballot, announcing its vote to the group as he did so.

It would not be necessary to consider unpremeditated murder.

Solemnly, St.Amour directed the accused and his counsel to rise. The senior panelist read aloud from the court-provided worksheet upon which he had recorded the members' findings.

"Two-thirds of the members present concurring, this general court-martial finds you, of [count] one: guilty." Schwarz betrayed no emotion. "Of [count] two: guilty," and so on, until the colonel had announced twelve findings of guilt of premeditated murder. The members found Schwarz not guilty of the four homicides at the first hooch, where they accepted that he had been inside when the firing began. Since only the required minimum of two-thirds concurrence is announced, there is no way to know if the vote was unanimous or otherwise, nor why they accepted the truth of Schwarz's account concerning one hut, but not the other two. It didn't matter.

But it mattered to Boyd, whose own general court martial would soon begin. Released to confer with counsel, Boyd had been informed that there was a decision in the Schwarz case, and he was standing just outside the courtroom door. Upon hearing the guilty verdict he broke down, shouting through his sobs, "They're a bunch of pigs, man! A bunch of pigs!"[3] Boyd pressed open the courtroom door, saying, "I want to look at them! I just want to look at the pigs!"[4] Restrained by his armed chaser and ignored in the courtroom, Boyd was led back to his lawyer's office.

Herrod, whose offer to testify for Schwarz had been rejected, later wrote, "Schwartz's [*sic*] defense had been
based solely on the fact that I had given the orders to
fire—an accurate account of what had happened, though
an incomplete one. What I didn't realize at the time was the
degree to which all of the others—Schwartz, Green, Boyd,
and Krichten—were still ignorant of the true sequence of
events. Since their lawyers had not even questioned me,
but had proceeded to build their own defenses without
hearing the full story, no one really had enough information
to put together a legitimate defense based on the fact that
we had been fired on and were protecting our lives. . . . I
should have anticipated the results of Schwartz's trial, but I
didn't."[5]

But Schwarz *had* asserted he was being fired upon, and
that he had returned fire in self-defense. He simply wasn't
believed. Maybe he didn't tell it right.

Schwarz still remained to be sentenced. Although it was
Sunday evening, the members told St.Amour they wanted
to continue and conclude the trial. In military practice, sentencing is by the same panel that decides guilt. Like the
findings stage, it is adversarial, both sides offering evidence
relevant to punishment and arguing an appropriate sentence. Because the evidence the prosecution may introduce
in that stage of the trial is limited to data from the accused's
official record, the procedure usually favors the defense.
But not this time.

Schwarz had an amazingly poor disciplinary record. In
other times he would have been administratively discharged years before for his constant, metronomic involvement with military authorities, misconduct that indicated
his basic unsuitability for military service. But not in 1970,
not in Vietnam.

With the members present, Jevne admitted into evidence Schwarz's history of non-judicial punishments
(NJPs) stretching back two years: two for failures to go to
formation (which no doubt actually reflected strings of

other overlooked and unpunished "failures to go"); a two-week unauthorized absence; a twelve-day UA; and, in Recon Battalion in Vietnam, a drunk and disorderly. The NJPs were minor offenses resulting in minor punishments. The surprise was that Schwarz also had three prior courts-martial! He had a minor summary court for breaking restriction, and two not-so-minor special courts-martial: one for again breaking restriction, repeatedly; the other for two two-month UAs. But now he was in the big league, where a special for a two-month UA paled into insignificance.

Jevne argued for confinement for life, citing the obvious justifications. LeGear, with absolutely nothing to work with, not even a letter from a former teacher or minister extolling Schwarz's virtues, could only plead for mercy and leniency.

As the members filed back into their deliberation room to discuss and vote a sentence, no one left the courtroom. It seemed likely that this wouldn't take long.

While the jury was out, Jevne and St.Amour became embroiled in a heated on-the-record disagreement. The prosecutor pointed out that the judge, in his sentencing instructions, told the members that the maximum punishment they could impose for twelve premeditated murders was twenty years to life. In fact, the correct maximum sentence was mandatory life—nothing less. Inexplicably, Jevne had not raised this point before the panel left the courtroom, but he vehemently urged the judge to recall them and correct his sentencing advice. St.Amour acknowledged his mistake, but hoping to avoid a messy corrective session on the record, coolly refused to recall the members. It was unnecessary, he told Jevne, intimating that the error would make no difference. He was correct.

A few minutes later, Schwarz and LeGear again stood facing the senior member, who read from a sentencing work sheet. "Pvt. Michael A. Schwarz, this general court-martial sentences you to be confined at hard labor for the length of your natural life; to forfeit all pay and allowances; and to be dishonorably discharged from the Marine Corps."

The court was dismissed. The trial was over.

Outside the courtroom, as he was led away by his chaser, Schwarz said to the waiting reporters, "If we did such a hell of a crime, down there, how can they give a man immunity, when he was there with us, when he was firing with us?" Hands cuffed behind his back, he laboriously climbed into the waiting Mighty Mite for the ride to the III MAF brig.

Ron Ambort, as he watched Schwarz be driven away, said to a newsman, "If I'd been smart, I'd have told these guys down there not to talk unless they saw a lawyer. But I'm not smart. I told them to talk."[6]

Twelve time zones away, in Florence, Pennsylvania, Schwarz's parents learned their son's fate through a Sunday morning television newscast. His diabetic mother collapsed. His wife, Linda, was hospitalized with shock. His father lowered the American flag from the staff outside his rural farmhouse. "And that's how it'll stay from now on!" he told reporters. "If anything happens to my boy, if he dies in prison, they better not put a flag on his casket. I'll tear it off and stomp it in the ground! . . . I don't like this a goddamn bit! . . . The charge is really ridiculous. I don't buy one iota of it. That boy couldn't shoot a dog."[7]

But his boy stood convicted of having shot twelve noncombatant human beings to death; convicted of playing a central part in the Marine Corps' worst war crime in the Vietnam War.

Throughout Schwarz's GCM no one, judge advocate, witness, or reporter, mentioned the term "war crime." Nor did those words appear on his charge sheet. Was his crime, then, no more than a multiple premeditated murder—if multiple murders can be considered as "no more than"?

There is no international legal code listing war crimes. However, the 1949 Geneva Convention IV and 1907 Hague Convention IV provide legal protections for civilians in time of war, the Geneva Convention prohibiting "in particular murder of all kinds."[8] Geneva only formalized what the Nuremberg and Far East tribunals adjudicated countless times after World War II: the murder of noncombatants, be they civilians, disarmed soldiers, or cobelligerents, is a war crime and a grave breach of the law of war.[9]

On the battlefield there are crimes, there are war crimes, and there are grave breaches. One soldier punching another in an argument, or the theft of personal property—those are simple crimes, whether committed in a combat zone or elsewhere.

War crimes, on the other hand, are acts considered violations of the customary law of war, or the law of war embodied in multinational treaties such as the four 1949 Geneva Conventions. On a basic level, battlefield war crimes include illegitimate violence and the mistreatment of prisoners, acts that remain criminal even though committed in the course of war, because they are outside the area of immunity prescribed by the laws of war. The term "war crime" is somewhat misleading, for most battlefield crimes of war would be crimes in peace as well.

Thus, for a soldier in combat to assault a fellow soldier is a crime; for him to assault an enemy prisoner is a war crime; for him to kill an enemy prisoner, or a noncombatant, is a grave breach.

The most serious war crimes are described as "grave breaches" in the 1949 Geneva Conventions. The significance of this classification is that the conventions' signatories are bound to enact domestic criminal legislation for the punishment of persons responsible for such acts, and to bring them to trial, or hand them over to another signatory for trial.

Congress has authority to define and punish "offenses against the Law of Nations,"[10] including law of war breaches. For U.S. military personnel, "violations of the law of war . . . usually constitute violations of the Uniform Code of Military Justice and . . . will be prosecuted under that Code."[11] The first two sentences of the 1969 *Manual for Courts-Martial* read, "The sources of military jurisdiction include the Constitution and international law. International law includes the law of war." The *Manual* goes on to emphasize that a GCM may try "any crime or offense against the law of war" and "adjudge any punishment permitted by the law of war."[12] That application, in conformance with U.S. obligations under the Geneva Conventions and their predecessors, has long been recognized by the Supreme Court[13] and by military appellate courts,[14] notably in the Calley–My Lai appellate opinions. In such prosecutions, the term "war crime" need not appear on the charge sheet.

Finally, where offenses against the law of war are involved, the verdict of a court-martial is more than an expression of military law. As Prof. Hans Kelsen notes, "The military court, by punishing the acts, executes international law even if it applies . . . its own military law. The legal basis of the trial is international law, which establishes the individual responsibility of the person committing the act of illegitimate warfare."[15]

In Vietnam, the UCMJ–law of war nexus was particularly evident by virtue of MACV and I Corps injunctions stressing its enforcement through regularly updated orders and directives, and by ongoing training requirements for U.S. personnel—although the ineffectiveness of that training was illustrated in 1/7. Still, by MACV directive, every serviceman in Vietnam was required to report incidents which might constitute war crimes.[16] In Vietnam, as elsewhere, "a war crime is the business of the United States, regardless of the nationality . . . of the victim."[17]

The problem for military justice personnel in Vietnam was learning of violations of the law of war. Guenter Lewy writes in *America in Vietnam,* "The reporting system for war crimes in effect required officers to report on their own deficiencies as combat leaders; enlisted men, too, were not anxious to expose their comrades to legal retribution for having killed Vietnamese civilians who generally were perceived as unfriendly."[18]

Elaborate measures were taken to inform MACV personnel of the more important provisions of the Geneva Conventions, but the efficacy of those measures was questionable. Pocket-size pamphlets on the topic were distributed. Cards outlining the law of war were given every soldier and Marine entering Vietnam. ("Nothing short of ludicrous," wrote Lt. Gen. William Peers, leader of the My Lai cover-up investigation.[19])

Nevertheless, GCMs convicted twenty-seven Marines of the murder or manslaughter of Vietnamese noncombatants. Ninety-five Army soldiers were convicted of the same offenses. Between January 1965 and September 1973 there were eighty-one substantiated cases, excluding My Lai, of war crimes involving U.S. Army personnel, and thirty one soldiers were convicted.[20] The Marine Corps kept no war crime records but no doubt had its fair share, which included the conviction of Pvt. Michael Schwarz.

What prevented South Vietnamese officials from asserting their own legal jurisdiction for the murder of South Vietnamese nationals? Vietnamese civil police and criminal courts continued to function throughout the American presence. Normally, territorial jurisdiction is exclusive and complete, yet there was no attempt by the Vietnamese to gain custody of, or to try, the men who murdered sixteen Vietnamese citizens.

Oddly, the United States and South Vietnam never entered into a status of forces agreement (SOFA), the usual document concerning U.S. military forces based on the soil of another nation. A SOFA specifies, among other things, the criminal and civil jurisdictions of the "host" and "guest" nations.

To define jurisdictional issues in South Vietnam, the United States and Vietnam looked to informal practice and the brief, loosely worded Agreement for Mutual Defense Assistance in Indochina, usually referred to as the "Pentalateral Agreement," instead of a SOFA. The Pentalateral Agreement was concluded between Vietnam, France, Cambodia, Laos, and the United States in 1950, when there were only 200 or 300 Americans in-country, long before the U.S. military landings in 1965. Less than six pages long, it had broad, general terms and, initially, granted U.S. forces no immunity from Vietnamese criminal prosecution.

General Westmoreland avers that "under agreements preceding American commitment . . . discipline of American troops was to be an American responsibility."[21] He apparently refers to an annex to the Pentalateral Agreement, amended by a unilateral 1958 U.S. addendum which, in claiming exclusive jurisdiction over U.S. troops, was contrary to normal international practice.[22]

Legalities aside, Vietnamese prosecutions of Americans were politically out of the question in 1970. U.S. public opinion would not have allowed Vietnamese trials of American servicemen for purported murders of Vietnamese. Instead, the United States would discipline her own troops, and that was that.

There was one more echo from the Schwarz courtroom. A few days after the trial's conclusion, a member of the panel, a lieutenant colonel, wrote a brief letter to the CG, who would soon review the case. The colonel pointed out Schwarz's very low GCT, and what appeared to him to be Schwarz's crippling inability to fully understand the progress of the trial and assist in his own defense. As allowed by the *Manual for Courts-Martial*, the member recommended clemency on that basis.

But Schwarz's sentence reflected the military community's assessment of an appropriate punishment. The colonel's letter represented but one community member's appeal for mercy.

RELUCTANT WARRIOR?

Since the general court-martial of Pfc. Thomas R. Boyd, Jr., had been scheduled weeks earlier, it was only coincidence that it was to begin on Monday morning, 22 June 1970, the day after Schwarz's trial concluded.

Tommy Boyd, a month past his twentieth birthday, was

a slender five foot nine. He was raised in Evansville, Indiana, the eldest of three brothers and two sisters, by his mother (his father had left long ago). One brother was in the Indiana Boy's School, the other in the Army, a veteran of Vietnam. At eighteen, Boyd had been convicted of disorderly conduct by a civilian juvenile court and received a suspended thirty-day sentence.

Boyd's intelligence was indicated by a GCT of seventy-six, two points higher than Schwarz's. He quit school after the tenth grade to join the Marines for a two-year enlistment. While service record books do not specify enlistment test scores, it is likely that Boyd, like Schwarz, was a cat four enlistee.

After boot camp and infantry training in San Diego, he went directly to Vietnam, arriving on 31 July 1969, eleven months before the convening of his GCM. He was promoted to private first class two months after arriving in-country and four days after his minor shrapnel wound. Unlike Schwarz and Herrod, Boyd had been in B-1/7 since coming to Vietnam.

Before the trial, Boyd's mother wrote her congressman and President Nixon on behalf of her son. "These kids were sent over to kill or get killed," she wrote. "And when they do, they get hanged for it. Whats this country coming to? . . . If my son along with the other mothers sons are punished for doing their duty I say Lets get a new president."[23]

In reply, Mrs. Boyd received a mollifying letter from an assistant secretary of the Navy; it was a personalized variation of the form letter sent to those concerned or complaining about some aspect of a loved one's treatment at the hands of military justice. "It is recognized," the letter read, "that, in a combat environment, a Marine is called upon to . . . perform his duties under the most arduous circumstances. However, the Marine Corps is not only responsible for adequately training its personnel to perform their combat mission, but also for imposing that degree of discipline which distinguishes a military force from an armed mob."[24] He assured her that all applicable legalities and high standards of justice, etc., would be observed in Thomas's case.

The Commandant of the Marine Corps, Gen. Leonard F. Chapman, Jr., responded to two additional congressional inquiries generated by Mrs. Boyd, with a letter prepared by judge advocates at Marine Corps headquarters. "The Marine Corps is fighting in Vietnam in the name of a nation which requires certain standards of civilized conduct," the Commandant wrote.[25] He promised to send Boyd's defense counsel the petitions Mrs. Boyd had forwarded through her congressman.

Meanwhile, on Hill 327, the case of *United States v. Boyd* proceeded toward trial, unaffected by letters written or received in the United States.

Boyd would be defended by Howard Trockman, a thirty-six-year-old lawyer from Boyd's hometown of Evansville, who was an outspoken critic of the war. Boyd's mother was referred to him by another lawyer. When she asked Trockman to assist her son, he readily agreed. He neither asked for nor received payment for his representation, and even paid his own expenses. Recalling the case years later he said, "It was truly one of the most rewarding experiences of my life."[26]

Trockman and Merrill had observed the closing stages of the Schwarz GCM. Trockman was disquieted by the members, whom he felt to be "tightly bonded together as a 'law and order' group which had little regard for Schwarz's defense of having carried out his leader's order. . . . I was certain that this defense would not fly." On the other hand, Trockman said, "I was impressed with the demeanor of the judge . . . attentive, kept copious notes, maintained a professional approach to the case."

While the Schwarz jury was determining its sentence, Trockman approached St.Amour as he sat on a hillside adjacent to the courtroom. It is dangerous to discuss a pending case with the judge *ex parte*—without the other party to the case being present. The risk of error arising from such

Pfc. Thomas Boyd (*right*), anticipating the worst, walks to trial with his military lawyer, Capt. Mike Merrill. *Associated Press*

a conversation is significant, should a conviction later result, because an aspect of the case might have been prejudiced or decided outside the bounds of the record, and with one side unrepresented.

But Trockman confidently asserts, "My conversation with the judge was professional and did not involve any discussion of the merits (or demerits) of the case. I asked him, simply, whether he would be willing to try the case solo, without a jury, and if he could hear the evidence in the Boyd case 'fresh' without in any way being affected by the previous trial. . . . He replied in the affirmative."

St.Amour noted that he did not even know who Trockman was, and besides, "I can say with absolute certainty that no aspect of the forthcoming Boyd trial was as much as mentioned."[27] There is no reason to doubt the legal innocuousness of their brief conversation.

After Trockman's conversation with the judge, he had a lengthy discussion with Boyd and Merrill. With Boyd making the final call, the three agreed to a significant gamble. Boyd's case would be tried "judge alone."

As in civilian courts, a military accused may opt to be tried either by members or by a judge sitting without members—judge alone. It is a tremendous burden for a judge to have to decide a murder case by himself. While issues of law may be straightforward, deciding the contested facts when life imprisonment is in issue imposes a grave responsibility on a single individual.

Judges, military and civilian, convict more often than do juries. In 1970, 94.6 percent of the Army's 2,647 GCMs resulted in conviction.[28] In cases involving "not guilty" pleas heard by Army judges sitting without members, conviction resulted 92 percent of the time; those decided by a military jury, 83 percent of the time.

Captain Merrill knew these things generally, if not in detail, but he concurred in going judge alone, acceding to Trockman's more experienced legal instinct. It was Trockman, after all, who would be presenting the defense case. By the time a case gets to trial it is essentially up to the lead counsel; Merrill, a twenty-eight-year-old from Nevada City, California, would assist where he could.

Escorted into the courtroom by his chaser, Boyd sat in the same chair his killer teammate had occupied hours before. He dropped his utility cover onto the deck beside the chair. He was neither surprised nor reassured to see on the bench the same Lieutenant Colonel St.Amour who had just presided over Schwarz's conviction.

Presuming a lack of bias, there is no legal impediment to the same judge hearing related cases.[29] As it happened, St.Amour was the only GCM judge posted to South Vietnam at that time. Two other judges, a Marine colonel and a Navy captain, made frequent trips from Yokosuka, Japan, to Vietnam to try cases. Sometimes a Navy judge advocate—commander came from the Philippines to fill in. But St.Amour was the lone in-country circuit-riding GCM judge, billeted in Navy quarters at Monkey Mountain on

Tien Sha Peninsula, working from a desk in the Navy's China Beach legal office.

If St.Amour was bothered by the heavy responsibility of deciding a multiple murder case without a jury, he did not show it on the day of trial.

"Court will come to order."

St.Amour looked up to find Trockman sitting at the defense table. While Trockman had always known who the judge would be, the judge had been unaware that Trockman was Boyd's defense counsel. "My first reaction . . . was one of amazement. . . . I had assumed [during the hillside conversation] that he was from the media,"[30] St.Amour later recalled. "Till that meeting in court, I had no notion whatever that Trockman was Boyd's counsel or, even, that he was a lawyer."[31]

In a judge-alone trial, there is no jury for the two sides to question and address, or for the judge to instruct, or usher in and out of the courtroom as evidentiary and procedural issues arise. Accordingly, the trial moves very swiftly, compared to a jury case.

St.Amour made no on-the-record mention of his *ex parte* conversation with Trockman because, he later said, "talking with counsel prior to any given case was the usual thing, particularly in a military setting where, inevitably, you knew the assigned counsel from previous experience, or socializing."[32] True enough. But should one discuss issues of the case with counsel in those situations? Not if one strictly followed the direction of the *Manual for Courts-Martial*.

But if defense counsel LeGear could room with chief prosecutor Jevne, St.Amour was on firm ground in not mentioning the conversation. As he suggests, a fact of military legal life is that friends and co-workers who do combat in the courtroom also socialize on a regular basis. Today's roommate and fellow prosecutor could be, and often is, moved to the defense section tomorrow; the two will remain roommates and friends. And, improper or not, they will most assuredly discuss their upcoming cases.

• • •

Captain Brown, second-seat in *Schwarz,* would represent the government. Captain Jevne, although still available in the area, was only days from his RTD—his rotation tour date, when he was scheduled to return to the United States. He was too "short" to become involved in the second Son Thang trial. Brown was assisted by Capt. Gary E. Bushell. The jury box was empty as the trial commenced.

The charge sheet reflected not sixteen separate counts of murder, but three, alleging four, six, and six homicides respectively, each count reflecting events at one of the three Son Thang hooches. Boyd's charge sheet would remain as it was. Although St.Amour preferred separate counts he, unlike members, would have no difficulty differentiating between particular victims and applicable defenses, if required by the evidence.

More significantly, the charge sheet reflected that Boyd was charged not with premeditated murder, but *un*premeditated murder. The difference, a lack of malice aforethought, would have little or no effect on the prosecution case, but would impact on sentencing.

Pretrial motions went more quickly than had Schwarz's. Trockman was going to concentrate on his defense theory and was largely unconcerned with several matters that LeGear had contested, such as copies of 1st Division message traffic. But like LeGear, he did seek to exclude the color photographs of the victims and, like LeGear, he was rebuffed. No matter, really. Everyone knew that St.Amour had seen them and could hardly forget them.

Trockman also charged improper command influence in refusing his motion for autopsies. Again like LeGear, Trockman contested the voluntariness of Boyd's written statements to Major Theer and, again, he was rebuffed. Trockman anticipated as much, but raised both objections to preserve the issues for appeal. He wasn't successful in asserting that improper command influence had been brought to bear in bringing the case, either. The government having prevailed on every pre-trial motion, it was shaping up like a prosecution cakewalk.

Prosecutor Brown admitted into evidence Boyd's 21 and 23 February written statements to Dick Theer without having to go through a day-long evidentiary hearing, the way Jevne had. The earlier statement, a page long, was entirely exculpatory, as were all of the team members' initial statements: the women and children were killed in a crossfire when the team was fired upon by VC snipers.

The second statement, four pages long, was taken after Boyd was confronted with Theer's assessment of what had actually happened—or had *not* happened. It addressed the events at the three huts in only eight hand-written lines. "R.H. [Randy Herrod] called the people out side and got them all together and opened up on them. . . . R.H. said to kill them and we opened up," times three. "We told the CO a lay becous we wear scard. . . . It was R.H. or M.S. [Michael Schwarz] idia to tell the CO that we had snipr fire."[33]

The prosecution opened its case-in-chief on Tuesday morning, its witness line-up much the same as in Schwarz's trial. Platoon Sergeant Meyers recounted the patrol's departure and return; Lieutenant Grant yet again told how he discovered the victims; his men recited how they recovered brass from U.S. weapons; and Theer repeated how he investigated, uncovered, and documented the sequence of events.

Krichten was the government's final major witness. This time around, however, he would surprise those who granted him immunity from prosecution.

A day or two before, Boyd and his lawyers had visited Krichten in sick bay, where he was being treated for a mild malaria attack. Trockman suspected that Krichten was merely being kept out of the way in sick bay, away from possible polluting influences, until the trials were concluded. He was probably correct. As was their right, the defense interviewed Krichten in sick bay to preview his testimony.

Krichten and Boyd were, of course, close friends. Before

Son Thang, they had been in the same eleven-man squad for almost seven months. They had joined that squad within four days of each other, undergone the intense summer combat of 1969 together, and both been wounded while in that squad. Krichten was Boyd's fire team leader. Theirs was a tie that civilians never know. They lived together, ate, slept, stood watch, and walked patrols together. And, if it had come to that, they would have died together. "One consistently finds the assertion that the bonds combat soldiers form with one another are stronger than the bonds most men have with their wives."[34] The union between infantry squad members in combat is difficult to define but impossible to overstate. Boyd and Krichten were tight.

Trockman recalled that in the sick bay meeting, "Krichten, at first, was reluctant to talk, but he did remember that Boyd had never fired his weapon during combat, to his knowledge, and on one particular occasion when Boyd was in grave danger, Boyd either froze or refused to use his weapon. Krichten . . . felt that Boyd fired high above the heads of the victims at Son Thang."[35]

Here was a dramatic, newly revealed aspect of Krichten's story. A failure to fire one's weapon, even in the face of possible death or wounding, is recognized and well-documented. S. L. A. Marshall's classic book, *Men Against Fire,* focuses on the phenomenon as do many other books and articles. As it would turn out, Boyd's pacific nature was not newly revealed to Trockman.

Krichten repeated his revelations in court. "Witness Says Pfc. Didn't Shoot Viets," the *Stars and Stripes* headlined an article, reporting that Krichten said Boyd "'fired well over their heads when they were already on the deck,' at all three hooches. . . . 'He was aiming over the people by about five feet, and was the last to fire in all three shootings.'"[36]

That testimony was a distinctly unpleasant turn for the government. "The prosecution was totally surprised," Trockman recalled with some degree of pleasure. Krichten also testified that Herrod at first had told the killer team he was going to bag the patrol—go out and set up in a secure site all night, allowing them to sleep. Instead, Krichten said, once in Son Thang-4, Herrod repeatedly ordered the team to fire on the victims.

Judge St.Amour said of Krichten's testimony, the only direct evidence potentially linking Boyd to the killings, "It became a pivotal factor in my ultimate determination of that case," even though "I was generally disbelieving of what he had to say."[37] He later wrote, "To say unequivocally that Boyd fired above the victims' heads was somewhat more than I could accept uncritically"; he found Krichten's testimony "at best, of marginal credibility."[38]

But who can say that Krichten lied? A military psychologist writes, "At close range the resistance to killing an opponent is tremendous. When one looks an opponent in the eye, and knows that he is young or old, scared or angry, it is not possible to deny that the individual about to be killed is much like oneself. . . . Now the killer must shoot at a person and kill a specific individual. Most simply cannot or will not do it."[39]

In any event, Krichten's sworn testimony was unrebutted evidence. There was no way the prosecution could prove that, contrary to their own witness's testimony, Boyd had actually killed any Son Thang victim. No ballistics, no autopsies. But perhaps the government would not have to prove it; not if they could show that Boyd was guilty of the murders as an aider and abettor. If they could show that he knowingly assisted the other team members who did kill, that would be sufficient for a conviction of Boyd, even if he had not himself killed. Aiding and abetting is the law's response to the getaway driver who pleads that he never entered the bank that his cohorts robbed. Had the government managed to show Boyd was an aider and abettor? The judge's verdict would answer that question soon enough.

The defense case was simple and direct. In his opening statement, Trockman had told the court that Boyd was essentially a pacifist, if not in the technical sense, certainly in a personal sense.

In support of that surprising assertion, he called Lt. Ron Ambort who related how Boyd had, as Krichten testified, actually "frozen stiff" in a firefight.

Other defense witnesses, Lieutenant Colonel Cooper again among them, emphasized the dangerousness of the Son Thang vicinity. In fact, the court heard, the helicopter recently dispatched to Son Thang to retrieve a Vietnamese witness for the trial had twice been turned back by enemy ground fire.

Then Trockman introduced depositions from an Evansville psychiatrist and a minister who knew Boyd. They confirmed that he was a religious sort who emphasized the commandment, "Thou shall not kill."

On Wednesday afternoon, Boyd, a clean-cut and emotional young man, took the stand in his own defense. He swore he had not shot any of the Son Thang victims "because it's wrong to kill anybody."[40] At each hut, he said, he shot over the heads of the Vietnamese. He also pointed out that in boot camp he had not even qualified with the rifle, and his record book showed that to be true. He explained his four-week unauthorized absence, just before coming to Vietnam, as an effort to avoid the combat zone, where he might have to kill.

Weeping intermittently throughout his testimony, Boyd offered that he joined the Marines because he wanted to show his mother he was a man, and because of his younger brother's Vietnam service. He testified to his strong religious beliefs, and his efforts to abide by the Ten Commandments. He said that, in Son Thang, he had waited until the victims had already fallen before he fired. That he fired at all was only because "I didn't want them to think I was a coward. I just wanted to get out. I was scared!"[41] He was, recalled Trockman, "a very good witness on his own behalf and left many courtroom observers in tears."[42]

Herrod, upon hearing of Boyd's account, was a disbeliever. "I had known him just long enough to be reasonably certain he was lying. But I don't blame him for trying. . . . Why, after all, would a conscientious objector spend his entire tour of duty being shot at by Vietcong when he could have announced his reservations and been reassigned? The prosecutor should have been able to rip him to shreds."[43] Herrod had a point.

Because enemy fire played no part in Trockman's defense theory, he offered no testimony asserting that machine-gun fire had been heard in Son Thang while the killer team was there.

As darkness fell, the GCM continued. In his closing argument, Brown emphasized Boyd's second written statement that, "I don't think that we did right and Im truly sorry I had a hand in it." Okay, maybe it is impossible to prove that Boyd actually shot and killed any particular victim, Brown argued. But don't those words prove that he knowingly helped, assisted, or facilitated the others, and is thus an aider and abettor? After all, those are his own words, written and sworn to only four days after the event. Are they not ripe with legal significance?

St. Amour closed the court to consider his verdict. He has since said, "My intuitive feeling at trial, and now, was/is that Boyd did at some time shoot at one or more of the victims. However, there was insufficient probative evidence introduced to this effect. Boyd's guilt was simply not established beyond a reasonable doubt."[44]

The judge called the parties back into the courtroom. Boyd and his lawyers stood and faced St. Amour. "Private First Class Thomas A. Boyd, it is my duty as military judge to inform you that the court finds you, of the charge and all specifications: not guilty."

Boyd collapsed sobbing into his lawyer's arms. "It was a tremendously emotional and tearful relief," Trockman said. It was "accompanied by the same reaction by the spectators, particularly the press corps, which included the *Stars and Stripes,* AP and UPI."[45]

Did Boyd tell it right, then? How does one reconcile the Schwarz and Boyd verdicts? The Son Thang facts had not changed. The same evidence suggesting the culpability of all involved was available to both sides in both cases.

The difference lay in the dissimilar postures of the facts the defense lawyers had to work with, and the defense strategies. LeGear was hobbled by his client's detailed written admission to the charges, and by a prosecution witness, Krichten, who unambiguously nailed his man in the act. St.Amour later noted that "Schwarz was much more active [than Boyd]. There was not available to Schwarz the notion that he had just been a passenger on the bus. There was direct testimony [Schwarz was] instrumental in a personal, direct way in shooting people, such as blowing the brains out of that two- or three-year-old kid."[46]

LeGear unwisely pressed a muddled defense theory combining obedience to orders and self-defense, which contradicted other substantial evidence; a theory that Trockman knew would not fly, and the judge considered absurd. But such assessments of courtroom tactics are easy for other lawyers to make after the fact. LeGear was handed bad facts and, though his wasn't the most artful of legal defenses, he did what he could with them.

Trockman, on the other hand, was burdened only with Boyd's ambiguous written admission, and was substantially aided by the unexpectedly friendly testimony of the prosecution's sole eyewitness. Further, he offered an imaginative defense, religious pacifism, that sidestepped the legal thickets of both superior orders and improbable self-defense.

What about Boyd's written words, "I'm truly sorry I had a hand in it"? They were certainly evidence suggesting culpability. But only someone who personally heard all of the evidence, someone like the judge, can accurately measure the weight and significance of those words. Did they rise to proof beyond a reasonable doubt? The one tasked with deciding that question, and trained to do so, thought not.

The Boyd trial was not so much lost by the government as it was won by the defense. As always in a criminal trial, the crux of the case was not whether the accused did it, but whether the prosecution could *prove* he did it. They couldn't.

The Novice Warrior

In Oklahoma City, Herrod's civilian lawyers, Stipe and Garrison, held a press conference to report their recent trip to Vietnam. My Lai was major news and Son Thang, so similar, inevitably drew significant press attention. Herrod writes in his book, "The coverage, carried in newspapers across the country, accomplished something else that was extremely important: Lt. Oliver North learned halfway around the world I was in trouble."[47] North writes in *Under Fire*, "When I read the defendant's name I practically fainted: the alleged killer was Randy Herrod, the machine gunner who had saved my life in Vietnam. . . . I couldn't believe Randy was guilty. For one thing, I had trained him better than that. For another, only a coward would murder unarmed civilians."[48]

First Lieutenant North was several months into his post-Vietnam tour as an instructor of newly minted officers at the Marine Corps' Basic School at Quantico, Virginia. North wrote lawyer Stipe, who immediately accepted his offer to help. The lieutenant began arranging his return to Da Nang. He would have to take annual leave and pay his own way to the West Coast. There he could catch a government flight back to the combat zone. He said of Herrod, "I owed him a tremendous debt, and . . . I would have a chance to repay it."[49]

In Cleveland, Pfc. Sam Green's civilian lawyer, James A. Chiara, sent numerous messages to Vietnam pressing for delay in his client's trial, just as Herrod's civilian lawyers were doing. All were accommodated, to a point. Green's GCM, scheduled next, was repeatedly set back to accommodate Chiara. It was Green's assigned defense counsel, Capt. John J. Hargrove, who actually had to face the court in submitting the requests for delay. In the end Chiara, citing a lack of funds, would not appear. It would be Hargrove's case.

On 13 August 1970, seven weeks after Boyd's acquittal,

Green and Hargrove sat in the same small courtroom on Hill 327. Boyd had been returned to B-1/7 to complete his Vietnam tour of duty. Green, too, would rather have been in the bush, taking his chances with the VC.

Private First Class Samuel G. Green, Jr., was an angry young man. He saw his predicament as the Marine Corps' fault, not his. He was eighteen years old. Born in Georgia, he and two younger sisters were raised in Cleveland. His youth was troubled, involving drug addiction and repeated minor run-ins with authority that finally resulted in a conviction for incorrigible truancy and two years confinement in an Ohio juvenile facility.[50]

Although reasonably intelligent, with a GCT of 98, Green quit school after the eighth grade to drift across the country, working at temporary jobs. His civilian confinement was served during this period. He eventually joined the Marines to break out of his life's unpromising pattern, he later said. His enlistment, however, is suspect.

During the war it was not uncommon for civilian courts to give young accuseds a choice between jail or military enlistment. Similarly, confinement was sometimes shortened if military enlistment immediately followed a prisoner's release. Though such enlistments were prohibited by service regulations, hard-pressed military recruiters often were parties to them.[51] Green's record of four juvenile proceedings, and his confinement, should have made him ineligible for enlistment. If his police and juvenile records were known to his recruiter, his enlistment was contrary to service regulations. If they were not known to his recruiter—and they are not reflected in his service record—Green materially misrepresented his background upon enlisting, with or without the connivance of his recruiter. In either case, his enlistment was voidable.

Enlistment proprieties aside, Green followed the familiar Vietnam-era path from Parris Island boot camp to ITR (where he was a model Marine, promoted to private first class), and directly to Da Nang.

The significant difference between Green and the other

killer team members was that he was no combat veteran. He arrived in-country on 21 January 1970, reported to B-1/7 ten days later and, with less than six months in Marine green, found himself on the Son Thang patrol nineteen days after that. S. L. A. Marshall writes, "It has happened too frequently in our Army that a line company was careless about the manner in which it received a new replacement . . . nor was there time for him to feel the friendly interest of his immediate associates before he was ordered forward with the attack. The result was the man's total failure in battle."[52] Herrod's killer team was the first patrol Green had been on. And his last.

Many British soldiers pass their entire military careers in the same regiment. Poet Robert Graves wrote of his World War I service in the Royal Welsh Fusiliers, "We all agreed that regimental pride remained the strongest moral force that kept a battalion going as an effective fighting unit, contrasting it particularly with patriotism and religion."[53]

But the British model was not for America, which held Vietnam duty to one year (until late in the war, a Marine's Vietnam tour was thirteen months long). "A limited tour is particularly desirable in Vietnam," General Westmoreland said in 1969, "because of the intensity of combat and the debilitating climate and environment of Southeast Asia."[54] A contrary view was expressed by Col. Bui Tin of the North Vietnamese Army: "Only one year! He spends six months learning. . . . About the time he is ready to fight, he was ready to leave! I do not understand such a policy."[55] Eventually, even Westmoreland agreed with Colonel Tin. "It may be that I erred."[56]

The folly of this replacement system and the limited Vietnam tours has been noted often since the war. Because every combatant, like Green, arrived as an individual replacement, "Morale, cohesion, and bonding suffered tremendously. All but the best of units became just a collection of men experiencing endless leavings and arrivals," according to psychologist Lt. Col. Dave Grossman. Another writer points out, "Strategists had lost sight of a fundamental truth of war: combat was not just a particularly toxic form of shift work to which soldiers could be rotated in assembly line fashion. Men in battle did not fight for a paycheck, the flag, or apple pie. . . . They fought and died for each other."[57] But Green went to Son Thang as just another Fucking New Guy, knowing no others.

Green's pretrial confinement in an Army stockade, rather than the Marine Corps' III MAF brig, reflected his anger. Confrontations with guards resulted, on at least one occasion, in his being tear-gassed and placed in straitjacket and leg irons, after which he enjoyed diminished rations for thirty days. All of this generated congressional inquiries when his mother, informed through his letters, complained to her congressman. Defense counsel Hargrove responded to the congrints, as did Green himself, as did Washington. Predictably, the responses did not jibe, which generated still more congrints.

The Commandant, in a confidential message to the CG of III MAF, complained, "We are in a difficult situation as result of conflicting info concerning treatment of Pfc. Green. . . . Congressman Stokes of Cleveland placed entry in Congressional Record of 10Aug70 which was highly critical."[58] The Commandant urged that Captain Hargrove's responses to congressional inquiries be coordinated with his client's, so as to avoid Marine Corps headquarters looking foolish, or worse, duplicitous, in its own responses, which they based on Hargrove's.

It was a hell of a way to run a war.

ONLY FOLLOWING ORDERS

Defense counsel John Hargrove was a tall, lean, deep-voiced twenty-eight-year-old from Babylon, New York. A 1967 Notre Dame law graduate, he had been in-country for nine months. His only other murder defense had resulted in an acquittal. Like all the defense counsel in the SJA's office, he had been an uncredited helper in the two prior Son

Thang GCMs. He knew what worked in those trials, and what had not. He would try to convince the court that Green, whom he found "very straightforward and honest,"[59] had not actually shot anyone. The government could not *prove* he shot anyone, Hargrove believed, and Green was far too junior and inexperienced to be considered an aider and abettor of the others.

This time, members would decide the case. Trockman had gone judge alone essentially on instinct. Hargrove had appeared before too many military judges to entrust one with a murder verdict.

The members were all new. No juror had prior association with, or detailed knowledge of, any aspect of the Son Thang incident, or the prior trials. This was ensured by Hargrove's close pretrial questioning of them, and, in fact, he reduced the original eight members to five, dismissing three because of their knowledge of the previous trials. Actually, all the panelists freely admitted knowing something of the case; the potential member who knew the most, a major, had just arrived in-country and had learned of the case in the States. But as long as their knowledge was only general, and did not relate specifically to Green's involvement, Hargrove correctly had no objection to their sitting.

Military law allows an accused to opt for a panel that includes enlisted members. If that option is exercised, at least one third of the members must be enlisted personnel. The theory is that enlisted men and women may tend to view the case from perspectives officers do not experience, that enlisted men and women are more truly judged by peers from the same community of rank. But "peers" are rare in any jurisdiction. As a prominent civilian trial lawyer has written, "Experienced litigators know no one is ever unbiased. What they are looking for are jurors who will be *partial* to their client's case and prejudiced against their opponent's."[60] Hargrove was an experienced litigator.

Enlisted jurors are a two-edged sword. The accused may require them, but the commander selects the group from which the litigants choose members. Seldom are any but

Capt. John Hargrove, Green's defense counsel. *Col. Robert J. Blum*

senior enlisted personnel assigned to that pool. Most accused prefer to take their chances with an officer panel, rather than risk the tender mercies of an unknown sergeant major. Judge advocates commonly believe that enlisted members more often vote for conviction, but there is no evidence that rank affects votes one way or another.

Nevertheless, Green wanted enlisted members. He got two first sergeants, one an amtracker, the other serving with 1st Medical Battalion. Also on his panel were two lieutenant colonels, one from division supply, the other from division communications, and a major from motor transport. Although none of the five had served in an infantry unit in Vietnam, three were on second tours of duty in the combat zone.

Once again, Lt. Col. Paul St.Amour would preside. Although Hargrove had not previously appeared before St.Amour, he considered him a mixed blessing. St.Amour's acquittal of Boyd demonstrated his lack of preconceived opinion of guilt. On the other hand, he had a reputation for querulousness and the occasional unanticipated ruling.

The *Manual for Courts-Martial* and military case law permitted St.Amour to preside over this third trial in the series of cases in which Green was heavily implicated. Although St.Amour had a detailed knowledge of the factual basis for the charges, the fact-finders would be the five members, not the judge. In other words, even if St.Amour by now had a bias (and there was no indication that he did), he could not indulge it because the panel, not he, would decide Green's guilt or innocence. Besides, there still weren't that many GCM judges in South Vietnam.

St.Amour, self-confident, prickly, and suffering fools badly, exemplified the old line about judges. he might be in error, but he was not in doubt. "The question of recusing [removing] myself I never really entertained, because I had not perceived any reason to do so. The closest I came to it was . . . the Green case and I decided that I would not."[61]

St.Amour had enlisted in the Navy for two years after finishing high school in Pawtucket, Rhode Island, in 1945. Eventually, after graduating from Providence College and Boston University law, he joined the Marine Corps and was commissioned in May 1950, a month before the Korean War began. In 1970 he was forty-two years old and already had been passed over for promotion to colonel more than once. He was unconcerned about pleasing either juniors or seniors. He just did his job.

"Court will come to order." As in *Boyd*, the charge was sixteen counts of *un*premeditated murder. The maximum possible confinement, if convicted, was life. The accused's plea: not guilty.

There was little new in the pretrial motions. Over defense objection, Green's written statement to Theer was admitted, as were the nine color photos. Hargrove moved for a change of venue based upon the case's publicity. Armed Services Vietnam radio station records and newspaper clippings were offered in support of the motion. Motion denied.

Captain Brown, again assisted by Capt. Gary Bushell, again presented the government's case. The prosecution had learned from Boyd. From opening statement onward, the thrust of its proof was that Green was guilty of murder as an aider and abettor. No effort was made to prove he had killed any particular Son Thang victim. That was not necessary. Instead, he was depicted, in the words of the *Manual for Courts-Martial*, as having "shared the criminal intent or purpose of the perpetrator."[62]

The one written statement made by Green during the first round of Major Theer's questioning was admitted into evidence and read by each member of the jury. Although the dictated statement penned by Theer was predominantly exculpatory, Brown wanted the jury to note Green's words regarding the final hooch: When he saw one of the women reach into the waistband of her trousers, he "opened fire on her and the group, emptying my magazine. As I began firing the rest of the patrol opened fire on them."[63]

The usual line-up of prosecution witnesses appeared, among them Krichten. The government was now leery of its principal witness, who had aided in Boyd's acquittal. But Green had no claim on Krichten's loyalty. The two had met only when the killer team assembled on the day of the incident. Still under a grant of immunity, Krichten testified that Green had fired at all three hooches, although Krichten did not actually see his rounds strike any woman or child. But that was fine with Brown, since it was sufficient for conviction if Green merely aided or encouraged the others in killing the victims. That made Green a principal to the murders, subject to the same penalties as the main actors. And Krichten's testimony showed Green a principal. As the appellate opinion phrased it, "the accused was convicted by testimony 'purchased' at a price of a grant of immunity."[64]

Hargrove said that in the defense case-in-chief, "I tried to focus . . . on the fact that Herrod and Schwarz were really the primary actors . . . keep Green in the background. He was there, but we weren't sure what he did. . . ."

Krichten helped out when he said 'I really didn't see Green shoot somebody.' . . . But he did say that Green did shoot."[65] It was as much a moral defense as one based upon law.

Green, testifying in his own defense, emphasized that, yes, he had fired his rifle, but he purposely aimed to miss, and fired in the first place only upon the repeated orders of Herrod, whom he believed to be an experienced NCO, a reliable source of combat guidance. He had followed the commands of his senior Marine. Obedience to orders was again an issue.

Lieutenant Colonel Cooper, once again testifying for the defense, said that in his experience he never recalled a Marine receiving instruction on when to *not* obey an order. Marines, he said, are instructed to obey orders at *all* times.[66]

Befehl ist Befehl! Orders are orders, SS Gen. Otto Ohlendorf claimed at Nuremberg.[67] But that was not what Cooper suggested. Any order to perform a military duty or act may be inferred to be lawful, yes, and is disobeyed at the peril of the subordinate. But that inference does not apply to a patently illegal order. An order, for example, to shoot unarmed, unresisting prisoners.

Like Schwarz and his lawyer, LeGear, Green and Hargrove opted to not raise testimony that machine-gun fire had been heard in Son Thang while the killer team was there.

Closing arguments followed the theories presented in the cases-in-chief. Brown urged that even if the panel found that Green did not personally shoot and kill any victim, he remained an aider and abettor in their deaths. And even if the facts were viewed in the light most favorable to the accused, Green was not merely present in Son Thang, he actively assisted in the killings, and shared the criminal intent of the others. Was it not Green who first opened fire at the third hooch, emptying his M-16 into the Vietnamese? Did he not admit on the stand what Krichten confirmed: that he fired at each hooch, not just at the third?

He cannot pass off his actions as mere compliance with Herrod's orders, Brown argued. As the judge would instruct, a Marine is a thinking agent, under a duty to exercise judgment in obeying orders. When the order given is obviously illegal, when the order is such that a man of ordinary sense and understanding would *know* it to be illegal, obedience can be no defense.

Hargrove argued for understanding and compassion. What was Green to do, in the dark night of Son Thang? He had five months in the Marine Corps, less than one in Vietnam, and was on his first patrol. Not knowing those he was with, not knowing how to behave in combat, what choice did he have but to look to the others for guidance and example? Did we really know what part Green took in Son Thang? Krichten testified he saw no specific individual hit by Green's fire. Did he hit *anyone*? Is there any proof? Ordered to fire by his team leader, Green fired. Is that aiding and abetting murder? No, Hargrove argued, Green was merely there, at the wrong time, in the wrong place.

By now, instructions were all but decided before the cases-in-chief were concluded. "My instructions," St.Amour said, "were essentially the same in both the Schwarz and Green cases."[68] After three trials, there were few evidentiary surprises.

Notably, the defense requested no instructions. Even after twice being queried by St.Amour on the specific point—a broad hint that lawyers usually heed—Hargrove declined to request an instruction on accomplice testimony. Such an instruction would have warned the jury to accept Krichten's account only with great caution. The lack of that instruction would be noted on appeal, to Green's detriment.

St.Amour instructed the members on the law of mistake of fact, obedience to orders and, of course, aiders and abettors, among other matters. Then, after three days of trial, the court closed for deliberations. Green's panel, unlike Schwarz's, deliberated nearly all day.

When they finally returned, Green was found guilty of fifteen counts of unpremeditated murder, acquitted only of killing the woman shot first by Herrod and finished off by Schwarz. St.Amour agreed with the verdict.[69]

Now expecting the worst, Green and Hargrove braced themselves for the other shoe, the panel's sentence. And it was a surprise. After deliberating for two and a half hours, the five members returned to the courtroom. Green's sentence: reduction to private, loss of all pay and allowances, a dishonorable discharge, and confinement at hard labor for five years. Shaking his head, Green said, "Five years for *that*?"[70]

Green thought it a stiff sentence. No one else did. Five years for fifteen murders. Schwarz got life for twelve.

An inherent problem in military law, and in many civilian jurisdictions, is the lack of sentencing guidelines or mandatory minimum sentencing direction for jurors. How are laymen to know what is an appropriate sentence for a particular offense? They are informed of the maximum confinement the law allows, or the permitted range, say two-to-fifteen years in a civilian case. But there is no benchmark to which they may refer, no gauge by which to compare their case with similar cases. There is no barometer suggesting how much sentence enhancement prior convictions merit, or what this particular case's circumstances are worth in terms of punishment. Prosecutors urge a specific level of punishment, but defenders urge another, and the judge stands mute.

Judges have the experience and background to enable them to tailor a sentence to the individual criminal. Mandatory sentencing aside, judges can mete out punishment commensurate to the crime while also meeting the needs of society and the individual miscreant.

Supreme Court Justice Harry A. Blackmun wrote in a 1989 opinion: "Compassion need not be exiled from the province of judging."[71] Perhaps Green's panel demonstrated the wisdom of the jury system, tempering its punishment to reflect the community's assessment of what was fair and just. "The sentence . . . might well account for just that level of innate concern and understanding," St.Amour suggested, "notwithstanding such a matter not having been formalized at trial."[72] Others may argue that the sentence simply did not reflect the gravity of the crime. More often than one would care to acknowledge, when the victims were Vietnamese, courts-martial acquitted or imposed light sentences out of sympathy for the frustrations experienced by the infantryman dealing with a hostile indigenous population.

Military juries are never asked in any official way to explain their sentences, or their reasoning in reaching them. Green's members gave him the benefit of his youth and combat inexperience in their sentence, if not in their verdict.

ALL MARINES ARE GREEN?

Sam Green was the only black among the Son Thang accused. The only other black directly involved in the cases was Captain Williams, Herrod's appointed defense counsel, who was marginalized by the Oklahoma lawyers who took over the case.

In 1970, blacks constituted about 13 percent of the draft-age American population, and 11.2 percent of Marine enlisted strength. The Marine Corps reputedly had undergone greater integration in the twenty years preceding the Vietnam War "than the larger society managed in over 100 years."[73] Still, blacks, often lacking a basis for deferment, were more likely than whites to be drafted, to serve in infantry units and, hence, to be killed or wounded.[74] For example, the Marine Corps's 11.2 percent black population constituted 20.1 percent of its infantry population.

As the Vietnam War grew more unpopular with the American civilian populace and the world at large, discord

Pfc. Samuel G. Green, Jr. *(right)*, and his military lawyer, Capt. John J. Hargrove, anxiously await the verdict at the conclusion of Green's trial. *Associated Press*

grew in the military. By 1970, racial unrest had begun to hinder the fighting effort,[75] and racial violence, including intramural firefights, became a major problem in the combat zone.[76] Afro haircuts, "dapping," "passing power," and black power symbols were common. Marine Corps records confirm that in Vietnam, between April and June of 1969, there was an average of one "large-scale riot" per month.[77] Racially motivated fraggings and white-versus-black armed confrontations were normal cases on the dockets of III MAF judge advocates. Today, it is difficult to recall the fearful tenor of those times.

Racial problems were beginning to ease by 1970, as Vietnamization progressed and major Marine units returned to the United States. Still, 1,060 violent racial incidents occurred throughout the Corps that year, resulting in serious injury to seventy-nine Marines and two deaths, all at the hands of other Marines.[78]

Military justice also suffered racial strains during this period. Bernard Nalty, who chronicled the integration process in the armed services, notes that "statistics indicated that blacks were more likely than whites to run afoul of regulations. Furthermore, black servicemen had the greater probability of undergoing trial by court-martial ... being convicted, and receiving long sentences. ... The malfunctioning of the justice system ... resulted from the systemic racial discrimination that pervaded American society."[79] These disparities existed despite genuine efforts on the part of the armed forces to ensure equal treatment.

But there is no suggestion of racism in Green's case. The crime, and his involvement in it, were obvious; the charges clearly merited trial; the evidence supported a conviction; and his sentence could hardly have been more lenient. Schwarz certainly considered it light.

Green's defense: I was too insignificant a cog to have been of help, legally speaking, in the acts of the others, and besides, you can't prove I shot anyone. It was a slender reed upon which to stake one's freedom, and it ultimately resulted in the war crimes conviction of one more American.

In Washington, D.C., a Georgetown University law student read of Green's conviction. As a Vietnam veteran, James Webb took interest in the trial. Something about it struck him as not right, as unfair. He decided to look more closely into the case.

In Vietnam, Herrod was next up, and Capt. Brown knew it would not be an easy trial—not with the legal forces arrayed against the government. Now message traffic said that there would be not two, but *four* civilian lawyers defending Herrod.

7 | U.S. v. Pvt. R. D. Herrod

Law in a Combat Zone

Why were young, relatively new judge advocates prosecuting multiple murder cases in the first place, let alone opposing a phalanx of civilian criminal lawyers? Where were the older, trial-hardened judge advocates, the majors and lieutenant colonels?

Col. Bob Lucy, the 1st Marine Division's Staff Judge Advocate, readily admitted that his captain-lawyers "were not real experienced lawyers, there's no doubt about that."[1] In a briefing at the Marine Corps's Pacific headquarters in Hawaii, Lucy noted, "Sixty-six percent of all our crimes are crimes of violence—and they're serious!"[2] His captains tried as many murders in the first six months of 1970 as in all of 1969. But most alarming, he said, was the raw inexperience of his young lawyers.

Instead of breaking in with special courts-martial for a year or so at a stateside command, three out of four judge advocates came to Vietnam directly from law school, with only a ten-week pause at Naval Justice School where, in yet another classroom, they learned the rudiments of military practice. "That's a very, very bad policy," Lucy conceded. "We're in the big leagues now." Experienced civilian lawyers were defending many serious Vietnam courts-martial, and novice military lawyers could not learn their craft in murder cases against polished pros. But that was the situation in Vietnam in 1970.

Looking at it from a judge's vantage point, Lt. Col. St.Amour could only shake his head. "Junior lawyers I encountered in Vietnam were trying 'heavy' cases without prior trial experience."[3] Imagine taking a driver's license test in a Formula One racer, or attempting major surgery as a new intern. Law school is only the first stage of a lawyer's education. Military law, a subcategory of federal criminal law, requires time and experience to master, like any other specialty. Few judge advocates who were rushed to the combat zone were afforded the time to acquire that experience before they were trying major felonies under field conditions. Their problem was that of all military occupational specialties in all the armed services in Vietnam: the war ate manpower. There were not enough uniformed lawyers to meet military needs.

Inexperience should not be confused with ineptitude, however. These were smart kids, graduates of America's finest law schools, many of them with honors. Some civilian lawyers, in displays of egocentric ignorance, condescendingly presume that military law is an inferior species of quasi-jurisprudence, evoking images of sailing ships and Billy Budd. In Vietnam, judge advocates often lost cases to civilian lawyers, not because service lawyers were intellectually or professionally inferior, but because they lacked vital trial seasoning.

On the other hand, many judge advocates, in Vietnam and elsewhere, also had the pleasant experience of meeting supercilious civilian attorneys in trial and quietly kicking their legal asses.

All judge advocates, then and now, are graduates of

American Bar Association–approved law schools and have passed a state bar examination and a service-taught military law course. The percentage of additional specialist law degrees is far higher in military ranks than in the civilian population. Judge advocates argue before the Supreme Court of the United States—whose clerk, William K. Suter, is a former acting judge advocate general of the Army and a Vietnam veteran. Many who leave uniformed ranks upon completion of their contractual duty enjoy bright civilian careers. F. Lee Bailey, once a Marine fighter pilot, first tried cases as a non-lawyer court-martial prosecutor. Brendan V. Sullivan, defender of Lt. Col. Oliver North, broke in as an Army JAG, as did his Williams & Connolly law firm associate, Aubrey Daniel, who, as a captain, brilliantly prosecuted Lt. William Calley. David Brahms, Harvard Law, was as fine a Marine Corps Vietnam lawyer as ever rose to the rank of brigadier general, and John Hargrove, Green's defender, became a distinguished judge of the United States Bankruptcy Court.

As in any professional community, some judge advocates shine brighter than others. But the common attributes of virtually all judge advocates in Vietnam were dedication and hard work.

Vietnam was the first sustained test of the UCMJ's reformed procedures under combat conditions, and even without the staffing problems, the test was not an unalloyed success. Often it wasn't possible to examine the scene of a war crime, or search for Vietnamese witnesses, because the crime scene was in an unsecure area. Court recording equipment, dependent upon electrical power, often failed due to gasoline-fed generator problems, leading to a loss of the mandatory verbatim record of trial, leading, in turn, to a reversed conviction. When a belt-style recorder broke, as it did with regularity in Vietnam's extreme heat, dust, and humidity, "you [couldn't] even get the goddamn thing fixed!"[4] St.Amour exclaimed. The division's law library could be contained in a footlocker, and new case reports were what you read in *Stars and Stripes*. Incoming enemy fire was just an unscheduled recess. Even the production of Marine witnesses was problematic—they were often transferred, wounded, or killed before trial, and there is no provision in the UCMJ for such occurrences. A missing crucial witness simply meant a failed defense or prosecution. Documents lost to combat action were considered just that: lost. And in an era before copy machines, when multiple carbon copies were high-tech, the rules of evidence were neither set aside nor relaxed for reason of combat.

Worse, the fledgling judge advocates had almost no one to look to for professional advice, other than similarly handicapped tyros. What about the more senior judge advocates? St.Amour observed, "They should have had one of those major or lieutenant colonel lawyers they had floating around . . . or somebody who had trial experience who could . . . put [a case] in a posture for trial, ricky-tick!"[5] But the majors and lieutenant colonels were deputy SJAs and administrative lawyers, occupied with their own paper chores. Junior Reserve officers on their first and last tours of military duty, a year out of law school, were too often left to fend for themselves. By and large those "can do" hardchargers did a fine job, but it was a poor use of resources and its cost was measured in failed prosecutions and unpunished criminality.

Just prior to Herrod's trial, Col. Bob Lucy completed his tour of duty as the 1st Marine Division's staff judge advocate. He was supplanted by Col. Donald E. Holben. The SJA plays no direct role in the actual prosecution of cases but, like a battalion commander, he sets the tone for the activities of those "in the pits," the trial-level judge advocates who do daily courtroom battle.

Lucy was fortunate to depart Vietnam without being closely questioned, on the record, about his irregular activities in the Son Thang cases. St.Amour said, "I was surprised that Colonel Lucy's involvement, personal involvement in the case, and particularly the investigation thereof, was not made a basis for a motion in the three cases I sat on. I was very much surprised."[6] Lucy's undocumented trip to FSB Ross just after hearing about the case, and his procedural advice to Lieutenant Colonel Cooper and Major Theer, were probably entirely explainable. But the visit raised an appearance of possible improper command influence, and a disqualifying bias in any Son Thang conviction that Lucy might eventually review. But he was a kindly, intelligent, and supportive leader, popular with his lawyers, and the issue was never raised.

Lucy's replacement, Don Holben, was another Naval Academy graduate. A decidedly new broom, Holben seemingly viewed unpleasantness as a virtue. Subordinates soon learned that his gruff exterior was actually bone-deep—but no one accused him of not knowing how to run a law office. If there was any unexamined prosecutorial bias in his predecessor it would not continue in Holben, nor in his eventual legal reviews of the Schwarz and Green trials—nor of Herrod's, should Herrod be convicted. Holben was a hard man, but not unfair. His assumption of the SJA's duties was significant in that he, rather than Colonel Lucy, would oversee the drafting of Schwarz's and Green's trial reviews. His legal judgments tended to be a bit more harsh than those of his predecessor.

Lieutenant Colonel Cooper was another absentee. He left Vietnam for his next assignment in Washington a few days before Herrod's GCM. Upon his departure, Cooper was selected for promotion to colonel and awarded the Legion of Merit and the Vietnamese Cross of Gallantry.

OF LAWYERS AND JUDGES

In Oklahoma, interest in her native son's case was high. A petition signed by 160,000 citizens urging the release of Herrod and the other "unjustly confined" Son Thang accused was sent to the Commandant. Oklahomans from Calvin, Herrod's home town, raised funds to allow his elderly grandfather to visit him in Da Nang.

Pvt. Randy Herrod during his general court-martial.
Author's collection

Like Boyd's family, Herrod's divorced parents peppered congress with demands for justice for their son. In a letter to Texas senator John Tower, Herrod's mother, then living in Texas, asked that the senator inform her of the legal background, trial experience, and capabilities of her son's military lawyer. Furthermore, she asked that the commanding general of the 1st Marine Division (who, as required by law, had signed Herrod's charge sheet) "be charged with gross misconduct in the performance of his military duty and removed from his command immediately"[7] for charging her son with murder prior to an investigation. In the usual congressional-military service gavotte, Tower forwarded the letter to Marine Corps headquarters, asking that staff to "review her letter and documents, which I am enclosing [and] provide me with a report that I may use."[8] At headquarters a notation was made on the cover sheet for Tower's letter: "Personalize the stock reply." A standard "personalized" response was written and returned to the senator, who in turn sent his constituent his own stock reply based upon the Marine Corps' stock reply.

Given the volume of correspondence that such issues generated, little more was feasible. It is impossible to compose original responses to every letter received, and no real purpose would be served by doing so. The concerns raised by parents, relatives, and friends of servicemen caught up in the military justice system are, after all, sadly similar and predictable. Still, the cynicism of political expediency that often permeates congressional relations with constituents is repellent, especially when expedited by willing military handmaidens.

Thus, letters from Herrod's parents to Representatives George Bush and Carl Albert, Senators Fred Harris and Henry Bellmon, and Attorney General John Mitchell received similar treatment and similar replies. ("Herrod is an outstanding young man from a well-known family," Albert inventively wrote.[9]) None of the heartfelt letters from Herrod's loved ones, or from the president of the Inter-Tribal Council of the Five Civilized Tribes, had an impact on his court-martial or its processing. A GCM is a federal criminal trial, not a matter of electoral politics.

In the Korean War, Army captain Denzil D. Garrison had been pulled from a crashed and burning aircraft by Randy Herrod's uncle. Twenty years later, Garrison was happy to answer the call to defend his friend's nephew. By then, Garrison was a veteran trial lawyer and the Republican leader of the Oklahoma state senate. He quickly recruited his friend Gene Stipe, a Democratic state senator from

Oklahoma State Senator Denzil Garrison, who assembled Herrod's civilian legal team, on Hill 327. *Author's collection*

McAlester whose background included years of experience as a defense attorney. Garrison and Stipe, besides being good lawyers, are outgoing, sincere, and likable individuals. Those positive personal qualities don't show up in a record of trial, but are significant matters in a jury case, where personality can affect verdicts. There is a degree of truth in the jest that a jury trial is a contest to see which side's lawyer the jury likes best.

Stipe had prior military trial experience. He had defended a Vietnam fragging case at a GCM at Camp Pendleton, California, after the 1st Marine Division returned there from Vietnam. His man was convicted, but the trial gave Stipe a familiarity with military practice that he would use to good advantage in Vietnam. He was quoted as saying

The accused and his defense lawyers outside the 1st Marine Division courtroom: *(from left)* Harry Palmer, appellate specialist; Richard Miller, legal researcher; Gene Stipe, lead counsel; Capt. Bob Williams, assigned military defense counsel; Herrod; Denzil Garrison, co-lead counsel. *Denzil D. Garrison*

of Herrod: "A local boy half-a-world away from home being tried for murder. At that time everybody was beginning to have second thoughts about the war and they felt one way to purge their conscience was to prosecute these kids. I felt they were picking on some people who didn't have a helluva lot to say about their destiny."[10] Stipe and Garrison believed in the innocence of Randy Herrod.

Like Howard Trockman, Stipe and Garrison paid their own ways to Vietnam, making three journeys by government air to assess the case, observe the trials of Schwarz and Boyd, and prepare Herrod's defense. They also made their way to Washington, where they fruitlessly lobbied Representative Carl Albert, Speaker of the House, and Mendel Rivers, chairman of the powerful Senate Armed Services Committee, on Herrod's behalf.

As the trial date approached, the defense team was augmented by two other Oklahoma volunteers, Harry Palmer and Dick Miller. Palmer, a corporate lawyer experienced in appellate law, would concentrate on potential issues for appeal. Miller, crippled by polio, moved about on crutches and leg braces, which would be no small task on Hill 327. He would concentrate on legal research. Palmer and Miller also paid their own freight. Captain Williams, still Herrod's assigned defense counsel, would cover military aspects of the case. Stipe would be lead counsel. With five lawyers present, the defense table would be crowded.

The prosecution was already fending off written pretrial defense motions—something military lawyers were not used to doing. In the early 1970s military justice, not surprisingly, was practiced almost exclusively by military rather than civilian lawyers, especially in the combat zone. But in any venue, military law lacked, and continues to lack, the significant motions practice common to civilian jurisdictions. What few motions there were in courts-martial were always submitted in court, orally, and to put it gently, casually. Unlike their civilian counterparts, military law offices do not have a "motions file," where canned motions, and canned responses to opposition motions, may be found and easily produced when needed. Each military motion and each military response is the wheel invented anew.

This is partially explained by the military lawyer's lack of secretaries and copy machines, and the scarcity of clerks. In 1970, there were no personal computers with standard motions software, either. Other factors include the lack of experience at the trial level, and the failure of senior military lawyers to require a motions file, or formal motions practice at trial. Consequently, responding to Stipe and company's paper flurry added to the prosecution's burden, distracting it from other aspects of trial preparation.

Like the defense, the prosecution was reinforced for Herrod's GCM. Capt. Charlie Brown would again be lead prosecutor, this time assisted primarily by Capt. James L. "Len" Skiles, twenty-seven years old and two years out of law school. Capt. Gary Bushell would again provide back-up. Every judge advocate in the prosecution section would lend a hand in one way or another, just as the unassigned military defense lawyers assisted Herrod's defenders behind the scenes. Schwarz's prosecutor, Franz Jevne, had by now returned to the States, his Vietnam tour completed.

Lt. Col. Paul St.Amour would not be on the bench for the Herrod trial, or for any other Vietnam case. Days before the trial was to begin he was, without warning, transferred to Iwakuni, Japan, a relatively minor command. It was months before St.Amour's Vietnam tour was scheduled to end.

"If you really want to stir up the muck," St.Amour later suggested, "ask Faw whether or not my transfer to Japan was in any way related to the pending Herrod trial."[11] Gen. Duane L. Faw was the Marine Corps' senior lawyer, director of the Judge Advocate Division, in Washington, D.C. St.Amour's comment could be interpreted as suggesting that his acquittal of Boyd had earned him a midnight transfer to a backwater billet where he could do no further harm, which would have been an improper and unethical manipulation of judging assignments.

But that was not the case, and St.Amour eventually conceded as much.

In fact, Marine Corps headquarters, and General Faw in particular, had for some time been wrestling with issues generated by St.Amour and unrelated to the Son Thang trials. St.Amour's brusque personality and independent bent, combined with his wide-ranging authority as a GCM judge, sometimes made him a thorn in the side of his Vietnam legal contemporaries.

In June, just before the Schwarz case commenced,

St.Amour judged two fragging cases at Fleet Logistic Command (FLC), a major unit headquartered in Da Nang. Four racial agitators had tossed a fragmentation grenade into an enlisted men's club crowded with men watching a USO show. One Marine was killed, fifty-two hospitalized.

The eventual prosecutions were anchored by the immunized testimony of one of the four agitators against the other three. Despite this considerable advantage, two Marine panels acquitted the first two to be tried. FLC, unwilling to meet the expense and effort of another trial in what appeared a losing cause, did not even prosecute the remaining accused.

The SJA of FLC was mad as hell. Despite what appeared to be a winning case, he had lost not once, but twice—not a single person punished for a murder and fifty-two assaults with intent to commit murder. Despite suggestions that his own lawyers had used questionable tactics, the SJA believed that in-court comments and rulings by St.Amour had been decisive in both acquittals. Given the considerable influence of judges over jurors, it was possible. The SJA, who also had grievances regarding other St.Amour cases, made formal complaint to General Faw, urging the judge's relief. He supported his complaint with typed portions of verbatim records of the lost fragging prosecutions to illustrate what he perceived as St.Amour's judging sins. The SJA also barred St.Amour from assignment to future FLC cases by ensuring that the commanding general, who fully agreed, would sign no court convening order if St.Amour was to be the judge.

General Faw, asked about St.Amour's transfer, was reticent in discussing the issue. An officer of integrity and probity, Faw would only say that FLC's complaints, justified or not, were not the sole reason for St.Amour's departure. "Military justice is sufficiently difficult, in combat, when the command, the attorneys, and the courts have a mutual respect for the reliability of the other two to do their job in a professional manner," Faw said. "This situation did not exist in Vietnam [with St.Amour]."[12] Faw relieved and transferred him.

Herrod's defense counsel, Stipe, took another notunreasonable view of St.Amour's transfer. "We had cause to be concerned about command influence, because the general had just fired the judge and run his butt plumb out of the country!"[13]

Military judges lack tenure and thus may be reassigned for virtually any reason. While that is hardly conducive to an independent judiciary, there are no documented instances in the naval service of judicial transfers for improper motives. St.Amour's move, its suspicious timing notwithstanding, appears unrelated to his rulings in any Son Thang case.

The new judge would be a sailor, the GCM judge based at the Navy Legal Services Office in Subic Bay, the Philippines. Marine cases are usually tried by Marine judges, but the sister services occasionally provide judges and lawyers for each other's cases, and the burgeoning GCM caseload in Vietnam had long since required Navy judging assistance.

Cdr. Keith B. Lawrence was thirty-eight years old, a graduate of Willamette University Law School in Salem, Oregon. He had already sat in numerous Vietnam Marine Corps cases, many of them murder trials. Only a few months before he had judged eight Marine trials in succession, seven of them attempted murders, the eighth an aggravated arson. In 1970 Vietnam, serious crime was a growth industry.

The replacement of St.Amour by Lawrence was even more significant than Col. Lucy's replacement by Holben as SJA. Lawrence, who was to become a cleric upon retirement from active duty, differed from St.Amour in personality. Less aggressive and less driving, Lawrence allowed far more leeway on the lawyers' part in both his courtroom and his rulings.

A War Crime Prosecution

The GCM of Pvt. Randy Herrod, last of the Son Thang killer team members, began at 0900 on 20 August. Oral pretrial motions were heard before the members became involved. The familiar small courtroom was filled with lawyers—five for the defense, three for the prosecution, and the judge—as well as a court reporter, a bailiff, and eight news-media reporters on the two spectator benches. Soon, seven members would join the throng. In his 1989 book, *Blue's Bastards*, Herrod recalls his GCM and the events leading up to it. He writes, "Counting everybody, there were twenty-eight of us in the room when the trial was in full swing, all of us inhaling the same meager supply of oxygen. . . . There were no windows. It was August. The temperature was easily 110 degrees. And the only thing we had to cut the heat was a single ceiling fan that churned the air just enough to keep a swarm of flies from settling."[14] Actually, there was a struggling wall-mounted air conditioner, but its effect was negligible. The room remained hellishly uncomfortable.

The memorable, oily aroma of burning shitters did little for Hill 327's judicial ambiance. Plywood two-, three-, and four-holer outhouses, known to pious chaplains and coarse Marines alike as "shitters," dotted the division headquarters area. Each day, the cut-down fifty-five-gallon drums of waste beneath each hole were dragged from the shitters, doused with kerosene, and set alight to burn away the waste matter. It was hard to say whether the smell was worse before, during, or after the burning.

Herrod was charged with the war crime of premeditated murder of sixteen Vietnamese noncombatants, fifteen of the sixteen counts naming the alleged victim. The sixteenth victim was described simply as "an unknown female child."

To all counts, Herrod's plea was not guilty.

As in the preceding three trials, a charge sheet endorsement signed by the officer convening the court, the CG of the 1st Marine Division, stipulated, "This will be treated as a Non-Capital case." In other words, the maximum possible punishment faced by Herrod, if convicted, was confinement for life. As required by the UCMJ, a copy of the charge sheet, with the general's endorsement, had been served on Herrod in May. Herrod's later assertions that he was fighting for his life, "with a firing squad waiting at the end of the line," and that "the Marines might just take me out and shoot me before I could file an appeal. Greater fuck-ups had occurred," are not true.

In fact, there has not been a military execution since 1961, and the last Marine put to death pursuant to a court-martial sentence was one William Boyington, in 1817, a century and a half before Herrod's trial.

From the outset, it was clear the Herrod defense was going to be aggressively pressed. Before the members were selected, Stipe rigorously questioned the new military judge in an effort to determine and ensure his fairness. This examination, a process known as *voir dire,* is allowed by the *Manual for Courts-Martial.* Earlier, Stipe had submitted a motion to the Court of Military Appeals in Washington, the military's highest court, for a change of venue and a further postponement of trial, and challenging the constitutionality of the military jury system and other provisions of the UCMJ. The motion had been denied. The court wrote in its denial: "Other requests are not supported by averments sufficient to demonstrate the necessity of intervention by this Court."[15] But Stipe's early and unusual resort to the military appellate system foreshadowed the intensity of the defense team's preparation and resolve, and made them especially careful in their questioning of Commander Lawrence.

Stipe did all he could to discover any bias harbored by Judge Lawrence. "I'll tell you," Stipe later marveled, "the Code's got a provision that enables you to *voir dire* the judge—it's a helluva tool! We don't have anything similar to that in civilian practice. I'd just love to *voir dire* the judges I appear before. Goddamn! I spent three days, I think, *voir diring* [Lawrence]."[16] The questioning actually took somewhat less than three days, but Stipe and Garrison were finally satisfied that Lawrence would do.

Subsequent defense motions were numerous, often supported by witnesses, always by legal authority. There were motions for a new Article 32 pretrial investigation (denied), a renewed change-of-venue motion based upon prejudicial pretrial publicity and command influence (denied), a motion for production of service records and "housing assignments" of those involved not only in Herrod's case, but also in Schwarz's, Boyd's, and Green's (personnel records denied, billeting assignments granted), a motion for Herrod's release from confinement (denied), a motion for copies of all GCM convening orders in the division in the past year (granted), a motion for production of all messages, classified and otherwise, that mentioned the Herrod case (granted as to unclassified messages; thirty-seven classified messages to be provided the judge to review for prejudicial matter were instead declassified and provided, at the direction of the CG of Fleet Marine Force, Pacific),[17] a motion for clerical assistance (a typist was provided for the defense, to the frustration of the prosecution, which had to scramble for its own clerical assistance), and a catch-all motion for "relief from all of the other oppressive procedures of the UCMJ" (denied). Along with a variety of other, lesser motions, the dispositions, in total, took four in-court days.

A significant tactical victory for the defense reflected a difference between the judicial philosophies of Commander Lawrence and Lieutenant Colonel St.Amour. Stipe moved to keep from the jury the nine color photographs of the Son Thang victims. Military appellate authority clearly supports the admission of such exhibits, gory as they might be. St.Amour certainly never slowed down in admitting the pictures into evidence in the Schwarz, Boyd, and Green trials. But it's the judge's call and Lawrence, allowing the defense greater maneuvering room, granted the motion to exclude, depriving the prosecution of a potent evidentiary weapon.

The defense eventually withdrew motions to force Colonel Lucy's return to Vietnam to testify, and to require autopsies, and for the presence of the CID sergeants who assisted Major Theer in questioning the nighttime mobile ambush. (The Marine Corps and the prosecution, sensitive to the image raised in the press by the term "killer team," had deleted the expression from its lexicon. "It had a pretty bad connotation when I was talking to the media about this thing,"[18] Lieutenant Colonel Cooper said. Instead they now employed the sanitized euphemism "nighttime mobile ambush" in court and in press releases.)

At the beginning of the second day of trial, Brown handed Stipe and Garrison the messages, the convening orders, and the billeting assignments required by previously granted motions. He also gave them copies of the prosecution's working files and, at the judge's direction, audio tapes of the prior trials. The defense already had been provided with detailed maps and diagrams of Son Thang-4, as well as a selection of specially taken eight-by-ten aerial photographs that clearly delineated every hooch, tree, and trail.

Years before civilian jurisdictions adopted disclosure rules, the UCMJ required prosecutors to, in effect, open their files to the defense. In this instance "in effect" was "in fact." The defense knew everything the prosecution knew; would have copies of every written statement relating to the case, whether or not their maker had testified; would have a copy of Krichten's grant of immunity; would have copies of every report and official form prepared for the initial investigation, for the Article 32, and for the trial itself. There would be no surprise prosecution witnesses and no unanticipated prosecution evidence. Trial by prosecution ambush is prohibited in military law.

The defense was required to give the government a list of its witnesses.

Just before the prospective members were brought in, the defense once more raised or renewed several motions. Stipe argued that the judge, rather than the prosecutor, should administer oaths to the jury and to witnesses. He asked for sixteen peremptory challenges—removals of jurors for any reason whatever—rather than the usual single peremptory. Moreover, he urged, the jurors should be selected at random from all ranks in the division headquarters, or, alternatively, should be composed entirely of enlisted men. And, in a last-minute move, Stipe also requested government funding for a civilian psychiatrist-expert witness.

The subjects of all the defense motions, except the last, were settled issues in military law and all were promptly denied. Lawrence did grant Stipe's request for government funds to pay for a defense psychiatrist. Lawrence was unaware that the defense, as part of their savvy case preparation, had already secured the services of a prominent Oklahoma psychiatrist. It was going to be a steep learning curve for the prosecution.

One more time, Stipe made a stab at changing the trial's location, renewing his change-of-venue motion yet again. This time he surprised the prosecution by calling a Marine officer to testify in support of the motion.

First Lt. Oliver L. North strode to the witness stand, took the oath, and sat down to relate an extraordinary tale.

In the messhall and the officers' club a few nights before, North testified, he had approached a number of officers, roughly thirty, and casually raised the topic of the Herrod trial. North had been discussing the change-of-venue issue with the defense. His unstated purpose in the O-club was to sound out the command's attitude toward the trial of his former platoon member. In his 1991 autobiography, *Under Fire*, North recounts that "nearly every man told me the same thing—that Randy Herrod didn't stand a chance. . . . I was shocked when Herrod's defense counsel cited my unscientific opinion poll as evidence that a fair trial was not possible."[19]

Shocked or not—having been prepped, no witness should be "shocked" by the questions of the lawyer who calls him—North testified to his poll readily enough. He omitted that he had been escorted to the door of the

O-Club by a senior officer who had discovered his purpose and was less than pleased to learn he was being set up as a GCM-accused's defense stratagem.

Judge Lawrence was unmoved and so was the trial. Motion denied. But North's testimonial evidence was on the record for appellate review, in case of conviction—and all concerned, including Herrod and his defense team, were reconciled to conviction. But they also knew that appellate issues would be numerous and that the chances of reversal, or at least a reduction of sentence, would be fair to substantial.

A defense request for a fifteen-day continuance to appeal this latest denial of the change-of-venue motion—Stipe was not one to give up a good legal issue—was also denied.

The court recessed for the day, reopening at 1320 the next, a Sunday. During the night, VC 122mm rocket fire straddled Division Ridge, where Oliver North and the defense team bunked in a SEAhut, a raised plywood hut with wire screen sides and a corrugated tin roof. Although a regular occurrence anywhere near Da Nang, Katyusha rockets were new to the civilian lawyers. But they were undisturbed. "It was kinda like watching fireworks,"[20] Stipe coolly allowed.

The next morning eight officers, a colonel, two lieutenant colonels, four majors, and a captain, filed into the courtroom's rough jury box. Sweat-stained camouflage utilities were still the uniform of the day for Marines; the judge's Navy work uniform was plain green. The questioning of the prospective members by the judge, the government, and the defense lawyers began. Four and a half hours later, one of the lieutenant colonels was dismissed. The remaining seven would be Herrod's jury, although Stipe felt uneasy about the member he noticed reading *Atlantic Monthly*.

Oliver North had previously urged the defense lawyers to select only officers with combat experience because "only men who had served in combat could appreciate the pressures that Herrod must have been under," he was quoted as saying. "In the end, every member of that [panel] was a decorated combat Marine."[21]

James Webb, himself a decorated infantry officer and Vietnam veteran, agreed with North's view of members. In a law review article about the Son Thang case, Webb wrote, "Combat is a unique experience. To understand the reactions of a person [in combat] . . . a trier of fact should have some understanding of the immense difficulties and frustrations inherent in small-unit infantry operations."[22] International legal scholar L. C. Green goes further: "It may even be questioned whether a military code, manual, or directions to courts-martial drafted by lawyers . . . who carry military ranks merely because they serve in the Judge Advocate's . . . Departments, but who have no idea of the realities of service life, particularly in action, are the proper persons to be responsible for preparing these regulations."[23]

Such criteria for war crime jurors, however, would have excluded most of the post–World War II Nuremberg judges, several Calley members, and most of the Vietnam War's military judges. Combat is unquestionably a unique and emotional experience, but the North-Webb-Green viewpoint suggests that its effects cannot be appreciated by any except those who experience it firsthand as infantrymen.

More than 448,000 Marines served in Vietnam, although far fewer actually saw combat. One study asserts that no more than 71 percent of all Vietnam veterans saw any combat at all.[24] Combat itself may be defined on a sliding scale. At what point on such a scale would one merit "combat juror" status?

The traditional jury has never given complete satisfaction anywhere. But the officers and enlisted men who decided the Son Thang cases were as random, and as much the peers of the accused, as any civilian jury. One need not be a business executive to be a fair juror in a white-collar crime case, nor a police officer to decide a charge of excessive force. To require only combat-experienced jurors in war crimes cases injects elements not meant for inclusion in the weighing of guilt or innocence. The Honorable Walter T. Cox, Chief Judge of the U.S. Court of Appeals of the Armed Forces, and a civilian with Army experience, notes that "there are certain biases and prejudices in favor of letting the war criminal go, if you try him in the battle zone."[25] Might that bias be the point of one's desire for combat-experienced jurors?

At any rate, Herrod got his all-combat-vet jury. The colonel was a grizzled thirty-year Marine, an enlisted veteran of World War II, an officer in Korea and Vietnam. He was the division G-4, the senior supply officer. Herrod described him as "a legitimate combat hero." The lieutenant colonel, wounded in action as an enlisted man in Korea, was commissioned during that conflict and had pinned on his silver oak leaves only a few weeks before Herrod's trial. One of the four majors was a mustang, commissioned after his Korean service and now at his terminal rank. The captain, too, was ex-enlisted, a former staff sergeant with six years commissioned service. All of them had been around the block.

At 0902 Monday morning, 24 August, Charlie Brown opened the government's case-in-chief, after the normal procedural preliminaries. This was effectively a trial already tried, employing thrice-tested tactics—prosecution tactics that, in a sense, called for the cooperation of the opposition.

The Herrod prosecution was a straightforward chronological recitation of events that led the members down a narrowing vortex of facts, at the center of which stood Randy Herrod, waiting to be swept away by a guilty verdict. The "cooperation" the prosecution required for best results would be a similarly simple defense consisting of equal and opposite reactions: when the prosecution would posit that there was no enemy fire, a compliant defense would respond, yes, there was; if the government said Herrod ordered fire on the civilians, the defense would reply, no, he ordered fire on the distant enemy. The prosecutor would close: our witness Krichten says yes; the defense: our accused says no. Gentlemen of the jury, what we have here is a swearing contest—who do you like?

More often than not, the prosecution wins such contests. But those simple, tested prosecution tactics had already been found wanting with Boyd, when the defense took a different, more imaginative tack by raising an unanticipated and plausible defense. Boyd didn't rise to the prosecution's there-was-enemy-fire/there-wasn't-enemy-fire option. Boyd didn't care if Herrod had or had not ordered fire on the victims. Boyd's defense, religious pacifism, slipped the government's punches, giving the fact-finder another option. Fatally, that option was largely unopposed by a prosecution which was, correctly enough, concentrated on proving the elements of the offense, but unprepared for anything other than the obvious defenses of enemy fire and Herrod-made-me-do-it.

Alan Dershowitz, Harvard law professor and appellate lawyer of note, writes in *Reasonable Doubts,* "A criminal trial is anything but a pure search for truth. When defense attorneys represent guilty clients—as most do, most of the time—their responsibility is to try, by all fair and ethical means, to *prevent* the truth about their client's guilt from emerging. Failure to do so . . . is malpractice."[26] No one would accuse Gene Stipe or Denzil Garrison of malpractice.

No prosecutor can anticipate every defense gambit, but one mark of an accomplished trial lawyer is the nimbleness of legal wit to absorb and counter, on the fly, the ploys an opponent unexpectedly raises. That ability is one difference between a journeyman and an expert, a skill developed case by case, often through painful experience. In 1970, in Vietnam, judge advocates were low on experience and feeling the pain.

Would Herrod's defense team be any less resourceful and imaginative than Boyd's? That possibility probably never occurred to the young prosecutors. On-the-job training can exact its own high price.

· · · ·

Brown's opening statement for the prosecution was brief and unemotional. As Herrod wrote, "He told how we had gone out into the field with orders to exact revenge for the death of Sergeant Lyons. (True.) How we'd come upon the small village of Son Trang-4 [*sic*]. (True.) How we'd found nothing but women and children there. (True.) How we'd herded them all out into a clearing in the woods. (True.) And how, without the slightest provocation, we had shot them down, killing sixteen. (Half-true.) Indeed, except for Brown's assertion that we were not provoked in any way, I had no quarrel with his summary of the case."

Captain Williams made the defense opening statement, a similarly concise presentation that stressed the dangers of Son Thang-4, the number of Marines recently killed and wounded near there, and the anticipated deficiencies in the prosecution's case. And, he said, the defense would *prove* Herrod had been fired upon.

The taking of evidence commenced.

The first government witness was platoon sergeant Harvey Meyers, now in his eighteenth month in the combat zone. As in previous trials, he related the formation and departure of Herrod's "nighttime mobile ambush." He told the members that he and Lieutenant Carney put Herrod, a private as far as they knew, in charge because, as Meyers had testified at Schwarz's GCM, "he did a good job, and he knows what's going on, so we thought he'd be the best man for the job."[27] It was the first time Herrod had led any B Company patrol, Meyers said. The fact that every patrol member was apparently senior to the patrol leader—Lance Corporal Krichten, Privates First Class Boyd and Green, and, by time in service, Private Schwarz—was not considered.

Meyers repeated that, having heard about Ambort's inflammatory briefing to "pay the little bastards back," he warned Herrod to not do anything foolish, "just go out and do your job, and get some."[28]

Meyers told the members how, upon the patrol's return to Hill 50 from Son Thang-4, Herrod told him the team had "gotten some," leading him to believe Herrod had confirmed VC kills. Only later, Meyers said, did he understand Herrod was misleading him by neglecting to say that the "some" he got were unarmed women and children.

Herrod writes, "I had been deliberately evasive in my report of the action. Clearly I'd been trying to cover up something. My behavior seriously undermined my credibility. I couldn't quarrel with either the facts or with the logic of [Meyers's] conclusion."

It was Stipe's cross-examination that revealed a new defense direction. He questioned Meyers's recollection of hearing automatic fire from the vicinity of Son Thang while the team was there: 100 to 160 rounds, lasting thirty to sixty seconds, and from more than one weapon, Meyers said. Meyers had testified to the same effect in the prior trials, but had never been quizzed on the matter before.

Lieutenant Grant, the next prosecution witness, reprised his testimony regarding discovery of the victims the morning after Herrod's patrol. The officer Herrod describes as "a by-the-numbers bastard, the 90-day-wonder whose report had gotten us all into trouble in the first place," detailed the bodies' horrific wounds, the brass from U.S. weapons, and how his patrol helped the Vietnamese bury their dead.

Cpl. Gary Bowler, a member of Grant's patrol, was called. As in prior trials, he related picking up .45 brass, M-16 brass, and a spent M-79 buckshot cartridge. (Herrod, the members were later told, had carried an M-79 and buckshot rounds.) Bowler said he and the others in Grant's patrol found only U.S. brass in Son Thang, and that it was retrieved from all three sites where the Vietnamese bodies lay.

HM1 Milton Jones, also from Grant's patrol, substantiated finding brass from American weapons—including another M-79 cartridge—where the bodies lay.

Bowler and Jones were both cumulative witnesses, offering nothing to which Grant had not already testified, and repeating each other's testimony in the bargain. But the prosecution was not done, although the court recessed for the day.

The next afternoon, after a 1515 start required by the usual difficulties in getting Vietnamese witnesses to Hill 327 by helicopter, the court heard the testimony of two female Son Thang residents. The first, who had testified in the other GCMs, related through an interpreter her observation of Americans, presumably the Herrod killer team, in Son Thang-4 on the night of the killings. The second woman repeated the same account. Although the Vietnamese did not attempt to identify Herrod, they nailed down the presence of a U.S. patrol in the ville, ruling out the possibility of American brass left by VC using U.S. weapons.

Under Stipe's wide-ranging cross-examination, one of the women admitted that her daughter, one of the patrol's victims, lived with a VC member. He was not with the daughter on the night of the killings, she said. Nevertheless, her testimony lent legitimacy to the defense assertion that there often were VC in Son Thang-4. Although the prosecution had anticipated Stipe stressing the common presence of VC in the ville, the possibility of Herrod having been fired upon by VC was a bit more credible as that court day ended.

The next morning, LCpl. Michael Krichten, the government's inside man, returned to the stand to detail his story for the fourth and final time.

As in the Schwarz trial, Krichten repeated Ambort's "little bastards, get some" briefing, and the sequence of shootings in Son Thang-4: at the hooch where the first shooting occurred, Herrod dropped a running woman with a shot from his M-79, Krichten said, then told Schwarz to finish her off. Then, he testified, despite his and Boyd's protestations, Herrod ordered the team to fire on the remaining three women and children.

At the second hut, Krichten continued, Green fired first, then Herrod again ordered the hesitant team to kill the six

Vietnamese at point-blank range. "Kill 'em all," Krichten said, repeating Herrod's words: "That's what the lieutenant told us to do, and we're going to do it."[29]

The third hooch was a deadly replay of events at the second, Krichten continued, with Herrod telling Schwarz to silence the crying child after the other Vietnamese had been cut down. So swore Krichten. And he recalled for the court precisely who fired at each hooch, and where they stood while doing so. An impressive performance.

The members listened to Krichten's recitation with hushed intensity. This was the first time they had heard the killings described in detail. Captain Brown had roughed out the homicides in his opening statement. Grant, Bowler, and Jones spoke of the bodies. But nothing could prepare the panel, no matter how combat-experienced, for the cold starkness of this participant's account.

The prosecution had not admitted Herrod's written statement to Major Theer. That was because throughout the investigation and work-up to trial, Herrod stuck to his initial, relatively innocuous statement, relating that at the first two hooches civilians were hit when the team returned sniper fire; at the third, the victims were shot as part of the sniper's initial set-up.

As Krichten walked out of the courtroom and into the growing mass of reporters, the government rested.

The brevity of the prosecution case was striking: seven witnesses, their testimony and cross-examination completed in little more than six hours in aggregate. For a contested trial of sixteen premeditated murders that's a decidedly swift prosecution. In defender Denzil Garrison's perhaps biased opinion, it was also a "sophomoric prosecution."[30]

But trials are not judged by the clock. In terms of evidence, what more was there for the prosecution to present? Major Dick Theer, perhaps, who had determined that no enemy sniper could have been present near Son Thang that night. But Theer, already once recalled to Vietnam to testify in two trials, was being saved for rebuttal, this time. So, was

Oklahoma State Senator Gene Stipe, architect of Herrod's defense, on the final day of the general court-martial. *Author's collection*

there not sufficient evidence to convict as to each element of the charged crime? Brown thought there was.

Without a recess, the defense set out to convince the members otherwise.

DEFENDING THE INDEFENSIBLE

One of the members, the junior major, recalled that at this point, Gene Stipe rose and walked a few paces to the large easel-mounted map, a blow-up of the Son Thang vicinity. The prosecution had earlier introduced it in evidence, using it to lead the jurors step-by-step through the incident. "The first thing the civilian lawyer did," recalled the juror, "was to turn the map ninety degrees, to reorient it so that 'North' was up." Embarrassed snickers were smothered all around the courtroom.

Stipe's first two witnesses immediately established the principal defense thrust. Sgts. Bruce Fay and Ronald Butler, NCOs from another 1/7 company who did not know Herrod, took the stand in turn. There is no indication of how they were located by the defense team, but it was a good job. Their testimony proved vital.

Fay and Butler related that ten days after the Son Thang-4 incident their platoon had been operating in the same vicinity. They had come under fire—fire from an M-60 machine gun. More importantly, they could prove it was an M-60: During the ensuing engagement the Marines killed several VC in a cave about 700 meters from Son Thang, and actually captured the American weapon. It had been taken from a downed U.S. helicopter, they testified. The VC, to avoid revealing the M-60's position, had even substituted ball ammo for the tracers placed, U.S. fashion, every sixth round in the ammunition belts.

Stipe asked Fay to characterize the Son Thang area. The sergeant replied, "Everything that's in there is VC or they're helping the VC. There's no doubt about it."[31]

Herrod writes, "As the lance corporal [sic] told his story, everything fell into place for the jurors—or so I hoped. Here was proof that . . . they had a machine gun, that they fired on American troops." Garrison concurred, "This was a very important facet of evidence. Schwarz and Green did not have that testimony to corroborate their story."[32]

Brown's cross emphasized that the sergeants had no way of knowing if the machine gun had been brought to the area that day, that week, or that month. They only knew it had been there on the day they captured it. Does the fact that a machine gun was captured in 1/7's tactical area, Brown's questions implied, mean that a machine gun was fired on Herrod, and that it forced him to return fire with civilians in his line of fire?

The Fay-Butler testimony hurt the prosecution. Still, no

killer team member had ever before suggested anything more than four shots being fired at them, even in their initial and admittedly false written statements. Certainly *machine-gun* fire had never been mentioned. In fact, Schwarz, Boyd, and Krichten all admitted—had sworn, in their second statements—that there had been no enemy fire at all. Green, in his written statement, alleged two rounds fired at the first hooch and two at the second. In Herrod's own statement, which Brown now quickly admitted into evidence, Herrod wrote that only three rounds were fired at the team: "A shot zinged over our heads," he wrote of the first hooch. "Two shots rang out," he wrote of the second, and no shots rang or zinged at the third. So the sergeants' evidence was not necessarily a fatal blow to the prosecution.

But the written statements of Schwarz, Boyd, Green, and Krichten were not in evidence. Nor was there testimony from the religiously disposed Boyd, or from Schwarz or Green, both of whom might have won reduced sentences in exchange for brief prosecution-oriented testimony. Krichten had already testified in Herrod's GCM and remained obligated to testify as often as required in return for his continued immunity. True, Krichten had told Herrod's jury that the team received no enemy fire. But that statement was not made in refutation of this particular defense assertion of M-60 fire. What the prosecution badly needed was a specific denial by Krichten of the machine-gun fire. If Schwarz, Boyd, or Green could be induced to join Krichten in such a denial, even better.

But the jury never heard such a refutation. Nor did the jury learn that, in their written statements, three of the four team members, independent of each other, unambiguously agreed there had been no enemy fire whatever, and that none of them mentioned a machine gun.

Beyond the issue of the machine gun, Sergeant Fay asserted that the entire Son Thang vicinity was peopled by VC and their sympathizers. The same opinion was later advanced by Lt. William Calley when he said in a book on My

Lai, "*These people, they're all the VC.* . . . If those people weren't all VC then prove it to me. Show me that someone was for the American forces there. Show me that someone helped us and fought the VC. Show me that someone wanted us: one example only!"[33]

The response to Calley's plea and Fay's assertion, and the aggression they implicitly justified, is in the judge's instructions to the jury at Calley's general court-martial: "Noncombatants detained by the opposing force, regardless of their loyalties, political views, or prior acts, have the right to be treated as prisoners until released, confined, or executed in accordance with law. . . . Summary execution of detainees or prisoners is forbidden by law."[34] In terms that applied equally to the Son Thang incident, the appellate opinion in Calley's case added, "Slaughtering many for the presumed delicts of a few is not a lawful response . . . Villagers [of toddler age] were indiscriminately included in the general carnage. . . . The argument is in essence a plea to permit summary execution as a reprisal for irregular villager action favoring the Viet Cong."[35] Would Herrod's members appreciate as much? Or might the Fay-Butler testimony make it a moot issue?

At 1400, the judge granted a defense continuance until Lt. Col. Charles Cooper arrived. He was expected from the States at any moment.

When court was called to order at 0900 the next morning, Cooper, who now had appeared for the defense in all four trials and in Ambort's Article 32, was the day's first witness. "I insisted from the very beginning," Cooper later said, "that I wanted to testify at these trials, and I didn't care who it was for. I just wanted to look those members in the eye and explain to them that all of *you* might not have been able to tell what to do, but particularly if you were twenty years old, and you had just come from the 3d Division."[36] No prosecutor was likely to call Cooper for that testimony.

Dick Theer, Cooper's battalion operations officer who single-handedly first documented what happened in Son

Thang, was unaware of his commander's continuing involvement in the defense case. Upon being told of it years later, he was incensed. He wrote, "I was also very disturbed to learn . . . that Lt. Col. Cooper had been an important defense witness for Herrod."[37] Theer saw the case as a slaughter of defenseless Vietnamese, their political allegiance being immaterial. Cooper concentrated on the accused killers, their youth, and the difficulty of their situation.

In his testimony, Cooper again emphasized the extreme danger faced by the men of 1/7 in and around Son Thang, and the hamlet's infestation with VC. He later wrote, "My philosophy had been to question what 'murder' actually was when we had called in air strikes, mortar and artillery fire on this hamlet before this patrol ever entered the area."[38]

The moral and legal difference between air and artillery strikes and premeditated murder were the crux of the charges Herrod faced, of course. But through Stipe's direct examination, the colonel's point was made clear to the members.

Cooper then returned to the Pentagon and his assignment to the Office of the Joint Chiefs of Staff, and went on to a distinguished military career, retiring in 1985 with the three stars of a lieutenant general.

Cooper was followed by 2d Lt. Bob Carney, still a B-1/7 platoon commander. Carney repeated much of what Cooper had described, adding that he heard a long burst of automatic fire from Son Thang that night. The shots he heard had a deeper crack to them than M-16 rounds, he said. He thought it sounded like an M-60, and that the team had walked into an ambush.

In quick succession, 1st Lts. Peter Kimmerer (leader of another B-1/7 platoon) and Ron Ambort testified, both reiterating the dangers of Son Thang, both relating hearing machine-gun fire there.

Adding further weight to the defense version of events in Son Thang, Stipe introduced into evidence Schwarz's M-16 and argued its two points of damage. Obvious bullet impacts, he said, holding the weapon up for the members to see. If the team was not under enemy fire, how was that damage to be explained?

Throughout the day, television and print reporters quietly moved in and out of the courtroom. They had agreed among themselves to a rotation system that allowed their large and growing number to observe at least portions of the trial. Son Thang and Herrod, particularly, were major stories not only in the *Pacific Stars and Stripes,* but on network television, in major U.S. dailies, and in the participants' hometown papers.

If the prosecution was not worried, it should have been. Two NCOs had established the presence of a captured M-60 near Son Thang-4 within days of the Herrod patrol. Schwarz's M-16 allegedly had been hit by incoming fire. Witness after witness told the members they heard automatic fire from Son Thang that could not have been Herrod's weapons. The panel was not likely to ignore the assertions of experienced officers and NCOs who were there; assertions that precisely fit the defense version of events. Nor was this something for the prosecution to try to counter in closing argument. Firm testimonial evidence in refutation was needed, and quickly.

After court recessed for the day, one prosecutor could have hustled to the III MAF brig to see Schwarz, another to the Army stockade to see Green. In the presence of their military defense lawyers, the Herrod prosecutors could have made both convicted men an SJA-approved offer they could not refuse: a chance to testify in the government's rebuttal case that there had been no machine-gun fire in Son Thang, presuming they concurred that was the truth. That's all. In return, the SJA would formally recommend that their confinement be substantially reduced. By the time they testified they would have the specific sentence reduction they agreed to in writing, approved and signed by the CG, who had such authority. Schwarz and Green, already convicted and sentenced, would have nothing to lose but much to gain by agreeing.

There is no way of knowing if such a tactic was considered. The subsequent absence of both Schwarz and Green suggests it was not.

The next defense witness was 1st Lt. Oliver North. Herrod writes, "I knew more than my civilian lawyers just how important his testimony would be. . . . North's endorsement of my character and my conduct under fire would be crucial."

So North's role was to tell the members that conduct like that charged against Herrod, his previous subordinate, was entirely out of character; that from his close knowledge of the man, Herrod could not have murdered sixteen human beings in cold blood.

North would not mention that he had known the accused only for the seventy-four days the two had been in the same battalion. In combat, seventy-four days can be a lifetime. Still, it was a brief period upon which to base a staunch assertion of innocence. And veterans like those on the jury would know that the kind of close relationship asserted by North is rarely formed between officers and privates first class, as Herrod was when he knew North.

But North knew his role. In *The Nightingale's Song*, Robert Timberg writes, "When his time came to testify, North put on the kind of performance the nation would see seventeen years later when he faced John Nields, the chief House counsel of the congressional Iran-Contra committees. Chin up, feet flat on the floor, hands on his knees, he was, said [Herrod defense lawyer] Harry Palmer, 'two right angles.' Said Denzil Garrison, 'He was the most believable witness I've ever seen.'"[39]

If nothing else impressed the members, they certainly listened up when they heard North say he paid his own way cross-country, while on leave, to testify for Herrod. That alone said much.

In response to Stipe's questioning, North ran with the testimonial ball, describing Herrod in glowing terms. A model Marine, obedient to orders, routinely courageous, always disciplined in his actions. "I explained," North writes

During a court recess: 1st Lt. Ron Ambort *(left)*, Pvt. Randy Herrod, and 1st Lt. Oliver North, who returned to Vietnam to testify for Herrod at his court-martial. *Denzil D. Garrison*

in his autobiography, "that the charges of murder against Herrod were totally inconsistent with the qualities I had seen less than a year earlier. I also pointed out that he had been trained in a different war. We saw very few civilians in the northern part of the First Corps Tactical Zone, where the rule of thumb was: it's either us or the NVA, and if it moves in the killing zone of an ambush—*shoot!*"[40] (advice not appreciably different from that Herrod received in Ambort's briefing, in the southern part of the tactical zone).

The defense had earlier moved to admit a copy of Herrod's Silver Star citation, a motion properly denied by Judge Lawrence, as it had no bearing on whether or not Herrod had committed the offenses. But North now detailed for the members the action for which the medal was awarded—or at least had been approved—and how Herrod had saved his life.

Now the panel understood why North was there. And a pretty damn good reason it was.

The defense was pleased with North's testimony. Not only was it highly favorable, but his very presence was an impressive testament to an officer's loyalty to one of his men, as well as to Herrod's courage under fire. Garrison considered Brown's cross-examination of North ineffective, saying, "He [Brown] was like a bear cub playing with his you-know-what."[41] Even those unaware of what bear cubs play with would know what a you-know-what was.

As well as it had gone for the defense so far, they weren't done.

Stipe moved to admit two previously secret messages the prosecution had provided him. One, from the 1st Division CG to the CG of Fleet Marine Force Pacific, was sent shortly after the case broke. It read, "Vietnamese district and province officials are not disturbed over the incident since all the families involved in the incident are considered VC."[42] The other message, from the Division CG to the III MAF CG, reported (quite incorrectly) that the killer team had apparently followed the rules of engagement then in force.

The next morning, Randell Dean Herrod took the stand to testify in his own defense. Looking the judge in the eye, he raised his right hand and swore to tell the truth, the whole truth, and nothing but the truth.

Herrod looked good, a factor not to be discounted when testifying before a jury. Three weeks shy of his twenty-first birthday, he stood six foot four and was reed thin, as only an athletic young man can be. He had sandy brown hair and blue eyes.

Oklahoma-born, Herrod and his younger brother grew up in Holdenville, where their now-divorced parents had themselves been born and raised. Herrod designated his brother as his government insurance beneficiary. Cared for by his grandparents for much of his early youth, Herrod had graduated from high school four months before commencing his two-year Marine Corps enlistment. He was offered a basketball scholarship to Southeastern Oklahoma State but turned it down. He had never been in trouble.

At boot camp in San Diego, Herrod did very well, graded 4.9 of a possible 5.0 in both conduct and proficiency. His military intelligence test scores showed a GCT of 118, remarkably high for a nineteen-year-old enlistee. Promoted to private first class out of Infantry Training Regiment, he reached Vietnam in June 1969. All continued well in the 3d Marine Division with Oliver North's platoon in K-3/3 near the DMZ.

There was an incident involving Herrod's sleeping while on a listening post. In a combat zone, sleeping on post is an offense technically punishable by death. It was so commonly encountered in Vietnam, however, that Herrod's week of extra duty and twenty-five-dollar fine at nonjudicial punishment was typical, and not considered serious.

When 3/3 was pulled from Vietnam and returned to Okinawa, Herrod's real difficulties began. Too new in-country to depart with his battalion, he was promoted to lance corporal and transferred south to the 1st Marine Division and Ron Ambort's B-1/7. He brought with him a Purple Heart and a Silver Star recommendation. But, displeased with his new unit, Herrod left for his two-month UA. He was eventually tried at a special court-martial, defended by the same Captain Williams who now sat at his defense table with his four civilian lawyers. After his first court he returned to B-1/7, unaware that his bust to private was not yet in effect, but otherwise no worse for wear. Thirty-four days later, he had led the five-man killer team to Son Thang.

Herrod had been in custody since three days after the patrol—at this point, 186 days in confinement. He had spent much of this time in his lawyer's office, however, and so was outside the brig far more than other prisoners. Throughout his confinement he had corresponded with Karen W., a former high-school girlfriend, sometimes typing letters to her on the typewriter outside Captain Williams's office cubicle. He wrote her, "I figure I will be getting about 240 years. That sounds funny . . . because of all the things that I wanted to do and all the things I had planned. . . . I can take what they give me although I would rather die than spend my life in jail."[43] In a pensive mood difficult to imagine in the other killer team members, Herrod sent a poem to Karen:

> *Since I have gone so far away,*
> *A curious thing I find.*
> *The world is like a golden clock,*
> *That God forgot to wind.*[44]

It was a side of Randy Herrod that no one in Vietnam saw or suspected.

As he began his testimony, "I began to feel my stomach churning," Herrod writes in his autobiography. "I was a little shaky." But he proved an excellent witness in his own behalf. Prompted by Stipe's questions, Herrod related the same story he had told from the beginning. Male voices. At two hooches, women and children assembled. Enemy fire—but M-60 fire, now; not individual sniper rounds. The team returned fire, Vietnamese killed in the crossfire. At the third hooch, the Vietnamese killed as participants in the prior two shootings. "I do not now, and I did not then, feel that I had killed anyone it wasn't necessary to kill."[45]

There was a notable lack of emphasis on Ambort's belli-cose pre-patrol briefing. "What Ambort was doing [in his briefing]," Stipe later said, "was in keeping with what the whole goddamn strategy was, at that time." Besides, Am-bort's briefing only lent weight to the prosecution's version of events.

Neither was there any assertion that, in Son Thang, Her-rod had only been carrying out Ambort's all-but-explicit or-ders. Asked about that later, Stipe laughed good-naturedly and said, "I wouldn't describe our defense as one of supe-rior orders. . . . We did throw it in there, just for the jury to consider. You never know what a jury sinks their hooks in, to justify their acquittal. . . . We had a defense with a lot of options for the jury."[46]

Regarding his false report to Ambort that the team had ambushed a column of VC and killed six to eight of them, Herrod explained on the stand, "I was afraid he [Ambort] might think we had screwed up."[47]

Recalling his own testimony, Herrod writes, "By the time I had finished, I had explained the full complexity of our situation that night, and I was satisfied that anyone who had been in combat would understand what we had done."

Brown's cross-examination was aggressive and harsh. Again confronted with his initial false report to Ambort, Herrod again readily admitted his lie. Not wanting to ap-pear a screw-up, he was telling the company commander what he wanted to hear, Herrod said. But it was not an ef-fort to cover up sixteen cold-blooded, calculated murders.

Nor was the subsequent artillery mission called on Son Thang in hopes of destroying evidence of his crime, Herrod responded. Asked again why he had lied, Herrod repeated that he wanted to hearten Ambort with good news. There really wasn't any enemy fire, was there? Brown persisted. There was, answered Herrod.

Emphasizing what he saw as Herrod's willingness to tai-lor his words to the situation, Brown again sought clarification of Herrod's lie to Ambort. Herrod writes, "I know he asked that question fifteen or twenty times, and in a variety of ways. . . . Every time he asked the question, however, I answered calmly and with courtesy. I knew that if I lost my temper or seemed undisciplined, the officers facing me might begin to believe the picture he was trying to paint."

In the end, Herrod returned to his place beside his lawyers, unshaken in his story.

Oliver North briefly returned to the stand to tie up testimonial loose ends. Upon leaving the courtroom, North started the long trip back to Quantico, where his Basic School patrolling classes and a pregnant wife awaited. Whatever the GCM's outcome, North would read about it in the newspapers.

The government had paid for the next defense witness, Dr. Hayden M. Donahue. In compliance with the motion granted Stipe, the 1st Marine Division's budget paid Dr. Donahue's expert-witness fee, transportation from Oklahoma, and per diem. Dr. Donahue, a psychiatrist, was director of the Oklahoma Department of Mental Health and superintendent of Central State Griffin Memorial Hospital.

What could he possibly say, the prosecution wondered? It was too far into the trial to raise an insanity defense. Besides, Donahue, who had just arrived in-country, had not examined Herrod.

Stipe's direct examination established the white-haired, travel-rumpled psychiatrist as a leading expert on what World War II veterans called "battle fatigue." Well-published and long-experienced in the topic, Donahue told the court that, in his opinion, Herrod probably was suffering from battle fatigue on the night of the killings. Since Herrod had been in combat for months, had seen friends killed, and faced death on a daily basis, his reasoning had essentially been supplanted by instinct, the doctor said.

The prosecution's cross of Dr. Donahue reclaimed no ground. Effective cross-examination of an expert witness, particularly a medical expert, requires the lawyer's concentrated effort and study of the area of expertise, and review of the pertinent literature and texts beforehand. Copies of the expert's own writings can be mined for inconsistencies with in-court testimony, or differing interpretations of other experts' opinions. But Captain Brown had access only to a *Classic Comics* version of a law library, and he certainly had no psychiatric references. There was the division surgeon, a medical doctor, on Hill 327, and a psychiatrist at the major Army medical center adjacent to China Beach, half an hour's drive away. But those doctors had other, more pressing, duties. For the moment, Dr. Donahue's assessment of Herrod stood unchallenged.

While Donahue's opinions were, no doubt, well-grounded in general, they were of questionable validity as applied to Randy Herrod.

Throughout World War II, U.S. armed forces lost 504,000 men to mental collapse. In the 1973 Arab-Israeli War, nearly a third of Israeli casualties were psychiatric. Most psychiatrists and psychologists agree that psychiatric breakdown is directly correlated to length of time in combat and its attendant experiences.

But Vietnam's twelve-month tours of duty brought a far lower incidence of battlefield psychiatric casualties (as opposed to post-traumatic stress disorder, a different matter) than from any previous war of American involvement. That low incidence involved other factors—frequent hot meals, rapid casualty evacuation, R&R—but the limited-length tours are commonly credited with virtually eliminating battle fatigue from U.S. units in Vietnam. And in Herrod's case, less than five weeks before Son Thang he had been on his unauthorized absence, a free, two-month, in-country holiday complete with beaches, babes, and beer.

Not counting this UA period, Herrod had been on duty in Vietnam for just under 200 days when he led the killer team to Son Thang. There is no evidence that he suffered any of the classic manifestations of combat fatigue: physical exhaustion, unsociability, confusion, mood swings, conversion hysteria, obsessional anxiety, or compulsive morbidity or fixation. If Herrod was suffering combat fatigue, the 39,900 other Marines then in South Vietnam would have liked a dose.

But from a defense standpoint, Dr. Donahue's testimony was another option upon which the members might base an acquittal, and an appellate issue suggesting possible postconviction sentence reduction.

Defense attorney Garrison later wrote, "The psychiatric evidence we presented in Herrod's trial was very persuasive, I think."[48] But persuasive of what? Later, the defense would offer, and then withdraw, a motion to dismiss the charges against Herrod "due to a lack of mental responsibility on the part of the defendant,"[49] a motion based on the defense's civilian experience, but one not employed in military practice. Were the members persuaded that acquittal was warranted because Herrod was suffering combat fatigue? Not likely, but only they could say for sure. Herrod wrote, "Dr. Donahue had done what he had been brought to do."

Partial mental responsibility, akin to insanity, is a defense in military law that, if argued and found by the members, reduces premeditated murder to *un*premeditated murder. That, in turn, reduces the possible maximum sentence.[50] The parameters of partial mental responsibility were irrelevant in Herrod's trial as it was not raised by the defense, although combat is the ideal basis for such a plea.

A series of defense motions for mistrial, all grist for the appellate court, followed Dr. Donahue's departure from the stand: motions for mistrial for the prosecution's misconduct in examining Ambort (denied); for failure of the prosecution to provide all the material earlier ordered by the court (denied); and for the jury's prosecutorial bias and prejudgment of the case, as demonstrated by their written questions to various witnesses (denied).

It had been a long day: they had spent more than eight hours in the cramped, sweaty courtroom, breathing each other's air, with only an hour's break for chow. After ten straight days in trial it was now Friday, and the litigants faced another weekend in court. But the end was in sight, the defense winding down. One more witness, Stipe and Garrison assured Commander Lawrence. Then the defense would rest.

Tomorrow, Lawrence responded; we'll do it tomorrow. It was happy hour at the O-Club. The GCM adjourned at 1715.

On Hill 327, as at FSB Ross, Saturday was just another workday. Herrod's court convened promptly at 0800. The defense recalled Sgt. Ronald Butler as its final, brief witness in order to leave the jury with testimony supporting its major thrust. Under the guise of clarifying questions raised since Butler first testified, Stipe cannily had him reiterate being fired upon by the M-60, and capturing it.

Smart lawyering. The last words heard by the jury were those of a disinterested Marine NCO confirming the defense's argument explaining how the Vietnamese victims came to be killed.

The defense rested. They had finished strong.

The government's rebuttal witnesses were succinct. Cdr. Richard L. Weidenbacher, a Navy doctor, pointed out the implausibility of Herrod having been a victim of combat fatigue.

Maj. Dick Theer, workhorse of the case, once more returned to Vietnam from Quantico, this time to testify in rebuttal. He later said of his questioning by the prosecution, "I was really disappointed."[51] His brief examination, he thought, was perfunctory, with little point, and not worth his long trip.

Theer was asked about the possibility of a captured machine gun, but pre-examination preparation had left him unaware of details raised by the two sergeant defense witnesses. Theer knew of a machine gun captured by the 3d Battalion, 21st Infantry, 196th Brigade, an Army command fifteen miles south of Son Thang. But he couldn't understand why he was asked about that weapon, seemingly unrelated to the Herrod case. His responses must have left the members equally mystified, as it hardly squared with the testimony they heard from the two sergeants. Theer's presence that day was of little impact. Thanks to the prosecution lawyers, Herrod won his final round with the major. Theer left the Son Thang stage. Eleven years later Richard E. Theer retired from the Marine Corps as a lieutenant colonel.

The defense offered no rebuttal testimony. Instead, Stipe and Garrison closed by offering up, like sacrifices, still more motions: pro forma motions to dismiss for failure of the prosecution to prove a prima facie case, and for a finding of not guilty (denied and denied); their perennial motion, more persistent than a bad odor, for a change of venue (denied with a laugh); a motion, moved and then withdrawn, to dismiss for lack of mental responsibility; and two motions for a mistrial, one—again—for prejudgment of the case by the jury, the other for asserted misconduct of the prosecution in asking improper questions during Herrod's cross-examination (denied and denied). The government's appellate lawyers in Washington, who would have to address all of these points on appeal, were going to hate these guys.

On Hill 327 the hour was late, but all concerned, lawyers, members, and accused, could clearly see the trial's end. Drive on, they agreed. Brown stood to deliver the government's closing argument to the jury. Polished through three previous trials, he hit the prosecution high points and attacked the defense theories and assertions. The facts were clear, he argued, the law even clearer. The verdict could only be guilty. A cocksure Herrod wrote of Brown's closing argument, "He was a good lawyer and had done his homework; but he was clearly exhausted, and he and his teammates had been outclassed. Everyone knew that."

Brown had earned his exhaustion. He had lived with Son Thang for more than six months. A few days after the killings, he and coprosecutor Jevne accompanied Theer on his inspection of the ville. For weeks after that, in helmet and flak jacket, a loaded .45 on his hip, Brown interviewed

Marines at FSB Ross, at Ryder, and at Baldy, and searched out reluctant Vietnamese witnesses. With Jevne, Brown painstakingly assembled the prosecution's case, working without forensic specialists, without autopsies, without ballistics, without dedicated transportation, without reference materials, and with little tangible support from seniors in his own office. He shepherded the case through a joint Article 32 investigation, through Ambort's Article 32, and through the emotional highs and Stygian lows of four general courts-martial—all the while balancing his other felony cases and contending with the occasional rocket attack. With no overtime.

A contested trial is work of the hard variety. Brown had been in virtually constant contested trials for six months. Only in military law does a young lawyer gain so much responsibility so early in his or her career. But too much of a good thing can get pretty damned old, pretty damned quick.

Defense pretrial motions had taken five days. The prosecution's case-in-chief was presented over three days. The defense, also taking three days, offered eleven witnesses over a span of about twenty in-court hours.

Stipe delivered the defense closing argument. For nearly two hours he addressed each piece of evidence, each witness's testimony, minimizing the government's case, stressing its inevitable inconsistencies, pressing the defense view of the facts. In plain, folksy language, he brought years of trial experience to bear, at one point emotionally comparing Herrod with the then-current case of the Chicago Seven.

After final argument, the court gave the members their instructions. There was little disagreement from either side as to their content. Commander Lawrence had discussed instructions with St. Amour before the latter left Vietnam.

But to one who observed all four courts, there was a striking change of thrust in the instructions. Schwarz's instructions mirrored his defense, emphasizing the Marine as "a reasoning agent" who must not obey obviously illegal orders. Green's instructions minimized obedience to orders while emphasizing the law of aiding and abetting, consistent with the prosecution's theory of that case. Reflecting Herrod's basic denial of the impropriety of his acts, his court's instructions simply accented the basic requirement that the government prove the charges beyond a reasonable doubt, the highest form of proof known to the law. One war crime had generated four trials, each with starkly differing thrusts.

At 2130, Lawrence asked the members if they wished to begin their deliberations at that late hour. They did. But an hour later they wearily returned to the courtroom and asked to continue in the morning. Lawrence recessed the court and all hands slowly made their way through the warm and humid darkness to their quarters. Date night was over.

At 0800 sharp the next morning, Sunday, the judge again convened the court. At 0802 the seven-officer panel once more filed from the courtroom into the deliberating room at the building's rear.

Randy Herrod was finally facing justice.

THE QUALITY OF JUSTICE

After a jury trial is concluded and the verdict and sentence rendered, some lawyers make it a practice to thank jurors as they depart, and ask if any evidence or testimony particularly influenced their thinking. But other lawyers never do so, their past experience having revealed the unaccountable, even weird, things jurors sometimes seize upon in deciding cases; the litigators would just rather not know. Also, after a trial, jurors may consciously distort their true opinions and tailor their responses to what they think may please their questioner. There is no requirement that jurors talk to the lawyers, truthfully or otherwise, so they feel no particular obligation to be forthcoming.

Scientific research fares no better than individual attorneys in probing the dynamics of the jury process. Reid Hastie, an authority on jury research, writes in *Inside the Ju-*

ror, "We have discovered no unified description of the nature of the juror decision processes in the legal literature; certainly none has appeared in the major appellate decisions concerned with the right to trial by jury or in any of the major law reviews during the past fifty years."[52] Hastie later adds, "When the evidence is technical, sparse, or *if the charge involves emotion-provoking events,* the juror's sentiments are 'liberated' and extra-legal considerations (*e.g., the race of the defendant or victim,* the juror's attitude toward the applicable law, etc.) influence the judgment."[53] [Emphasis added.] In other words, while extra-legal factors may well affect verdicts, no one can offer a general theory of how juries reach their verdicts. They just do.

Twenty years after Herrod's trial, the four members who were still living were asked about their verdict.

When the seven officers had began their discussion of the case in the stifling August heat, it was immediately apparent to them that the prosecution was in trouble.

Apart from the facts of the case, the jurors were uniformly impressed by the defense team and its case. "He had a slick lawyer," one of the panelists remembered. "He [Stipe] was trying to take care of the hometown boy who was being railroaded. . . . He was a good ol' boy."[54] A second officer agreed, "Herrod's civilian lawyers did a brilliant job." A third said, "My strongest impressions of the trial are of the competency of the civilian defense team."

Their opinions of the prosecution, on the other hand, were not good. "I remember waiting, when the prosecution rested, for the defense counsel to move for a directed verdict of not guilty," said one member. "I simply did not see where a crime had been committed."[55]

What about Herrod's repeated orders to "kill them all"? "My recollection," one major responded, "is of testimony that each such utterance was preceded by some action on the part of the Vietnamese which could have been seen by the Marines as a hostile action, and that their response was as to an ambush. After the first incident, they appeared to me to have been a very frightened team." He concluded, "The prosecution had failed to show any deliberate act of unprovoked killing, and had been unable to overcome defense testimony that Herrod and his team truly believed themselves to be under hostile attack."

Different jurors often draw differing conclusions from the same evidence. In the course of any trial, juror attention wanders, snippets of testimony are missed, mis-heard, or misinterpreted, and different facts are seized upon by different individuals. The Herrod members recalled events in just such a way but, surprisingly, their differing perceptions were predominantly sympathetic to the defense.

"The machine-gun fire the patrol was subjected to was probably the most persuasive fact," allowed one member. But, other than Herrod's testimony with its obviously self-serving potential, there had been no evidence that the Son Thang patrol received machine-gun fire, and Krichten had sworn there was *no* enemy fire. Krichten's testimony was not recalled.

Another member was struck by a defense witness's testimony that the firing from Son Thang sounded like an M-16 on automatic and, with complete irrelevance, he wondered if modifications to the captured M-60 might have made its rate of fire similar to an M-16 on automatic.

Yet another member said, "The primary factors which influenced our decisions was the lack of definitive testimony as to what actually happened."[56] But, as Prof. Alan Dershowitz writes in *Reasonable Doubts*, "In a criminal trial, we are generally dealing with a decision that must be made under conditions of uncertainty. We will never know with absolute certainty."[57] The principal task of a jury, after all, is to decide cloudy or disputed facts.

All of those questioned agreed that Lieutenant North's testimony had no particular impact upon their verdict.

Concerning the possibility of a conviction, with its attendant publicity, a juror added, "Of course, there was some concern about the record of the Marine Corps . . . how it would look."[58]

During deliberations there was strong argument for Herrod's conviction. But too few of the seven saw it that way. "There was certainly enough evidence for conviction," one of the lieutenant colonels opined. "My impression was that he was certainly guilty. [But] he had a good defense and they had succeeded in . . . creating some reasonable doubt in the minds of some of the more senior members of the court."[59]

The panel's initial vote on the charge of premeditated murder was four to three, but the members' recollections are inconsistent as to whether for acquittal or conviction. In either event, since a two-thirds majority was required for conviction, the split constituted a finding of not guilty of that charge

As in civilian criminal trials, and in accordance with their instructions, the members then voted on a series of lesser included offenses. That is, if not guilty of the charged offense, premeditated murder, did they find Herrod guilty of the lesser offense of voluntary manslaughter? And if not voluntary manslaughter, of aggravated assault? Unaccountably, as the seven officers considered the lesser offenses, the vote swung not toward conviction of a less serious charge, as one would expect, but more strongly toward acquittal.[60]

The panel's discussion stretched toward noon as their consensus solidified. At 1055, two hours and fifty-three minutes after they had retired to deliberate that morning, the members filed back into a packed courtroom. Every lawyer in the 1st Marine Division was present, majors and above excepted. There were as many media representatives as could squeeze into the spectators' area beside the Marine judge advocates.

Herrod and his lawyers stood shoulder-to-shoulder facing Col. Miller M. Blue, a tough combat Marine and the senior member. Blue passed the findings worksheet, upon which the verdict was written, to the clerk, who handed it to Commander Lawrence. After briefly examining it, Judge Lawrence returned it to Blue, saying, "The findings are in order." Lawrence told the colonel to announce the verdict.

"Pvt. Randell D. Herrod, it is my duty as president of this court," Blue intoned, reading from the worksheet, "to advise you that the court, in closed session and upon secret written ballot, has found you not guilty of all specifications, and the charge."

Randy Herrod was found not to be a war criminal.

The courtroom "erupted in pandemonium," in the words of the *Washington Post* report. Herrod threw his hands in the air, then embraced his closest lawyer, Captain Williams. Over the tumult the judge ordered the accused released from custody. Lawrence formally closed the court and began to gather his books and manuals for his return to Subic. Herrod's chaser, now superfluous, unbuckled his duty belt with the holstered .45, slung it over his shoulder, and waited for a chance to wander back to his unit.

Gene Stipe later said of the court-martial, "Anytime you walk your man you can't be too damn critical of the way the system works."[61] "We walked the patrol leader,"[62] said defense counsel Garrison, seemingly amazed.

Beaming, Herrod and his defense team edged through the crowd surrounding the courtroom to answer reporters' questions in the noonday sun. The members weaved through the throng on their way back to their quarters—they wouldn't get much work done on a Sunday afternoon anyway. Herrod writes that as he responded to the media, he caught a glimpse of Boyd and Krichten walking away. "I would have shaken their hands. I didn't blame either one of them, wouldn't have blamed them even if I'd been found guilty. They were just a couple of poor rats who had found a way to wriggle out of a trap. I was just glad I had wriggled out too."

That afternoon, Gene Stipe climbed into a Marine Corps van to be driven to the airbase at Da Nang for his flight back to the States. Herrod, free after nine months in pretrial confinement, eased aside the armed Marine who

Post-trial interviews: as Herrod speaks, Lt. Ambort (hands behind back) looks on, flanked by civilian defense lawyers Richard Miller, Denzil Garrison (partially hidden), and Gene Stipe. *Author's collection*

was to ride shotgun, and got in the van, too. Herrod would act as security for his lawyer's departure.

How did Herrod's acquittal come about? Only the jury can say, and even the jurors do not agree.

Maj. Bob Blum, who conducted the joint Article 32 investigation, believed the acquittal was based upon Herrod's Silver Star, the Mere Gook Rule, and Judge Lawrence's exclusion of the photographs of the victims.[63]

Lt. Col. Paul St.Amour, who knew the Son Thang cases as well as anyone, uncharitably said of the acquittal, "The best defense in a court-martial has always been a weak [prosecutor] along with an inadequate judge."[64] As usual, he was correct.

Commander Lawrence himself opined that the acquittal was the jury's statement of "public policy,"[65] a term which, in that trial's context, suggests the Mere Gook Rule in more genteel words. As to the evidence, Lawrence said, "There was an element of self-defense, but I did not feel it was a strong element . . . because it lacked reasonableness." So much for enemy machine-gun fire, as far as the judge was concerned. Lawrence concluded, "There was adequate evidence of guilt to have supported a conviction, but the court concluded that to convict would result in an injustice."[66]

Was the verdict correct, as distinct from just? Not if one considers the second statements of the killer team as the best indicators of truth. Those statements were made just four days following the event, after advice of rights to silence and against self-incrimination and that their first statements could be withdrawn without penalty—and before they spoke to lawyers. And the independently given accounts of Schwarz, Boyd, and Krichten mesh in all significant details.

But, as Denzil Garrison replied when asked about his client's guilt, "I can only ask you the immortal question of Baron Munchausen, 'Vas you dere, Charlie?'"[67]

The doctrine of jury nullification allows jurors to refuse to enforce the law against defendants whom they believe in good conscience should be acquitted. Jury nullification is explicitly recognized in many civilian appellate opinions, but not in military cases.[68] Jeffrey Abramson writes in *We, the Jury,* "The jury should also acquit when it finds the broken law just but agrees that enforcing it against the particular defendant on trial would be unjust. . . . For anyone who takes seriously the jury as a bridge between community values and the law, jury nullification is a strong plank."[69]

Draft resistors were frequent beneficiaries of jury nullification in civilian courtrooms during the Vietnam era: they were acquitted despite their clear violation of unpopular laws. Jury nullification also has a darker side. In the 1950s, '60s, and early '70s, particularly, civil-rights violations and racially motivated crime were too often excused by sympathetic juries.

Vietnam military juries, prey to the Mere Gook Rule, were particularly open to jury nullification in cases involving Vietnamese victims. Prof. Guenter Lewy asserts, "If officers serving on courts-martial acquitted defendants or adjudged light sentences, their verdicts much of the time were the result of sympathy they felt for the frustrations experienced by the men . . . a tendency to close ranks and to protect fellow officers or comrades-in-arms from the enlisted ranks."[70]

Was Herrod's acquittal the expression of the jury's unwillingness to imprison a good-looking, articulate, heroic young man for the killing of mere Vietnamese—such killings occurring in combat a hundred times every day? Or was it no more or less than seven conscientious, combat-experienced officers empathizing with a junior Marine's difficult choices? Or did the prosecutors, inexperienced and in over their heads, simply fail to prove the charges beyond a reasonable doubt?

The Honorable Jack Weinstein, a U.S. district court judge, points out, "The legitimacy of the jury process demands respect for its outcomes, whatever they may be. Attempting to distinguish between a 'right' outcome—a verdict following the letter of the law—and a 'wrong' one—a 'nullification' verdict—can be dangerous, and this endeavor depends largely upon personal bias."[71]

As for Herrod's acts in a morally gray tactical situation, Colonel Cooper noted that, "The trooper rightly never understood why we could order an air strike on a village that was the source of fire, but a more definitive rule of conduct applied to the man with the rifle. There is a difference, a big difference, but can you explain that satisfactorily to a man who saw his best friend just killed in an ambush triggered by a 10-year-old with an AK-47?"[72]

Even presuming that Herrod had experienced such events, the answer is, yes, the difference *can* be explained. The trooper *must* be taught to recognize the essential difference between artillery fire on a legitimate target, which may have civilian victims, and pulling a rifle's trigger on a defenseless noncombatant. The difference is moral choice and intent—intent to kill another human being. Lawful conduct on the battlefield will never be universal, but there can be no excuse for military leadership not making every effort to reach that high goal.

The Marines and civilians involved in the trial process made little of their roles in the law of war, yet played them effectively. The UCMJ fulfilled its intended international law function effectively, its criminal sanctions brought to bear in the combat zone.

But what does Herrod's acquittal say about military justice and its duty to enforce America's obligations under the Geneva Conventions and the customary law of war? The acquittal says the same thing as the convictions of Schwarz and Green: that as a nation, America and her military forces did all they could to carry out international legal responsibilities.

The Son Thang trials were not show trials like, for example, the post–World War I trials in Leipzig, Germany. There was no cover-up of the crimes by Marine commanders. The acquittals of Herrod and Boyd merely reflect the unpredictable course of particular cases in any legal system. While one hopes for a general consistency of verdict and sentence, those cannot be ordered, even in a court-martial. The best one may expect are fair trials and vigorous representation by both sides, the results occurring as they may. That fairly describes the Son Thang courts-martial.

And if the courts-martial were described in a movie, or a play, the curtain would fall with the setting Vietnam sun. But neither military nor civilian trials end with the judge's gavel and his announcement, "This court is closed." Not in real life.

Significant post-trial events often take place in appellate courtrooms, away from media interest. This is not anti-climax; it is the normal progress of the law. The Son Thang cases were not over. There were still unanticipated hurdles for the killer team, and for the Marine Corps.

8

CLEMENCY GRANTED,
APPEAL DENIED

After his conviction of war crimes, Schwarz got a dishonorable discharge and confinement for life. Green got a dishonorable discharge and confinement for five years.

Herrod got a medal. But not when he should have.

After his acquittal on 30 August, Herrod returned to 1/7 while orders were cut to return him to the States. Although his enlistment would not be completed until 14 October, he was to be returned and discharged as soon as the paperwork could be processed—not because of his GCM, but because he was "short," with very little time-in-service remaining on his enlistment. He had already served more than his obligatory year in Vietnam. All Marines as short as Herrod were discharged immediately upon return to CONUS—the continental United States. The Marines recognized that it was fruitless and unwise to keep personnel in the combat zone when they were soon to be discharged, because their distraction could possibly result in injury or death to themselves or others.

Among the distractions were the "short-timer calendars" ubiquitous throughout Vietnam. They were mimeographs of poorly drawn figures of nude women in rudely seductive poses, their bodies divided into one hundred numbered segments. The short-timers patiently colored in a segment a day, working their way from the figure's extremities to the torso, counting down to zero—the scheduled day of departure. Zero was predictably centered on the pudendum.

Among Herrod's distractions during trial was the fact that he had not been given the Silver Star he earned early in his Vietnam service. In conformance with federal law, he could not be given the medal while he was undergoing disciplinary proceedings—but there was another reason.

On 6 January 1970, in an administrative screw up, Herrod's medal was sent to the 3d Marine Division, where he had earned it, for presentation. That was two weeks before the Son Thang incident but ten weeks after Herrod had been transferred to the 1st Marine Division. Compounding the confusion, it was also nine weeks after 3d Division headquarters had permanently departed Vietnam for Okinawa. Knowing only that the medal had not been awarded, the president of Oklahoma's Inter-Tribal Council of the Five Civilized Tribes instigated congressional correspondence concerning the matter. Senator Fred Harris queried the Commandant in June. General Chapman presumed the non-award was due to Herrod's court-martial and he replied to Senator Harris in that vein. Actually, it was not awarded because it was lost "in channels."

So for four months, while the 3d Marine Division was unscrambling the epic confusion engendered by relocating to Okinawa after three-and-a-half years in combat, no one realized that there was an unawarded Silver Star, meant for someone no longer on the division roster, rattling around the personnel officer's desk drawer. In Vietnam, the 1st Division, Herrod's actual unit, had no reason, or means, to know of the medal's award, or its misdirection. Herrod, not surprisingly, viewed the lack of award as the Marine Corps' final affront: a conscious refusal to give him the medal he risked his life in earning.

In March, five months before Herrod left Vietnam, the 3d Marine Division belatedly sorted out Herrod's location and forwarded his Silver Star to the 1st Division, which delayed its award, pending his court's outcome. The medal should have been awarded after Herrod's acquittal and before his return to the States, a period of less than seventy-two hours. It was not. That failure may have been the result of petty mean-spiritedness on the part of officers who believed Herrod should have been convicted. More likely, it was simply overlooked in the fleeting period when it might have been presented. As Herrod said in another context, greater fuck-ups had occurred.

Three days after his acquittal, on 2 September, Herrod boarded a civilian Flying Tiger 707 "freedom bird"; three days after that he reported aboard the Marine Corps Recruit Depot, San Diego, for out-processing. He had been in Vietnam four days short of fifteen months, UA for two of those months, and in custody awaiting his general court-martial for more than six months.

Three days after arriving at MCRD, with an entry in his service record noting that he was not recommended for reenlistment due to failure to achieve the rank of lance corporal, Herrod was handed an honorable discharge and a voucher for a ticket back to his home of record, Calvin, Oklahoma. Herrod's twenty-two months in the Marine Corps had been, as the Chinese curse puts it, interesting.

Three months after his discharge, the confusion surrounding his Silver Star was resolved when Marine Corps headquarters asked the 1st Marine Division why an endorsement indicating presentation of the medal had not been returned. The award was hastily located and sent back to Washington. Herrod received his well-deserved medal on 10 December 1970 at the Marine Barracks, U.S. Naval Ammunition Depot, McAlester, Oklahoma, in a ceremony attended by his grandfather, other relatives, and friends. As a military band played the Marines' Hymn, the citation was read out and the depot commanding officer, a Marine colonel, pinned the Silver Star on Randy Herrod's sport coat. Few of those present could have appreciated the irony.

LCpl. Michael Krichten completed his full tour of Vietnam duty, departing Da Nang on 13 September. He walked out the main gate of San Diego's Marine Corps Recruit Depot ten days later, with an honorable discharge. Pfc. Thomas Boyd, after serving one year, one month, and one week in Vietnam, had passed through the same gate six days earlier with a similar honorable discharge in hand. Both Krichten and Boyd returned to their pre-enlistment homes to continue their lives in quiet obscurity.

Schwarz and Green left Vietnam too. On 16 September they were transferred under guard to the brig at Camp Pendleton, California. As soon as the administrative groundwork was completed they were further transferred to the Navy Disciplinary Command at Portsmouth, New Hampshire, where long-term naval service prisoners served their time.

In Vietnam, print journalists and TV news crews moved on to other stories, other horrors. Son Thang's international notoriety faded, but the cases were not played out.

SEEKING EQUITY

Charles F. Widdecke had been a Marine for thirty years. A tall, thin Texan, he was a Marine raider in World War II, awarded his own Silver Star, plus a Navy Cross and Purple Heart. He first served in Vietnam in 1966. Now in his second tour, he was a major general, commander of the 1st Marine Division. He had held the billet since April, two months before the first Son Thang GCM. When he assumed command from Maj. Gen. Edwin Wheeler, the Son Thang cases were already on their administrative paths to general courts-martial; Krichten's immunity had already been granted; the legal ground had been staked out. From the beginning Widdecke had little room for maneuver, yet

Maj. Gen. Charles F. Widdecke, CG of the 1st Marine Division throughout the Son Thang courts-martial, troops the line with a South Vietnamese general in June 1970. A hundred meters away the Boyd trial had just convened. *U.S. Marine Corps*

it was *his* command that suffered months of adverse publicity for the crimes of a few men. The trials for "the Marine Corps My Lai" were never far from his mind.

Although his own son was to be a lawyer, Widdecke had no noticeable use for judge advocates. Cols. Bob Lucy and Don Holben, his successive staff judge advocates, did not enjoy a close command relationship with him. That having been said, it was with their legal advice that Widdecke made the decisions to try the Son Thang accused as noncapital cases.

Widdecke's assistant division commander, Brig. Gen. Edwin H. Simmons, had served with him before and knew him well. Simmons described the CG as "a fine, fine officer."[1] But Simmons recognized that Widdecke was a hard man, more interested in results than approval. "He was not a popular officer," Simmons conceded. "Demanding, impatient, and he made no particular effort to be pleasant. . . . Very much a loner . . . not at all satisfied with the caliber of officer or [enlisted] man that we had in the 1st Marine Division at that time. On at least one occasion, he quoted Wellington: he said, 'Scum! Wellington had it right. They're scum!'"[2]

Now it was up to Widdecke to conduct the first legal review of the Schwarz and Green convictions, with the advice of his SJA, Don Holben. Boyd and Herrod, having been acquitted, required no further administrative action. Their tape-recorded records of trial were not even typed, since only convictions require verbatim records for review purposes.

Under 1970 military law, special and general courts-martial required legal review by the convening authority—Widdecke—before their sentences (other than confinement) could be carried out. Any sentence including a bad-conduct or dishonorable discharge, as did Schwarz's and Green's, required a second, later review and affirmation by the Court of Military Review, in Washington. Throughout these reviews, the initial sentence of the court could never be increased, nor a "not guilty" finding be disturbed. Unlike civilian appellate systems, military reviews are automatic, and may exercise clemency, as well as review questions of law and fact.

Widdecke's review would be prepared by lawyers in his SJA's office. They would examine each contested issue, and its in-court resolution, for legal correctness. If no substantial error was found the SJA would recommend the CG approve the proceedings and order the sentence executed. A CG's disapproval of a guilty finding was unusual, but not unheard of. Sentence reductions, however, were common. And Widdecke was very concerned about the sentences of Schwarz and Green.

General Simmons, recalling his own reactions to the verdicts, and his discussions with the CG, exclaimed, "My

God! How inequitable! Appalling! Why is it that the person who seems should be most guilty is acquitted? . . . Where's the sense to it? And I saw other patterns. If you want to beat the court-martial, get yourself a prestigious, high-pressure civilian and he'll tie the young [judge advocate] captains into knots."[3]

Indeed, it remains disturbing that the two Son Thang accused represented by civilians were acquitted, while the two represented by military lawyers were convicted. A similar observation might apply to the Army's My Lai prosecutions, in which acquittals of Col. Oran Henderson and Capt. Ernest Medina were, in large part, due to their civilian lawyers, Henry Rothblatt and F. Lee Bailey. (An exception was the splendid prosecution of Calley by judge advocate Capt. Aubrey Daniel, opposed by Calley's inept civilian defender, George Latimer.)

As Widdecke pondered what action to take in regard to the convicted murderers, he was disturbed by the discrepancies in the outcomes of the four courts-martial. "These are the things that General Widdecke perceived," Simmons recalls. "We often talked about them, those brooding nights in the semi-gloom of his quarters. Jesus Christ, what the hell is happening here? How do you restore some kind of equity? And I think that's what he eventually tried to do."

Widdecke had the power to simply rubber-stamp the sentences, or to reduce them to any level he considered appropriate—in theory, even to disapprove the guilty findings.

Although General Widdecke did not know it, study after study documents that the Schwarz-Green sentences were not at all unusual.

During the Vietnam War, twenty-seven Marines were convicted of the war crime of murdering noncombatants, several cases involving multiple victims or associated crimes, such as aggravated assault or rape. The sentences in those cases had a wide range: confinement for life, for fifty years, for thirty, for twenty years. Only in seven cases was confinement imposed for fewer than ten years. Thus

Schwarz's life sentence was not remarkable. Green's lesser five-year confinement was.

Marine Corps war crime sentences were also consistent with civilian sentences for murder. In 1970, in Schwarz's and Krichten's home state of Pennsylvania, for example, sentences to confinement for murder ranged from one year to a high of only *six* years, and one death sentence.[4] So Marine sentences, imposed in a combat zone, cover a much higher range of years than Pennsylvania's. A comparison with murder sentences imposed by U.S. Federal district courts yields the same conclusion.[5] Nor was Schwarz's or Green's confinement significantly different from that of military personnel who murdered fellow soldiers or Marines outside Vietnam.

Similarly, the acquittal rate for homicides in Vietnam did not materially differ from the rate of acquittals in federal courts of the same period, as far as can be determined. The Son Thang acquittals, and the sentences imposed in the convictions, although disturbingly disparate, were no different from sentences and acquittals found in civilian America. As the authors of one civilian sentencing study point out, "the more culpable offense does not always receive the more severe punishment . . . [and] the huge differences in sanctions within the murder category would appear to offend any colorably coherent theory of punishment."[6]

General Widdecke, however, was unaware of and unconcerned with academic sentence comparisons and their rationales. He recognized an inequity when he saw one. Lieutenant Ambort had inflamed his young Marines, yet would return to civilian life in 1971 with no more than a nonjudicial punishment on his military record. Boyd and Krichten were enjoying safety and freedom. Herrod had returned to college, his tuition subsidized by the G.I. Bill. But Schwarz and Green . . .

What could Widdecke do? He turned to his SJA-prepared review. Attached was a "Brief in Behalf of Pvt. Michael A. Schwarz," submitted by two lawyers from a seven-man Pittsburgh law firm. They were working *pro bono*, and their brief reflected a low level of professional competence.

The law firm's earlier attempt at an end run—urging the Secretary of the Navy to take mitigating action—had been unsuccessful. Secretary John Chafee had suggested they stay within the congressionally established route for military judicial review and take their arguments to the convening authority.

With no other choice, they did so. To expedite review, the brief's authors wrote, they would avoid "technical discussions of abstruse legal concepts."[7] They surely did. Citing no cases, evidentiary rules, or legal authorities, they essentially argued that, in light of Herrod's acquittal, fair play required Schwarz's conviction be set aside. Treading a fine line just short of alleging incompetence on the part of Captain LeGear, the trial defense counsel, they related the evidence not raised in Schwarz's GCM that *was* raised in Herrod's, and urged that the Herrod evidence now be applied to the Schwarz case—a unique legal suggestion. "A review of the trial record of [Schwarz] would indicate a paucity of proof in support of his defense of obedience to a lawful order," they wrote. "A review of the trial record made in the Herrod case discloses a wealth of facts to cure the poverty of the Schwarz proof." (How the civilians knew what was raised in Herrod's trial is unknown since, contrary to their assertion, there never was a hard-copy verbatim record of that GCM.)

The civilian lawyers had low opinions of the acquitted team members, as well. Herrod was "the patrol leader who gave the orders to kill." Boyd, they said, was acquitted on a defense "that he was in fact a pacifist, a rather novel defense for a combat Marine." Krichten, "the informer . . . a characterless weakling whose incredible memory was only exceeded by his desire to save his own skin," was further depicted as "a remarkable Marine: he was able to describe in detail the position of every man in his patrol in each of three occasions."

The defense brief closed, "Private Schwarz now sits in the brig convicted of premeditated murder . . . because he obeyed the order of his patrol leader. Private Schwarz's patrol leader is now in college. . . . We respectfully request that the finding of the court be disapproved and the charges against Private Schwarz be dismissed."

But the judge advocates to whom they sent their brief weren't the pilgrims the Pittsburgh lawyers may have supposed. The SJA's thirty-page, single-spaced review of the evidence, findings, and sentence of Schwarz's GCM responded in detail to the civilian firm's arguments.

As to Schwarz's assertion that in Son Thang he only followed orders, Colonel Holben wrote that, given Schwarz's age and military experience, he could not have honestly believed Herrod's orders to fire on unarmed women and children were legal. Moreover, "Herrod's order and Private Schwarz's consequent acts were wholly unprovoked by enemy action."

The SJA did not write about it, but obedience to orders has been raised as a defense by soldiers since the inception of armies. In 1474, Peter von Hagenbach, appointed governor of Breisach by Duke Charles of Burgundy, pleaded that defense before his tribunal. Convicted of murder and rape, Hagenbach was put to death. After the Civil War, Maj. Henry Wirz, the Swiss doctor who was commandant of the Andersonville prisoner-of-war camp where 12,900 Union soldiers died, raised the defense of obedience to orders. He was convicted and shot, the only soldier of either side to be executed for war crimes. And so on, down to the twentieth century. In 1901, Lt. Harry H. "Breaker" Morant of the British Bush Veldt Carbineers was shot for law-of-war violations during the Boer War, after his defense of obedience to orders failed.

But strangely, obedience to orders was an absolute defense for American servicemen charged with war crimes in U.S. courts until late in World War II. The War Department's *Rules of Land Warfare, 1914* read, "Individuals of the

Armed Forces will not be punished for these offenses in case they are committed under orders or sanction of their government or commanders. The commanders ordering the commission of such acts . . . may be punished." Those 1914 rules remained in effect into World War II.

Finally appreciating that Nazis would soon be tried for war crimes, and would inevitably raise the defense of superior orders, the United States followed Britain's lead and, in November 1944, amended her approach. From then on, obedience to orders was *not* a defense to war crime charges.[8] The postwar Nuremberg International Military Tribunal, and the Subsequent Trials, nevertheless saw the defense of superior orders raised to an art form. Despite Article 8 of the Tribunal's charter ("The fact that the Defendant acted pursuant to order . . . of a superior shall not free him from responsibility"), many Nazis employed the defense and a few were acquitted on that basis.

In 1956, Field Manual 27-10, *The Law of Land Warfare,* articulated the current U.S. test for obedience to orders as a defense for war crimes. In his review of the Schwarz conviction, Holben agreed with the members that Schwarz had failed that test; as a man of ordinary sense and understanding Schwarz must have known that the acts ordered by Herrod were unlawful, and beyond the scope of Herrod's authority.

In textbooks and scholarly articles the soldier's dilemma is often explored, usually in drastic terms: "The position of a soldier is in theory and may be in practice a difficult one. He may . . . be liable to be shot by a court-martial if he disobeys an order, and be hanged by a judge and jury if he obeys it."[9] In fact, no American soldier will be either shot or hanged for disobedience of an order. At worst, the maximum punishment (rarely imposed) is five years.

Another professor protests, "It is easy to instruct men. . . . But there is no attempt to tell the soldier how he is to distinguish the noncombatant child from a boy soldier . . . the ordinary village population from guerilla units."[10]

Such ruminations belittle battlefield war crimes, which

are usually naked criminal acts by anyone's definition. There was no Vietnam-era murder prosecution for having mistaken a civilian for a combatant. Instead, at My Lai, Calley demanded of one of his soldiers, "Why haven't you wasted them yet?" In another case, an Army captain commanded, "Take [the prisoner] down the hill and shoot him."[11] "Kill all the bitches," Herrod shouted. Given those circumstances does a soldier require a class on Geneva Conventions to recognize the illegality of the order? Can possible disciplinary action for not obeying such commands excuse the obeying of them? Recognizing the illegality of such orders requires neither superior intelligence nor academic accomplishment. There are improper orders of less clear illegality, no doubt, subtle in their wrongfulness, requiring a fine moral discernment to avoid criminality in their execution. But they are rare on the battlefield.

At least two GCM judges in Vietnam even refused to instruct jurors on the superior orders defense when requested by the accused's counsel.[12] In both cases the charges involved shooting and killing detained Vietnamese upon the order of a superior. Appellate courts upheld both refusals to instruct, noting that "the killing of a docile prisoner taken during military operations is not justifiable homicide."[13] The appellate courts agreed that the orders were manifestly unlawful as a matter of law. In a 1958 opinion, an Israeli court wrote, "The distinguishing mark of a 'manifestly unlawful order' should fly like a black flag. . . . Not formal unlawfulness, hidden or half-hidden, nor unlawfulness discernable only to the eyes of legal experts. . . . [The] unlawfulness piercing the eye and revolting the heart, be the eye not blind nor the heart stony and corrupt—that is the measure of 'manifest unlawfulness' required to release a soldier from the duty of obedience."[14]

In his review, Holben concluded that Schwarz's attempt to excuse his acts by pleading Herrod's manifestly unlawful orders was legally ineffective.

On the sticky issue of Lieutenant Ambort's urging Schwarz, without a warning of rights, to "tell the truth," and the accused's resulting statement to Theer, Schwarz's own testimony was determinative, Holben wrote. Schwarz assured the court that Ambort did not make him feel compelled to make his admissions and his written statement was legally unobjectionable. Arguable as the point may have been, a case so otherwise strong was not likely to be overturned on such a close point.

The dismaying difference in outcomes in Schwarz's and Herrod's cases was considered. The team leader walks, the subordinate does life. Is that lawful? Clearly so.

Civilian and military law is replete with instances of differing verdicts in co-actors' cases. If two parties commit a crime together, one may be found guilty and the other innocent for a variety of reasons, each reason acceptable in both law and common sense. The Son Thang cases remain perfect examples. Different judges in companion cases, lawyers of differing ability, dissimilar evidentiary rulings, differing levels of involvement by the accused, juries with opposing perceptions—the possible explanations for dissimilar verdicts for the same acts are endless. Since laws are applied by humans, disparities will arise.

Nor was Holben overly concerned with the civilian lawyers' criticism of Schwarz's lawyer. "The derogatory assessment of Captain LeGear's conduct of the defense at the trial of this case," Holben declared, "is not novel in military law. In fact it has become common practice for losing litigants, provided with excellent hindsight." The criticism of LeGear's trial tactics was raised, Holben continued, only because of their lack of success.

Finally moving to Schwarz's sentence, Holben made a surprising recommendation, probably prompted by conversations with General Widdecke. "The accused was not the leader of the patrol, but was carrying out the orders of his patrol leader. While the orders . . . were patently illegal, there is no evidence the accused entered into a pre-planned conspiracy to commit murder. Another consideration is the accused's low level of basic intelligence." Taking these factors into consideration, Holben recommended that the dishonorable discharge, and forfeitures of pay and allowances, remain undisturbed, but that the sentence to confinement for life be reduced to twenty years.

There was no legal requirement for clemency, and no error was found in the trial. It was simply Holben's advice after comparing Schwarz's case with the others, and with similar cases. Coming from the CG's senior lawyer, the recommendation carried significant weight.

Few executives actually compose the official correspondence they sign. The 1st Division's SJA was no exception. Holben's review, with its clemency recommendation, was actually drafted by Capt. Gary Bushell, formerly of the prosecution section. Ironically, Bushell had been third-seat prosecutor in Herrod's trial, and second seat in Boyd's and Green's trials. The extent of Bushell's involvement, if any, in convincing Holben that clemency was merited for Schwarz, is unrecorded. Given the interchange of personal opinion and legal viewpoint between a convening authority, the SJA, and his review section, one suspects that former prosecutor Bushell had a significant part in the recommendation for leniency.

The SJA's review of Green's trial, recommending no reduction of his already notably light five-year confinement, followed within days of the Schwarz review.

Mercy, or License?

Widdecke, as it turned out, had his own ideas regarding clemency. Perhaps he knew that whether an order be lawful, unlawful, or manifestly unlawful, it is not an easy thing for a Marine to refuse to obey.

Military historian John Keegan writes in *The Face of Battle* that "'Battle,' for the ordinary soldier, is a very small-scale situation which will throw up its own leaders and will be fought by its own rules—alas, often by its own ethics."[15] In combat, a group dynamic sometimes overtakes individual judgment and one's normal behavior may become sub-

merged in the behavioral commonality of the unit, sometimes the lowest common behavioral denominator. As a
psychologist tells us, "The military group provides powerful
incentives for releasing forbidden impulses, inducing the
soldier to try out formerly inhibited acts which he originally
regarded as morally repugnant."[16]

Perhaps obedience is even greater in the Marine Corps,
which sees itself as an exclusive fraternity. Lt. Gen. Victor
Krulak writes, "Among Marines there is a fierce loyalty. . . .
Woven through that sense of belonging, like a steel thread,
is an elitist spirit. Marines are convinced that, being few in
number, they are selective, better, and, above all, different."[17] Vietnam war correspondent Morley Safer agrees:
"The bond, the loyalty to the Corps is almost mystical in its
power."[18]

The members of the Son Thang killer team, except for
Boyd and Krichten, had met each other only that afternoon.
Three of the five had been in the Marine Corps for little
more than a year, one for only six months. But they had a
shared military background, however brief. Their very presence in Vietnam and the 1st Marine Division was evidence
of an unconsciously shared attitude and ethos. They were
Marines, sharing the bond that the title "Marine" tradition-
ally imparts.

Of the five, the oldest was twenty-one. Three were
teenagers. The most senior among them was a lance corporal. Except for Herrod, the only high school graduate
among them, they revealed a marked lack of education and
intellect in their written statements. During the patrol they
were on their own, at night, beyond friendly lines. A member of their company had been killed hours before. What,
then, passed through their minds, when ordered to fire on
unresisting women and children? Who among the four be-
nighted subordinates might have mustered the presence
and courage to refuse Herrod's orders?

It has been said that in combat "the relatively abstract
commands of the [Geneva] Conventions are not likely to
bear much relation to reality in the mind of a serviceman

who is not . . . attuned to the niceties of the law,"[19] and the group's standards of behavior become those of the individual. In the study *Crimes of Obedience*, ethicists and sociologists suggest that "not only do normal moral principles become inoperative, but—particularly when the actions are explicitly ordered—a different kind of morality, linked to the duty to obey superior orders, tends to take over."[20] The need to obey is strengthened to the extent that others obey. In a combat situation, the man who refuses to obey an order that his comrades are carrying out is in a *very* difficult position. Classic scientific studies confirm that superior orders can override an individual's own sense of morality.[21] "Even when the facts of a situation are clear, moral choice may demand more moral courage than even a competent professional can muster."[22] Never underestimate the power of the need to obey.

How do ordinary men become extraordinary murderers? Christopher Browning, in *Ordinary Men*, his account of Nazi police reservists who engaged in genocide, suggests that "socialization through family, school, and military service, as well as a whole array of rewards and punishments within society generally, reinforces and internalizes a tendency toward obedience."[23] Grossman makes a similar point: "Killing another human being is an extraordinarily difficult thing to do. But if a soldier . . . can get others to share in the killing process (thus diffusing his personal responsibility by giving each individual a slice of the guilt), then killing can be easier."[24]

But tell that to the parents and families of the Son Thang victims. Improper orders *can* be refused. At My Lai, three soldiers, including a private first class and a specialist fourth class, refused Calley's despicable orders to murder. They were not rare individuals with a special capacity to resist authority, or assert moral autonomy. They were commonplace soldiers; ordinary men.

Could any Son Thang accused, however dull, however obedient, actually have failed to appreciate the magnitude of wrong he was ordered to carry out, not once, but three times? Michael Walzer points out in *Just and Unjust Wars*, "The right can in fact be recognized, since it often is, even in the chaos of combat. It is simply not true of soldiers, as one philosopher has recently written, that 'war . . . in some important ways makes psychopaths of them all.' . . . There is no general rule that requires us to make allowances."[25] Commenting on My Lai in terms that apply to Son Thang, Walzer writes:

> It has been argued on behalf of these soldiers that they acted, not in the heat of battle (since there was no battle) but in the context of a brutal and brutalizing war. . . . They had been encouraged to kill without making careful discriminations—encouraged to do so by their own officers and driven to it by their enemies, who fought and hid among the civilian population. These statements are true, or partly true; and yet massacre is radically different from guerrilla war. . . . This was not a fearful and frenzied extension of combat, but "free" and systematic slaughter, and the men who participated in it can hardly say that they were caught in the grip of war.[26]

General Widdecke's dilemma was that some who participated in Son Thang's slaughter were paying no price at all. "He really disdained these persons," Widdecke's assistant division commander recalled. "Having said that . . . he still wanted to see justice done, equity preserved, without excusing them for their actions."[27] And he thought he knew how to do it.

On 15 December, Widdecke sent a "Secret—Marine Corps eyes only" message to the Commandant. "A careful study of the [Schwarz] record of trial . . . has revealed certain mitigating factors."[28] Widdecke detailed the lack of a proper patrol briefing (although the killer team's briefing was as complete as that of any other Vietnam patrol); Schwarz's short time assigned to B-1/7 (although that had no bearing on criminal guilt or innocence); the harsh combat environment (also of no legal import), and the dissimilar sentence and verdicts in the companion cases. (Ah! Now we get to the heart of the matter.) Even considering Schwarz's egregious prior disciplinary record, wrote Widdecke, "the sentence awarded by the court appeared disproportionate."

With that warning to headquarters to brace themselves, Widdecke signed his review, referred to in military law as the convening authority's "action." Like the review, it was written by the SJA's office, but per the general's direction. It began with preliminary legal throat-clearing, then said of Ambort's Company B, "There seems to have been a conscious effort to create and maintain within this company an ambience and milieu of a unit operating at great danger in a treacherously hostile environment."[29] That was a harshly dismissive description of a company within an infantry battalion that, in the first three months of 1970 alone, suffered thirty-six KIAs and eighty-seven wounded, something more than an "ambience and milieu" of danger, one might conclude. But the CG's action *was* written by the SJA's office, and hell hath no fury like a noncombatant.

The action continued: "A superficial comparison of the results of the Schwarz trial with the results of the three companion cases suggests that the greatest guilt for the death of the sixteen civilians rested with Private Schwarz. Examination of the record in this case fails to support such a conclusion." Schwarz thought Herrod an NCO, and an experienced patrol leader. He was anxious to impress the others in the unit he had joined only days before, "a newcomer who went along with the patrol in both a literal and figurative sense."

Concluding, the action read, "The sentence awarded by the court appeared disproportionate and has accordingly been reduced." General Widdecke approved only as much of the sentence as provided for forfeiture of all pay and allowances, a dishonorable discharge—and confinement for one year.

The jury sentenced Schwarz to life. The SJA recommended twenty years. Widdecke gave him one year.

If six men rob a bank and three are captured, should the three in hand be released because of failure to apprehend the other three? If four Army officers and nine enlisted men murder 343 to 370 Vietnamese (depending on whose numbers are accepted) at My Lai, and three of the officers and two enlisted men are acquitted by courts-martial, should charges against the remaining eight therefore be dropped without trial—which is precisely what transpired? If Herrod, Boyd, and Krichten escaped penalty, should the Schwarz and Green sentences be reduced to time served?

This was not the first time a court-martial sentence had been reduced, of course. As commander-in-chief, President Lincoln frequently reduced penalties imposed by military tribunals.[30] After World War I, 28,000 courts-martial were reviewed by Special Clemency Boards and hundreds of sentences modified or disapproved. Following World War II, sentences of Nazi war criminals, whose enormity of evil beggars comprehension, were quietly reduced or wholly abated on the altar of international political expediency.[31] In Vietnam, other war crime sentences were cut almost as drastically as Schwarz's by other convening authorities, by appellate courts, by clemency boards, and by political appointees. For example, upon initial review Lieutenant Calley's sentence to life imprisonment was reduced to twenty years. President Nixon ordered his confinement held in abeyance. The Secretary of the Army next reduced his sentence to ten years. Calley then served a total of four months and three weeks in a stockade before being paroled for good.

The leniency of the military review process raises complaints that it weakens the deterrent effect of punishment. But military clemency is indistinguishable from civilian clemency. Professor Guenter Lewy notes in *America in Vietnam*, "It is well known that civilian parole boards often act . . . in response to political pressures and the currents of public opinion . . . no different in the case of servicemen convicted of atrocities or war crimes in Vietnam."[32]

• • •

By the date of Widdecke's action, 15 December, Schwarz and Green were inmates of the Naval Disciplinary Barracks at Portsmouth. With good time, Green's release date would be 3 June 1971. But even with his sentencing break, he was unhappy. "Green is a very angry young man,"[33] the CO of the disciplinary barracks wrote. "His civilian background during developmental years is replete with anti-social behavior. Prior drug addiction, [civilian] criminal record, and aggressiveness have all contributed to his personality." These problems notwithstanding, the CO noted, "imposition of a punitive [dishonorable] discharge in this case would negate whatever chance he may have for . . . any civilian career. Accordingly, I recommend remission of the dishonorable discharge and substitution of a general discharge."

Unlike a dishonorable discharge, a general discharge had no stigma attached; it was usually indicative of a character problem over which the service member had no control. It was a notch below an honorable discharge but still a discharge "under honorable conditions." Not many convicted multiple murderers received a general discharge. But Sam Green remained displeased. Appearing before a clemency board, he railed, "if I can't get a good discharge, don't disturb the DD through clemency—I'd rather have a DD than a BCD [bad conduct discharge]."[34]

Schwarz fared no better at Portsmouth. The CO found Schwarz, like Green, "angry about his conviction." He did not acknowledge "the most substantial reduction in his sentence."[35] Another assessment of Schwarz reported, "He feels he should not have been punished for this offense, as it was all political. . . . [He] gives the impression that all will be dropped at a later date. . . . Past record and present attitude preclude consideration for restoration and it is recommended that his punitive [dishonorable] discharge be executed."[36]

While Schwarz was confined at Portsmouth, Marine Corps headquarters received an inquiry from Congressman Thomas E. Morgan of Pennsylvania. Having been sentenced to forfeiture of all pay and allowances, Schwarz, the only married Marine among the Son Thang accused, received no further pay. Nor did his wife and young son receive the monthly allotment check that had been their primary income throughout Schwarz's enlistment. "It will be greatly appreciated if you will look into this matter to see if anything can be done,"[37] the congressman wrote.

Here was the hidden price of a court-martial conviction and perhaps its cruelest cost. In punishing the serviceman his family is penalized as well. A bust in rank means a reduction in pay, which equals a lessened allotment. Total forfeitures means no further family allotment. It is a matter that every military judge considers when deciding upon a sentence; a matter that occurs to few court-martial jurors. At least Schwarz's family was not living aboard a Marine Corps base in government-supplied housing. His sentence would have required their eviction at the same time their allotment was stopped.

Col. Verne "Bubs" Oliver, a Marine judge advocate and the legislative counsel to the Commandant, responded to Representative Morgan. Oliver's was one of the very few non-form official letters sent in the Son Thang cases. "By operation of law and regulation thereunder," he wrote, "the allotment to Mrs. Schwarz must regrettably be terminated as a result of the approved court-martial sentence." He went on to sympathize, suggesting possible avenues of financial support in the civilian community. His regret was clearly heartfelt.

At the end of the day, Schwarz's GCM sentence having been reviewed and approved, there was nothing of a financial nature the Marine Corps could have done for Linda Schwarz and her son, even had it been inclined to. From his first nonjudicial punishment less than a year into his enlistment, Schwarz had link-by-link forged the chain that imprisoned not only himself but his family.

Meanwhile, in Vietnam, in the SJA's office the guard had changed. The old hands involved in the Son Thang cases were gone, and new judge advocates had replaced them on

Hill 327. At his new duty station prosecutor Franz Jevne was awarded the Navy Achievement Medal for his Vietnam service, not only in the Schwarz case but for his other prosecutions as well. Prosecutors Charles Brown, Gary Bushnell, and Len Skiles received Navy Commendation medals. Defenders were recognized as well, Dan LeGear (Schwarz) and John Hargrove (Green) receiving Navy Commendation Medals. Mike Merrill (Boyd) received a Navy Achievement Medal.

Whether a judge advocate, a supply officer, an air controller, or a P.X. officer, if you were a Marine officer in Vietnam, if you didn't screw up in any major way, and you were reasonably affable, chances were good that you would receive a Navy Comm or a Navy Achievement. Capt. Bob "X" Williams, Herrod's lawyer, was a pain in the ass to his legal seniors. He got nothing.

A Washington Hearing

There was one more round of military appeals. It was automatic, its initiation requiring only the signature of the convicted Marine on a form attached to his record of trial. The appeal is free of cost and, with surprising frequency, results in a sentence reduction or even a reversal of conviction. Even if Schwarz and Green had already been discharged, the appellate process would not have been affected. The Navy Court of Military Review (NCMR) in Washington was still required by military law to review their convictions for legal error. Should their convictions be busted—overturned—their discharges would be upgraded, their lost pay returned (with interest), and apologies given for all that time lost in the brig.

Appellate judge advocates were assigned to brief the appeals. Green's was heard first, in March 1971. He was represented not only by an assigned lawyer, a Navy lieutenant, but also by James A. Chiara. Chiara was the same civilian who earlier was unable to reach Vietnam to defend Green at trial. Chiara had remained involved with Green's case, working without fee.

Green's appellate argument was heard by three black-robed judges in a dark wood-paneled courtroom at the Washington Navy Yard. The judges made up one of several panels that considered the cases that continued to hemorrhage from Vietnam. The sounds of helicopters arriving and departing from HMX-1, the presidential helicopter detachment at Anacostia Naval Station, drifted across the Anacostia River, a stone's throw from the courtroom door. The appellate hearing was about as far from Hill 327 as it could be. Sam Green was absent, in keeping with normal appellate procedure. He was still serving the last days of his sentence in the Naval Disciplinary Barracks. His lawyers, one in a sedate gray suit, the other in open-collar Navy whites, would argue on his behalf.

The issues were not the same as those considered in the convening authority's action in Vietnam. A more probing examination of possible legal deficiencies would be undertaken now. Six assignments of error were argued by Chiara. Opposing him was Marine captain Frank Kaveney, representing the government. Three years before, Kaveney had himself been on Hill 327, assigned to the Office of the SJA, 1st Marine Division.

The arguments, briefed in advance, lasted only a couple of hours. The judges had previously reviewed the opposing briefs and had few questions. The issues, except for one, were not demanding. Following the arguments, the parties exchanged pleasantries, then filed from the room as the next-scheduled appellate players replaced them.

On 19 May, the judges handed down *United States v. Samuel G. Green, Jr.*, an eighteen-page opinion deciding his appeal. After quickly recapping the events at Son Thang ("The evidence did not establish . . . that the team was under hostile fire"[38]), the opinion held that, contrary to the defense assignments of error, Judge St.Amour's instructions to the jury were satisfactory. His admission of the nine photos of the dead was approved, as was his refusal to grant the defense a change of venue. Nor did the acquittal of Herrod, "certainly a perpetrator of some of the offenses," require that Green's conviction be set aside. But the issue of obedience to orders split the judges.

In 1971, the Navy Court of Military Review consisted of ten senior Navy and Marine judge advocates, captains and colonels, and for most of the Vietnam War, at least one civilian jurist experienced in military law. Of the Navy captains, two were retired judge advocates returned to active duty to man the legal bilge pumps keeping the court-martial system afloat. It would be fair to say that the three Marine colonels assigned to each NCMR panel were not noted for a pro-defense orientation. But that is usual, be the court civilian or military.

In *Green*, civilian jurist J. Fielding Jones dissented. The court's majority found St.Amour's obedience-to-orders instruction unobjectionable; Jones did not.

St.Amour's instruction tasked Green's jury with deciding if a man of ordinary sense and understanding would have honestly believed that Herrod's orders were legal. The jury decided that such a man would have recognized the orders as illegal, and could not have honestly believed them otherwise. But, Jones argued, Green was "a pure novice. This was his first mission."[39] He should not have been judged by the standard of the imaginary "man of ordinary sense and understanding." The jury should have been instructed, Jones held, to ask if Green, the particular accused before them, not some illusory legal construct, would have recognized the orders as illegal, or could have believed them other than illegal. As Jones pointed out, "the fictional man of ordinary sense and understanding is never a criminal."

But Judge Jones's point is merely the first-year law school issue of reasonableness, cloaked in law of war terms. The "reasonable man" standard is the only practical means of judging accused criminals. Jurist Richard Posner writes, "The social concern is with the deed . . . rather than with the mental state that accompanies it. . . . There is no anomaly in sometimes imposing criminal liability on the pure of heart or the empty of mind. . . . To decide [individual mental states] would require a type of investigation that is not conducted in criminal trials."[40] Harsh, but correct. Oliver Wendell Holmes agreed that "public policy sacrifices the individual to the general good."[41] In other words, if Green did not know that what he was doing in Son Thang was wrong, he *should* have known.

Dissenting opinions are dissents because they fail to convince the majority. Green's appeal was rejected: "Accordingly, the findings of guilty and the sentence approved on review below are affirmed." Nor was there anything about his case that might cause the judge advocate general of the Navy to refer it to the military's highest appellate forum, the United States Court of Military Appeals. Two petitions for further review of Green's case by that court were denied. His legal string had run out.

On 2 April 1971 Schwarz completed serving his sentence. He was transferred to Quantico, Virginia, to await word on whether his discharge would be upgraded by the Discharge Review Board, which was statutorily established to review military discharges. Upon finding that a discharge was improperly or inequitably issued, the DRB may order it upgraded.

Following his conviction, Schwarz had been confined for 286 days—nine and a half months—at "hard labor," which consisted of trash and maintenance details as well as vocational classes on a variety of rehabilitation-oriented topics.

The same month Schwarz completed his sentence, Widdecke was transferred to Camp Pendleton and relinquished command of the 1st Marine Division. Ed Simmons, his assistant division commander, said, "He was a disappointed man, a disillusioned man, when he left."[42] As were many Vietnam veterans. Two years later, while on a Mexican fishing trip, Major General Widdecke died of a heart attack.

A month after Schwarz made the trip from the Naval Disciplinary Barracks to Quantico, Sam Green followed, his sentence also completed. At Quantico the pair whiled away the summer days, assigned to Casual Company, again on trash and maintenance details, but free. Having completed serving his sentence on 4 May, Green had been jailed for 263 days—nine months, less one week—of post-trial confinement.

In June, Schwarz was discharged from the Marine Corps. The Discharge Review Board, having considered his disciplinary record that included five courts-martial, and the prior reduction of his sentence from life to nine and a half months, granted no further clemency. He returned to Pennsylvania with a dishonorable discharge.

If Sam Green was sincere when he told the clemency board that if he couldn't have a "good" discharge he would rather have his DD, on 28 July 1971, he was gratified. Not yet twenty years old, he was released with a dishonorable discharge. The DRB granted no clemency. But to the end Green performed well, given final proficiency and conduct marks of 4.6 and 4.7, respectively. His page twelve, the page in one's service record book that records disciplinary actions other than courts-martial, remained clean. Had it not been for Son Thang Green's military service would have been exemplary.

At about this time, Jim Webb's interest in the case was aroused.

James H. Webb, Jr., is a remarkable Marine. Graduating high in his Naval Academy class, he was a contemporary of Oliver North. The two were not close. Webb was commissioned a Marine lieutenant, graduating first in his 243-man Basic School class. Sent to Vietnam, he was an infantry platoon commander and company commander in the 1st Marine Division. He knew the Son Thang area, having operated there, and throughout all of Quang Nam Province. Webb returned to the States with a Navy Cross, a Silver Star, two Bronze Stars, and two Purple Hearts. Any Marine will appreciate what those awards represent. Deep-selected for captain, Webb also returned with the experiences that would form the core of his 1978 book, *Fields of Fire*.

While fighting a medical discharge, Captain Webb was assigned to the office of the Secretary of the Navy. Among his duties was the review of courts-martial such as Schwarz's and Green's that might merit SecNav action. Robert Timberg writes in *The Nightingale's Song*:

> Webb saw incredible injustice at play. Herrod, the patrol leader . . . had been found not guilty even though he admitted giving the order to shoot and acknowledged blasting away with an M-79 grenade launcher loaded with buckshot. Green, an eighteen-year-old inner-city black with eleven days in Vietnam at the time of the shootings, had been convicted even though no testimony was presented that he actually killed anyone. Green, moreover, was of marginal intellect; there was evidence that he could not spell his own middle name. He had been in trouble as a civilian, but . . . Green joined the Marines in hopes of moving beyond his youthful transgressions and making something of himself.[43]

What could Webb do? Less than a year later he was himself medically retired. He entered Georgetown University Law Center, but he did not forget Sam Green.

His continuing interest was evidenced in an award-winning article in *Res Ipsa Loquitur,* Georgetown's Review of Law and Public Interest. Webb argued that as a newcomer to combat, Green had no basis for appreciating the illegality of Herrod's orders, or for refusing to obey them. "The local inhabitants, including women and children, were not 'innocent civilians' in the traditional sense of the word," Webb wrote, "but . . . a tightly-knit, essential element of the Vietcong Infrastructure. . . . In the short time that Green had been with Company B there had been three direct encounters involving women or children."[44]

Just as dissenting opinions represent unavailing viewpoints, law review articles win no cases. But Webb was just beginning his effort on Green's behalf.

APPELLATE CONCLUSIONS

Schwarz's appeal was heard by two of the NCMR judges who heard Green's. Commitment to other cases required that Fielding Jones, Green's dissenting judge, be replaced. Captain Kaveney again argued for the government. The Pittsburgh lawyers who submitted a brief for Widdecke's action in Vietnam represented Schwarz, this time in person.

If civilians often whipped-up on military lawyers in Vietnam, they did less well on appeals. Schwarz's civilian paladins did what they could, but their assignments of error lacked both originality and legal imagination. The point that fairly begged for judicial review, the voluntariness of Schwarz's self-incriminating statement to Major Theer after Ambort's unwarned exhortation to come clean, went unquestioned. Instead, they revisited issues that had already failed at trial, failed in the convening authority's action, and failed in Green's appeal. And they failed again.

In *United States v. Schwarz* the court's synopsis of the Son Thang facts was more melancholy than it had been in *Green*. It noted the shooting of the blind Vietnamese girl led onto the patio by her younger brother, the wounded woman whose screaming ended at the firing of Schwarz's .45, and the baby whose crying stopped in the same circumstances.

The court readily agreed that these acts were at the specific orders of Herrod but, as in *Green*, Schwarz's guilt lay in his obedience to those directions. In now-familiar words the panel held, "the accused could not have honestly and reasonably believed that Herrod's order to kill the apparently unarmed women and children was legal."[45] Crystalizing its assessment of criminal responsibility, the court added, "The record . . . before us shows beyond any doubt that Herrod's orders to kill the unarmed women and children were patently illegal and were recognized as being so by members of the patrol including Private Schwarz." The opinion was handed down on 21 June 1971. It concluded,

"The findings of guilty and the sentence approved on review below are affirmed." There was no dissenting opinion.

Sam Green may have departed Vietnam, but he never left Vietnam behind. Through the early 1970s, while attending fashion design school, he had consultations at military medical facilities at the direction of the Naval Clemency Board and the Discharge Review Board. He had been discharged, but his continuing appeals of his dishonorable discharge kept his case alive.

A March 1972 psychiatric report found him "angry and anxious," adding, "he feels that he is quite innocent and that even a dishonorable discharge is completely unjust." The report noted, "This individual is essentially normal [but] there are clearly some psychological problems."[46]

Meanwhile, attorney James Chiara continued to barrage military, legal, and political authorities with pleas for reconsideration of Green's conviction and for upgrading of his dishonorable discharge. The U.S. Court of Military Appeals denied Chiara's petitions for writs of prohibition[47] and extraordinary relief.[48] His request for an injunction was denied. A District of Columbia complaint for declaratory judgment was summarily dismissed. A Naval Clemency and Parole Board petition failed. The Supreme Court denied his petition for *certiorari*. Chiara's beseeching mail to President Nixon, reflecting more political naiveté than legal merit, went unanswered.

Chiara's problem was basic—he had no new evidence, only new deliveries of old arguments which had already been considered and dismissed by a court of competent jurisdiction. The lawyer's plea of last resort, "it isn't fair," rarely persuades. There was simply no reason why any court should either set aside the conviction or upgrade the DD.

But give Chiara this: for years, alone and on his own dime, in the face of repeated rejection, he carried the fight on behalf of Green, a young man he barely knew. Not for reward or recognition, but because he believed in Green's cause. In doing so, Chiara lent dignity to the profession of law.

In 1975, in his final year of law school at Georgetown, Jim Webb re-entered the fray. He wrote a 22,000-word brief, arguing that Green's conviction involved constitutional error requiring the civilian courts to reverse the military conviction. Chiara filed Webb's brief in the federal jurisdiction where Green was then residing, the U.S. District Court for the Northern District of Ohio. Some of the arguments were novel, most were familiar. The court denied the motion to overturn the conviction, although the judge was sufficiently impressed with Webb's impassioned argument to write a memorandum to the Secretary of the Navy urging clemency. But once again, no action followed. Something along the lines of divine intervention would be required to rid Green of his dishonorable discharge.

In March 1972, Ron Ambort was again a topic of discussion at Marine Corps headquarters.

Officer promotions are decided by boards that meet annually in Washington. There are two promotion boards for each rank, one for regular and one for reserve officers. Senior officers are assigned to sit on the various boards and review the records of those eligible for promotion. Votes are taken, and some candidates are selected for promotion, others passed over.

The 1972 promotion board for Marine Corps Reserve captains met in the Headquarters Battalion buildings across the street from the Navy Annex, which housed Marine Corps headquarters. Built in World War II for temporary occupancy, the wooden buildings were cramped and uncomfortable. Four regular, active-duty officers and five reservists, all lieutenant colonels except the senior member, were grouped around a conference table. It was only luck of the draw that all the regulars had served in Vietnam and all the reservists had not. Untidy stacks of OQRs, Officer Qualification Records, were piled before each board member. Arthur N. Nehf, Jr., the senior member, sat at the head of the large table that virtually filled the room. Nehf, a Marine aviator, had enlisted before Pearl Harbor and was commissioned in 1942. Now he was one of the twelve most senior colonels in the Corps. His board was considering promotions to captain for reserve first lieutenants not on active duty.

Each board member had previously reviewed his share of the OQRs, and each was tasked with briefing the others on his candidates, recommending a yea or nay vote on promotion. Since no board member could review every OQR, the recommendation of the briefing officer was almost always accepted. The many candidates for promotion dictated that each case be considered only briefly, generally for two or three minutes, before voting.

The case of 1st Lt. Louis R. Ambort, discharged from active duty on 1 August 1971, was briefed by one of the reservists. Ambort had a problem in Vietnam, the lieutenant colonel noted, but otherwise was a good officer. A letter of reprimand was, to a degree, offset by two glowing Bronze Star recommendations written by a Lt. Col. Charles Cooper—although the Bronze Stars were never approved. The briefer omitted any mention of the letter of reprimand, and recommended Ambort's promotion. The others, relying on his assessment, supported the recommendation unanimously.

The board's recorder, the non-voting record-keeper of the panel's decisions, was Capt. W. Hays Parks. A judge advocate, Parks had been chief prosecutor of the 1st Marine Division the year before the Son Thang incident. He remembered the case, and Ambort's involvement.

"At the lunch break, I pulled Ambort's file to read it," Parks later said. "I do not recall any reports other than those written by Cooper. . . . Based on them alone, Ambort certainly merited promotion."[49] Parks crossed the street to the Navy Annex, just up the hill from the Pentagon, and visited the offices of the director of the Judge Advocate Division. Col. Jim King, Ambort's Article 32 investigating officer, was now the division's deputy director. (There were only about 340 Marine Corps lawyers on active duty in 1972; it was a relatively small community.) King refreshed Parks's recollection of Son Thang. "After reviewing the case I met privately with Colonel Nehf," Parks recalled. "I told him that, while the board had voted on Ambort, I felt there was more to the case."

Nehf, whose instructions as senior member included the admonition to be aware of matters that might adversely reflect upon the Marine Corps, looked over Ambort's OQR. A year previously, Lieutenant Calley's GCM had ended in conviction. The media frenzy was fresh in every officer's mind.

When the board reconvened that afternoon, Nehf said that information had arisen meriting reconsideration of a selectee. After Ambort's involvement in Son Thang was recounted and his letter of reprimand disclosed, a new vote was taken. The four active duty board members, Vietnam veterans all, voted to not promote Ambort. The five reserve members voted yes. "I found the split ironic," Parks said.

Ambort was promoted to captain in the inactive Marine Corps Reserves.

Son Thang faded from the memory of all but those who were involved. But the case did not dim for Jim Webb. After gaining his law degree, Webb published his first novel, *Fields of Fire*. Nominated for the Pulitzer Prize, the book was a thinly veiled account of Webb's combat experiences in the Son Thang area.

Alternating between periods of writing and government service, Webb soon became minority counsel for the House Veterans Affairs Committee, and later an assistant secretary of defense. In April 1987, he became the sixty-sixth secretary of the Navy.

But in 1977 and 1978, while writing *Fields of Fire*, Webb also devoted considerable energies to Green's case. Having worn the same uniform and trod the same killing ground as Sam Green, Webb pursued what he considered equity for a young man without the means to do so for himself. Green could not have wished for a better ally.

Nor was Green's the only cause Webb championed. In 1977 Dale Wilson, a former member of Webb's platoon, received a Silver Star Medal initiated in Vietnam eight years before. The award was the result of Webb, then a congressional staffer, shaking the system until the medal was disgorged. Ten years later, Secretary of the Navy Webb awarded the Bronze Star to another of his Vietnam platoon members, Mac McDowell. The unjustly belated recognition was again due to Webb's prodding of the bureaucracy. Unlike the Greens, Wilsons, and McDowells of the world, Webb knew where the levers of power were, and when he perceived a wrong, he was in a position to work them.

In 1978, Webb appeared before the Board for Correction of Naval Records on behalf of Green. BCNR, which reports only to the Secretary of the Navy, has the authority to correct any error in a Navy or Marine Corps record, the Board determining what constitutes "error." Their corrections are final and conclusive, if accepted by SecNav, as they almost always are. Significantly, BCNR is composed of civilians, and the members who hear cases are not lawyers, although they are advised by legal counsel.

On 17 January, in a third floor office in the Navy Annex in Arlington, Virginia, Webb sat with a three-member BCNR panel, asserting the injustice of Green's DD. That was the sole issue. The board discovered the young lawyer to be a persuasive advocate.

Webb knew that Green's wrongdoing was undeniable. Nor would he make an effort to excuse Green's actions. Instead, he urged the panel to view Son Thang through Green's eyes, in a context of first-time combat pressure, laced with the heavily coercive effect of military authority. Yes, Webb argued, the actions of Herrod, the experienced veteran and Son Thang moving force, merited the charge of murder. But Green? At that point in Green's military experience, in those circumstances, surely *his* acts amounted to no more than negligent homicide—a careless and reckless disregard for the consequences of his actions that tragically resulted in death. But that's not murder. Consider the circumstances, Webb urged. Consider Green's youth; his combat inexperience; the compulsion to obey Herrod, as the others did. What Green did was wrong. But considering all he had now undergone was it fair, was it just, that he bear the burden of a dishonorable discharge for all his life, as well? Webb argued not to excuse Green, but to give the panel a realistic context in which to view his acts. They listened, faces impassive, until Webb finished.

A month later, BCNR sent its recommendation to the Secretary of the Navy for his pro forma approval. That which judge advocates, civilian lawyers, courts, and other boards could or would not do, BCNR did.

After mentioning the crimes of which Green, "the Petitioner," stood convicted, the recommendation pointed out that at the time of the offenses he was eighteen, a Marine for only five months, in Vietnam for only twenty-nine days. In Son Thang, BCNR wrote, he was "forced to choose between following orders given by a respected and experienced fellow Marine or disobeying those orders."[50] Depicting Herrod as "respected and experienced" reflected the board's bias and direction.

The recommendation continued, "Undisputed evidence showed that the leader gave the orders to kill and himself shot some of the victims, yet [he] was acquitted." Then, relating key legal issues in erroneous ways, BCNR noted that Herrod was acquitted while his obedient subordinate was convicted; that "inflammatory color photographs" were admitted in evidence against Green but not Herrod; and that there was no evidence that Green actually killed any victim. Herrod was represented "by two influential state senators . . . [Green] by detailed military counsel." (Influential state senators? Stipe and Garrison influenced judge and members not through political position, but by legal skill and insight.) Herrod, the board continued, was "a combat-experienced Marine who had been recommended for a silver star and by virtue of that experience probably made a better impression than Petitioner, who was an inexperienced black Marine from a poor background."

Acknowledging the impact of Webb's involvement, the recommendation added, "It should also be noted that counsel's summary of facts and argument before the Board were very persuasive, particularly in light of counsel's own Marine Vietnam experience in the same general geographical area. . . . The Board was most impressed with counsel's summary of the emotional climate, the constant danger from Vietnamese who appeared to be 'civilians' but were not, and his assessment of Petitioner's lack of combat experience as it pertained to his ability to disobey an order from an experienced leader." Few lawyers, including Chiara, whose similar petition BCNR had rejected, were favored with such respect.

BCNR concluded, "There was an unequal rendition of justice. . . . The Board now finds the existence of an error or injustice warranting corrective action. . . . It seems manifestly unfair that . . . Petitioner should bear the continuing stigma of a dishonorable discharge." BCNR's recommendation was approved by SecNav, and Green's DD was replaced with a general discharge.

From a legal perspective, Green's guilt remains unquestionable and, as Chiara found, unassailable. But BCNR thought that insufficient: Sam Green went to trial seeking justice. Instead, he found the law.

The lawyer's plea of last resort, "it isn't fair," had prevailed after all. It was something along the lines of divine intervention. Impelled by Webb, BCNR saw how Green had been forced into a near-impossible position in Son Thang. Did Green really have a choice other than to follow the others and obey the supposedly experienced killer team leader? A man of more maturity, of stronger character, of greater intelligence, might have refused to obey . . . one hopes. Even in the face of sixteen murdered children and women, it remains a difficult question.

But, as Grossman writes, "The psychological trauma of

living with what one has done to one's fellow man may represent the most significant toll taken by atrocity."[51]

BCNR's letter announcing the upgraded discharge was sent to the Petitioner's mother in Cleveland, rather than to Green. Three years before, in July 1975, after the Ohio federal court refused to overturn his conviction, Sam Green had shot and killed himself.

CONCLUSIONS

The 1949 Geneva Conventions require signatory states to prosecute grave breaches of the law of war. The U.S. executes its law-of-war obligations through the Uniform Code of Military Justice. From the standpoint of international law, the Son Thang prosecutions effectively met America's obligation; discovered battlefield war crimes were vigorously prosecuted in a timely manner. Acquittals and negligible sentences, reached in good faith, are part and parcel of the common law's adversarial system and do not detract from the integrity of the process. By prosecuting Herrod's killer team we affirm that what happened at Son Thang-4 was an aberration that, as a civilized society, we will not tolerate. The trials were reminders of humanity's aspiration to do justice.

On a more basic level, however, the Son Thang trials were a failure. Not because the military justice system was unable to police the military; the system carried out its prosecutorial function. But the results betray that it did so deficiently, its effort wanting in several significant respects.

Initially, even though the 1st Division's staff judge advocate was personally aware of the potential charges—offenses of the most serious nature known to the law—the legal system failed to itself investigate the charges. Because the critical first investigation and interrogations were left to non-lawyer personnel in 1/7, an infantry battalion in combat, the resulting statements of the accused became legal issues that could have ended the trials before they began. A judge less practical and aggressive than Paul St. Amour could *very* easily have found the suspects' rights warnings deficient, or found Ambort's unwarned inquiries of the team objectionable, and kept the team's pivotal statements out of evidence.

Allowing an offender's parent command to investigate the delicts of its own men suffices for most crimes, but someone in the SJA's office, if not the SJA himself, should have appreciated that allegations of multiple murder called for the immediate involvement of judge advocates.

The Marine Corps' Judge Advocate Division, in Washington, did not ensure the assignment to Vietnam of lawyers of sufficient skill and experience to competently prosecute and defend GCMs like the Son Thang cases. This was not a one-of-a-kind incident. Murders of noncombatants were dismayingly frequent in Vietnam. It must be acknowledged that, to an extent, the personnel assignment conundrum was beyond the Judge Advocate Division's power to remedy, as there were only so many lawyers assignable to Vietnam and Washington couldn't manufacture accomplished advocates.

But within Vietnam, and within the 1st Marine Division, the leadership failed to assign its experienced lawyers to the trials. The 1st Division's lawyer-majors, and even lieutenant colonels, who might have tried the cases were assigned to other duties in the SJA's office. Given the gravity of the charges, experienced advocates should have been broken loose and sent to the courtroom.

If the 1st Division lacked the requisite specialists, then prosecutors, defenders, and administrators sufficient to the task should have been brought to Hill 327 from other incountry commands, even from stateside commands, if necessary. It had been done before when multiple homicides were to be tried.[1]

The system failed to provide oversight and guidance for those inexperienced captains it did assign to prosecute the Son Thang cases, even when alerted to problems by loss of the Boyd case. These were strong cases supported, thanks to infantry officer Dick Theer, by interlocking, incriminating written statements by the accused themselves, and by the prosecution-oriented testimony of one of the crime's participants. True, no trial is too difficult for the lawyer who doesn't have to try it, but these were all cases with a strong potential for convictions.

Oversight and guidance were likewise absent for the defense advocates, who were no more experienced than the prosecutors. Criminal lawyers joke among themselves, "At the end of this trial someone's going to jail, just make sure it ain't you." But it's no joke when the client faces the possibility of life in prison. In a system that assigns an advocate to its accused, those clients merit a high standard of representation.

In retrospect, the system too quickly embraced Krichten for immunity. In fairness to the prosecution, the need for, or strength of, his testimony was at first unknown, although that only highlights the wisdom of waiting to decide if his testimony was really required. As it turned out, Krichten was an unconvincing witness, perhaps by his own design, and he was either disbelieved or disregarded in two of the four cases in which he appeared.

Immunized witnesses require prosecutorial handling that is firm, even bullying, to avoid surprise testimony like that Krichten gave in Boyd. If there is any suggestion of indecisive testimony—and the prosecutor must know through close interviews precisely what the immunized witness will say on the stand—the witness and his lawyer must be reminded of the terms of the immunity and the assurance of its loss, and swift prosecution, if the terms are not executed in full good faith. That is not to suggest that the immunized witness be coerced into saying anything untrue, or with a prosecution spin. But neither can he be allowed to hold back or tailor testimony to favor a friend, or minimize or disguise any criminality he is aware of. Dealing with an immunized witness calls for a prosecutorial veteran with an awareness of legal ethics combined with hard-nosed aggressiveness.

The culpability of Lt. Ron Ambort was never determined at a trial. Maj. Jim King's opinion that no jury in Vietnam would have convicted Ambort of an offense is quite probably correct. But Ambort's inflammatory briefing played a significant role in Herrod's bellicose direction of the killer team. Despite King's scrupulous balancing of the equities in recommending nonjudicial punishment rather than trial, Ambort, like Lieutenant Calley's superior, Captain Medina, should have been made to account for his actions. If, like Medina, he be acquitted, so be it.

The military justice system failed to provide its judge advocates in Vietnam with the tools to do the job asked of them. As is often the case in the Marine Corps, lawyers labored in an expeditionary environment with Spartan administrative support, makeshift law libraries, inadequate scientific and medical forensic support, and without dependable witness transportation—the latter not as minor a point as it sounds. While the division CG dined on Hill 327 "in baronial splendor," as one embarrassed general officer put it, on linen tablecloths, with silver place settings and candelabra, actually served wine by white-jacketed Marine waiters, judge advocates were trying felonies on a shoestring; hitchhiking to the brig for client interviews; living in SEAhuts with screened sides open to typhoon-driven rains; and relieving themselves in shitters cheek-to-cheek with other Marines. Granted, lawyers lived well compared to infantrymen. But even allowing that it was a war zone, the lack of adequate facilities and support hobbled not only the lawyers, but justice.

Army and Marine judge advocates have questioned whether it is practical, or even possible, to effectively apply the UCMJ in a combat zone. The UCMJ became law a month before the outbreak of the Korean War. Most cases tried in that conflict were conducted in Japan, not the tactical arena. Vietnam was the first real application and test of the code under combat conditions.

Brig. Gen. John R. DeBarr, a GCM judge in Vietnam and later director of the Marine Corps Judge Advocate Division, notes that modern judicial process can no longer easily be moved to a secure area outside the combat zone. As he points out, trials should be held where the crime was committed, because witnesses and evidence are there, and commanders wish to stay apprised of the administration of military justice, which remains a function of command.[2]

But more important than the place of trial is the workability of the system. Did the UCMJ really work in Vietnam? Clearly, it worked in the sense that thousands of courts-martial were tried. But opinion remains divided. Today, a quarter-century after the war, the UCMJ reflects most of the evidentiary and procedural benefits of the civilian jurisprudential system. But Vietnam demonstrated that application of the UCMJ's then-lesser protections in combat could be accomplished only unevenly and with great difficulty.

Many of those most experienced in the UCMJ's expeditionary employment decry the results: "[A] consistent source of concern in recent years has been whether the complex procedure-rich system created by the Code can survive in a major combat environment."[3] In a seminal law review article, Vietnam veteran Maj. Gen. George Prugh, former judge advocate general of the Army, and Gen. William Westmoreland write, "The Uniform Code of Military Justice is not capable of performing its intended role in times of military stress."[4] Marine Col. Don Holben, Son Thang SJA, says, "The system does not work, from a military viewpoint. . . . Under no circumstances will it work in an all-out war."[5] Brig. Gen. William Tiernan, another former director of the Judge Advocate Division, holds, "It's totally unworkable in a combat environment."[6] Soldier-turned-academic Archibald King writes, "The law should provide in advance for an automatic change on the outbreak of war from the peacetime procedure to that of wartime."[7]

British military law allows for "field general courts-martial" permitting latitude in the application of evidentiary and procedural rules. British field experience demonstrates the practicality of those provisions and provides a proven model. The Son Thang results might have been no different had such modifications been in place in 1970, but those results would have been achieved with substantially equal justice and, one suspects, far less difficulty for both sides. While "difficulty" is no criterion for modifying the UCMJ, difficulty that results in ineffectiveness is.

But it is unlikely that there will be major change to the UCMJ or to the *Manual for Courts-Martial* to render them more effective in war zones. The code is an excellent system that has proved itself for nearly fifty years. Still, it has opponents and critics. Political reality makes it too difficult to contemplate broad or innovative change. The military will make do with what it has, in peace and war. But other, more modest, improvements are possible.

The Son Thang trials, representative of many similar GCMs, make a case for the establishment of multi-service war crime teams staffed by judge advocates with special law-of-war training. The captains involved in the Son Thang GCMs were unaware they were even trying war crimes, viewing them as simple homicides. Other than obedience to orders, the special legal issues and defenses that war crimes raise—*respondeat superior,* duress, reprisal, necessity, and issues of *mens rea,* for example—were unexamined.

In February 1945, a U.S. Army War Crimes Group was established in the European Theater of Operations.[8] It grew to nineteen War Crime Investigating Teams and a strength of 2,000 personnel. By 1948, they had tried 489 Nazis for war crimes. A similar War Crimes Division was formed during the Korean War. But not in Vietnam.

Today, in a greatly expanded Department of Defense

Law of War Program, the Army has primary responsibility for the trial of enemy war crimes. Presumably it could try Americans charged with war crimes, as well. War crime teams are primarily manned by reservists in time of war, although manning levels appear inadequate to the assigned task, except in short-lived conflicts like the Gulf War. The Marine Corps Reserve includes a Law of War Detachment that provides invaluable training to Marines, but it can hardly investigate and prosecute war crimes as well.

Realistic plans for the prosecution of war crimes, including those of U.S. troops, must be formalized in advance of hostilities. Although the Army is responsible for trials, complementary war crime teams should be planned by the Marine Corps—the other armed service having contact with enemy ground forces and noncombatants. Cross-service attachment of Marines to Army teams should be mandated. Interservice coordination of teams should be considered, as well.

But planning for administrative contingencies that are not immediately foreseeable is not a military strength. The military "Seven *P*'s" apply: Proper Prior Planning Prevents Piss-Poor Performance.

The final word may be that of Brig. Gen. Charles Cushman, a Marine and the former assistant judge advocate general of the Navy. Asked if the UCMJ would work effectively in a future war, he gave an answer that strikes a familiar chord in any military officer: "Would it work? Of course it would work. It would work with major flaws and major difficulties and major delays, but . . . you would *make* it work!"[9]

Which again raises the matter of performance of the judge advocates who defended and prosecuted the Son Thang cases. The loss of the Herrod and Boyd cases and, for that matter, the convictions of Schwarz and Green, cannot fairly be laid at the doorstep of the "losing" lawyers. Each counsel was functioning within professional limitations of which, as newly minted lawyers, they were not even aware.

For the defense, *Schwarz* was probably unwinnable. Of the other three cases, the price of those professional limitations was paid by Green and, in the Boyd and Herrod cases, paid by the government.

Will there be another Son Thang in another war? To answer "of course" is not cynicism so much as recognition of the reality of war. As long as nations give weapons to very young men there will be war crimes. We must train our warriors as best we can, not only in the use of arms, but in the morality of their use. That training cannot be accomplished by the military alone.

Finally, the true Son Thang losers remain the sixteen Vietnamese civilians and their survivors. It bears reminding that "war is not a series of case studies that can be scrutinized with objectivity. . . . War is the suffering and death of people you know, set against a background of suffering and death of people you do not."[10]

Notes

Chapter 1. 1/7, 1st MarDiv

1. Except where otherwise indicated, all quotations and descriptions in this chapter of events occurring in the 1st Battalion, 7th Marines, are from one of three verbatim records: Joint pretrial (art. 32) investigation, *U.S. v. Pvt. Randell D. Herrod, Pvt. Michael A. Schwarz, LCpl. Michael S. Krichten, Pfc. Thomas R. Boyd, Jr., and Pfc. Samuel G. Green, Jr.,* and the written, sworn statements therein; pretrial (art. 32) investigation, *U.S. v. 1st Lt. Louis R. Ambort;* or record of trial, *U.S. v. Pvt. Michael A. Schwarz.* [The latter hereafter: Schwarz record of trial.]
2. Record of pretrial (art. 32) investigation, *U.S. v. 1st Lt. Louis R. Ambort,* 55. [Hereafter: Ambort pretrial investigation.]
3. Ibid., 203.
4. Ibid., 207.
5. *U.S. v. Pfc. John D. Potter, Jr.*
6. *U.S. v. Plt.Sgt. Roy E. Bumgarner.* Upon appeal, the sentence was lessened to reduction to private and forfeiture of $97 per month for six months. Pvt. Bumgarner was then reenlisted.

7. *U.S. v. Cpl. Ronald J. Reese,* and *U.S. v. LCpl. Stephen D. Crider.*

8. 16 June 1970.

9. 17 June 1970.

10. Smith, *U.S. Marines in Vietnam, 1969,* 6.

11. Spector, *After Tet,* 54.

12. Gen. Robert H. Barrow interview, 30 Jan. 1987, cited in Smith, *U.S. Marines in Vietnam, 1969,* 81.

13. Cosmas and Murray, *U.S. Marines in Vietnam, 1970–1971,* 45.

14. Ibid., 22.

15. 1/7 Command Chronology, Aug. 1970, Combat Records Section, Marine Corps Historical Center, Washington, D.C. [Hereafter: MCHC.]

16. Three other 1/7 Marines were posthumously awarded the Navy Cross: one in 1969, and two in Feb. 1970.

17. Hord, interview. Dowd also was awarded an earlier Silver Star Medal, Legion of Merit, and Purple Heart.

18. After the My Lai massacre, Capt. Eugene M. Kotouc, a staff officer in Lt. William Calley's parent unit, was charged, *inter alia,* with being a principal to murder for standing by while South Vietnamese soldiers murdered two civilians suspected of being VC. He was acquitted. Peers, *The My Lai Inquiry,* 222; and U.S. Army, *Preliminary Investigation into My Lai,* n.p.

19. Nolan, *Death Valley,* 80.

20. This account based upon a 6 Jan. 1970 report in the 7th Marines Command Chronology; 1/7 Command Chronology, Jan. 1970; and interviews of personnel involved, on Tape 4734, Oral History Collection, MCHC.

21. Richard E. Theer, letter to author, 24 Feb. 1989.

22. Ambort, interview.

23. Theer, letter to author.

24. Other factors may have influenced the characterization of Clark's relief. The CO of 2/7 had been relieved for cause less than five months before. A second such firing of a battalion CO could focus unwanted atten-

tion on the relieving officer, the regimental CO, Col. Gildo S. Codispoti.

25. Kelley, interview. Gen. Kelley was the 28th Commandant of the Marine Corps.

26. Cooper, interview, session 10 transcript, 24, 26. Except as otherwise indicated, all Cooper quotations are from sessions 10 or 11 of this interview. [Hereafter: Cooper interview.]

27. Theer, letter to author.

28. Nolan, *Death Valley*, 80.

29. Hord, interview.

30. Ambort pretrial investigation, 39.

31. Schwarz record of trial, 343.

32. 1/7 Command Chronology, Feb. 1970 operations journal, entry serial no. 143.

33. Theer, letter to author.

34. Record of joint pretrial (art. 32) investigation, *U.S. v. Pvt. Randell D. Herrod, Pvt. Michael A. Schwarz, LCpl. Michael S. Krichten, Pfc. Thomas R. Boyd, Jr., and Pfc. Samuel G. Green, Jr.*, 532. [Hereafter: Joint pretrial investigation.]

35. Properly, higher "grade" controls. Rank refers to seniority of position within the same grade. The more common, if not strictly correct, usage is employed throughout this volume.

36. Little, "Buddy Relations and Combat Performance," 213.

37. Cooper, letter to author, 12 Sept. 1988.

38. Herrod, *Blue's Bastards*, 120–21.

39. Ibid., 129.

Chapter 2. Son Thang-4

1. There is reference to "hunter-killer teams" in *U.S. v. Schultz*, and to "killer teams" in occasional professional articles, e.g., Wily, "Light Infantry and Vietnam."

2. Except as otherwise indicated, all quotations in this

chapter are from either the Schwarz record of trial or the joint pretrial investigation.

3. A policy of shooting anyone who is encountered, without question, has been held a violation of the customary law of war: *In re Lippert*.

4. Smith, *U.S. Marines in Vietnam, 1969*, 7.

5. Herrod, *Blue's Bastards*, 8. Herrod's book is riddled with error and misstatement. Although it reveals Herrod's thinking on certain subjects, it is of little value as an historical source. Except as otherwise indicated, all Herrod quotations in this chapter are from this volume.

6. FMFPac Awards Alpha Roster, 24 Aug. 77, Book 2 of 4, n.p. (MCHC).

7. Pvt. Randell D. Herrod, Special Court-Martial Order No. 1–70, dated 22 Feb. 70.

8. Theer, letter to author.

9. Pvt. Michael A. Schwarz, Service Record Book, page 11, entry dated 700116.

10. *Green v. Wylie*.

11. Spector, *After Tet*, 209.

12. Westmoreland, *A Soldier Reports*, 152.

13. Bilton and Sim, *Four Hours in My Lai*, 60.

14. Ambort pretrial investigation, 92.

15. This account of events in Son Thang-4 is based upon the sworn, verbatim trial testimony of LCpl. Krichten and Pvt. Schwarz, Schwarz record of trial, 279–314 and 397–432, respectively; HM2 Milton M. Jones, joint pretrial investigation; and the sworn, written statements of Pfcs. Boyd and Green, two of LCpl. Krichten, and three of Pvt. Schwarz, and South Vietnamese death certificates, joint pretrial investigation.

16. Ambort pretrial investigation, 18.

17. 1/7 Command Chronology, Feb. 1970, operations journal entry 192030H.

18. Ambort pretrial investigation, 81.

19. Ibid., 27.

CHAPTER 3. DISCOVERY AND INVESTIGATION

1. Ambort pretrial investigation, 15 (unusual testimony by a prosecuting judge advocate, Capt. Charles Brown, detailing interviews he conducted of Lt. Ambort, a suspect, in the presence of Ambort's defense counsel, Capt. Frank G. Roux).
2. Prugh, *Law at War*, 102.
3. Taylor, *Nuremberg and Vietnam*, 134. Neither Taylor nor Major General Prugh is entirely correct. Art. 4 of 1949 Geneva Convention IV does indicate that nationals of a cobelligerent are not protected persons. But protected status does not turn on the hostile character of territory, as Taylor suggests, even under the Hague Conventions he apparently refers to ("Law & Customs of War on Land," 29 July 1899, and 18 Oct. 1907, supplemented by Geneva Convention IV, art. 154). But General Prugh's assertion that the killings were not war crimes, as that term is commonly defined, is too narrow, in my opinion. See, e.g., *U.S. v. Calley* (ACMR), which nominates My Lai, the murder of South Vietnamese cobelligerent civilians, a war crime. Even under the 1949 conventions, the POW Convention was arguably breached in both My Lai and Son Thang, where noncombatants, whose status was reasonably in doubt, should have been accorded POW status. This approach is explicitly supported by MACV Directive 20-5 of 15 Mar. 1966, par. 19, as well as MACV Directive 381-46, Annex A.
4. "The term 'war crime' is the technical expression for a violation of the law of war by any person or persons, military or civilian. Every violation of the law of war is a war crime." U.S. Dept. of the Army, *The Law of Land Warfare*, par. 499.
5. Paust, "My Lai and Vietnam," 108.
6. Rich, interview.
7. Kelley, interview.
8. Parks, "Crimes in Hostilities," part 1, 21.

9. Suter, interview.
10. Cooper, interview.
11. Westmoreland, *A Soldier Reports*, 288.
12. George S. Prugh, letter to author, 29 Nov. 1991.
13. Marshall, *Men Against Fire*, 78.
14. Ambort pretrial investigation, 64–65.
15. Unless otherwise indicated, all subsequent quotes in this chapter are from: joint pretrial investigation, the written statements of Herrod, Boyd, Green, Krichten, and Schwarz, investigation exhibits 34, 36, 38, 39, 41, 43, 45, and 47.
16. Ambort pretrial investigation, 24–25.
17. Unless otherwise indicated, all Herrod quotations in this chapter are from his book, *Blue's Bastards*.
18. An account of an epic 1966 patrol led by Theer is related in a condensation of a book by Andrew Jones, "Where Do We Get Such Men?" *Reader's Digest* (Sept. 1985): 216–18.
19. "Worst" is a matter of judgment. On 23 Sept. 1966 a 1/5 patrol from Chu Lai raped and shot one Vietnamese and murdered five others, including a baby. See *U.S. v. Potter*.
20. CG 1st MarDiv message to CG III MAF, 20 Feb. 1970.
21. The rights and warnings actually given: to remain silent; that any statement made could be used as evidence against the maker; to consult with a lawyer before being interviewed—either a civilian lawyer, at the individual's expense, or a military lawyer; to have that lawyer present at the interview; to have a military lawyer appointed free of charge, if the suspect has no lawyer; to end the interview at any time. Additionally, a suspect must be advised of the offense of which he is suspected.
22. Ambort pretrial investigation, 67.
23. Shay, *Achilles in Vietnam*, 39.
24. Shanor and Terrell, *Military Law in a Nutshell*, 114.
25. Son Thang Daily Report #6, CG 1st MarDiv message to CMC, 4 Mar. 1970. [Hereafter: Daily Report.]

26. MACV Directive 20-4, 25 Mar. 1966; MACV Directive 335-1 (BACKLASH), 5 Jan. 1966.
27. Daily Report #2, 27 Feb. 1970.
28. Cooper, interview.
29. Daily Report #7, 5 Mar. 1970.
30. 10 U.S. Code §6249, first enacted in 1919, reads: "No medal . . . may be awarded or presented to any person . . . if his service after he distinguished himself has not been honorable."
31. Daily Report #3, 1 Mar. 1970.
32. Daily Report #11, 13 Mar. 1970.
33. Robert J. Blum, letter to author, 11 July 1995.

CHAPTER 4. PRE TRIAL

1. Herrod, *Blue's Bastards,* 143.
2. Michael Krichten to President Nixon, 24 Mar. 1970.
3. Krichten to Nixon, 2 Apr. 1970.
4. Herrod, *Blue's Bastards,* 150.
5. Stipe, interview.
6. Daily Report #14, 8 Apr. 1970.
7. Except where otherwise indicated, all succeeding quotes in this chapter are from Ambort pretrial investigation.
8. *U.S. v. Brig. Gen. J. H. Smith,* an unreported case described at S. Doc. 213, 57th Cong., 2d sess., 5–17.
9. *In the Matter of the Application of General Tomoyuki Yamashita,* actually a writ of habeas corpus application. The court did not consider the guilt or innocence of Yamashita.
10. Eckhardt, "Command Criminal Responsibility," 18; and Lewy, *America in Vietnam,* 360.
11. Fleming, *U.S. Marine Corps in Crisis,* 4.
12. Simmons, interview.
13. See Lewy, *America in Vietnam,* 268; Spector, *After Tet,* 196; Palmer, *The 25-Year War,* 125; and DeLupis, *The Law of War,* 328.

14. Joint pretrial investigation, 659.
15. Timberg, *The Nightingale's Song,* 152.
16. Brig. Gen. James P. King, letter to author, 20 Jan. 1991.
17. Lt. Col. James P. King, Article 32 Interim Report to CO, 7th Marines, 18 Apr. 1970.
18. Hammer, *One Morning in the War,* 71.
19. Hammer, *The Court-Martial of Lt. Calley,* 392.
20. Taylor, *Nuremberg and Vietnam,* 171.
21. Cassady, interview.
22. Green, "Aftermath of Vietnam," 142, 172.
23. Best, *Humanity in Warfare,* 220.
24. Peers, *The My Lai Inquiry,* 230–31; to the same effect, Karsten, *Law, Soldiers, and Combat,* 35.
25. Grossman, *On Killing,* 158.
26. Kelman and Hamilton, *Crimes of Obedience,* 163.
27. Daily Report #17, 11 May 1970.
28. Daily Report #16, 9 May 1970.
29. CG 1st MarDiv letter of reprimand to 1st Lt. L. R. Ambort, 15 May 1970.
30. 1st Lt. L. R. Ambort, Officer Fitness Report, 25 July 1970.
31. 1st Lt. L. R. Ambort, Bronze Star Medal recommendation, n.d.
32. Lucy, interview.
33. Rare exceptions were two Army officers involved in the My Lai massacre, Capt. Eugene M. Kotouc (see ch. 1, fn. 18) and 1st Lt. Thomas K. Willingham, who were initially charged with violations of the law of war. The charges were otherwise worded as ordinary UCMJ offenses. Eventually Willingham's charges were dropped, and Kotouc was acquitted of lesser offenses. U.S. Army, *Preliminary Investigation into My Lai,* testimony of Kotouc (designated by code letters "BX") and Willingham (code letters "WT"), n.p.
34. Art. 18, Jurisdiction of General Courts-Martial, reads in pertinent part, "General courts-martial also have jurisdiction to try any person who by the law of war is

subject to trial by a military tribunal and may adjudge any punishment permitted by the law of war." U.S. Dept. of the Army, *Law of Land Warfare*, par. 507.b, to similar effect.

35. Kelsen, *Peace Through Law*, vol. 4, 147, 149.
36. See the 1907 Hague Convention IV, art. 46; U.N. War Crimes Commission, *Law Reports of Trials of War Criminals*, vol. 15, 85–86; *The Hadamar Trial (Trial of Klein, et al.)*, IV; and 1949 Geneva Conventions common art. 3, pertaining to armed conflict *not* of an international nature.
37. See *U.S. v. Schultz*, a Marine Corps case.
38. Lucy, interview.
39. *Stars and Stripes* (Pacific), 21 May 1970.
40. Daily Report #19, 20 May 70.
41. Lucy, interview.
42. Cooper, interview.
43. King, interview.
44. Daily Report #21, 26 May 1970.
45. *U.S. v. Hedges*, a case involving jury tampering by a commander.
46. Figures are unavailable because the sole source, Report of the Judge Advocate General of the Navy, in *Annual Report of the U.S. Court of Military Appeals, 1970*, 26–30, lumps together Navy and Marine Corps statistics.
47. Col. Max G. Halliday, Head, Military Law Branch, JAD, letter to Mrs. Kenneth D. Coffin, 19 Mar. 1970, cited in Cosmas and Murray, *U.S. Marines in Vietnam, 1970–1971*, 347.

CHAPTER 5. U.S. v. SCHWARZ

1. Memorandum for the record, Casualty Section, Personal Affairs Branch, HQMC, n.d. (MCHC).
2. Puller, *Fortunate Son*, 77.
3. Harry G. Summers, *Stars and Stripes* (European ed.), 15 Nov. 1995.

4. There is no way to determine an individual's mental group by examining the service record book. The SRB relates a General Classification Test (GCT) score, not the enlistment test score from which mental category position derives. The two are not the same.

5. Brig. Gen. Jonas M. Platt, Manpower, G-1 presentation, General Officers' Symposium, HQMC, 1967, tab II-E-1, p. 9. By 1968, however, the Marine Corps was having difficulty finding qualified volunteers and, absent changes in Selective Service deferment policies, might well have lowered standards in any event, as it did during the Korean conflict, when it accepted many category fours.

6. Lewy, *America in Vietnam,* 331.

7. Palmer, "The General, At Ease," 34.

8. Kitfield, *Prodigal Soldiers,* 126.

9. Cushman, interview transcript, 344, 361.

10. Tompkins, interview transcript, 93–94.

11. Gen. Leonard F. Chapman, Jr., opening remarks, General Officers' Symposium, HQMC, 1970, tab E, p. 19 (MCHC).

12. Powell, *My American Journey,* 148.

13. *Washington Post,* 17 June 1970.

14. Jevne, interview.

15. Lt. Col. Paul A. A. St.Amour, USMC (Ret.), letter to author, 4 Mar. 1991.

16. Ibid.

17. Unless otherwise indicated, this and all succeeding quotes in this chapter are from the verbatim record of trial, *U.S. v. Pvt. Michael A. Schwarz.*

18. St.Amour, interview.

19. Lanning and Craig, *Inside the VC and the NVA,* 62.

20. Pike, *PAVN,* 215.

21. Trullinger, *Village at War,* 51–52.

22. Santoli, *To Bear Any Burden,* cited in Grossman, *On Killing,* 267.

23. 1/7 Command Chronology, Feb. 1970, entry 171315H, 20.

24. Ibid., entry 151115H, 19.
25. Ibid., entry 141620H, 18.
26. H.E.S. was a MACV computer rating system to evaluate the loyalty of villages, and to determine the progress of pacification. Ratings ran from A (loyal to Saigon) to V (VC controlled). The reports were frequently falsified to favor the South Vietnamese government.
27. *Los Angeles Times*, 27 Feb. 1970.
28. Cooper, letter to author, 24 July 1995.
29. Grossman, *On Killing*, 211–12.
30. Blum, letter to author, 2 Mar. 1989.
31. Lynch, "Fish Rot from the Head," 73.
32. St.Amour, letter to author.
33. St.Amour, interview.
34. *Trials of the Major War Criminals Before the International Military Tribunal*, vol. 22, 271.

CHAPTER 6. U.S. v. BOYD AND U.S. v. GREEN

1. *Los Angeles Times*, 21 June 1970.
2. Daily Report #22, 28 May 1970.
3. *Los Angeles Times*, 22 June 1970.
4. *Phoenix Gazette*, 22 June 1970.
5. Herrod, *Blue's Bastards*, 153.
6. *Phoenix Gazette*, 22 June 1970.
7. Ibid.
8. Art. 3, sec. 1(a) and Annex arts. 43–53, respectively.
9. "Grave breach," the most serious of war crimes, is a term of legal significance, defined in the 1949 Geneva Conventions (arts. 50, 51, 130, and 147, respectively) as including "willful killing."
10. U.S. Constitution, art. I, sec. 8.
11. Dept. of the Army, *Law of Land Warfare*, par. 507.b.
12. *Manual for Courts-Martial, United States, 1969*, 4-4,5; 27–48.
13. E.g., *Ex Parte Quirin* (1942).

14. E.g., *U.S. v. Fleming* (ABR, 1951); *U.S. v. Schultz* (USCMA, 1952); *U.S. v. Dickensen* (USCMA, 1955); *U.S. v. Potter* (USCMA, 1967); *U.S. v. Keenan*; *U.S. v. Schultz* (USCMA, 1969); *U.S. v. Mitchell* (USCMA, 1972).

15. Kelsen, *Peace Through Law,* 77.

16. MACV Directive 20-4, 18 May 1968, "Inspections and Investigations: War Crimes." Also applicable were Directives 27-5, 17 May 1966, "Inspections and Investigations: PoWs—Determination of Eligibility"; 27-5, 2 Nov. 1967, "Legal Services: War Crimes and Other Prohibited Acts"; 335-1, 5 Jan. 1966, "Reports of Serious Crimes or Other Incidents"; and 20-5, 15 Mar. 1966. Paragraph 19 of the latter directive is particularly significant in the Son Thang cases. It directed that Geneva Convention POW protections should be extended to "persons who when detained were not openly engaged in combat and whose status may be: innocent civilian, returnee, prisoner of war, or civil defendant."

17. Axinn, *A Moral Military,* 126.

18. Lewy, *America in Vietnam,* 372.

19. Peers, *The My Lai Inquiry,* 230, fn.1.

20. Prugh, *Law at War,* 74.

21. Westmoreland, *A Soldier Reports,* 247.

22. This complex topic was addressed by: MACV Directive 27-1, 30 Sep. 1965, ch. 1, "SOP for Litigation Actions under the Pentalateral Agreement," which treats U.S. jurisdiction over U.S. military personnel as a *fait accompli.* The interested reader is referred to Lazareff, *Status of Military Forces under Current International Law,* 51; Prugh, *Law at War,* 118; and Hooker and Savasten, "The Geneva Convention of 1949; Application in the Vietnamese Conflict."

23. L. Boyd, letter to President Nixon, 13 Mar. 1970.

24. Robert A. Frosch, letter to L. Boyd, 18 Mar. 1970 (a notably prompt response).

25. CMC to Rep. Roger H. Zion, 8 Apr. 1970.

26. Howard Trockman, letter to author, 17 Apr. 1991.
27. St.Amour, letter to author, 20 July 1992.
28. Brookshire, "Juror Selection under the Uniform Code of Military Justice," 86.
29. *U.S. v. Bradley; U.S. v. Jarvis; U.S. v. Davis.* Subsequent case law suggests, however, that a judge who has presided over the trial of a co-accused in which the current accused was heavily implicated may require re-cusal.
30. St.Amour, interview.
31. St.Amour, letter, 20 July 1992.
32. St.Amour, interview.
33. Joint pretrial investigation, exhibit 38.
34. Grossman, *On Killing,* 149, quoting Richard A. Gabriel, *No More Heroes.*
35. Trockman, letter.
36. *Stars and Stripes,* 25 June 1970.
37. St.Amour, interview.
38. St.Amour, letter, 4 Mar. 1991.
39. Grossman, *On Killing,* 118, 119.
40. *Stars and Stripes,* 25 June 1970.
41. Ibid.
42. Trockman, letter.
43. Herrod, *Blue's Bastards,* 156.
44. St.Amour, letter, 4 Mar. 1991.
45. Trockman, letter.
46. St.Amour, interview.
47. Herrod, *Blue's Bastards,* 152.
48. North, *Under Fire,* 122.
49. Ibid., 110.
50. *Samuel G. Green v. J. C. Wylie.*
51. *U.S. v. Catlow* and *U.S. v. Russo,* companion post-Vietnam cases which made such enlistments, when discovered, voidable. "Constructive" enlistments often resulted, however.
52. Marshall, *Men Against Fire,* 42.
53. Graves, *Goodbye to All That,* 157.
54. Westmoreland, "The State of the Command," 242.

55. Safer, *Flashbacks*, 23.
56. Westmoreland, *A Soldier Reports*, 417.
57. Kitfield, *Prodigal Soldiers*, 62, 64.
58. CMC message 211751Z Sep. 70 to CG III MAF, in Son Thang Daily Report file (MCHC).
59. Hargrove, interview.
60. Grutman and Thomas, *Lawyers and Thieves*, 122.
61. St.Amour, interview.
62. MCM, 1969, par. 156.
63. Joint pretrial investigation, exhibit 39.
64. *U.S. v. Green*.
65. Hargrove, interview.
66. Webb, "The Sad Conviction of Sam Green," 16
67. *The Einsatzgruppen Case* (*U.S. v. Ohlendorf, et al.*) (1947), U.S. Military Tribunal, Nuremberg, TWC, IV. Asked about the legality of orders to kill Russian prisoners who were Jews or Communists, Ohlendorf replied, "I do not understand your question; since the order was issued by the superior authorities, the question of illegality could not arise in the minds of these [subordinate] individuals, for they had sworn obedience to the people who had issued the orders." Found guilty of war crimes, in 1951. Ohlendorf was hanged.
68. St.Amour, letter, 14 Feb. 1991.
69. St.Amour, letter, 4 Mar. 1991.
70. *New York Times*, 16 Aug. 1970.
71. *DeShaney v. Winnebago County*.
72. St.Amour, letter, 4 Mar. 1991.
73. Perry, *Racial Discrimination and Military Justice*, 80.
74. Palmer, *The 25-Year War*, 83.
75. Binkin and Eitelberg, *Blacks and the Military*, 37.
76. Racial violence including murders, fraggings, and intramural firefights are detailed in Solis, *Marines and Military Law in Vietnam*, 110–11, 127–31, 134–38, 193–96.
77. Ibid., 130.
78. Ibid., 171.
79. Nalty, *Strength for the Fight*, 329.

Chapter 7. U.S. v. Herrod

1. Lucy, interview.
2. Col. Robert M. Lucy, FMFPac briefing, tape 4814, Oral History Section (MCHC).
3. St.Amour, letter, 4 Mar. 1991.
4. St.Amour, interview.
5. Ibid.
6. Ibid.
7. Mrs. P. J. Snow, letter to Sen. John Tower, 8 Mar. 1970.
8. Sen. John G. Tower, letter to legislative assistant to the Commandant, 13 Mar. 1970.
9. Rep. Carl Albert, letter to legislative assistant to the Commandant, 5 May 1970.
10. Bradlee, *Guts and Glory*, 88.
11. St.Amour, letter, 14 Feb. 1991.
12. Brig. Gen. Duane L. Faw, letter to author, 13 July 1991.
13. Stipe, interview.
14. Unless otherwise indicated, all Herrod quotations in this chapter are from his book, *Blue's Bastards*.
15. Complaint for Writ of Prohibition, *Herrod v. Convening Authority*.
16. Stipe, interview.
17. CG FMFPac secret message 232135Z Aug. 70 to CG 1st MarDiv, Son Thang Daily Report file (MCHC).
18. Cooper, interview.
19. North, *Under Fire*, 123.
20. Bradlee, *Guts and Glory*, 90.
21. Ibid., 123–24.
22. Webb, "The Sad Conviction of Sam Green," 18.
23. Green, "Superior Orders and the Reasonable Man," 101.
24. Martin, "Who Went to War."
25. Cox, interview.
26. Dershowitz, *Reasonable Doubts*, 166. Emphasis in original.

27. *U.S. v. Schwarz*, 548.
28. Ibid., 549.
29. *Washington Post*, 27 Aug. 1970.
30. Denzil Garrison, letter to author, 4 Jan. 1996.
31. *Washington Post*, 27 Aug. 1970.
32. Gene Stipe, letter to author, 15 July 1988.
33. Sack, *Lieutenant Calley: His Own Story*, 79. Emphasis in original.
34. Jury instructions, *U.S. v. Calley*, quoted in Friedman, *The Law of War*, 1703, 1721.
35. *U.S. v. Calley*.
36. Cooper, interview.
37. Theer, letter.
38. Cooper, letter, 24 July 1995.
39. Timberg, *The Nightingale's Song*, 190.
40. North, *Under Fire*, 124.
41. Timberg, *The Nightingale's Song*, 190.
42. *New York Times*, 28 Aug. 1970.
43. Karen W., letter to Sen. Henry Bellmon, 12 May 1970.
44. Ibid.
45. Bradlee, *Guts and Glory*, 92.
46. Stipe, interview.
47. *Washington Post*, 28 Aug. 1970.
48. Garrison, letter to author, 22 Aug. 1988.
49. *U.S. v. Herrod*, 991.
50. *Manual for Courts-Martial, 1969*, par. 120.c, and *U.S. v. Chappell*.
51. Theer, interview.
52. Hastie, *Inside the Juror*, 4.
53. Ibid.
54. McDermott, interview.
55. Maj. David W. Hardiman, letter to author, 20 June 1991.
56. Maj. Al G. Borlan, letter to author, 24 June 1991.
57. Dershowitz, *Reasonable Doubts*, 38.
58. McDermott, interview.
59. Ibid.
60. Borlan, letter.

61. Stipe, interview.
62. Timberg, "The Private War of Ollie and Jim," 144, 152.
63. Blum, letter to author, 20 Feb. 1989.
64. St.Amour, letter to author, 14 Feb. 1991.
65. Keith B. Lawrence, letter to author, 19 Mar. 1991.
66. Ibid.
67. Garrison, letter, 4 Jan. 1996.
68. See Korroch and Davidson, "Jury Nullification," and Warren and Jewell, "Instructions and Advocacy."
69. Abramson, *We, the Jury*, 61.
70. Lewy, *America in Vietnam*, 327.
71. Weinstein, "Considering Jury 'Nullification,'" 339, fn. 1.
72. Cooper, letter, 12 Sep. 1988.

CHAPTER 8. CLEMENCY GRANTED, APPEAL DENIED

1. Simmons, interview.
2. Ibid.
3. Ibid.
4. Zimring, Eigen, and O'Malley, "Punishing Homicide in Philadelphia," 227, Table VI, 234. The table's percentages have been translated into discrete numbers here.
5. Hindelang and others, *Sourcebook of Criminal Justice Statistics, 1973*, Table 5.38. (1973 was the first year for which such statistics were compiled.)
6. Zimring, Eigen, and O'Malley, "Punishing Homicide," 242.
7. Civilian brief for appellant at 1, *U.S. v. Schwarz*.
8. U.S. Dept. of War, *Rules of Land Warfare, 1914*, change 1, 15 Nov. 1944, par. 345.1.
9. Dicey, *Introduction to the Study of the Law of the Constitution*, 303.
10. Green, "Aftermath of Vietnam," 172.
11. *U.S. v. Griffen*.
12. *U.S. v. Schultz* and *U.S. v. Griffen*.

13. *U.S. v. Griffen*, 588.
14. *Chief Military Prosecutor v. Melinki and others,* cited in *A.G., Israel v. Eichmann.*
15. Keegan, *The Face of Battle,* 47.
16. Janis, "Group Identification."
17. Krulak, *First to Fight,* 175.
18. Safer, *Flashbacks,* 105.
19. Rubin, "Legal Aspects of the My Lai Incident," 265.
20. Kelman and Hamilton, *Crimes of Obedience,* 16.
21. Milgram, "Behavioral Study of Obedience."
22. Hartle, *Moral Issues in Military Decision Making,* 123.
23. Browning, *Ordinary Men,* 173.
24. Grossman, *On Killing,* 153.
25. Walzer, *Just and Unjust Wars,* 307.
26. Ibid., 309–10.
27. Simmons, interview.
28. CG, 1st MarDiv-CMC message 151000Z Dec. 1970 (MCHC).
29. General Court-Martial Order No. 68-70, 15 Dec. 1970; case of Pvt. Michael A. Schwarz.
30. Lurie, *Arming Military Justice,* vol. I, fn. 32.
31. Buscher, *The U.S. War Crimes Trial Program in Germany, 1946–1955* is a particularly fine examination of that failure of justice.
32. Lewy, *America in Vietnam,* 371.
33. NDC Clemency Recommendation, 16 Feb. 1971; case of Green, Samuel George.
34. Ibid.
35. NDC Clemency Recommendation, 16 Feb. 1971; case of Schwarz, Michael Allen.
36. NDC Prisoner Status Report, 30 Dec. 1970; case of Schwarz.
37. Congressman Thomas E. Morgan to Col. William P. Oliver, Legislative Counsel, OLA, HQMC, 4 Jan. 1971.
38. *U.S. v. Green,* 7.
39. Ibid., 16.
40. Posner, *The Problems of Jurisprudence,* 168–69.

41. Holmes, *The Common Law*, 48.
42. Simmons, interview.
43. Timberg, *The Nightingale's Song*, 191.
44. Webb, "The Sad Conviction of Sam Green," 15.
45. *U.S. v. Schwarz*, 852.
46. Report of psychiatric examination, Dept. of Neuropsychiatry, U.S. Army Hospital, Ft. McPherson, Ga., 28 Mar. 1972.
47. *Green v. Convening Authority*.
48. *Green v. Wylie*.
49. Parks, letter to author, 7 Apr. 1995. Parks later became special assistant for law-of-war matters to the judge advocate general of the Army.
50. Chairman, BCNR, to SecNav; Subj: Green, Samuel G., former Pvt., USMC; review of naval record, 20 Feb. 1978.
51. Grossman, *On Killing*, 222.

Conclusions

1. Solis, *Marines and Military Law in Vietnam*, 80, 200.
2. Col. John R. DeBarr, FMFPac debriefing, 9 June 1969, tape 4254, Oral History Collection (MCHC).
3. Gilligan and Lederer, *Court-Martial Procedure*, vol. 1, 24.
4. Westmoreland and Prugh, "Judges in Command," 4.
5. Holben, interview.
6. Tiernan, interview.
7. King, "Changes in the UCMJ," 49.
8. Lancaster, "Enemy War Crimes."
9. Cushman, interview.
10. McDonough, *Platoon Leader*, 139.

GLOSSARY

Article 32 In military legal practice, a pretrial proceeding often compared to a civilian pretrial hearing; roughly, the military analogue of a grand jury proceeding, except open, without the civilian grand jury's secrecy. A GCM must be preceded by an Article 32. The government must present sufficient evidence to convince an investigating (presiding) officer that an offense has been committed and that the accused committed it. An excellent discovery vehicle for the accused, who need not present evidence. Following the Article 32, the investigating officer submits a report to the convening authority, recommending the further disposition of the case, if any. The recommendation does not bind the convening authority.

Many of these definitions are from the excellent reference *Words of the Vietnam War: The Slang, Jargon, Abbreviations, Acronyms, Nomenclature, Nicknames, Pseudonyms, Slogans, Specs, Euphemisms, Doubletalk, Chants, and Names and Places of the Era of United States Involvement in Vietnam,* by Gregory R. Clark (Jefferson, N.C.: McFarland, 1990).

Brig. Gen. Brigadier general; a one-star general.

CA Convening authority.

CG Commanding general.

Chieu Hoi "Open Arms," a Government of South Vietnam program granting amnesty to defecting NVA and VC soldiers. Some Chieu Hois became scouts for U.S. units and were also known as Kit Carson scouts.

CID Criminal Investigations Division. The military organization that investigates criminal activity within the military.

CMA See: USCMA.

CMR Court of Military Review; military appellate court. Each armed service has its own CMR, served by appellate judge advocates and staffed by military judges from its own service. The Marine Corps and Navy combine in the Navy Court of Military Review. (In 1994, Congress altered the name to the Court of Criminal Appeals.)

CO Commanding officer.

COC Combat operations center. Command center responsible for coordination and operation of combat units assigned to it.

Convening authority In military legal practice, the officer possessing legal authority to convene a court-martial. In the case of special courts-martial and general courts-martial, the convening authority also has the power to appoint court personnel and members (jurors). Under procedure in effect until 1984, the convening authority took the initial action (review) on the court-martial record of trial before it was forwarded to CMR.

CP Command post.

DOD Department of Defense.

FSB Fire support base; usually given a name which follows the term, e.g., FSB Dotty. In a combat zone, the base serving as headquarters area of a battalion or larger-sized infantry or artillery unit, from which elements of that unit are dispatched on combat missions. Usually remotely located, temporary, self-contained, and supplied by air; containing a helicopter landing zone (LZ), FSBs are interchangeably referred to as LZs, using the same name; e.g., LZ Dotty.

FSB Ross The FSB at which the headquarters element of the Son Thang patrol's parent unit, the 1st Battalion, 7th Marines, was located. Thirty kilometers south and sixteen kilometers west of Da Nang, near Que Son District Headquarters, it commanded much of the Que Son Valley, the scene of heavy fighting.

GCM General court-martial, one of the three levels of court-martial, the other two being the special court-martial and the summary court martial. The most serious offenses, including war crimes, are tried by GCMs.

HE High explosive.

HQMC Headquarters Marine Corps, Washington, D.C.

IO Investigating officer. The presiding officer at an Article 32 investigation. Usually a judge advocate major, or above, although the MCM requires no specific grade, nor that the IO be a judge advocate.

JA Judge advocate, a military lawyer. In military practice, an officer who has graduated from an accredited civilian law school and a military legal training course, who is a member of a state bar association and has been certified by his/her service's judge advocate general as competent to act as a military lawyer.

Judge Advocate Division That section of Marine Corps headquarters having oversight of all Marine legal activities, with personnel assignment authority (along with the Headquarters personnel section) over legal personnel. Commanded by a brigadier general who has powers and authority akin to the other armed services' judge advocates general (JAGs). The Marine Corps, by federal law part of the naval service, has no JAG, instead looking to the Navy's JAG in those matters that specifically require the action of a JAG, such as the certification of counsel.

KIA Killed in action. Because the action in Vietnam was not a declared war, U.S. combatants killed as a result of enemy action were officially listed as "Killed in Hostile Fire." Although technically unauthorized, the term "KIA" was universally used to describe both enemy and friendly troops killed in combat.

Lt. Col. Lieutenant colonel. Insignia of rank, a silver leaf.

Lt. Gen. Lieutenant general; a three-star general.

MACV Military Assistance Command, Vietnam. The U.S. Army headquarters in Saigon (Tan Son Nhut) that exercised overall administrative command and, to a degree, tactical command of all armed services in South Vietnam.

Maj. Major. Insignia of rank, a gold leaf.

Maj. Gen. Major general; a two-star general.

MARS Military Affiliated Radio Stations. A network of ham radio stations that allowed free phone calls from Vietnam to the U.S., by radio, via the U.S. Signal Corps. Connections were made over a two-way radio using standard radio procedure, e.g., callers could not talk at the same time, turns indicated by saying "over."

MCHC Marine Corps Historical Center, Washington, D.C.

MCM *Manual for Courts-Martial, United States.* The manual containing rules for courts-martial, military rules of evidence and procedure, and reprinting the UCMJ. Promulgated by the president as an executive order, it has the force of law pursuant to UCMJ Article 36. Versions have been published and made effective in 1951, 1969, and 1984.

Member In military legal practice, an individual ordered to hear a particular court-martial case; essentially the same as a civilian juror. At trial, members decide issues of fact; issues of law are decided by the military judge. Members are usually, though are not required to be, commissioned officers, unless the accused requests that enlisted members be included on his/her panel, in which case at least one-third of the members must be enlisted personnel. Members are initially selected by an administrative officer on the staff of the convening authority, the selection being ratified by the convening authority by his signature on the completed roster. At least five members hear general courts-martial. There is no statutory maximum number, but usually a panel consists of no more than seven or eight.

Military judge The court-martial trial judge, with powers similar to those of a federal trial-level judge. Decides all issues of law, rules on motions, and has overall responsibility for conduct of the proceedings.

M-79 A 40mm, smooth-bore, single-shot shoulder weapon weighing 6.5 pounds, with an effective range of 300 meters. Resembling a shotgun, it is designed to fill the gap between a rifle and a mortar. It fires antipersonnel rounds, i.e., high explosive, tear gas, and buckshot.

NCMR Navy Court of Military Review, which considers the appeals of both Marine Corps and Navy cases. See: CMR.

NCO Noncommissioned officer. In the Marine Corps, the grades of corporal, sergeant, staff sergeant, gunnery sergeant, master sergeant, first sergeant, and sergeant major.

NDC Naval Disciplinary Command, Portsmouth, N.H.

NVA North Vietnamese Army, connoting organized, uniformed, regular enemy troops, as opposed to VC irregulars.

1/7 Common designation for the 1st Battalion of the 7th Marines; pronounced "one-seven." A battalion-size infantry unit.

ROEs Rules of engagement. Directives issued by military authority which delineate the circumstances and limitations under which U.S. forces will initiate and/or continue combat. In Vietnam, ROEs often changed.

RPG Rocket-propelled grenade. Soviet-made antitank weapon firing a shaped charge. Shoulder-fired, single-shot, and reloadable, widely used by the VC/NVA.

Sapper Specially trained NVA/VC commandos. Their prime function was the destruction of enemy fortifications and equipment. The satchel charge was their primary weapon. Experts in infiltration techniques, booby-traps, and mines. Sappers cleared paths through minefields for attacking troops. Many sapper missions were suicidal but effective.

Satchel charge Explosive device containing blocks of explosives designed to detonate simultaneously. Carried in a pack, detonated by a timer or a burning fuse. Placed by hand or thrown at the target.

SJA Staff judge advocate. The senior military lawyer on the special staff of a Marine Corps division, or larger unit (for aviation units, a wing, or larger). Not to be confused with a judge advocate, above. All SJAs are judge advocates; few judge advocates are SJAs.

SOFA Status of Forces Agreement. A bilateral agreement between "host" and "visiting" nations that specifies their relationship, as well as the legal rights, duties, and responsibilities of each. The concept arose in 1941 when the United States leased bases in Great Britain in exchange for destroyers; it was refined in the North Atlantic Treaty SOFA of 1951.

Spotrep Spot report, or situation report. Means by which field units maintained periodic contact with their headquarters, informing them of their position, proposed course, or enemy situation, updated as the combat situation changed.

TAOR Tactical area of responsibility. The designation for a specific area under command and control of one headquarters.

Trial counsel In military legal practice, the term denoting the military lawyer assigned as court-martial prosecutor in a particular case; the officer of the court who represents the United States.

UCMJ Uniform Code of Military Justice. The basic statute governing military criminal law in all of the armed forces. Formulated by Congress, enacted by the president, codified in Chapter 47, Title 10, U.S. Code, it is federal law. It includes the military legal system's jurisdictional basis, substantive offenses, and basic procedural structure. First effective in May 1951, it is periodically amended by congressional action through presidential executive orders. Major modifications were made effective in August 1969 and September 1984.

USCMA The United States Court of Military Appeals, the highest military appellate court. It considers appeals from all the military services. Established under Article I of the U.S. Constitution, the court was created in May 1950. Composed of five civilian judges (three, during the Vietnam War era) appointed by the president with the advice and consent of the Senate, the court sits in Washington, D.C. (In 1994, Congress altered the court's name to the United States Court of Appeals for the Armed Forces.)

VC Viet Cong; derogatory contraction of the Vietnamese phrase meaning "Vietnamese Communists." The combat arm of the National Liberation Front (NLF). The enemy's irregular, often loosely organized guerrilla force, without uniform or distinctive identifying insignia, that operated throughout South Vietnam.

BIBLIOGRAPHY

BOOKS

Abramson, Jeffrey. *We, the Jury: The Jury System and the Ideal of Democracy.* New York: Basic Books, 1994.

Axinn, Sidney. *A Moral Military.* Philadelphia: Temple University, 1989.

Best, Geoffrey. *Humanity in Warfare: The Modern History of the International Law of Armed Conflicts.* London: Weidenfeld and Nicolson, 1980.

Bilton, Michael, and Kevin Sim. *Four Hours in My Lai: A War Crime and Its Aftermath.* London: Viking, 1992.

Binkin, Martin, and Mark J. Eitelberg. *Blacks and the Military.* Washington, D.C.: Brookings Institution, 1982.

Boulanger, Ghislaine, and Charles Kadushin, eds. *The Vietnam Veteran Redefined: Fact and Fiction.* London: Lawrence Erlbaum Associates, 1986.

Bradlee, Ben, Jr. *Guts and Glory: The Rise & Fall of Oliver North.* New York: Donald Fine, 1988.

Brookshire, Maj. R. Rex, III. "Juror Selection under the Uniform Code of Military Justice: Fact and Fiction." *Military Law Review* 58 (1972): 71.

Browning, Christopher R. *Ordinary Men: Reserve Police Battalion 101 and the Final Solution in Poland.* New York: Harper Perennial, 1992.

Buscher, Frank M. *The U.S. War Crimes Trial Program in Germany, 1946–1955.* Westport, Conn.: Greenwood Press, 1989.

Clark, Gregory R. *Words of the Vietnam War: The Slang, Jargon, Abbreviations, Acronyms, Nomenclature, Nicknames, Pseudonyms, Slogans, Specs, Euphemisms, Double-talk, Chants, and Names and Places of the Era of United States Involvement in Vietnam.* Jefferson, N.C.: McFarland and Co., 1990.

Clark, Ian. *Waging War: A Philosophical Introduction.* Oxford: Clarendon Press, 1990.

Cosmas, Graham A., and Lt. Col. Terrance P. Murray. *U.S. Marines in Vietnam: Vietnamization and Redeployment, 1970–1971.* Washington, D.C.: GPO/U.S. Marine Corps, 1986.

DeLupis, Ingrid D. *The Law of War.* Cambridge: Cambridge University Press, 1987.

Dershowitz, Alan M. *Reasonable Doubts: The O.J. Simpson Case and the Criminal Justice System.* New York: Simon and Schuster, 1996.

Dicey, Albert V. *Introduction to the Study of the Law of the Constitution.* 10th ed. London: Macmillan and Co., 1959.

Eckhardt, Col. William G. "Command Criminal Responsibility: A Plea for a Workable Standard." *Military Law Review* 97 (1982): 1.

Falk, Richard A., ed. *The Vietnam War and International Law.* Vol. 4, *The Concluding Phase.* Princeton: Princeton University Press, 1976.

Fleming, Keith. *The U.S. Marine Corps in Crisis: Ribbon Creek and Recruit Training.* Columbia: University of South Carolina Press, 1990.

Friedman, Leon, ed. *The Law of War: A Documentary History.* Vol. 2. New York: Random House, 1972.

Gabriel, Richard A. *No More Heroes: Madness and Psychiatry in War.* New York: Hill and Wang, 1987.

Gilligan, Francis A., and Fredric I. Lederer. *Court-Martial Procedure.* Vols. 1 and 2. Charlottesville, Va.: Michie, 1991.

Graves, Robert. *Goodbye to All That.* London: Jonathon Cape, 1929; Penguin Classics, 1960.

Green, Leslie C. "Aftermath of Vietnam: War Law and the Soldier." In Falk, ed., *Vietnam War and International Law.* Vol. 4.

———. "Superior Orders and the Reasonable Man." *Canadian Yearbook of International Law* 8 (1970): 61.

Grossman, Lt. Col. Dave. *On Killing: The Psychological Cost of Learning to Kill in War and Society.* Boston: Little, Brown and Co., 1995.

Grutman, Roy, and Bill Thomas. *Lawyers and Thieves.* New York: Simon and Schuster, 1990.

Hammer, Richard. *The Court-Martial of Lt. Calley.* New York: Coward McCann and Geoghegan, 1971.

———. *One Morning in the War: The Tragedy at Son My.* New York: Coward-McCann, 1970.

Hartle, Anthony E. *Moral Issues in Military Decision Making.* Lawrence: University Press of Kansas, 1989.

Hastie, Reid, ed. *Inside the Juror: The Psychology of Juror Decision Making.* Cambridge: Cambridge University Press, 1993.

Herrod, Randell D. *Blue's Bastards: A True Story of Valor under Fire.* Washington, D.C.: Regnery, 1989.

Hindelang, Michael J., and others, eds. *Sourcebook of Criminal Justice Statistics, 1973.* Washington, D.C.: GPO/U.S. Dept. of Justice, 1973.

Holmes, Oliver W., Jr. *The Common Law.* Boston: Little, Brown and Co., 1881.

Hooker, Wade S., and David H. Savasten. "The Geneva Convention of 1949: Application in the Vietnamese Conflict." *Virginia Journal of International Law* 5 (1964): 243.

Janis, I. L. "Group Identification under Conditions of External Danger." *British Journal of Medical Psychology* 36 (1963): 227.

Janowitz, Morris, ed. *The New Military: Changing Patterns of Organization*. New York: Russell Sage Foundation, 1964.

Jones, Andrew. *Where Do We Get Such Men?* Book condensation, *Reader's Digest*, September 1983.

Karsten, Peter. *Law, Soldiers and Combat*. Westport, Conn.: Greenwood Press, 1978.

Keegan, John. *The Face of Battle*. London: Jonathon Cape, 1976; Penguin, 1978.

Keijzer, Nico. *Military Obedience*. Alphen aan den Rijn, Netherlands: Sijthoff and Noordhoff, 1978.

Kelman, Herbert C., and V. Lee Hamilton. *Crimes of Obedience: Toward a Social Psychology of Authority and Responsibility*. New Haven: Yale University Press, 1989.

Kelsen, Hans. *Peace through Law*. Vol. 4. Chapel Hill: University of North Carolina Press, 1944.

King, Col. Archibald. "Changes in the Uniform Code of Military Justice Necessary to Make It Workable in Time of War." *Federal Bar Journal* 22 (Winter 1962): 49.

Kitfield, James. *Prodigal Soldiers*. New York: Simon and Schuster, 1995.

Korroch, Lt. Cdr. Robert E., and Maj. Michael J. Davidson. "Jury Nullification: A Call for Justice or an Invitation to Anarchy?" *Military Law Review* 139 (1993): 131.

Krulak, Lt. Gen. Victor H. *First to Fight*. Annapolis, Md.: Naval Institute Press, 1984.

Lancaster, Col. Steven F. "Enemy War Crimes: How to Investigate and Prosecute." Study Project, U.S. Army War College, Carlisle Barracks, Pa., 1988.

Lanning, Michael Lee, and Dan Craig. *Inside the VC and the NVA: The Real Story of North Vietnam's Armed Forces*. New York: Fawcett Columbine, 1992.

Lazareff, Serge. *Status of Military Forces under Current International Law*. Leyden, Netherlands: A. W. Sijthoff, 1971.

Lewy, Guenter. *America in Vietnam*. Oxford: Oxford University Press, 1978.

Little, Roger W. "Buddy Relations and Combat Performance." In Janowitz, ed., *The New Military*.

Lurie, Jonathon. *Arming Military Justice*. Vol. 1. Princeton: Princeton University Press, 1992.

Lynch, Maj. Gen. J. D. "Fish Rot from the Head." U.S. Naval Institute *Proceedings* (Feb. 1995), 73.

Marshall, Brig. Gen. S. L. A. *Men against Fire: The Problem of Battle Command in Future War*. Alexandria, Va: Byrrd Enterprises, 1947.

Martin, Randy. "Who Went to War." In Boulanger and Kadushin, eds., *The Vietnam Veteran Redefined*.

McDonough, James R. *Platoon Leader*. New York: Bantam Books, 1985.

Milgram, Stanley. "Behavioral Study of Obedience." *Journal of Abnormal and Social Psychology* 67 (1963): 371.

Nalty, Bernard C. *Strength for the Fight: A History of Black Americans in the Military*. New York: Free Press, 1986.

Nolan, Keith William. *Death Valley: The Summer Offensive, I Corps, August 1969*. Novato, Calif.: Presidio Press, 1987.

North, Oliver L., with William Novak. *Under Fire: An American Story*. New York: Harper Collins, 1991.

Palmer, Gen. Bruce. *The 25-Year War*. Lexington: University Press of Kentucky, 1984.

Palmer, Laura. "The General, at Ease: An Interview with Westmorland." *MHQ, The Quarterly Journal of Military History* 1 (Autumn 1988): 34.

Parks, Col. W. Hays. "Crimes in Hostilities." Pt. 1. *Marine Corps Gazette* 60 (August 1976): 16.

Paust, Capt. Jordan J. "My Lai and Vietnam: Norms, Myths and Leader Responsibility," *Military Law Review* 57 (1972): 99.

Peers, Lt. Gen. William R., USA (Ret.). *The My Lai Inquiry*. New York: Norton, 1979.

Perry, Ronald W. *Racial Discrimination and Military Justice*. New York: Praeger, 1977.

Pike, Douglas. *PAVN: People's Army of Vietnam*. Novato, Calif.: Presidio Press, 1986.

Posner, Richard A. *The Problems of Jurisprudence*. Cambridge: Harvard University Press, 1990.

Powell, Colin L., with Joseph E. Persico. *My American Journey*. New York: Random House, 1995.

Prugh, Maj. Gen. George S. *Law at War: Vietnam, 1964–1973*. Washington, D.C.: U.S. Dept. of the Army, 1975.

Puller, Lewis B., II. *Fortunate Son*. New York: Grove Weidenfeld, 1991.

Rubin, Alfred P. "Legal Aspects of the My Lai Incident." *Oregon Law Review* 49 (1970): 260.

Sack, John. *Lieutenant Calley: His Own Story*. New York: Viking, 1970.

Safer, Morley. *Flashbacks*. New York: Random House, 1990.

Santoli, Al. *To Bear Any Burden*. New York: Dutton, 1985.

Shanor, Charles A., and Timothy P. Terrell. *Military Law in a Nutshell*. St. Paul, Minn.: West Publishing, 1980.

Shay, Jonathan. *Achilles in Vietnam: Combat Trauma and the Undoing of Character*. New York: Atheneum, 1994.

Smith, Capt. Arthur M. "Fear, Courage, and Cohesion." U.S. Naval Institute *Proceedings* (Nov. 1994), 65.

Smith, Charles R. *U.S. Marines in Vietnam: High Mobility and Standdown, 1969*. Washington, D.C.: GPO/U.S. Marine Corps, 1988.

Solis, Lt. Col. Gary D. *Marines and Military Law in Vietnam: Trial by Fire*. Washington, D.C.: GPO/U.S. Marine Corps, 1989.

Spector, Ronald H. *After Tet: The Bloodiest Year in Vietnam*. New York: Free Press, 1993.

Taylor, Telford. *Nuremberg and Vietnam: An American Tragedy*. Chicago: Quadrangle Books, 1970.

———. *The Anatomy of the Nuremberg Trials: A Personal Memoir*. New York: Alfred A. Knopf, 1992.

Timberg, Robert. *The Nightingale's Song*. New York: Simon and Schuster, 1995.

———. "The Private War of Ollie and Jim." *Esquire* (March 1988), 144.

Trials of the Major War Criminals before the International Military Tribunal. Vol. 22. Nuremberg, Germany: 1947–49.

Trullinger, James W. *Village at War: An Account of Conflict in Vietnam.* Stanford: Stanford University Press, 1994.

United Nations War Crimes Commission. *Law Reports of Trials of War Criminals.* Vols. 4, 15. London: U.N., 1947–49.

U.S. Court of Military Appeals. *Annual Report of the U.S. Court of Military Appeals and the Judge Advocates General of the Armed Forces, January 1, 1970, to December 31, 1970.* Washington, D.C.: GPO, 1971.

U.S. Dept. of the Army. *Review of the Preliminary Investigation into the My Lai Incident.* Vol. 2, books 16, 20. Washington, D.C.: Pentagon, n.d.

———. Field Manual 27-10, *The Law of Land Warfare.* Washington, D.C.: GPO, 1956.

U.S. Manual for Courts-Martial, 1969. Rev. ed. Washington, D.C.: GPO, 1969.

U.S. Dept. of War. *Rules of Land Warfare, 1914.* Washington, D.C.: War Dept., 1914.

Walzer, Michael. *Just and Unjust Wars: A Moral Argument with Historical Illustrations.* 2d ed. New York: Basic Books, 1977/92.

Warren, Maj. Michael D., and Lt. Col. W. Gary Jewell. "Instructions and Advocacy." *Military Law Review* 126 (1989): 147.

Webb, James H. "The Sad Conviction of Sam Green: The Case for the Reasonable and Honest War Criminal." *Res Ipsa Loquitur* (Georgetown University Law School) 26 (Winter 1974): 11.

Weinstein, Jack B. "Considering Jury 'Nullification': When May and Should a Jury Reject the Law to Do Justice?" *American Criminal Law Review* 30 (1993): 239, 339 n. 1.

Westmoreland, Gen. William C. *A Soldier Reports.* New York: Doubleday, 1976.

———. "The State of the Command." *Report on the War in Vietnam,* sec. 2. Washington, D.C.: GPO, 1969.

————, and Maj. Gen. George S. Prugh. "Judges in Command: The Judicialized Uniform Code of Military Justice in Combat (A Draft Code Amendment)." *Harvard Journal of Law and Public Policy* 4 (1976): 199.

Wily, Col. Michael D. "Light Infantry and Vietnam." *Marine Corps Gazette* 74 (June 1990): 58.

Zimring, Franklin E., Joel Eigen, and Sheila O'Malley. "Punishing Homicide in Philadelphia: Perspectives on the Death Penalty." *University of Chicago Law Review* 43 (1976): 227.

Unpublished Material

Interviews

Ambort, Lewis R. Telephone interview by author. Tape recording, 18 Sept. 1992.

Barrow, Gen. Robert H., USMC. (Ret.) Tape recording transcript, 30 Jan. 1987. Oral History Collection, Marine Corps Historical Center, Washington Navy Yard, Washington, D.C. [Hereafter: MCHC]

Cassady, Col. David J., USMC. Interview by author. Tape recording. Arlington, Va., 4 Nov. 1986.

Cooper, Lt. Gen. Charles G., USMC (Ret.). Interview by Benis M. Frank. Tape recording transcript, sess. 10, 14 Aug. 1986; sess. 11, 15 Aug. 1986. Oral History Collection, MCHC.

Cox, Judge Walter T. Interview by author. Tape recording. Washington, D.C., 7 Dec. 1990.

Cushman, Brig. Gen. Charles A., USMC. Interview by author. Tape recording (tape 6481). Alexandria, Va., 4 Dec. 1986. Oral History Collection, MCHC.

Cushman, Gen. Robert E., Jr., USMC (Ret.). Interview by Benis M. Frank. Tape recording transcript, n.d. 1984. Oral History Collection, MCHC.

Hargrove, Lt. Col. John J., USMCR. Telephone interview by author. Tape recording, 29 Aug. 1991.

Holben, Col. Donald E., USMC (Ret.). Interview by author. Tape recording (tape 6472). Oceanside, Calif., 13 Oct. 1986. Oral History Collection, MCHC.

Hord, Col. Raymond A., USMC. Interview by author. Tape recording. Quantico, Va., 8 May 1990.

Jevne, Franz P. Telephone interview by author. Tape recording, 31 Oct. 1995.

Kelley, Gen. Paul X., USMC (Ret.). Interview by author. Tape recording. Washington, D.C., 12 Dec. 1990.

King, Brig. Gen. James P., USMC (Ret.). Interview by author. Tape recording (tape 6478). Arlington, Va., 5 Nov. 1986. Oral History Collection, MCHC.

Lawrence, Capt. Keith D., JAGC, USN (Ret.). Telephone interview by author. Tape recording, 9 Jan. 1996.

Lucy, Col. Robert M., USMC (Ret.). Telephone interview by author. Tape recording, 22 June 1991.

McDermott, Lt. Col. John J., USMC (Ret.). Telephone interview by author. Tape recording, 17 Dec. 1991.

Rich, Brig. Gen. Michael E., USMC. Interview by author. Tape recording. London, 26 Aug. 1990.

Simmons, Brig. Gen. Edwin H., USMC (Ret.). Interview by author. Tape recording. Washington, D.C., 10 May 1990.

St.Amour, Lt. Col. Paul A. A., USMC (Ret.). Interview by author. Tape recording. Bedford, Mass., 13 Nov. 1992.

Stipe, Gene. Telephone interview by author. Tape recording, 14 Dec. 1990.

Suter, Maj. Gen. William K., JAGC, USA. Interview by author. Tape recording. Alexandria, Va., 11 Dec. 1990.

Theer, Lt. Col. Richard E., USMC (Ret.). Telephone interview by author. Tape recording, 4 Feb. 1996.

Tiernan, Brig. Gen. William H. J., USMC (Ret.). Interview by author. Tape recording (tape 6484), 14 Oct. 1986. Oral History Collection, MCHC.

Tompkins, Maj. Gen. Rathvon McC., USMC (Ret.). Interview by Oral History Unit, History Division, USMC. Tape recording transcript, 13 Apr. 1973. Oral History Collection, MCHC.

Index of Cases

INDEX

About the Author

GARY SOLIS served in the Marine Corps for twenty-six years. As an assault amphibian officer he twice served in Vietnam, in 1964 as a platoon leader, and in 1966–1967 as a company commander.

After becoming a lawyer, he served eighteen years as a Marine judge advocate. He was chief prosecutor for the 3d Marine Division, then the 1st Marine Division, trying more than 450 cases. Later, at Marine Corps Headquarters, he headed the military law branch of the Judge Advocate Division. Finally, he completed two tours as a general court-martial judge, sitting in another 300 cases. He retired as a lieutenant colonel.

His 1989 book, *Marines and Military Law,* is the Marine Corps' official history of judge advocates and courts martial in that conflict. During his research for that volume he became interested in Son Thang-4.

Following retirement from the Marine Corps, Lt. Col. Solis lived in London, where for three years he taught British Law at the London School of Economics and Political Science, as well as U.S. law for the University of Maryland in Europe. He hosted a weekly television show on legal issues for Sky News, and was a law commentator for BBC radio.

Solis holds law degrees from the University of California at Davis (J.D.), George Washington University (LL.M), and the London School of Economics and Political Science

(Ph.D.). He's a member of the bars of Virginia, Texas, Maryland, Pennsylvania, the District of Columbia, and the Supreme Court of the United States.

He currently teaches law at the U.S. Military Academy at West Point. His home is in Alexandria, Virginia.

The fascinating true stories behind these extraordinary public figures

IT DOESN'T TAKE A HERO: *The Autobiography*
by General H. Norman Schwarzkopf with Peter Petre

Rarely does a figure appear of such compelling leadership and personal charisma as to capture the imagination of an entire nation. Now, in this candid, outspoken, and eagerly awaited autobiography, General Schwarzkopf reveals the full story of his remarkable life and a career spanning nearly four decades.

_____56338-6 $6.99/$7.99 in Canada

YEAGER: *An Autobiography*
by Chuck Yeager with Leo Janos

From his humble West Virginia roots to his role as the test pilot who first broke the sound barrier, this is the story of the man who rose to lead America into space.

_____25674-2 $7.50/$9.99

MARINE! *The Life of Chesty Puller*
by Burke Davis

This is the explosive true story of the most courageous and controversial commander of them all-- the only marine in history to win five Navy crosses. Here is the fabulous tale of a real life hero.

_____27182-2 $6.99/$8.99

Ask for these books at your local bookstore or use this page to order.

Please send me the books I have checked above. I am enclosing $_____ (add $2.50 to cover postage and handling). Send check or money order, no cash or C.O.D.'s, please.

Name _____

Address _____

City/State/Zip _____

Send order to: Bantam Books, Dept. WW 9, 2451 S. Wolf Rd., Des Plaines, IL 60018
Allow four to six weeks for delivery.

Prices and availability subject to change without notice.

WW 9 9/98

Vivid, compelling narrative histories of some of
America's most memorable decades

VOICES OF FREEDOM
An Oral History of the Civil Rights Movement
from the 1950s through the 1980s
by Henry Hampton and Steve Fayer

Martin Luther King Jr. and Malcolm X, JFK and LBJ. From the bus
boycott in Montgomery to busing in Boston, from the marches
on Selma to the riots in Miami, *Voices of Freedom* illuminates the
long, impassioned, sometimes painful, sometimes joyful struggle
for a truly democratic society that continues today.
_____35232-6 $19.95/$27.95 in Canada

"Utterly fascinating. *Voices of Freedom* tells the greatest American story
ever told. These voices are extraordinary. So is the book."
—Pat Conroy, author of *The Prince of Tides*

THE GLORY AND THE DREAM
A Narrative History of America, 1932–1972
by William Manchester

A narrative history that spans four unforgettable decades.
_____34589-3 $27.95/$41.95

"A fascinating work of history . . . Solidly researched, bold and
imaginative in its conception, it is written with a fine sensitivity to
the nuances of the American experience in the 40 years before,
during and after the Second World War." —William L. Shirer

Ask for these books at your local bookstore or use this page to order.

Please send me the books I have checked above. I am enclosing $_____ (add $2.50 to
cover postage and handling). Send check or money order, no cash or C.O.D.'s, please.

Name _____

Address _____

City/State/Zip _____

Send order to: Bantam Books, Dept. NFB37, 2451 S. Wolf Rd., Des Plaines, IL 60018
Allow four to six weeks for delivery.
Prices and availability subject to change without notice.   NFB 37 9/98